THE SOCIAL ORIGINS OF THOUGHT

Methodology and History in Anthropology

Series Editors:
David Parkin, Fellow of All Souls College, University of Oxford
David Gellner, Fellow of All Souls College, University of Oxford
Nayanika Mathur, Fellow of Wolfson College, University of Oxford

Recent volumes:
Volume 43
The Social Origins of Thought: Durkheim, Mauss, and the Category Project
Edited by Johannes F. M. Schick, Mario Schmidt, and Martin Zillinger

Volume 42
Franz Baermann Steiner: A Stranger in the World
Jeremy Adler and Richard Fardon

Volume 41
Anthropology and Ethnography Are NOT Equivalent: Reorienting Anthropology for the Future
Edited by Irfan Ahmad

Volume 40
Search after Method: Sensing, Moving, and Imagining in Anthropological Fieldwork
Edited by Julie Laplante, Ari Gandsman, and Willow Scobie

Volume 39
After Society: Anthropological Trajectories out of Oxford
Edited by João Pina-Cabral and Glenn Bowman

Volume 38
Total Atheism: Secular Activism and Politics of Difference in South India
Stefan Binder

Volume 37
Crossing Histories and Ethnographies: Following Colonial Historicities in Timor-Leste
Edited by Ricardo Roque and Elizabeth G. Traube

Volume 36
Engaging Evil: A Moral Anthropology
Edited by William C. Olsen and Thomas J. Csordas

Volume 35
Medicinal Rule: A Historical Anthropology of Kingship in East and Central Africa
Koen Stroeken

Volume 34
Who Are We? Reimagining Alterity and Affinity in Anthropology
Edited by Liana Chua and Nayanika Mathur

For a full volume listing, please see the series page on our website:
http://berghahnbooks.com/series/methodology-and-history-in-anthropology

THE SOCIAL ORIGINS OF THOUGHT

Durkheim, Mauss, and the Category Project

Edited by
Johannes F. M. Schick, Mario Schmidt, and Martin Zillinger

berghahn
NEW YORK • OXFORD
www.berghahnbooks.com

First published in 2022 by
Berghahn Books
www.berghahnbooks.com

© 2022, 2026 Johannes F. M. Schick, Mario Schmidt, and Martin Zillinger
First paperback edition published in 2026

All rights reserved. Except for the quotation of short passages
for the purpose of criticism and review, no part of this book
may be reproduced in any form or by any means, electronic or
mechanical, including photocopying, recording, or any information
storage and retrieval system now known or to be invented,
without written permission of the publisher.

Library of Congress Cataloging-in-Publication Data

A C.I.P. cataloging record is available from the Library of Congress
Library of Congress Cataloging in Publication Control Number:
2021062576

British Library Cataloguing in Publication Data

A catalogue record for this book is available from the British Library

EU GPSR Authorized Representative

LOGOS EUROPE, 9 rue Nicolas Poussin, 17000, LA ROCHELLE, France
Email: Contact@logoseurope.eu

ISBN 978-1-80073-233-9 hardback
ISBN 978-1-83695-572-6 paperback
ISBN 978-1-80758-365-1 epub
ISBN 978-1-80073-234-6 web pdf

https://doi.org/10.3167/9781800732339

In memory of N. J. Allen
1939–2020

We extend our gratitude to the family of Tommy McRae-Yakaduna and the Koorie Heritage Fund to reproduce the cover image *Buckley Ran Away from ship*, and to Anna Brus for bringing this work to our attention. Tommy McRae (c. 1835-1901) produced his outstanding art works in the contact zone between indigenous Australians and European settlers and crafted several depictions of ceremonies referred to as *corroborees* in Emile Durkheim's work. In this drawing, he took up the then famous story of William Buckley, who—imprisoned for fraud and shipped to Australia—took refuge and lived among a Wathaurung community. In this scene, the figure of Buckley is marked by white color, and moves in time with the dance movements of his Wathaurung companions; he is stripped of his European clothes, except for his hat, and wears the body paint that presumably marks him as an initiated member of society. Hovering over the scene is the ship that brought Buckley to Australia. McRae thus reverses the then famous and widely circulating narrative of Buckley's discovery as "wild white man" and instead depicts the assimilation of the European man into society from the perspective of First Australians. We could not think of a better image for this book. "Mankind erected its mind by all possible means: technical and non-technical, mystical and non-mystical; using its mind (senses, sentiment, reason), [and] using its body" (Marcel Mauss, *Real and Practical Relations between Psychology and Sociology* 33). Tommy McRae's image, drawn in the 1880s, reminds us that this work is not only "complex [and] hazardous" but continuously transforming and shaped by encounter.

CONTENTS

List of Figures   x

Introduction. The Durkheim School's "Category Project": A Collaborative Experiment Unfolds   1
    Johannes F. M. Schick, Mario Schmidt, and Martin Zillinger

Part I. Silenced Influences and Hidden Texts

Chapter 1. Kantian Categories and the Relativist Turn: A Comparison of Three Routes   29
    Gregory Schrempp

Chapter 2. Hidden Durkheim and Hidden Mauss: An Empirical Rereading of the Hidden Analogical Work Made Necessary by the Creation of a New Science   44
    Nicolas Sembel

Chapter 3. *Mana* in Context: From Max Müller to Marcel Mauss   57
    Nicolas Meylan

Chapter 4. Durkheim, the Question of the Categories, and the Concept of Labor   70
    Susan Stedman Jones

Chapter 5. Inequality Is a Scientific Issue When the Technologies of Practice that Create Social Categories Become Dependent on Justice in Modernity   86
    Anne Warfield Rawls

Chapter 6. Experimenting with Social Matter: Claude Bernard's Influence on the Durkheim School's Understanding of Categories   113
    Mario Schmidt

Part II. Lateral Links and Ambivalent Antagonists

Chapter 7. Freedom, Food, and the Total Social Fact: Some Terminological Details of the Category Project in "Le Don" by Marcel Mauss 131
   Erhard Schüttpelz

Chapter 8. Durkheimian Thinking and the Category of Totality 156
   Nick J. Allen

Chapter 9. Durkheimian Creative Effervescence, Bergson, and the Ethology of Animal and Human Societies 170
   William Watts Miller

Chapter 10. "It Is Not My Time That Is Thus Arranged...": Bergson, the "Category Project," and the Structuralist Turn 187
   Heike Delitz

Chapter 11. "Let Us Dare a Little Bit of Metaphysics": Marcel Mauss, Henri Hubert, and Louis Weber on Causality, Time, and Technology 207
   Johannes F. M. Schick

Part III. Forgotten Allies and Secret Students

Chapter 12. The Rhythm of Space: Stefan Czarnowski's Relational Theory of the Sacred 227
   Martin Zillinger

Chapter 13. *La Pensée Catégorique*: Marcel Granet's Grand Sinological Project at the Heart of the *L'Année Sociologique* Tradition 242
   Robert André LaFleur

Chapter 14. Drawing a Line: On Hertz's Hands 257
   Ulrich van Loyen

Chapter 15. Between Claude Lévi-Strauss, Pierre Bourdieu, and Michel Foucault, or: What Is the Meaning of Mauss's "Total Social Fact"? 274
   Jean-François Bert

Chapter 16. From Durkheim to Halbwachs: Rebuilding the Theory of Collective Representations 283
   Jean-Christophe Marcel

Chapter 17. Durkheim's Quest: Philosophy beyond the
Classroom and the Libraries 295
   Wendy James

Index 313

FIGURES

12.1. *Ager Romanus Antiquus* (after Alföldi 1965: 297, in Ziółkowski 2009: 99).   232

12.2. Ager. In Paulys Realencyclopädie der classischen Altertumswissenschaft (1893), 788.   235

12.3. Ager. In Paulys Realencyclopädie der classischen Altertumswissenschaft (1893), 788 (concentric circles added by the author).   237

17.1. The Blue Nile Borderlands. Wendy James, *War and Survival in Sudan's Frontierlands: Voices from the Blue Nile* (Oxford: Oxford University Press, 2007).   302

17.2. The fun of the *pumbulu*. © Wendy James 1975.   305

17.3. The Gumuz leopard celebration, 1975. © Wendy James 1975.   307

Introduction

THE DURKHEIM SCHOOL'S "CATEGORY PROJECT"

A COLLABORATIVE EXPERIMENT UNFOLDS

Johannes F. M. Schick, Mario Schmidt, and Martin Zillinger

> The study of the categories of collective thought is our originality.
> —Henri Hubert, "Texte autobiographique de Henri Hubert,"
> [1915] 1979

In his "Intellectual Self-Portrait" written around 1930, Marcel Mauss mentions a topic that he considers of "utmost importance": the question of the social origins of the categories of thought. This issue had preoccupied himself, Émile Durkheim, Henri Hubert, and other members of the Durkheim School since the second volume of the *Année sociologique* published in 1899 (Mauss [1930] 1998: 40).[1] Several scholars, some of whom have contributed to this volume, have published extensive monographs on how the social origin of the categories is treated and analyzed in the thought of Émile Durkheim or Marcel Mauss. Nick Allen (1998; 2000), in particular, but also Iris Därmann (2005), Marcel Fournier (2006), Bruno Karsenti (1994; 2011), Anne Rawls (2005), Warren Schmaus (1994; 2004), and Susan Stedman Jones (2000; 2001; 2006) have reconstructed the project's argumentative structure and how it was embedded in the sociological, anthropological, and philosophical context of its time—and they have, at times, advanced differing readings of the main sources, influences, and the epistemological argument of the category project itself. Yet, we still lack a comprehensive history of how the category project developed over time as a collaborative work of different scholars.

The difficulty of writing such a history of what we call the category project[2] is already indicated by the term *project*. The Durkheim School's preoccupation with the categories always had the character of something left to be done. While developing the category project, the Durkheim School—"a 'group'—in the full force of the term" (Mauss [1925] 2016: 29)—kept postponing its completion as if they had recognized the impossibility of their task to replace philosophy with anthropology as Mauss had announced in 1923 (Mauss 1923b: 26). As an intellectual project, it always remained fragmentary—"a ruin of speculation" (Schüttpelz 2005: 218).

The intellectual history of the project's impact remains to be written. We find its direct repercussions in the classical writings of French anthropology—from André Leroi-Gourhan through, of course, Claude Lévi-Strauss to Pierre Bourdieu, but also in Michel Foucault, Gilbert Simondon, and the more recent works of Philippe Descola and others. Also, as Wendy James has rightly emphasized, the translation of major works into English, initiated by E. E. Evans-Pritchard and systematically pursued by Rodney Needham and Robert Parkin, has been crucial for the development of British Social Anthropology and shaped one of the major intellectual currents of the twentieth century, that is, the "rationality debate" (Tambiah 1990) with its echoes in the recent ontological turn. Not least, the emphasis on classification in contemporary science and technology studies (STS) literature, as exemplified by Geoffrey Bowker and Susan Leigh Star, cannot do without referencing Durkheim and Mauss (Bowker and Star 2000).

Be that as it may, we do not find a canonical model of how to write the internal history of the Durkheim School's interest in the categories of thought in the current scientific landscape. Such an internal history of the Durkheim School is not only missing because of the historical ruptures of World Wars I and II and the death of a large number of members of the Durkheim School, but also because of the loose form of their cooperation. The project had never been spelled out systematically and remains to be reconstructed as a collective effort spanning almost fifty years and including the work of a dozen scholars. The Durkheim- or Mauss-centrism of many sociologists and anthropologists (notable exceptions are Hörl 2005; Moebius 2006: 73–115) has also impeded the writing of a history of the category project. This focus on individual scholars obscures that the category project has not only been a quest for the social origins of thought, but originates itself in social relations. The published texts are just the tip of the iceberg, which consists of debates at the Société Française de Philosophie (SFP), informal meetings, letters, book reviews, and hidden references.

We distinguish four structural phases that exemplify the dynamics of the project as a comparative experiment. In a largely neglected passage Durkheim explains: "When, on the other hand, the production of facts is something beyond our power to command, and we can only bring them together as they have been spontaneously produced, the method used is one of indirect experimentation, or the comparative method" (Durkheim [1895] 1982: 147; see Durkheim 1888: 41).

The work that has been initiated by Durkheim and Mauss from the 1890s to the late 1930s was a realization of the comparative method as "indirect experimentation." As categories are the result of the bodily and mental cooperation between members of specific social groups, who unite rhythmically in rituals, the argument that categories are of social origin could not be proved through direct experimentation. Following Claude Bernard, Durkheim conceived of direct experimentation as an actively controlled manipulation of the object of knowledge (see Schmidt this volume). Instead of directly working on the social body of the Third French Republic—an endeavor Durkheim pursued in his pedagogical work—the Durkheimians started to compare different ways of how societies developed their categories in social practice.

Applying this method to the development of the category project results in four phases of the category project, which are: (1) building a hypothesis (until 1903–04), (2) conducting crucial experiments (1904–07), (3) formulating a theory and defending it against alternatives (1907–14), and (4) solidifying the theory empirically and comparatively as well as establishing links to other disciplines (1920–39).

It is important to remember that these phases cannot be reduced to historical periods. We nevertheless suggest mapping them loosely onto the four historical phases mentioned above. Until 1903–1904, the Durkheim School was focusing on different categories while not yet having a comprehensive account of their systematic endeavor. During this time, they also started to build the hypothesis of the categories' social origin without explicitly saying so, namely in Durkheim and Mauss's essay on classification (Durkheim and Mauss 1903a). In the second phase of crucial experiments, lasting until 1906–1907, individual scholars worked on those categories that can legitimately be considered central for a European history of thought: space, cause, and time. The period from 1906–1907 to World War I can be seen as the third phase in which the category project comes to its first fruition. Durkheim's *Elementary Forms* is the most coherent and systematic formulation of the theory of the social origin of the categories. At the same time, Marcel Mauss, Henri Hubert, Robert Hertz, Antoine Bianconi, and others tested the hypothesis of the social origins of thought in diverse empirical settings ranging from Bantu languages to Polynesian cosmologies until World War I had its devastating impact. After World War I and Durkheim's death in 1917, in the project's fourth period, Mauss was left to continue, refine, and open the category project for new historical and scientific developments such as the introduction of long-term fieldwork in anthropology, and interdisciplinary debates with psychology, linguistics, technology, and historical sciences.

The Beginnings: Formulating a Hypothesis (until 1903–1904)

Mauss dated the beginning of the category project to the second volume of the *Année*. He probably referred to two articles published in that volume: Durkheim's "De la définition des phénomènes religieux" (Durkheim 1899) and Hubert and Mauss's "Essai sur la nature et la fonction du sacrifice" (Hubert and Mauss 1899). The latter is generally considered to be the first monographic work dealing with the notion of the sacred and retrospectively has often been presented as possessing categorical status. Later on, however, Mauss ([1930] 1998: 40) acknowledged that the Durkheim School's fault had been to reduce the problem of the categories to the question of the sacred and vice versa.

Stefan Czarnowski (1925) mentions an alternative starting point of the project in his article "Le morcellement de l'étendue et sa limitation dans la religion et la magie." He makes a reference to the fifth volume of the *Année* published in 1902 in which his teacher Henri Hubert writes:

> Since religious acts are in fact performed in *space* and *time*, one of the enigmas of the ritual is the reconciliation of these ineluctable conditions with the infinity and theoretical immutability of the sacred. . . .
> In fact, the study of the notions of time and space should logically be combined with the study of representations. (Hubert 1902b: 248)[3]

Hubert's contribution to the collective endeavor of the category project remains highly underrated, even though he was the first to address the question of the categories systematically. His methodological stance is central to the category project and exemplifies how categories such as *space* and *time* have to be understood in relation to the study of representations, which include, among other notions and concepts, categories. In his introduction to the new rubric "Représentations religieuses d'êtres ou de phénomènes naturels," (Hubert 1902c), Hubert adds the category of the *person* as one of the notions to be included in the table of categories:

> We could add what we have written above on the religious representation of space and time, indicate here some works relating to nature and, by extension, to the fate of the soul and discuss the concepts involved in magic. . . . The representation of personality is one of the studies that we would like to be able to classify under this heading soon. (ibid.: 269)

In 1902, the same year Durkheim attained a prominent position in Paris, where he was appointed to the chair of education at the Sorbonne, he asked Mauss in a letter to collaborate with him on the "Essay on Primitive Classification." Acknowledging the difficulty of the task, he suggested a structure of the "Essay" and pointed to the core of the hypothesis of the social origins of the categories: "The mental operation called classification was not formed as one piece in the human brain. . . . Classes are not given in the things. They are created" (Durkheim 1998: 320). In the famous essay on classification, we then find the answer to the question of how things are classified and by whom:

> It has quite often been said that man began to conceive things by relating them to himself. The above allows us to see more precisely what this anthropocentrism, which might better be called sociocentrism, consists of. The centre of the first schemes of nature is not the individual; it is society. (Durkheim and Mauss [1903a] 1963: 51)

Here, we have the basic formula for the category project. Foundational concepts of thought such as classes are neither psychological achievements nor transcendental givens. They are developed in relation to social facts such as the structure of clans. The second introduction to the rubric "Représentations religieuses d'êtres ou de phénomènes naturels" from the *Année sociologique VI*, an addendum to the "Essay on Classification," however, shows that Durkheim and Mauss had not yet defined a set of categories to be studied. They argue for a "study of tales, cosmologies, in general of science, the notions concerning the soul, time, space, cause, law" (Durkheim and Mauss 1903b: 225–26).

Already visible here is what could be called the "containment" of the question of categories in the analysis of religious thought. This might be a result of Durkheim's attempt to distance himself from historical materialism as Nathan Schlanger argues (2006: 5–15), but one can also sense a certain hesitation to directly address the question of the categories. In a letter to Xavier Léon dated 24 July 1908, that is, after he had begun to prepare *Elementary Forms* (Watts Miller 2006: 3), Durkheim writes:

> I intend to indicate . . . some of the social elements that served to constitute some of our categories ([. . . ?] causality, the notion of force, the notion of personality). This question has preoccupied me for a long time and I do not dare, for the moment, to address it head-on. I believe that it is possible to approach it through religious thought. (Durkheim 1976: 467)

Religion thus provided the empirical ground to test a hypothesis with a much broader claim, namely Durkheim's frontal attack on the tradition of both a transcendental as well as empiricist explanation of the origin of categories: "For these philosophers, in fact, categories preform reality, whereas for us, they summarize it. According to them, they are the natural law of thought; for us, they are a product of human art" (Durkheim 1909: 757). Henri Hubert summarizes the Durkheim School's sociocentric explanation of the origin of human thought with explicit reference to categories as early as 1904:

> This ever-present idea of the sacred is of higher value than a simple notion. We are tempted to consider it as a true category in the Aristotelian sense of the word. It is in religious representations what notions of time, space and cause are in individual representations. (Hubert 1904a: xlvii)

In the next phase, the Durkheim School focused on a "sociocentric" analysis of time, space, and cause—exactly those categories mentioned by Hubert in 1904. While Durkheim used the work on religious phenomena as a shield behind which he mercilessly prepared his attack on Western philosophy in both its transcendental and empiricist outlook, he sent Marcel Mauss, Henri Beuchat, and Henri Hubert out as scouts to ascertain whether the hypothesis of the social origins of thought could be verified.

Crucial Experiments on Individual Categories: Time, Space, Causality (1904–1906)

Hubert and Mauss's "General Theory of Magic" ([1904] 2005), Mauss and Beuchat's *Seasonal Variations of the Eskimo: A Study in Social Morphology* ([1906] 1979), and Hubert's "Essay on Time" ([1905] 1999) are three interlinked experiments attempting to verify the hypothesis of the categories' social origin. While the "Essay on Magic" deals with the category of *mana*, which simultaneously unites quality and substance and forms the basis for causality (Hubert and Mauss [1904] 2005: 134–138), the "Eskimo Essay" and the "Essay on Time" show, always in reference to the "Essay on Magic," how the Kantian forms of *intuition*, *space*, and *time*, are generated through social practices. Evidence was established through the comparison of empirical material gained indirectly by means of travel reports and ethnographic descriptions. The three young men confidently presented themselves as the founders of a new comparative science of the social.

In the "General Theory of Magic," Mauss explored *mana*, like the idea of the sacred, as "a kind of category of collective thinking which is the foundation for our judgments and which imposes a classification on things, separating some, bringing together others, establishing lines of influence or boundaries of isolation" (Hubert and Mauss [1904] 2005: 149). This observation is systematized in Hubert and Mauss's "Introduction to the Analysis of Some Religious Phenomena" first published in 1906 and again in 1909 as an introduction to a collection of contributions by Mauss and Hubert to the sociology of religion (Hubert and Mauss [1906] 1968). Here, the working twins, *les jumeaux de travail*, seem to have become even more self-assured of their own theoretical endeavor. They present *mana* as a kind of "primordial category":

> But *mana* is not only a special category of primitive thought, and today, in the process of reduction, it is still the first form that other categories, still at work in our minds, have taken: those of substance and cause. What we know about it therefore makes it possible to conceive how categories present themselves in the minds of primitives. (Mauss and Hubert 1968 [1906]: 29)

With regard to the category of time, Hubert's expertise in Celtic and Roman myths and his interest in calendars and religious rhythms was crucial (see Hubert 1901; 1902a). Time is not conceived as a "form of intuition" but as a product of social convention: "In brief, the division of time entails the maximum of convention and the minimum of experience. Ultimately, experience lends it additional authority" (Hubert [1905] 1999: 70). A mere year later, Mauss and Beuchat published their *Seasonal Variations of the Eskimo: A Study in Social Morphology*, which deals with space as a category originating in social relations and links the question of space to the category of quantity by discussing the notion of social density and the idea of a law of the rhythm of social life.

It is unsurprising that Mauss and Hubert are, at the same time, interested in the concept of number, which is testified by reviews they wrote in the *Année* (Mauss 1904; Hubert 1905). As shown by Hubert's statement, which appears in a review of Roscher's "Die Sieben und Neunzahl im Kultus der Griechen" (1907), the Durkheim School's hypothesis of the social origin of thought had been refined. Compared to the rather cautious and empirically embedded arguments of his "Essay on Time" (see Hubert [1905] 1999: 80), Hubert phrases the argument of the social origin of time, number, and *mana* in a more abstract and philosophical tone:

> These are arbitrarily constructed numbers, which apply both to the division of space and to that of time and which are not given by even imperfect experiments. The elements of this construction are undoubtedly experimental, but the objective experience from which they emerged is infinitely distant and has been infinitely elaborated. They are intellectual constructions that are the work of men in groups, like classification, like the idea of mana, like the idea of time itself. I am only talking about the elements of the collective mentality whose formation we have so far studied. It is not, in my opinion, in the objects of experience, but in the logic of the collective spirit that their origin must be sought. (Hubert 1907: 314)

The argument is now based upon solid empirical evidence that allows the Durkheimians to advance their project. As Robert Hertz writes in a review of Mauss and Hubert's "Mélanges d'histoire des religions": "What Hubert has done for time, others have done or will do for the other categories of reason; thus a new theory of knowledge is gradually emerging, truly positive and experimental" (Hertz 1909: 219). This marks an important step toward the full-fledged theory of the "Elementary Forms."

Formulating a Theory and Fending off Criticism: From the "Elementary Forms" to the "Categories of the Black" (1907–1914)

After Mauss, Beuchat, and Hubert had shown that three of the most influential concepts of Western philosophy should be studied from a sociocentric perspective, the Durkheim School focused on two complementary strategies. While Durkheim was preoccupied with summarizing the epistemological intentions of the category project, which led to the publication of *The Elementary Forms of Religious Life* ([1912] 1995) other members of the Durkheim School started to broaden the geographical and topical scope of the project. While Robert Hertz explored the categorical status of "left" and "right" in different cultures (Hertz [1909] 1960), Mauss began his work on the relation between numbers, language, and food by analyzing Vedic poetry (Mauss 1911).[4]

Another, so far neglected, scholar, Antoine Bianconi, started to explore African Bantu languages,[5] which divide the world's entities into different classes. Bianconi demanded that sociological facts be integrated into linguistic studies and started to explore what he called *categories de noir* (Bianconi 1910: 219; see Bianconi 1913).[6] Alongside broadening the category project empirically, Durkheim started to develop a proper sociology of knowledge. In the eleventh volume of the *Année*, for example, Durkheim and Celestin Bouglé introduced the rubric "Les conditions sociologiques de la connaissance." They understood this rubric as the successor of the above-mentioned "Religious Representations of Being and of Natural Phenomena" (see Clammer 2000). It anticipated the program of the "Elementary Forms":

> If it is for the first time that the abovementioned rubric appears in "l'Année," it is because the issue it raises has remained foreign to us until the present time. The topic, however, has stood for a long time in the first rank of our preoccupations. Without speaking of our study "Primitive Classification," which appeared in these pages, and Hubert's "Etude sommaire de la représentation du temps dans la religion et dans la magie" ... the reader will find each of these volumes classified under the "Religious Representations of Being and of Natural Phenomena," in addition to a certain number of books and articles reviewed from this very point of view. Now, since religion is essentially a social phenomenon, in order to seek what religious factors have entered into our representation of the world, we have rigorously attempted to determine some of the sociological conditions of knowledge. (Durkheim and Bouglé 1910, quoted in Nandan 1980: 106–7)

Directly after this introduction, the Durkheimians placed a review of the "Soziologie des Erkennens" of Wilhelm Jerusalem (Durkheim 1910). This shows the extent to which they aimed at integrating their category project into a wider international discussion of the social conditions of knowledge.

Ultimately, the work of the Durkheim School on the social origins of thought culminated in *Elementary Forms*. This book represents a systematic account of the category project. There, Durkheim situates the project with respect to the philosophical tradition of Aristotle, Immanuel Kant, and Georg W. F. Hegel mediated through Charles Renouvier, Octave Hamelin (Stedman-Jones 2000), and the French spiritualist tradition (Schmaus 2004). Considering the boldness of both argumentation and rhetorical style, it is unsurprising that contemporary scholars started to discuss the Durkheim School's category project right after the publication of *Elementary Forms*. The reactions were, however, not at all approving.[7] They rather show the multitude of different criticisms and attacks the self-described "pack of ... dogs" (Mauss 1923b: 25) had to fend off.

A case in point is Durkheim's presentation at the SFP on 4 February 1913. Durkheim was confronted with arguments against his theory of the genesis of intelligence, religion, and society from very different philosophical and theological corners. The *Elementary Forms* threatened, on the one hand, the authority of philosophy as first science since Durkheim claimed competences for the new science of sociology that formerly had been reserved for philosophy. On the other hand, Durkheim had challenged the authority of Western thought in general and of Christianity in particular by demonstrating that the allegedly most rational and individualistic monotheistic religion was but a variety of religious thought in the history of mankind. Durkheim's position seemingly advocated a social constructivism that, according to his contemporaries, would ultimately lead to relativism. The discussion at the SFP illustrates the hostile intellectual climate in which the Durkheimians attempted to establish sociology as a foundational science.[8]

While the philosopher and psychologist Henri Delacroix rejects Durkheim's idea that effervescent rituals are to be held responsible for the genesis of categories and reason itself (Durkheim 1913: 78), Edouard Le Roy tried to push Durkheim to acknowledge a vital force as a principle for a creative evolution (1913: 92–93). Jules Lachelier followed Le Roy and saw the authority and moral high-ground of Christianity threatened by Durkheim's theory, a position also held by Abbot Lucien Laberthonnière, who claimed that primitive rituals have merely material goals, while Christian rituals aim at the spiritual transformation of the individual (1913: 102).

Alphonse Darlu brought forward the most interesting and systematic critique of Durkheim's work. He accused Durkheim of not differentiating between two versions of his argument. One version was commonly accepted by most social scientists while the other, being more radical, was rejected:

> The first idea . . . can be stated as follows: religious, moral and even logical conceptions are of social origin in the sense that they are given in collective thought; they reside in this synthesis of individual consciousnesses which is social consciousness, and social consciousness imposes them on the belief of individuals. The individual mind is immersed in the social mind. . . . But the second idea . . . must seem exorbitant to most of us; because it offends all our mental habits. Religious, moral, logical conceptions are of social origin in the second sense that they are primitive and essentially conceptions of social things, conceptions formed on the model of social things. (Durkheim 1913: 87–88)

The reaction of Durkheim to these critiques is striking. According to him, all of them were based on a general misunderstanding of *Elemen-*

tary Forms and did not discuss his central argument. Durkheim was disappointed that his critics did not take the claim seriously that religion has a dynamogenic character, that is, it generates phenomena that are spiritual and rational (1913: 80–81). Analogously to Darlu, Louis Weber also criticized Durkheim for putting too much emphasis on social force when explaining the genesis of the human intellect (Weber 1913; 1914; see Schick, this volume). If the social is required for the generation of categories such as causality, can we still have any objectivity in the world (Weber 1914: 71–72)? It was precisely this tension between the empirical genesis of the categories and the ideal faculties of the intellect, between the two different interpretations of Darlu as well as the difference between socially constructed and cognitively hardwired categories, that allowed Mauss to fruitfully continue the category project and to give it its own spin.

Engagement with Other Disciplines: Psychology, History, Linguistics (1918–1939)

World War I had devastating effects on the Durkheim School. While several members such as Robert Hertz (1881–1915) and Antoine Bianconi (1882–1915) died in the trenches of the Great War, Émile Durkheim (1858–1917) suffered a stroke and died in November 1917. The legacy was left to Marcel Mauss, who honored his dead friends in the first volume of the new edition of the *Année* (Mauss [1925] 2016). However bleak their scholarly and personal futures must have looked after the grim experience of World War I, the category project was immediately taken up by different members of the Durkheim School:[9] Maurice Halbwachs, Marcel Granet, and Paul Fauconnet. Halbwachs, for example, summarizes the project of Durkheim's *Elementary Forms* with a focus on the question of categories in his article "La doctrine d'Émile Durkheim," which quotes Durkheim's text almost verbatim:

> There are in our mind eminent concepts, which play a fundamental role in knowledge: these are the most general frameworks of our thinking, which Kant has referred to as categories, or forms: notions of cause, substance, space, etc. Durkheim sees in their very importance a reason to consider these categories as "social in the second degree." For, they do not only express the attitude of social thought towards things but the very things they represent and that society thinks are characters or aspects of society: the object of thought is social, as the subject who thinks it. (Halbwachs 1918: 387)

A similar reference was made by Paul Fauconnet, who stressed the historical character of the categories and called them "centers of intelligibility" (1922: 20):

> Durkheim calls them categories, mother-notions, centers of intelligibility that are the frames or the tools of logical thought.... We cannot see how these categories should be innate to the human mind. They have a history: they have been gradually built during the course of evolution of civilization and, in our civilization, through the development of the physical and moral sciences. (Fauconnet 1922: 201–2)

At least of equal importance was Marcel Granet. Granet's work might even be seen as the most consistent attempt to follow Durkheim's program of the "Elementary Forms" (see Schüttpelz and Zillinger 2017). While Mauss and Durkheim had been introduced to Chinese cosmology through the work of the Dutch sinologist Jan Jakob Maria de Groot (see Mauss 1899), Granet opened up French sinology for sociological thought (Granet 1920). Retrospectively, he even claimed that the "Classification Essay" "will be marked as a date in the history of sinological study" (Granet [1934] 1994: 485).

Granet's work seeks to verify Durkheim's theory of the genesis of the categories by applying it to Chinese thought. As Robert LaFleur stresses in this volume, Granet added movement to "the conceptual power of Durkheim's and Mauss's classificatory schemes.... Far from being static, platonic forms, yin and yang are always moving.... Marcel Granet's powerful response to *Les classifications primitives* establishes the overwhelming theme of *mouvement*." (LaFleur, this volume).

Mauss himself, following in the footsteps of Bianconi and with the help of Antoine Meillet, launched what could be called the category project's linguistic and historic turns (Mauss 1923a; 1924). He began to be interested in the relation between language and cognitive mechanisms[10] and the degree to which categories are shaped and altered in the course of history. This interdisciplinary outreach of the category project is epitomized in the following passage in which Mauss comments on a short statement by Meillet:

> One thing is well demonstrated: it is impossible to write the history of the abstracting, categorizing activity of the human mind, without taking these facts of linguistics and collective psychology into account and, above all, without taking into account the way in which these phenomena, being simultaneously social as well as psychological, are interdependent with the other phenomena of the history and very structure of societies. (Mauss [1923] 1964: 127)

This opening up of the category project took inspirations not only from linguistics, psychology, and history but also from technology. In 1927, Mauss explicitly criticized the claim that categories have a single source such as religion and urged us to take technical practices into account as well:

> The notion of class or genre is mainly juristic in origin, as Durkheim and I have assumed; as Hubert has said, the notion of time, and as Durkheim wrote in the "Elementary Forms of the Religious Life," the notion of soul and, in some pages of the same book, which have been too little noticed, the notion of the Whole are mainly religious or symbolic in origin—none of these arguments mean to say that every other general notion has had the same kind of origin. We do not at all believe that. There remain to be studied many other categories, both living and dead, deriving from many other origins, and in particular categories of a technical nature. To cite only the mathematical concepts of Number and Space, who will ever say enough and with sufficient exactitude the part which weaving, basket-making, carpentry, nautical art, the wheel and the potter's wheel have had in the origins of geometry, arithmetic and mechanics? . . . We would never come to an end of listing the various activities and also the various ideas whose forms are at bottom general ideas, including those which are still at bottom of our own ideas. These studies of the forms of thought, primitive or not, should appear at the end, to crown and to synthesise our studies. (Mauss [1927] 2006: 50)

Two of Mauss's last texts, the essay on matter as well as the essay on the category of the person, also begin with explicit references to the category project (see Mauss [1938] 1985: 1–2). Of special interest is Mauss's "Conceptions which Have Preceded the Notion of Matter" ([1939] 2006) in which he summarizes the main argument of the category project and extends its raison d'être to the study of science as a social milieu in itself (Schick et al. 2015). Mauss thereby broke ground for the social study of science *avant la lettre*. Introducing the notion of substance Mauss had been interested in at least since 1899 (see Allen 1998), he writes:

> Philosophies and sciences are languages and it is merely a matter of making use of the best language available. Language itself and the categories of thought are "extractions" from the modes of thought and feeling of a given social milieu. . . . Moreover, if our way of thinking derives at every moment from all that constitutes social life, we ought not to keep apart from it the scientific mentality, so intimately it is connected to the mentality as a whole. (Mauss [1927] 2006: 141–2)

By including Western science in their argument about the social origin of human thought, the Durkheim School took it to its logical extreme foreshadowed in Durkheim's *Elementary Forms*. It is no longer society that is built after models of nature but vice versa: the universe itself is modeled after the social (Durkheim [1912] 1995: 442–43). The legacy of the Durkheim School's category project thus extends well into the present—and beyond.

Contributions to This Volume

This volume has three sections. The first, "Silenced Influences and Hidden Texts," assembles contributions dealing with unknown or unmentioned influences that were, by accident or on purpose, concealed by Durkheim and Mauss. The second section, "Lateral Links and Ambivalent Antagonists," discusses the fact that the category project was an integral part of the renewed European urge to (re)establish the humanities against the "hard sciences." It is thus not surprising that the controversies within and between disciplines produced antagonists as well as "partners in crime." The alliances were often fluid and dynamic. Although, for instance, Henri Bergson and Durkheim appear as antagonists retrospectively, it seems that both shared the aforementioned goals while their evaluation of the empirical sciences differed. The last section, "Forgotten Allies and Secret Students," pays tribute to scholars who are often marginalized in scholarly debates focusing mainly on Durkheim and Mauss: Marcel Granet, Robert Hertz, Maurice Halbwachs, and Stefan Czarnowski.

Silenced Influences and Hidden Texts

Gregory Schrempp discusses three trajectories that situate the category project of the Durkheim School within the history of the general philosophical question of universalism and relativism. He understands the Durkheimian account of the categories as simultaneously universalist and relativist. Schrempp contrasts Durkheim's account with the work of Max Müller and Franz Boas, who have been influenced by the Kantian a priori account of the categories, as well as with David Hume's fundamental critique of causality and its influence on anthropology, especially on E. B. Tylor and James Frazer. Finally, Schrempp contrasts the relativist-universalist Durkheimian theory with contemporary research in the cognitive sciences, namely George Lakoff and Mark Johnson's famous work on the embodied character of knowledge, where the focus shifts from the bodily experience of society to the individual experience of the body.

Nicolas Sembel uses the term "hidden" to point out unacknowledged texts, persons, concepts as well as intellectual and social links shaping the development of Durkheim and Mauss. Sembel bases his work on findings in the library loan registers during Mauss and Durkheim's period in Bordeaux as well as on texts whose publication had been suppressed and were only discovered recently. This provides a new perspective on the collaboration of Mauss and Durkheim. While Hubert and Mauss both had their own field of specialization—the labor was divided, so to speak—Durkheim and his nephew were from the very beginning closely collaborating, having the same intellectual background and the same goal in mind: developing a general sociology.

The relation of the Durkheim School to British Anthropology is explored via the notion of *mana* in Nicolas Meylan's contribution. Meylan traces the notion of *mana* back to the work of Max Müller, who used *mana*—similar to Mauss and Hubert—to argue, against Tylor and Frazer, that religion is not based on reason but has its origin in another faculty (for Müller in poetry and feeling). This argument against Tylor and Frazer can also be found in the works of John King and Robert Ranulph Marett and contextualizes Hubert and Mauss's account within a general tendency in British Anthropology.

Susan Stedman Jones's article aims at understanding the question "how are categories laboriously forged?" She refers to the work of Renouvier, who was a major influence for Durkheim, in order to clarify the role of categories as collective representations and the importance of labor to generate categories. The categories of relation and becoming are fundamental for Renouvier and were adapted by Durkheim to develop his theory. Collective labor can thus be characterized as the effort to create, synthesize, stabilize, and differentiate relations through rituals and group actions.

Anne Rawls shows that the work on the categories already started, if not explicitly, in Durkheim's "Division of Labour," which analyzes the central role of constitutive practices of modern and premodern societies for the creation of categories. She identifies the independence of situated practice from structure as a central point of Durkheim's theory, which influenced the work of Talcott Parsons and Harold Garfinkel. While in the 1930s value neutrality had become the paradigm for scientific research, Rawls demonstrates with Durkheim, Parsons, and Garfinkel that statistics, like crime records in the United States, are social facts imbued with and building upon moral judgements. Rawls argues with Durkheim for a self-reflexive sociology that recognizes the moral implications of the creation of social facts and thus exposes unjust moral relationships and the practices that produce them.

Mario Schmidt's contribution concludes this section by suggesting that the notion of *expérience* refers not only to "experience" but also to the understanding of "experiments" at the turn of the nineteenth to the twentieth century. Schmidt points out that Durkheim was well acquainted with the works of Claude Bernard and that an interpretation applying the concept of experiment to rituals of effervescence paves the way for a new perspective on the category project. Categories are interpreted as intersubjectively experienced experiments on social matter.

Lateral Links and Ambivalent Antagonists

Erhard Schüttpelz stresses the importance of the "Essay on the Gift" and the notion of the "total social fact" for the category project. The "total social fact" combines the Durkheimian category of totality with the notion of the social fact in order to address the essential fluidity of societies. The social force, which is presupposed as underlying any social situation, is prevalent in gift exchange. It thus reveals a collective force that obligates the participants of the exchange and simultaneously provides them with a certain amount of freedom. The "holism of the gift" thereby transcends modern divisions and, as Schüttpelz points out, it is precisely this aspect that constitutes societies.

Totality is also at the core of Nick Allen's contribution. He applies this Durkheimian category to kinship, draws the consequences of totality for sociology as a science and uses it to interpret Indo-European myths. Totality as a starting point provides an alternative to egocentric kinship models. Allen's tetradic theory offers the simplest form of classification of a society on the basis of marriage. It presupposes the existence of the societal body as a whole in which the society's members participate and which can be ritually divided. In Vedic literature one finds the fictitious ritual of the sacrifice *of* and *to* Puruṣa, where the category of totality is rather an ontological property than a mere abstraction.

William Watts Miller engages Durkheim with Bergson and recent research on primates to shed new light on the origins of social life and the genesis of the notion of effervescence. Watts Miller points to a paradox within Durkheim's work that argues against spontaneous creation and for a strong distinction between animal and human life. While Bergson shares the interest in creativity with Durkheim, his strong opposition of instinct and intelligence does not provide a convincing argument. Rather, it is an obstacle to understand the genesis of social behavior. The comparison of Durkheim with contemporary research in the cognitive sciences allows Watts Miller to stress the importance of creative effervescence as a social phenomenon in hominin evolution. As he argues, there was not a single moment when human beings stepped out of their animality, but rather multiple creative social attempts and solutions.

The relation of Bergson and Durkheim is also at center stage in Heike Delitz's contribution that focuses on the social origins of the category project itself. The polemical tension between Bergson and Durkheim is considered essential at the *moment philosophique of 1900*, not only for the development of the category project but also for Bergson's sociology thirty years later. While Bergson had to be sociologized by Durkheim and his followers, such as Hubert and Halbwachs, this process of polemics, interpretation, and transformation also left its marks within the thought of the Durkheim School. Delitz describes these reciprocal influences and aversions along the lines of the phenomena of time, memory, and the genesis of societies.

Johannes F. M. Schick's article discusses the categories of causality, time, and technology against the background of a controversy between members of the Durkheim School and some philosophers. The debate revolved around the question of whether or not the genesis of intelligence, and consequently of the categories, is a social process or whether it is the material engagement of human beings that generates intelligence. Louis Weber, a forgotten but historically important critic of Durkheim, argued for the independence of a technical intelligence prior to any form of sociality. This dualistic conception is contrasted with Mauss and Hubert's holistic ontology. They argue for the concomitance of the social and the technical generating differences, categories, and concepts that are in a recursive relationship with the human body and its sociotechnical practices. These practices are illustrated with the genesis of the category of time, where the human body serves as the medium on which time operates.

Forgotten Allies and Secret Students

Martin Zillinger focuses on the category of space in Stefan Czarnowski's almost forgotten lecture "Le morcellement de l'étendue et sa limitation dans la religion et la magie" (Czarnowski 1925). Zillinger shows that this text is crucial for rethinking Durkheim's notion of "the sacred" in non-essentialist, relational terms and that it already entails positions the sociologists of the Collège de Sociologie defended ten years later. Czarnowski's study of space results in a theory of boundaries and thresholds, where the "sacred" is distributed into a concentrated (*sacré concentré*) and an unbound form (*sacré libre*). In moving from a center, the *sacré concentré* transforms into a *sacré libre* that faces competing forces coming from outside. The forces of the wilderness are represented at all units of a graduated social space, while the forces of the social are found in different intensities within *and* without. The "rhythm of space" thus constituted changes with the person and their gods defining the center of their world.

Robert LaFleur's contribution situates Granet's œuvre within the tradition of the *Année sociologique* and stresses the importance of movement as a classificatory category. Granet's imaginative ethnography is based upon Durkheim's *Elementary Forms* and his "Division of Labour." The detailed account of religious life in China appears as "part of a larger analysis of social dynamics fueled by the intellectual life of the *Année sociologique*" (LaFleur in this volume). The full force of Granet's work, however, is the interpenetration of sociological and sinological analysis that illustrates the dynamism of social life and of the categories.

Ulrich van Loyen relates Hertz's ([1909] 1960) classical study "Pre-eminence of the Right Hand" to questions of gender and inequality. He reads Hertz' essay as a praxeology of classification which understands human beings as natural symbols embedded into a cosmos that has to be "handled." Inequality is explained as resulting from the "idea that by inviting one hand to do the same all the time one enables a regime of stability as the basis for cosmological distinctions that otherwise would collapse" (van Loyen in this volume). Gender distinctions are also an expression of the stabilization of this pre-eminence. It is, however, precisely this need of the *homo duplex* to multiply themselves constantly through polar distinctions that allows for a reflexive stance toward these practices and makes fellow human beings similar in their shared strategies of world-making.

Jean-François Bert interprets the notion of the "total social fact" through readings of Lévi-Strauss, Bourdieu, and Foucault. While Lévi-Strauss stresses the mutual dependency of the individual and the social that is expressed by a total social fact such as gift exchange, Bourdieu reproaches Lévi-Strauss's position for not considering the question of time in the process of reciprocity. According to Bourdieu the total social fact focuses on the complexity of situations and avoids a priori replications of dualisms such as history and sociology or understanding and explaining. For Foucault, the notion overcomes the *homo duplex* and provides an archaeological account, which he integrates into his own method and—without mentioning Mauss—develops further in his genealogy. The intersection of the three readings allows a clearer picture of what Mauss was trying to convey with the concept of the "total social fact."

Jean-Christophe Marcel argues that Halbwachs continues Durkheim's program of the "Elementary Forms" and his social ontology. His theory of collective memory extends Durkheim and Mauss's theory of collective representations. Halbwachs specifies the cognitive powers of collective representations and describes how they are built and combined in collective consciousness. This "collective psychology" deals with collective representations that are extended and crystallized in spatial relations. Collective thought, according to Halbwachs, is to remember, which is always related to other members of the group and to matter. Material artifacts are apt to store memories and participate in the stabilization of a society.

The concluding chapter by Wendy James takes the category project to the "field" by illustrating how the Durkheimian approach can instruct and inspire fieldwork as discovery of other social worlds. Especially the notions of effervescence and of sociality as cooperation are useful to conceptualize ethnographic material such as the use and reinvention of instruments and rituals, for example, the musical practices of the Uduk (Sudan) and the Gumuz (Ethiopia) in refugee camps as means to produce sociality. James reminds us that the systematic claim of the category project arises precisely from the fact that it cannot be completed as such. The search for new categories always remains possible and necessary. The human mind is characterized by the dynamic quality of creating new intellectual formations and needs those new and different categories to decenter itself:

> The Aristotelian categories are not indeed the only ones which exist in our minds, or have existed in the mind and have to be dealt with. Above all it is essential to draw up the largest possible catalogue of categories; it is essential to start with all those, which it is possible to know man has used. It will be clear that there have been and still are dead or pale or obscure moons in the firmament of reason. The big and the small, the animate and the inanimate, the right and the left have been categories. . . . All the categories are merely general symbols, which, like other symbols, have been acquired only by mankind very slowly. This work of constitution needs to be described. . . . For this work was itself complex, hazardous, chancy. Mankind erected its mind by all possible means: technical and non-technical, mystical and non-mystical; using its mind (senses, sentiment, reason), using its body; at the whim of choices, things and times; at the whim of nations and their achievements or ruins. Our general concepts are still unstable and imperfect. I sincerely believe that it is by concerted efforts, but from opposite directions, that our psychological, sociological and historical sciences will one day be able to attempt a description of this painful history. And I believe that it is this science, this sentiment of the present relativity of our reason, that will perhaps inspire the best philosophy. Allow me to conclude in this way. (Mauss [1924] 1979: 32–33)

Johannes F. M. Schick is scientific coordinator of the CRC 1187 Media of Cooperation since January 2022. He was head of the research project "Action, Operation, Gesture: Technology as Interdisciplinary Anthropology" at the a.r.t.e.s. Graduate School for the Humanities (University of Cologne) from October 2017 to February 2021. His research focuses on interdisciplinary (techno-)anthropology (from Bergson, Espinas, and Mauss to Simondon, Bergson's philosophy of life), French epistemology, and the relation of anthropology to philosophy. He has published in journals such as *Parrhesia: A Journal of Critical Philosophy* and most recently in *Techné: Research in Philosophy and Technology*.

Mario Schmidt is a Postdoctoral Fellow at the a.r.t.e.s. Graduate School of the Humanities at the University of Cologne. He has published in distinguished academic journals such as *Africa*, *Journal of Eastern African Studies*, *Ethnohistory*, and *Journal of Cultural Economy*. Currently, he is editing a German anthology on the Durkheimian category project with Johannes F. M. Schick, Ulrich van Loyen, and Martin Zillinger that will be published by Matthes & Seitz.

Martin Zillinger is Professor of Social and Cultural Anthropology at the University of Cologne. His major field research has been in Morocco on trance, ritual, and new media. In his publications he addresses issues at the intersection of anthropology, media studies, and practice theory. His works on the history of anthropology and the Durkheim school are published in journals such as *Durkheimian Studies*, *HAU—Journal of Ethnographic Theory*, the *Zeitschrift für Ethnologie*, as well as the *Zeitschrift für Kulturwissenschaften*.

Notes

This publication has been supported by the German Research Foundation (DFG)—Project Number 262513311—CRC 1187, Media of Cooperation, University of Siegen, the a.r.t.e.s. Graduate School for the Humanities (University of Cologne), the Fritz-Thyssen Foundation, and the Gerda Henkel Foundation (Project Number 49/V/17). It was realized within the ongoing work of the "Werkstatt Praxistheorie" (University of Cologne and University of Siegen, with Ole Reichardt, Anne Rawls, Erhard Schüttpelz, and Martin Zillinger). As editors we would like to thank Julian Pieper, Annette Steffny, and Ole Reichardt who, by supporting us in our editorial tasks, made our work much easier.

1. We are well aware that Durkheim's focus on the categories may even have started earlier, that is, with his "Division of Labor," as Anne Rawls

and Susan Stedman-Jones both argue convincingly from different perspectives; but we here focus on the development of the category project as described by the members of the Durkheim School themselves, that is, as a history of a collaborative project closely connected to the journal *Année sociologique*.
2. Our work on the category project is a collective endeavor that would not have seen the light of day without the inspiration of and continuous dialogue with Erhard Schüttpelz.
3. All quotes were translated by the authors if not referenced otherwise.
4. For Mauss, the genesis of numbers and the categories of "left" and "right" actually belonged together: "At the basis of the abstract concept of number, we find a mystical egocentric concept that was gradually analyzed, increased and enriched. First comes the number 2, coming from internal sensations of the 'double self', right and left, or rather front and back" (Mauss 1904b: 313).
5. Mauss had already started to be interested in African cultures earlier. In a review of R. E. Dennett's "At the Back of the Black Man's Mind," he writes:
   > According to him, among the Bavili there exists a complete system of classifications, of categories in which all nature is organized. A complete philosophy, conscious of the world, in which things are grouped into families, principles, governing couples of causes and effects; each of these coupled elements is distinguished to the male and female. . . . The six categories are: water, earth, fire, procreation and movement, fertility. (Mauss 1907b: 306)
6. In his review of E. Pechuel-Loesche's "Die Loango Expedition," Bianconi explicitly links his linguistic explorations to Durkheim and Mauss's essay on classification, thereby filling a geographical gap in that essay (Bianconi 1910: 219).
7. The contemporary fame and global impact of *Elementary Forms* is also shown by the fact that Maurice Leenhardt, a follower and critic of the Durkheim School, whom unfortunately we cannot discuss at length, had been sent a copy by his family. He received it on his birthday, 9 March 1914, in his New-Caledonian office (Clifford 1992: 92).
8. Steven Lukes provides a detailed description of this discussion in his seminal "Emile Durkheim: His Life and Work. A Historical and Critical Study" (Lukes 1985: 506–11).
9. As Jean-Christophe Marcel has recently shown, Céléstin Bouglé, Maurice Halbwachs, and François Simiand played an important role in the transformation of the *Année sociologique* to the *Annales sociologiques* (Marcel 2019). Due to the limited scope of this introduction, we merely focus on Granet, Fauconnet, and Halbwachs. The role of Simiand and Bouglé in the development of the category project calls for further exploration.
10. How much the category project had been infused with linguistic problems can also be seen by Mauss's review activity in the second volume of the postwar *Année*. Here, he reviews C. K. Ogden and I. A. Richards's

"The Meaning of Meaning" as well as Ernst Cassirer's "Philosophie der symbolischen Formen" and writes approvingly: "All admit that the categories of thought have taken on different forms in history and that their critique is impossible without studying these forms. All admit that they have varied mainly due to the ways in which men have lived, spoken and thought collectively (*en commun*)" (Mauss 1925: 256).

References

Note: Volumes of the *Année sociologique* are cited as *AS*. Volumes of the *Revue philosophique de la France et de l'étranger* are cited as *RP*.

Work by the Durkheim School on Categories

Bianconi, Antoine. 1910. "Review of Pechuel-Loesche (1907): 'Die Loango-Expedition, III.'" *AS* 11: 218–27.

———. 1913. "Review of Dennett (1911): 'Notes on West African Categories.'" *AS* 12: 37–40.

Czarnowski, Stefan. 1925. "Le morcellement de l'étendue et sa limitation dans la religion et la magie." *Actes du Congrès international d'histoire des religions: tenu à Paris en octobre 1923 I*, 339–59. Paris: Librairie Honoré Champion.

Durkheim, Émile. [1895] 1982. *Rules of Sociological Method*. New York: The Free Press.

———. 1888. "Cours de science sociale: Leçon d'ouverture." *Revue international de l'enseignement* 15: 23–48.

———. 1899. "De la définition des phénomènes religieux." *AS* 2: 1–28.

———. 1909. "Sociologie religieuse et théorie de la connaissance." *Revue de métaphysique et de morale* 17(6): 733–58.

———. 1910. "Review of Jerusalem (1909): 'Soziologie des Erkennens.'" *AS* 10: 42–45.

———. 1912. *Les formes élémentaires de la vie religieuse, le système totémique en Australie*. Paris: Félix Alcan. [1995. *The Elementary Forms of Religious Life*, trans. Karen E. Fields. New York: The Free Press.]

———. 1913. "Le problème religieux et la dualité de la nature humaine." *Bulletin de la société française de philosophie* 13: 63–113.

———. 1976. *Textes 2. Religion, morale, anomie*. Paris: Minuit.

———. 1998. *Lettres à Mauss. Présentées par Philippe Besnard et Marcel Fournier*. Paris: Presses Universitaires de France (PUF).

Durkheim, Émile, and Marcel Mauss. 1903a. "De quelques formes primitives de classification." *AS* 6: 1–72. [1963. *Primitive Classification*, ed. and trans. Rodney Needham. London: Cohen & West].

———. 1903b. "Représentations religieuses d'êtres et de phénomènes naturels (L'âme, la vie, la maladie, le temps, l'espace, etc.)." *AS* 6: 225–26.

Fauconnet, Paul. 1922. "L'œuvre pédagogique d'Émile Durkheim." *RP* 93: 185–209.
Granet, Marcel. 1920. "Quelques particularités de la langue et de la pensée chinoise." *RP* 89: 98–195.
———. [1934] 1994. *La pensée chinoise*. Paris: Albin Michel.
Halbwachs, Maurice. 1918. "La doctrine d'Émile Durkheim." *RP* 85: 353–411.
Hertz, Robert. 1909. "La prééminence de la main droite: Étude sur la polarité religieuse." *RP* 68: 553–80. [1960. "The Pre-eminence of the Right Hand: A Study in Religious Polarity." In Robert Hertz, *Death & The Right Hand*, ed. Rodney Needham and Claudia Needham, 89–113. Glencoe: The Free Press.]
———. 1909. "Review of Hubert and Mauss (1909). 'Mélanges d'histoire des religions.'" *Revue de l'histoire des religions* 60: 218–20.
Hubert, Henri. 1901. "Review of Fowler (1899): 'The Roman Festivals of the Period of the Republic.'" *AS* 4: 234–39.
———. 1902a. "Review of Kellner (1901): 'Heortologie oder das Kirchenjahr und die Heiligenfeste in ihrer geschichtlichen Entwickelung.'" *AS* 5: 252–56.
———. 1902b. "Introduction (à la section 'Le Rituel')." *AS* 5: 247–48.
———. 1902c. "Introduction (à la section 'Répresentation religieuses d'êtres ou de phénomènes naturels')." *AS* 5: 269.
———. 1904a. "Introduction à la traduction française." In *Manuel d'histoire des religions* by Pierre D. Chantepie de la Saussaye, v–xlvii. Paris: Armand Colin.
———. 1904b. "Review of Usener (1903): 'Dreiheit'; McGee (1900): 'Primitive Numbers' and Thomas (n.d.): 'Numeral Systems of Mexico and Central America.'" *AS* 7: 308–14.
———. 1905. "Review of Kewitsch (1904): 'Zweifel an der astronomischen und geometrischen Grundlage des 60-Systems.'" *AS* 8: 337–38.
———. [1905] 1999. "Étude sommaire de la représentation du temps dans la religion et dans la magie." *Annuaire de l'École pratique des hautes études, section des sciences religieuses*, 1–39. Paris: École des hautes études en sciences sociales (EHESS). [1999. *Essay on Time*, trans. Robert Parkin. Oxford: Durkheim Press.]
———. 1907a. "Review of Roscher (1905): 'Die Sieben- und Neunzahl im Kultus der Griechen.'" *AS* 10: 314–15.
———. 1907b. "Review of Dennett (1906): 'At the Back of the Black Man's Mind.'" *AS* 10: 305–11.
———. [1915] 1979. "Texte autobiographique de Henri Hubert." *Revue française de sociologie* 20(1): 205–7.
Hubert, Henri, and Marcel Mauss. 1899. "Essai sur la nature et la fonction du sacrifice." *AS* 2: 1–28.
———. 1904. "Esquisse d'une théorie générale de la magie." *AS* 7: 1–146. [2005. *A General Theory of Magic*, trans. Robert Brain. London: Routledge.]

———. [1906] 1968. "Introduction à l'analyse de quelques phénomènes religieux." In Marcel Mauss, *Œuvres I. Les fonctions sociales du sacré*, ed. Victor Karady, 3–39. Paris: Minuit.

Mauss, Marcel, and Henri Beuchat. [1906] 1979. "Essai sur les variations saisonnières des sociétés Eskimos, Étude de morphologie sociale." *AS* 9: 48–132. [1979. *Seasonal Variations of the Eskimo: A Study in Social Morphology*, trans. with foreword by James J. Fox. London: Routledge.]

Mauss, Marcel. 1899. "Review of de Groot (1891, 1894, 1897): 'The Religious System of China, I, II, III.'" *AS* 2: 221–26.

———. 1904. "Review of Usener (1903) 'Dreiheit', McGee (1900) 'Primitive Numbers' and Thomas (n.d.) 'Numeral Systems of Mexico and Central America.'" *AS* 7: 308–14.

———. 1911. "Anna Viraj." In *Mélanges d'indianisme offerts par ses élèves à M. Sylvain Lévi*, ed. unknown, 333–41. Paris: Leroux.

———. 1923a. "Contribution à la discussion sur la présentation de M. Antoine Meillet 'Le genre féminin dans les langues européennes.'" *Journal de psychologie normale et pathologique* 20: 943–47. [1964. "On Language and Primitive Forms of Classification." In *Language in Culture and Society: A Reader in Linguistics and Anthropology*, ed. Dell Hymes, 125–27. New York: Harper & Row Publishers.]

———. 1923b. "Contribution à la discussion sur la présentation de M. Lucien Lévy-Bruhl 'La mentalité primitive.'" *Bulletin de la société française de philosophie* 23: 24–29.

———. 1924. "Rapports réels et pratiques de la psychologie et de la sociologie." *Journal de psychologie normale et pathologique* 21: 892–922. [1979. "Real and Practical Relations between Psychology and Sociology." In Marcel Mauss, *Sociology and Psychology. Essays*, trans. Ben Brewster, 1–34. London: Routledge & Kegan Paul.]

———. [1925] 2016. "In Memoriam: The Unpublished Work of Durkheim and His Collaborators." In Marcel Mauss, *The Gift: Expanded Edition*, ed. Jane I. Guyer, 29–51. Chicago: Hau Books.

———. 1925. "Review of Ogden and Richards (1923): 'The Meaning of Meaning'; Ranulf (1924): 'Der Eleatische Satz vom Widerspruch' and Cassirer (1923): 'Philosophie der Symbolischen Formen.'" *AS* (2nd series) 1: 256–60.

———. [1927] 2006. "The Divisions of Sociology (1927, extracts)." In Marcel Mauss, *Techniques, Technology and Civilisation*, ed. Nathan Schlanger, 49–54. New York: Durkheim Press/Berghahn Books. [*AS* (second series) 2: 98–176].

———. [1930] 1998. "An Intellectual Self-Portrait." In *Marcel Mauss, A Centenary Tribute*, ed. Wendy James and Nicholas J. Allen, 29–42. Oxford: Berghahn.

———. [1934] 1974. "Catégories collectives et categories pures." In Marcel Mauss, *Œuvres 2, Représentations collectives et diversité des civilisations*, ed. Victor Karady, 148–54. Paris: Éditions de Minuit.

———. [1938] 1985. "Une catégorie de l'esprit humain: La notion de personne celle de 'moi.'" *The Journal of the Royal Anthropological Institute of Great Britain and Ireland* 68: 263–81. [1985. "A Category of the Human Mind: The Notion of Person, the Notion of 'Self.'" In *The Category of the Person: Anthropology, Philosophy, History*, ed. Michael Carrithers, Steven Collins, and Steven Lukes, 1–25. Cambridge: Cambridge University Press.]

———. [1939] 1945. "Conceptions qui ont précédé la notion de matière." *Onzième semaine international de synthèse*, 15–23. Paris: PUF. [2006. "Conceptions which Have Preceded the Notion of Matter (1939)." In Marcel Mauss, *Techniques, Technology and Civilization*, ed. Nathan Schlanger, 141–46. Oxford: Berghahn.]

Nandan, Yash, ed. 1980. *Emile Durkheim: Contributions to L'Année sociologique*. New York: Free Press.

Weber, Louis. 1913. *Le rythme du progrès*. Paris: Félix Alcan.

———. 1914. "Y a-t-il un rythme dans de progrès intellectuel? (Séances du 29 Janvier et 5 Février 1914 à la Société Française de Philosophie, avec la participation de Parodi, Meyerson, Le Roy, Belot, Darlu, Leclère)." *Bulletin de la société française de philosophie* 14: 61–140.

Scholarly Work on the Category Project

Allen, Nicholas J. 1998. "The Category of Substance: A Maussian Theme Revisited." In *Marcel Mauss, A Centenary Tribute*, ed. Wendy James and Nicholas J. Allen, 175–91. Oxford: Berghahn.

———. 2000. "Mauss and the Categories." In *Categories and Classifications: Maussian Reflections on the Social*, ed. Nicholas J. Allen, 91–100. Oxford: Berghahn.

Bowker, Geoffrey C., and Susan Leigh Star. 2000. *Sorting Things Out: Classifications and Its Consequences*. Cambridge: MIT Press.

Clammer, John. 2000. "The Categories of Knowledge in the 'Année sociologique.'" *Durkheimian Studies / Études Durkheimiennes* 6: 27–42.

Clifford, James. 1992. *Person and Myth: Maurice Leenhardt in the Melanesian World*. Durham, NC: Duke University Press.

Därmann, Iris. 2005. *Fremde Monde der Vernunft: Die ethnologische Provokation der Philosophie*. München: Wilhelm Fink Verlag.

Fournier, Marcel. 2006. *Marcel Mauss: A Biography*. Princeton: Princeton University Press.

Hörl, Erich. 2005. *Die heiligen Kanäle: Über die archaische Illusion der Kommunikation*. Zürich: diaphanes.

Karsenti, Bruno. 1994. *Marcel Mauss. Le fait social total*. Paris: Presses Universitaires de France.

———. 2011. *L'homme total: sociologie, anthropologie et philosophie chez Marcel Mauss*. Paris: Presses Universitaires de France.

Lukes, Steven. 1985. *Emile Durkheim: His Life and Work. A Historical and Critical Study*. Stanford, CA: Stanford University Press.

Marcel, Jean-Christophe. 2019. "Editorial Practices and their Links with Recruitment and Intellectual Networks in the Durkheimian Journals." *AS* 69(1): 143–80.

Moebius, Stephan. 2006. *Die Zauberlehrlinge: Soziologiegeschichte des Collège de Sociologie, 1937–1939*. Konstanz: UVK.

Rawls, Anne W. 2005. *Epistemology and Practice: Durkheim's The Elementary Forms of Religious Life*. Cambridge: Cambridge University Press.

Schick, Johannes, Mario Schmidt, Erhard Schüttpelz, and Martin Zillinger. 2015. "Werkstatt: Unbekannte Monde am Firmament der Vernunft." In *Zeitschrift für Kulturwissenschaften "Begeisterung und Blasphemie,"* 233–59. Bielefeld: Transcript.

Schlanger, Nathan. 2006. "Introduction. Technological Commitments: Marcel Mauss and the Study of Techniques in the French Social Sciences." In Marcel Mauss, *Techniques, Technology and Civilisation*, ed. Nathan Schlanger, 1–29. New York: Berghahn.

Schmaus, Warren. 1994. *Durkheim's Philosophy of Science and the Sociology of Knowledge. Creating an Intellectual Niche*. Chicago: Chicago University Press.

———. 2004. *Rethinking Durkheim and His Tradition*. Cambridge: Cambridge University Press.

Schüttpelz, Erhard. 2005. *Die Moderne im Spiegel des Primitiven: Weltliteratur und Ethnologie 1870–1960*. Munich: Fink.

Schüttpelz, Erhard, and Martin Zillinger. 2017. "The Bodily Efficacy of the Categories. Durkheim's and Mauss's Intervention into the History of Philosophy." *Durkheimian Studies* 23: 106–27.

Stedman-Jones, Susan. 2000. "Representations in Durkheim's Masters: Kant and Renouvier. I: Representation, Reality and the Question of Science." In *Durkheim and Representations*, ed. William S. F. Pickering, 37–58. London: Routledge.

———. 2001. *Durkheim Reconsidered*. Cambridge: Polity Press.

———. 2006. "Action and the Question of the Categories: A Critique of Rawls." *Durkheimian Studies* 12: 37–67.

Tambiah, Stanley J. 1990. *Magic, Science and Religion and the Scope of Rationality*. Cambridge: Cambridge University Press.

Watts Miller, William. 2006. "A Note on Durkheim's Creation of 'Les Formes Élémentaires.'" *Durkheimian Studies* 12: 1–7.

PART I

Silenced Influences and Hidden Texts

Chapter 1

KANTIAN CATEGORIES AND THE RELATIVIST TURN

A COMPARISON OF THREE ROUTES

Gregory Schrempp

"Relativist" is a troubled term, beset by a popular inclination to assume that the message is "anything goes." For want of an alternative, I invoke "relativism" here to mean a readiness to entertain just two possibilities: first, that there may exist multiple, equally viable epistemologies or ways of constructing knowledge of the world; and second, that principles we think of as fundamental to thought (case in point, the Aristotelian/Kantian categories) may not be uncaused causes magically given in human intellect, but rather may be traceable to—that is, relative to—some facet of human existence lying outside of intellect proper. Even though Kant announced his scheme of categories as an alternative to Aristotle's, there is considerable overlap between their lists. For my purposes, it makes no great difference whether we call them Aristotelian or Kantian, though I tend to default to the latter as the proximate source through which the idea of such categories became an inescapable topic of epistemology in the nineteenth and early twentieth centuries.

Historical self-understanding is a necessary component of any intellectual project. Three pivotal thinkers—Aristotle, Immanuel Kant, and Émile Durkheim—would offer a sort of minimum starting point for imagining a linear history, a tracing through time, of the idea of the categories. But there is also a lateral way of thinking about history, which involves one in looking for the issues that are "in the air" and energize a particular epoch. Epistemological relativism was such an issue in the twentieth century; it is the "new thing" that the idea of the categories—born as a quest for a fixed and complete set—has had to contend with in the modern world. Of note is the fact that the Aristotelian/Kantian categories figure in the relativist turn in more than one way and in more than one intellectual tradition. I will here offer a sketch that attempts to contextualize the Durkheimian route in relation to two other routes that led to relativist perspectives in the early and mid-twentieth century; and then I will quickly add a few comments on a fourth trajectory that developed recently. All of these, though in very different ways, implicate the Aristotelian/Kantian categories.

First Route: Social Morphology

Given the makeup of this volume, the Durkheimian route does not really need much of an introduction, so I will outline only its most defining qualities. The most distinctive characteristic of the Durkheimian route to relativism, vis-à-vis the others considered here, lies in the linkage of the categories to "social morphology." The latter term points to social structure but also draws in such factors as spatial and calendrical organization and ritual life. As exemplified especially in Durkheim's *The Elementary Forms of Religious Life* (1995), the categories of time, space, class, and cause are argued to arise not in the course of some lofty ideational endeavor, but rather from a realm more basic and possessing a sort of visceral quality: the experience of membership in a group lying within a tribal boundary, of regimentation through calendrical rhythms, of being seized by the effervescence of ritual action. The social-experiential bases of the categories as set out in *Elementary Forms* are rather generic—tribal territory rather than a particular tribal territory, for example. They are highly abstract and, for the most part, treated as universal.

But in other works, such as Émile Durkheim and Marcel Mauss's *Primitive Classification* (1972), the concern lies specifically with variations between the classificatory systems of different societies—variations that bespeak, indeed are almost tantamount to, variations in social morphology as revealed through comparative ethnography. Giving rise to the notion of variation in social morphology is the recognition of anatomical variation in the biological realm; the similarities and differences between principles of classification in the sociological and biological realms are set out in Durkheim's *The Rules of Sociological Method* (see, e.g., 1966: 76–88). There is, in sum, a distinctly Durkheimian route to relativism: it originates in the idea of a sociology organized in part around comparative social morphology, inspired via analogy to the biological study of anatomical variations between different species of organisms.

There is no irresolvable contradiction in the fact that in the Durkheimian tradition categories, and indeed the idea of social morphology, are approached both universalistically and relativistically. The studies of variation do not so much challenge the highly abstract, generic characterizations of categories offered in *Elementary Forms*, as reveal the range of variations possible within them, made visible through the addition of further ethnographic specificity. All societies ipso facto employ the category of a "set" or "class," for example, but only some add to it the notion of moieties, or the rule that every member of the society, and by extension everything in the cosmos, must belong to either an "A" or a "B" subset. The universalist and relativist moments operate at different levels. The mental molds through which humans understand the world take their form from universal conditions of social life but also from the more particular categorical configuration that, within those universal conditions, have been devised through time and space by different societies.

The categories serve multiple functions in the Durkheimian school: they offer a focus for elaborating on the necessarily social character of human knowledge, which in turn provides sociology's claim to a place, if not the place of *regina scientiae*, within academia; practically they provide a grid for comparative sociology's internal division of labor and a sort of periodic table for organizing social facts; and they offer a venue to argue for a moral theory grounded in social being. And most importantly for present purposes, they offer a starting point for posing questions concerning the universality versus relativity of human knowledge and life.

Second Route: Natural Language

A second route to a socio-cultural relativistic perspective is much less direct. Specifically, I suggest that Kant's notion of a priori categories provided a model of cognition that conditioned or contributed to the way that language scholars thought about how categories implicit in natural languages shape human experience. Though I suspect one could find other, and earlier, examples of this sort of influence from Kantian philosophy on linguistics, here I will consider just two instances, both of which, though in quite different ways, influenced late nineteenth- and early twentieth-century anthropological theory by offering alternatives to the dominant E. B. Tylor/James Frazer social-evolutionist line. My first example is Friedrich Max Müller,[1] who was trained in the tradition of German philosophy and language science but whose scholarly career unfolded mostly in England. While at Oxford, Müller wrote a number of works on Indo-European language and mythology and on the nature and development of language generally, corresponded and debated with major English thinkers including E. B. Tylor and Charles Darwin, and, among many other activities, completed a translation of Kant's *Critique of Pure Reason*. He referred to the latter as his "constant companion through life" (Müller 1922: xxxiv), and through his translation he hoped the English philosophical scene could move beyond a situation that, borrowing Kant's metaphor, Müller described as pre-Copernican (xxxvi).

A popular idea in Müller's time was that all of the Indo-European languages, and perhaps all the languages of the world, could be traced to a set of original morphemic "roots" (the number of these becoming a matter of intense debate). Müller is a circuitous expositor, and I was not able to pin down exactly how he thought of the relationship between philosophy and linguistics. However, Müller often reached from the one realm to the other—for example, saying in the commentary to his translation of Kant that there now needs to be a parallel "Critique of Language"—and in general Müller seemed to think about language as working in approximately the same way as Kant's version of human reason. In particular, the roots of language, for Müller, have roughly the same status as the categories of reason as set out by Kant: both are portrayed by Müller as ultimate mental molds that delimit, unify, and impart form to the human experience of the world. There is both a universalist and relativist angle in Müller's science of language, the universalism residing in these original language roots, the relativism in their diversifying into the different languages of the world, so that the original language can no longer be understood—thus his theory of a "disease of language," one of the more memorable phrases produced by the romantic degenerationist strain of nineteenth-century social theory.

I am not the only commentator to speculate on a Kantian influence in comparative culture and language study. Another pertinent example is discussed by historian of anthropology George Stocking who writes about the possible influence of Kantian epistemology on Franz Boas, a linchpin figure in American anthropology. Stocking mentions the neo-Kantian revival during Boas's education in Germany and various other connections to Kantian philosophy, as well as the colorful detail of a claim by Boas to have taken a copy of Kant along on his first field expedition to Baffinland in the Canadian arctic (Stocking 1982: 143). Although this is the sort of ethnographer's aside that begs for mythologizing, Stocking argues against seeing Baffinland as a conversion experience, the scales suddenly falling from Boas's eyes. Rather, Stocking suggests that Kantian epistemology may be one factor among others, including his dissertation work on the problem of observer-objectivity in physics, that contributed to Boas's recognition of the role of culture and language in shaping the ways that humans apprehend the world. In his introduction to the *Handbook of American Indian Languages*, Boas espouses the principle that Indo-European grammatical categories should be avoided in favor of categories adduced from the inner-form of each language.

To the extent that Kant's idea of a priori categories influenced Boas, then, the route would seem to be, as in Müller, less through the specific list of categories proffered by Aristotle or Kant than through a *general model* of how the relation between categories and experience should be envisioned: the model should recognize the active agency of mind or language in imposing categories on experience, rather than posit the mind or language as mere passive receptors.

The emphasis on approaching any particular language from within runs parallel, and perhaps gave rise, to a Boasian skepticism of cross-cultural analytical concepts, Alexander Goldenweiser's challenge to the ethnographic concept of totemism being the best-known example. But there is also a countervailing theme, one that works against claims of ultimate incommensurability between different languages or categories. Though famous for his contributions to the "Sapir-Whorf hypothesis," Boas's student Edward Sapir, for example, argues that the variability of different languages culminates not in differences in what *can* be said, but in what can be said *readily*. Tellingly, Sapir invokes the example of Kantian philosophy, and specifically the concept of causality, one of Kant's categories. Sapir treats cause as though it is part of the structure of all languages, present in mechanisms that express causal relationships even in cases in which causality as an abstraction does not appear as a specific vocabulary item. Such an absence, Sapir argues, would stem not from language incapacity, but from lack of interest by some peoples, given their ways of life, in such a vocabulary item—which at any time could be easily borrowed or developed from within if the need arose. "Hottentot and Eskimo possess all the formal apparatus that is required to serve as matrix for the expression of Kant's thought" (Sapir 1985: 154). And even more venturously, "it may be suspected that the highly synthetic and periodic structure of Eskimo would more easily bear the weight of Kant's terminology than his native German" (154). Even though such pronouncements place a limit on relativism, they simultaneously support it, sometimes with hyper-corrective flare, by emphasizing the highly variable ways different languages can achieve similar ends, and by attesting, with Kantian philosophy as a sort of litmus test, to the equal potential of distant languages for intellectual gravitas.

Third Route: Epistemological Skepticism

Continuing on with the category of cause, I turn to the third route to relativism, which might be described as the route not taken, or at least not pursued in systematic fashion. I recall my initial reaction, as a student of anthropology rather than of philosophy (or more precisely, of ethnographic as opposed to philosophical anthropology) on reading David Hume's *An Enquiry Concerning Human Understanding* (2008a): it was that Hume had set out brilliant and radical groundwork for a relativistic understanding of human knowledge considered cross-culturally—one that would appeal to anthropologists through the crucial role it accords to custom. Comments on many of Aristotle's categories are scattered through Hume (we cannot yet call them Kantian, since it was Hume who awakened Kant from dogmatic slumber rather than the other way around). But Hume's fame centers on one of these categories: cause. In a version of the so-called problem of induction—or the impossibility of logically deriving with certainty a general principle from a set of particular instances—Hume claimed that what we think of as cause can never be anything more than habitual or customary associations of events conjoined by likeness or contiguity. With this in mind, it seemed that an ethnologist might proceed under the assumption that the associations discovered by humans in different historical and physical circumstances, and with different interests, might be expected to be quite varied without any of them necessarily being the lesser for that. There would be no way to pass judgment except perhaps by comparing the viability of total ways of life. If causation is customary, where is the basis for distinguishing false from true causation—the distinction that underlies Tylor and Frazer's dichotomy of magic versus science?

But in the *Enquiry* we also encounter considerable epistemological judgmentalism, fueled by Hume's sense of the "supine indolence of the mind, its rash arrogance, its lofty pretensions, and it superstitious credulity" (Hume 2008a: 30), and this assessment turns out to be the thin edge of a wedge when read in terms of Hume's earlier *A Treatise of Human Nature* and his later *Dialogues and Natural History of Religion* (2008b), which was to become a favorite of the coming generation of social evolutionists. In these works, we find outpourings against the usual Enlightenment targets: idolatry, papism, polytheism, women's gullibility to superstition, human susceptibility to fables, and the anthropomorphizing of nature, all set out along with a sense of assurance regarding the "natural progress of human thought" and the "improvement of human society, from rude beginnings to a state of greater perfection" (Hume 2008b: 135). We also find elaborately developed criteria for distinguishing better and worse customary associations. Hume reduces cause to custom, yes, but in the process, custom becomes the locus for distinguishing higher from lower understanding—in his terms, the wise from the vulgar. The stage is set for Tylor and Frazer's dichotomies of magic versus science, their social evolutionism generally, and Frazer's view of magic as working through likeness and contiguity, which became for decades the default characterization of magic, one that still lingers in the background.

Hume's position is clearly morally problematic—less, however, because he distinguishes between better and worse custom than because of the anthropologically myopic way in which he does so. A particularly important strand in Hume's criteria is that the associations formed by any mind become wise in part by being reflectively checked against the experiences of other minds; and Hume in effect disenfranchises large sectors of humanity from this possibility through the pivotal role he accords to writing. Writing, Hume says, offers a means of fixing the experience of other minds such that it does not degrade through time. Quoting Hume's *Treatise*, "If belief consisted only in a certain vivacity, convey'd from an original impression, it wou'd decay by the length of the transition, and must at last be utterly extinguishe'd" (Hume 1981: 145). But *writing*, Hume contends, can freeze that original impression, making it available to future minds.[2]

Perhaps the most oft-cited and obvious difference between James Frazer's and Henri Hubert and Marcel Mauss's portrayals of magic resides in the individual versus collective emphases accorded by these scholars respectively. But some of the entailments of Hubert and Mauss's elaboration of the collective dimension strike me as more important than the mere fact of that dimension. Notably, in their classic exposition (Mauss 1975: 108–10), *mana* is presented as a concept held by a collective, but, more than that, as a concept that, even in the absence of writing, rests upon debate, testimony, systematizing, and a dialectic of theory and practice. Though they do not phrase it this way,

Hubert and Mauss's exposition makes a case that, by many of Hume's own criteria, systems of thinking and practice developed around *mana* could lay claim to being customs of the wise. Something similar could be said of Claude Lévi-Strauss, who in delineating the "science of the concrete" cites Hubert and Mauss and E. E. Evans-Pritchard (Lévi-Strauss 1970: 11–13) on magical thought, and in essence rechristens magic as a prior form of science, one which, like its modern counterpart but unlike Frazer's "proto-science," offers objective, efficacious, rigorously accumulated, and expandable results.[3]

Hume's skeptical approach to the concept of cause carries into ideas about "connexion"—a term that for Hume summarizes theories that propose an overarching force or substance, lying beyond mere association in habit or custom, linking antecedent and consequent—as though humans everywhere cannot resist formulating these.[4] Overarching theories adjudged as uncertain/unprovable by Hume run from the religious "every thing is full of God" (Hume 2008a: 52), such that it is ultimately divine influence that transfers the movement of one billiard-ball to a second, to concepts such as "*power, force, energy, or necessary connexion*" (45, original emphasis). Even if, or perhaps especially if, one wants to follow Hume in concluding that all such ideas of connection are subject to the same kind of uncertainty, this very skepticism opens up the possibility of a level space in which, suspending or at least moderating judgment, one could explore and compare the imaginaries of different societies in regard to the ultimate forces, or classes of forces, that hold the cosmos together and allow it to function. The many cross-cultural juxtapositions, comparisons, and analogies offered by ethnologists in trying to characterize concepts of connection—from indigenous concepts such as *mana*, *orenda*, and *wakan*, to western scientific concepts such as gravitation, energy, and electricity[5]—suggest a long-standing fascination with such a possibility for comparative ethnology, and with the character of such concepts as "social facts" or, in some cases perhaps, "total social facts." It is as though Hume did all he could to close off the territory his insights about the category of cause opened, leaving it for later thinkers, especially during and after the Frazerian interlude, to reopen it in a more sympathetic spirit.

Relativism and Universalism

In comparing the three routes, it is clear that the Durkheimian one preserves most intact the original concept behind the categories: although ethnographically open to variations within and the possibility of yet other categories, the idea of a complete, systematic inventory remains a guiding ideal or heuristic. For thinkers inclined toward analytical systematicity and/or the possibility of universals, this might be seen positively; for those skeptical of universals it might be regarded as suspect. But in this context it is important to once again emphasize that the other two traditions compared above, each in its own way, acknowledge a limit to the relativist angles that they open up. A main Boasian route to relativism is through the lexical and structural variability of different natural languages; but in moments such as the ruminations of Sapir discussed above, we encounter the view that even in their deep variability, languages convergently attest to core principles such as cause.[6] If, in Hume's approach, cause amounts to custom, then it is the comparison of customs that allows for determination of which customizations of cause are wise and deserve to be retained. As I suggested above, Hume's insights about the concept of cause strike me as particularly radical, even bringing to mind the notion of "deconstruction" (a term I use sparingly). If Durkheim undercuts assumptions about the origin of the categories, Hume undercuts assumptions about their very epistemological character and value. Yet, even in the dethroning, Hume implies that not only will all societies hit on habitual associations that functionally amount to causes, but that all societies will also develop some sort of metaphysical doctrine of connection—some sort of attempt to close the unclosable—around these. Though in a way that would leave at least some philosophers feeling bereft, the deconstruction thus ends up attesting to the universality of one of the Kantian categories. In juxtaposing and analogizing theories of connection drawn from different societies, ethnological theorists too typically convey a limit—a sense that on this topic cross-cultural comparison reveals convergence along with divergence; Hubert and Mauss argue that *mana*-like conceptions originally were present everywhere (Mauss 1975: 112–18; Meylan 2017: 67–68).

However Hume stacks up against Durkheim and Boas on such issues, I do not see in Kant any cross-culturally relativizing gesture as radical as that furnished by Hume's take on the category of cause—provided of course that we put aside Hume's own sabotaging of that potential, magnified over time by Frazer and Tylor's readiness to grab onto the social evolutionism and glide over the epistemological skepticism. And if some later social thinkers took from the Kantian categories a model for thinking about the relativity of human knowledge, Kant's own larger interest seems to lie more in the categories as a frame in which universal agreement might be pursued—the cosmopolitan ideal in other words, which Kant sought to defend against the blow he perceived to have been struck by Humean epistemology! There is, then, at least a little irony in the respective aftermaths of Hume and Kant as these played out in ethnology and anthropology, for in both of these philosophical giants one finds core epistemological arguments that in fundamental ways are the reverse of the programs that later social thinkers drew from them respectively.

Categories and the Body

The three considered routes are part of the formative period of modern ethnology. At this point, I will add some brief comments about a late twentieth-century reappearance of the categories in a context that is cognitive science first and not ethnological except incidentally.[7] Specifically, the late twentieth century saw a controversial enterprise, with popularizing appeal, led by George Lakoff and Mark Johnson, to demonstrate the "embodied" character of all knowledge. Within their arguments the Aristotelian/Kantian categories of time, space, class, and cause—the four that dominate in Durkheim's *Elementary Forms*—reappear in passages reminiscent of Durkheim, except that the categories are now seen as emanating not from social morphology but from what might be termed corporo-morphology. The category of "kind" or "class" emanates not from the experience of being within a tribal boundary, but of the body as a container that, like formal logic, organizes things with reference to a "within" and a "without." The prototypical experience of "cause" is no longer the feeling of collective force generated in ritual effervescence, but the bodily experience of force in everyday life, from opening a car door to being slugged in the arm.

Similarly, compare these two passages on the category of time, the first formulated by Durkheim with reference to social calendrical rhythms, the second by George Lakoff and Mark Johnson from the perspective of personal use of time:

> For example, what if one tried to imagine what the notion of time would be in the absence of the methods we use to divide, measure, and express it with objective signs, a time that was not a succession of years, months, weeks, days, and hours? It would be nearly impossible to conceive of. (Durkheim 1995: 9)

> Try to think about time without thinking about whether it will *run out* or if you can *budget* it or are *wasting* it.
>
> We have found that we cannot think (much less talk) about time without those metaphors. That leads us to believe that we conceptu-

alize time using those metaphors. . . . What, after all, would time be without flow, without time going by, without the future approaching? (Lakoff and Johnson 1999: 166)

Both passages assert the impossibility of thinking about time except through the experientially based means (concepts in one case, metaphors in the other) through which we organize and fit ourselves into it. Lakoff and Johnson's appeals are often rhetorically parallel to Durkheim's, the similarities no doubt arising at least in part from the fact that, like Durkheim, Lakoff and Johnson are trying to achieve a meta-disciplinary status for their approach. The two traditions, via their respective foci, both claim to lay before us the experiential ground on which all knowledge-claims ultimately rest.[8]

Superficially it might seem that Lakoff and Johnson, under the mantra of embodiment, are attempting to undo Durkheim's sociologizing of epistemology, wresting it back for individualism. While there may be something to that, actually the situation is more complex. Individualism is not an adequate description of Lakoff and Johnson's perspective, because the body they are talking about for the most part is a generic body, which as such affords the grounds for a universal level of epistemological and ethical theorizing. The body also figures importantly in the Durkheimian tradition; think of Robert Hertz's arguments about right and left or Mauss's about "techniques of the body," and most importantly the visceral way Durkheim himself characterizes collective force. The contrastive foci of Durkheim versus Lakoff and Johnson might better be described as the bodily experience of society versus the bodily experience of the body, though even this is ultimately inadequate.

There is also both a universalizing and a relativizing impetus in both Durkheim and Mauss and Lakoff and Johnson, and in both cases it can be difficult to determine where the one ends and the other begins. For Durkheim, the universalizing pole amounts to the congruence between certain categories (such as that of a class or set of entities) and the generic condition of any society (that society is necessarily a collection of members); while the relativizing pole arises from recognition of variations in the way classes of entities might be organized or configured by different societies. On this point the arguments of Durkheim and Mauss are at least rhetorically more convincing than those of Lakoff and Johnson. For Lakoff and Johnson, the universalizing dimension derives from the congruence of categories with the generic condition of any body (that it must have an inside and an outside, for example). If Lakoff and Johnson were entirely parallel to Durkheim, we would expect their relativism to derive from morphological differences in body types, so that, for example, fuller-figured people might be expected to gravitate toward spherically elaborated space as contrasted with the vertical linearity of your lithe, slender types. Lakoff and Johnson do not go this route; and given the background of nineteenth- and early twentieth-century attempts to correlate intellectual with varying corporal traits, notoriously with respect to different head shapes, this can only be seen as a wise choice. Lakoff and Johnson acknowledge socio-cultural variability more than they attempt to systematically account for it. While Durkheim and Mauss belong to a generation that with some urgency grappled to fill the analytical void created by increasing recognition of the inadequacies of universal schemes of socio-cultural evolution, Lakoff and Johnson belong to a generation for which some degree of socio-cultural relativism is a given of the academic *conscience collective*.

The traditions that I have juxtaposed to the Durkheimian tradition all pose interesting challenges. Boas is strong on categories, but is probably the least robust voice on *the* categories, that is, universal categories. Lakoff and Johnson converge with Durkheim and Mauss in the usefulness of *the categories* at least as a starting point for comparative analysis, and also in dismissing the notion of pure a priori categories in favor of an experiential grounding of them, but they point toward different experiential grounds. Hume, now as then, remains the most troubling, because in his perspective cause—one of the most central principles in epistemological debates and seemingly in the conduct of life generally—turns out to be something different, and also something less, than humans, seemingly everywhere, think it is.

Durkheim and the Categories: Closing Thoughts

The Durkheimian school produced a body of social theory that continues to intrigue and inspire; it was able to do so in part because of a stance on the categories that, while non-dismissive, was also non-dogmatic. Also, Durkheim's approach would have received at least a degree of support from the intellectual milieu in which he and his students worked, since other scholars were also grasping for ways of more explicitly incorporating socio-cultural variation without giving up the possibility of general theory. In addition to the approaches already discussed, the same epoch gave us Max Weber's notion of "ideal types" and a little later Ludwig Wittgenstein's "family resemblances," a term which Mauss does not use but which, I suggest, articulates the unifying principle behind the diverse systems of exchange Mauss brings together in his essay *The Gift* (1967). Finally, though, in accounting for the cogency of the Durkheimian project, one cannot escape mention of one more factor: the brilliance of the practitioners—including their special gift for recognizing and incorporating complexities and uncertainties in ways that only strengthened their cause.

Gregory Allen Schrempp is Professor Emeritus of Folklore and Ethnomusicology at Indiana University Bloomington. Having earned his doctorate at the University of Chicago as a student of Marshall Sahlins, his work has located a host of fresh connections between folklore, philosophy, science, and myth. He is the author of, among others, *The Ancient Mythology of Modern Science* (2012), *The Science of Myths and Vice-Versa* (2016), and, most recently (with Tok Thompson), *The Truth of Myth* (2020).

Notes

1. My larger findings are summarized in Schrempp (1983).
2. So, in a loose way, Hume and Durkheim might agree that its collective character is what gives thought efficacy. But in stark contrast to Durkheim, that collective dimension, for Hume, does not lie at the base of thought, but is added—at least in critical, reflective form—only through time and in a way that leaves most of humanity behind. Durkheim acknowledges progress of science over religion, yet both of these ventures, in his view, are rooted in categories that are social in their origin and in their very constitution; and, moreover, the categories at the core of science remain those first born in the collective effervescence of religion. Durkheim's views on the relation of science and religion are set out with particular force in the conclusion of his *Elementary Forms*.
3. Recent ethnographers have made other claims, in different realms of knowledge and practice, that would challenge Hume's assessment. For example, inspired by Jacques Derrida's "Of Grammatology," David Shorter, in *We Will Dance Our Truth*, has demonstrated the way rituals of the Yoeme peoples of what is now the southern US/Mexico border region, vividly and memorably encode history in ritual, where it is arguably preserved with more original vivacity than one typically encounters in conventional historical writing (see Shorter 2009: 197–209). Such technically preliterate forms of marking, or arche-writing in Derrida's formulation, are at the core of the latter's critique of Western logocentrism. Hume's claims offer prime evidence of the metaphysics of presence that, Derrida claims, imbues Western ideologies of writing.
4. And we might also consider Kant's insistence (especially in elaborating the "transcendental dialectic" in the *Critique of Pure Reason*) that the cat-

egory of cause itself is not applied ad hoc or piecemeal, but inescapably draws us into further causes and series of causes. It would seem but one more step from this realization to the positing of some sort of essence or substance uniting diverse instances of causation.

5. See Meylan (2017) for a fascinating and wide-ranging survey of the many related concepts, from both indigenous societies and modern sciences, that have been drawn into ethnological debates about *mana*.

6. At one point Boas made a parallel unity-in-diversity argument regarding comparative ethics and aesthetics: "The student of the forms in which human affairs present themselves in different cultures is easily led to a relativistic attitude in which nothing appears as stable. The judgments of men as to what is beautiful or ugly, good or bad, even as to what is useful or harmful, differ so much that there might seem to be no common ground on which to base absolute standards. In this view it is generally overlooked that the *ideas* of good and bad, beautiful and ugly, duty and freedom, praiseworthy and condemnable are present and that they persist, however much their forms may vary" (Boas 1939: 21).

7. For a greatly extended comparison of the two projects considered here (Durkheim and Mauss's and Lakoff and Johnson's), see Schrempp (2012: chap. 4).

8. The fact that there is no mention by Lakoff and Johnson of the Durkheimian tradition prompts the question of whether Durkheim was the underlying target. Lakoff (personal communication) says that the target was not Durkheim in particular but Western philosophy generally.

References

Boas, Franz. 1939. [untitled] In *I Believe; the Personal Philosophies of Certain Eminent Men and Women of Our Time*, ed. Clifton Fadiman, 19–29. New York: Simon and Schuster.

———. 1991. "Introduction." *Handbook of American Indian Languages*. Lincoln: University of Nebraska Press. (Bound with John Wesley Powell, *Indian Linguistic Families of America North of Mexico.*)

Durkheim, Émile. 1966. *The Rules of Sociological Method*, trans. Sarah A. Solovay, John H. Mueller, and George E. G. Catlin. New York: The Free Press.

———. 1995. *The Elementary Forms of Religious Life*, trans. Karen E. Fields. New York: The Free Press.

Durkheim, Émile, and Marcel Mauss. 1972. *Primitive Classification*, trans. Rodney Needham and Claudia Needham. Chicago: University of Chicago Press.

Hume, David. 1981. *A Treatise on Human Nature*. Oxford: Oxford University Press.

———. 2008a. *An Enquiry Concerning Human Understanding*. Oxford: Oxford University Press.

———. 2008b. *Dialogues and Natural History of Religion*. Oxford: Oxford University Press.

Kant, Immanuel. 1965. *Critique of Pure Reason*, trans. Norman K. Smith. New York: St. Martin's Press.

Lakoff, George, and Mark Johnson. 1999. *Philosophy in the Flesh*. New York: Basic Books.

Lévi-Strauss, Claude. 1970. *The Savage Mind*. Chicago: University of Chicago Press.

Mauss, Marcel. 1967. *The Gift*. Trans. Ian Cunnison. New York: W.W. Norton.

———. 1975. *A General Theory of Magic*, trans. Robert Brain. New York: W.W. Norton.

Meylan, Nicolas. 2017. *Mana: A History of a Western Category*. Leiden: Brill.

Müller, F. Max. 1922. *Immanuel Kant's Critique of Pure Reason*. New York: Macmillan.

Sapir, Edward. 1985. "The Grammarian and His Language." In *Selected Writings of Edward Sapir in Language, Culture, and Personality*, ed. David G. Mandelbaum, 150–59. Berkeley: University of California Press.

Schrempp, Gregory. 1983. "The Re-education of Friedrich Max Müller." *Man* 18(1): 90–110.

———. 2012. *The Ancient Mythology of Modern Science*. Montreal: McGill-Queen's University Press.

Shorter, David D. 2009. *We Will Dance Our Truth*. Lincoln: University of Nebraska Press.

Stocking, George W. 1982. *Race, Culture, and Evolution*. Chicago: University of Chicago Press.

Chapter 2

HIDDEN DURKHEIM AND HIDDEN MAUSS

AN EMPIRICAL REREADING OF THE HIDDEN ANALOGICAL WORK MADE NECESSARY BY THE CREATION OF A NEW SCIENCE

Nicolas Sembel

To Willie Watts Miller, to whom I owe the term "hidden" and so many other Durkheimaussian things and to Louise Durkheim Dreyfus, the hidden worker.

It offends all our mental habits.
—Émile Durkheim, French Philosophical Society, 1913

To be able to hold an empirical dialogue via the archives with important deceased authors is an opportunity. Although at times challenging, such a dialogue offers unequalled perspectives. Regarding Émile Durkheim and Marcel Mauss, the discovery of the library loan registers of their period in Bordeaux implicated a considerable amount of work. I had to produce data on the basis of a corpus of material that was as rich as it was thankless to deal with and later crosscheck it with already existing archives.

However, it also enabled me not only to revisit their respective works and trajectories but also their intellectual relationships, their joint work, their collaborations and exchanges, their positions in the field, and also their School.[1] As with any empirical investigation, there is a time when the material itself gives the "orders." A new corpus of material forces us to revisit, confirm, or invalidate old hypotheses and lays the foundation for new hypotheses, fed by original data, which often make it possible to propose unexpected results. If the material gives the orders, the data, at the end of a research process that transforms the material into meaning, finally fall into place. Our main result is the discovery, with respect to Durkheim and Mauss, of "hidden work" that is revealed by their working practices. This hidden work opens up a new intellectual horizon for the whole of sociology up to the present day.

Every intellectual who publishes takes part in this dialectic of visible work and hidden work—the citations in published writings forming a visible structure while the reading notes stored in files and put into relation constitute an invisible structure. All intellectuals who publish submit their writings to a "game" of citations whose strategic dimension is as important as its intellectual one. The main consequence is that the citations selected for publication only partially reflect the reading that has been done to feed the writing, through its various stages, up to the final version. We have ascertained this empirically by comparing Durkheim's loans and the citations in his works (Sembel 2013). We also find a variant of this "hidden" work in Mauss while he was studying in Bordeaux (Sembel 2015) and at the Sorbonne in Paris, with loans concerning his thesis, as he was "officially" preparing for his *licence* and his *agrégation*, and similarly by Durkheim's student loans at the École normale supérieure de Paris (ENS) and the Sorbonne.

Their work is hidden from us who, until recently, were unaware of the scale, diversity, and structure of their borrowings. It is deliberately hidden by them, those who select their citations. Finally, it is hidden from them too as they obviously have not made their loans a subject of reflection, much less study. More generally, the accumulation of conscious borrowing choices produces a largely unconscious borrowing structure. The overall activity is more than the sum of the partial and conscious tasks that constitute it.

By extension, the metaphor of the hidden takes on other forms: hidden texts, put aside (for example, Durkheim [1887] 1975), disappeared or forgotten due to the hazards of circumstance (see "(Re)Discovered and missing texts" at the end of this chapter); the names contained in these texts accordingly also remain hidden, invisible, or forgotten (e.g., Eugène Gley); there are names published in "visible" texts that otherwise have remained invisible (e.g., Leo the Hebrew); there are also concepts that have known the same treatment (e.g., *dynamogénie*); and there are the intellectual and social links implicated by these names and concepts that therefore also remain hidden and need to be reconstrued.

The reconstruction of these intellectual links among loans, names and concepts, which reflect practices of work, networks of sociability, and the arrangement of ideas and arguments, opens up perspectives that are fascinating, because they contribute to the description of an intellectual horizon and social spirit of an era. By considering all the references and the pages of writing in which these references occur as a target population and sampling this population according to variables (the main one being the intellectual interest of Durkheim and Mauss),[2] that is, by further developing Carlo Ginzburg's (1990) "indexical" method and Clifford Geertz's (1973) "thick" description, we refine—in an uninterrupted process of cross-checking, hypothetical deduction, and comprehension—the production of reliable data and representative citations. Finally, thanks to this grid and to this method, a comparison with the other loans and readings of Durkheim and Mauss, ranked in the same way, can be made (Durkheim's borrowings from the ENS and the Sorbonne and from Mauss, and soon probably also his borrowings in Berlin and Leipzig). Similarly, for Mauss's personal library, and again for the citations in both authors' writings, a rereading of all the publications, and, eventually, a rereading of the reception of the two men's works can be envisaged. By finally combining these working practices with biographical elements and taking into account the writings of Durkheim and Mauss a kind of sociobiography begins to emerge.

The Hidden Work in Durkheim

Durkheim's hidden work became obvious to me at a certain point during the analysis of the material constituted by his Bordeaux loans ($n=505$): apart from cited works, there were theses and journals never or hardly ever mentioned in the published "visible" writings. While the former ($n=38$, loans of 33 different theses) sometimes later became works in their own right, not all of them achieved this editorial destiny and most remained more or less confidential. Thus, according to our hypothesis, Durkheim systematically consulted finished French theses and German "inaugural dissertations," even if he read only those that could provide him with new material, that is, theses that, according to his criteria, posed intellectual problems in an innovative way; which in practice, that is, after having thoroughly worked on the material, could be easily determined from the very first page of the theses (and the dissertations' titles).

The journals (n=29) constitute another type of material, which, because of its disparity, seemed even more suitable than the doctoral theses to be "brewed," "processed," and substantially "manipulaed" on the sociologist's "work bench," in the "kitchens of empiricism," so as to "make it speak" and transform it into data. According to our hypothesis, Durkheim carried out a "screening of documents" (to use today's expression) just as systematic for journals as for theses, in an identical movement of "real" work, as far away as possible from the academic canon of "prescribed" work, and read only those articles that interested him. Our main result is that he probably consulted the table of contents for a large number of journals, some even extremely far removed from his main interests such as the *Annales de science politique*, but from the dozens of articles in all likelihood he did not read more than two (which later were subject to a summary in *Année sociologique*); or such as the *Revue philosophique de la France et de l'étranger* from where he probably retrieved rare articles for reviewing that he neither read nor perused.

The methodical construction of the intellectual foundations of the "concrete general sociology" (as Mauss called it in the 1930s) in preparation in Bordeaux is not mirrored in citations. Insofar as these conform to rules as much academic and strategic as intellectual, they tell us little about the hidden work that Durkheim actually performed. Once unveiled, however, this hidden work tells us a lot about the intellectual universe and horizon not only of Durkheim, but also of Mauss, and about their method(s) of moving around in this universe: how they "sort out" (*débrouillent*), to use Claude Lévi-Strauss' term, their readings and then their files.[3]

In the end, the entire work of the two men can be revisited (we will come back to Mauss in the next section). For Durkheim, this applies to his relation to philosophy, in particular via his loans of the *Philosophy of the Unconscious* by Eduard von Hartmann (1884); his relation to Montesquieu, the loans indicating an extremely dense and concentrated work for the production of his thesis in Latin (with a decisive day in terms of consultative and then definite loans on 8 April 1892); his relation to British anthropology, to James Frazer, William Robertson Smith, Edward Tylor, Andrew Lang, and more, discovered and "embraced" through consultations and loans of the *Encyclopaedia Britannica*; his relation to the subject of "suicide," leading him to the phenomenon, the quantitative presentation (with the help of Mauss), and the published book, a comprehensive study on the entire medical field of the nineteenth century, including links to religious and especially mystic thought. Our main results are as follows: Durkheim criticizes von Hartmann in a written document but makes extensive use of his data and his general frame of thought; he does not waste time on his thesis in Latin but by its efficient realization expresses a decisive aspect of his sociological formalization; he exploits suicide, notably by quoting works he probably hardly read, as Massimo Borlandi (2000) has demonstrated, but by this book and the hidden work that contributed to turn it into a major intellectual achievement of the century he brings to fruition the encounter between emerging sociology, physiology, and those currents in medicine that despecify alienism; he reads articles popularizing science in the encyclopedia to invent, together with Mauss, the sociology of religions and modern ethnology (see for example, Durkheim and Mauss, [1910] 1974; [1913] 1974). Bringing to light these more or less unexpected academic working practices reveals a very specific working method and strategy for building a new science.

The Hidden Work in Mauss

Mauss does not limit himself to the status of philosophy student and nephew, both of which he officially was; neither does he limit himself to the academic tasks of bachelor's degree and the preparation for his *agrégation*, which he officially had to accomplish, but in working with Durkheim proves to be a full-fledged intellectual in his own right.

In Bordeaux, Mauss was working on his theses long before the institution required him to do so; this holds particularly true for his Latin thesis on the links between Spinoza and Leo the Hebrew (L'Hébreu, [1551] 2006), but also for his main thesis on the religious "oral ritual." During the year after his arrival and without any institutional obligation, Mauss, like Durkheim, graduated with a limited scientific baccalaureate (in physiology) intended for future doctors (which neither sought to become: it was physiology that interested them) and "only" licensed with the grade "quite good." His main interest lay elsewhere, as he judged retrospectively in a letter to Octave Hamelin. The work that preoccupied him instead remained hidden until today: the subject of the Latin thesis has only been known since 1979 with the publication of the text "L'oeuvre de Mauss par lui-même" (Mauss [1930] 1979), but it has not interested anyone; the baccalaureate in physiology appears in Mauss' administrative file, but not in his bibliography; the "Prière" is disconnected from his student work; his loan registers have only very recently been discovered and used. However, the work he did was not, of course, hidden for Durkheim, who supported Mauss in his second baccalaureate, then his thesis, with the help of Hamelin, and who from their Bordeaux period onward collaborated with him in jointly developing sociology. Mauss's hidden work in Bordeaux can be summed up by the following deliberately provocative formula: He is preparing a *licence*, an *agrégation*, and two theses not so much in philosophy but in Durkheimian sociology, or rather sociology with Durkheim; strictly speaking, sociology as such, or a sociology in the making.[4]

I suggest to call their common work "joint work" in order to distinguish it, for example, from work "as a pair," which, according to Jean-François Bert, links Mauss with his favorite co-author Henri Hubert. As Mauss himself wrote to Sylvain Lévi after Hubert's death: each one having his own field of specialization, remarkably complementary, but also clearly distinct. The "joint work" of Durkheim and Mauss was quite different. It probably began very early on as an intellectual project initiated by the former, less uncle than tutor, from the very first examples of intellectual socialization reported by the latter, less nephew or pupil than scientist in the making (very probably with writings by Auguste Daux [1877] and Louis Figuier [1860–1861] offered by Durkheim when Mauss was ten and fifteen years old respectively). Mauss's arrival in Bordeaux in the summer of his eighteenth birthday, directly after his first baccalaureate at Épinal, was immediately marked by new readings: Mauss cites Théodule Ribot, while Ribot's contemporary German psychology and the *Revue philosophique*, edited by him, are systematically borrowed by Durkheim, from the ENS, from the Lycée de Sens, and from the University of Bordeaux. The working practices revealed by his loans have been crosschecked with other empirical data from the "Mauss Fund." They all signal an inseparable working relationship with Durkheim. The density, modalities, scope, sustainability, joint and co-authored publications, the issues of *Année sociologique* that were largely co-directed by both of them are all characteristic for their collaboration, which in many respects was also hidden work. But the dogma separating Durkheim from Mauss has imposed a rather distinct visibility. For example, the only joint work really known and visible is their article on primitive forms of classification (Durkheim and Mauss [1903] 1974), whereas all the texts co-signed by Mauss and Hubert have become classics.

Let us conclude these first two points. As much as Durkheim's considerable hidden work tells us about the foundations of his pre-sociological thinking in the sense that he founded, as the "first sociologist," to use an epithet by Philippe Besnard, the new scientific recognition of a "general concrete" sociology, his approach can still be qualified, as we have done, as *"methodological* imagination." As much as Mauss's considerable hidden work, on the other hand, tells us about the projections of the sociological thought of the two men, in the sense that Mauss developed, as soon as he arrived in Bordeaux, into the "second sociologist," to use our own expression, the approach of the general concrete sociology, which Durkheim had just founded, can still be qualified, as we have done, as *"sociological* imagination."[5]

According to our hypothesis, these projections are just as hidden as their bases. While the latter are often wrongly identified keeping us from a full recognition of the intellectual horizon in which Durkheim and, in many respects, Mauss (whose main difference with his uncle was simply to be fourteen years his junior) have construed their general (concrete) sociology, the former are often subject to a highly questionable interpretation, as if each author's work, their conception of sociology, and so forth, were of a different nature. Our material certainly does not allow us to follow this path.

(Re)Discovered and Missing Texts

These following four texts have in common that they are fundamental, as shown by their content, and that they were discovered late; which means that most of the interpretations of Durkheim and Mauss were construed without these texts being known. Their reception thus sometimes poses considerable problems for a cumulative reading, often leading to a refusal to integrate them into the established interpretations, which they would modify or even invalidate. The irritation caused by these texts is proportional to the amount of time they have been buried.[6] In the afterlife of the works of Durkheim and Mauss, as in that of any renowned intellectual, there is a hierarchy of texts that confines some to historical oblivion (within the complete works).

The first example of a missing text is Durkheim's "Discours au lycéens de Sens" (Discourse to the high school students of Sens), written in 1883, published confidentially, and rediscovered by Edward Tiryakian in 1967 (Tiryakian 1967, also published as Durkheim 1975 [1883]). Although Tiryakian, in his short presentation, saw it as proof of the homogeneity of Durkheim's work rather than as an "early work" set aside from his later works, the "Discours" was later marked by the triple disadvantage of anecdotal text, early work, and educational purpose. In agreement with Tiryakian, we understand the text as the founding text of Durkheim's sociology of education and thus directly linked, via his sociology of knowledge (and in particular via the text written for the *agrégation* in philosophy in 1895), to his general sociology (and in particular to his book on the *Elementary Forms of Religious Life* ([1912] 1995); Sembel 2019a). His loan records certainly show that he was working on all these themes at the same time.

The second missing text "What General Sociology Should Be" was written by Durkheim in 1899 ([1899] 1998). It was the result of a symposium, published in a little-known Italian journal, and excavated in 1998 by Massimo Borlandi for the centenary of *Année sociologique*. This text, unique in its clarity, is proof of the direct links between Durkheim's *Division of Social Labour* (1893), his first insights into the sociology of religion, the *Elementary Forms*, which had already been announced but were yet to be published, and the general sociology that provided the title and main subject of the article. Borlandi's extremely well documented presentation (see Borlandi 1998) relativizes the content of the text in order to summarize the changes that general sociology has undergone among Durkheimians.[7]

The third text, two pages long, is entitled "As if . . ." (Mauss [1927] 1997). It was written by Mauss in 1927, not published, and discovered by Marcel Fournier in 1997. It was meant to conclude the text published by Mauss in the second issue of *Année sociologique*, second series. Mauss, however, decided not to publish the conclusion and left the initial text unfinished.[8] In addition to its general significance and great importance, this short text contains a decisive footnote on the scientific method used in sociology by Durkheim and Mauss, relegating the distinction between the so-called exact sciences and the so-called social sciences to the rank of unthinkable. Indeed, neither Durkheim nor Mauss would have built scientific sociology on the basis of such dichotomies.

The fourth of the vanished texts, Mauss's "Leçon d'ouverture au Collège de France," is both the last one written and the last one published (Bert 2012; Mauss 2012 [1931]). We have shown that it is at least as decisive as the text by Durkheim on general sociology. Mauss extends "As if . . ." and affirms as clearly as possible what characterizes sociology and Durkheimian general sociology and what will transcend them,[9] merging both within the same scientific work on very diverse objects, with cumulativity supplanting pluralism.

Three missing texts (perhaps destroyed), which to us seem important, are the course on religion of 1894–95, most likely written by Durkheim "for Mauss," Mauss's article on Spinoza and Leo the Hebrew of 1897, mentioned by Durkheim (or Milhaud), and Book Three of *La Prière* ([1909] 1968) ("*On Prayer*," Mauss' other thesis), cited more than fifty times in Book Two (Sembel, 2019b).

Conclusion: From Hidden to Visible as Scientific Categorization

In interpretations of Durkheim's as well as Mauss's work, exegesis has for long time replaced investigation, and too often formalism and dogmatism have suffocated archival work and the building of new hypothesis. The metaphor of the hidden is not scientific but, used as a trait of mind, it may alert us to the absence of scientific work.

We have to overcome the hidden by the scientific work of making visible: the "hidden" we refer to is like the needle in the haystack, the data in the material, the law in the fact, the universal in the case. The scientific work necessary to make the hidden visible is often routine, sometimes considerable routine. All the "hidden" elements listed in this text open up numerous scientific perspectives, in terms of results, philological readings, cumulativity, inventory, and socio-analysis. It becomes possible to revisit the intellectual horizon of Durkheim and Mauss, both in terms of ideas (their work[s] and beyond), as well as in terms of encounters, forming networks, fields, controversies, and a "hidden Durkheimaussian School" (as an "invisible college" e.g. L. Herr). In short, we have tried to reconstruct what Françoise Waquet (2015) has called the material order of knowledge. The broad structural and unconscious dimensions of this order distinguish our approach to science studies from the history of ideas, from the biographical approach, and more generally from everything that limits the sociological force of the social that we seek to reconstruct through the social origin of certain exemplary intellectual categorizations.

The prospects for future research therefore are also numerous. One possible path is tracing the hidden, because supposedly non-existent, improbable, or secondary links connecting Durkheim and Mauss with intellectuals or references that are more or less expected within their intellectual horizon. Restricting ourselves to the Durkheimian foundations and the Maussian extensions, we may put forward examples of research we have begun. The direct and lasting links between Durkheim and what was later to become pragmatism, since his time at the ENS and his reading of, most probably, William James, John Dewey and, possibly, the article of Charles Sanders Peirce about ideas in 1878).The links between Durkheim and his readings on mesmerism or the unconscious during the same period; and mysticism or the School of Nancy, before his time at the ENS; and Braidism, at the latest just after he left the ENS. The example regarding physiological psychology; and, before the end of the 1880s, between Durkheim and Freud (whom he probably met in 1889) or Pierre Janet (Durkheim's fellow student at the ENS, who defended his thesis on the subconscious in 1889, "against" the thesis of Bergson the same year). The family working links between the loans of Durkheim, his son André (for instance, *Berliner Studies* in 1886), and his nephew Marcel. Mauss's conception of knowledge set out in his penultimate public text on the notion of matter in 1939 and Durkheim's conception of knowledge set out sixty years before in his copy of the 1882 *agrégation*; the Maussian conception of aesthetics, the experimental one (Visher father and son), or "germinative" one (Grosse), discovered together with Durkheim in Bordeaux in the early 1890s and still taken up again in the *Manuel d'ethnographie* in the late 1940s (Mauss [1947] 2002). All these elements prove the existence of a hidden analogical work, by classification and generalization as sociological categories. Scientific creativity is also a matter of precocity, of selection, and of the most dynamic reiteration, that is, of a number of disparaged intellectual operations that are often hidden (minimized or made invisible by their authors or some of their commentators): Durkheim and Mauss have not escaped this logic; on the contrary, they are a perfect illustration of it.

Nicolas Sembel is Professor of Sociology at the Institut national supérieur du professorat et de l'éducation (Inspé) at Aix-Marseille University. He has edited several volumes on Durkheim and Mauss, such as *Les formes élémentaires de la vie religieuse, cent ans après* (2019, together with Matthieu Béra), on Mauss's thesis *La prière* (2019b, together with Florence Weber), or *"Education et sociologie"* (2022).

Notes

1. And this from a completely different perspective than that given, for example, by their "one-way" correspondence (since only Durkheim's letters are known while Mauss's letters have disappeared and remain "hidden" from us, so to speak).
2. As we understand it, trying to read as they have read, to prioritize their readings as they have done, to reconstruct their method, and, finally, to understand their habitus as readers.

3. Lévi-Strauss claims he had to "sort out" ("débrouiller," not "se débrouiller," or "bricoler") some 7,000 references to write the *Elementary Structures of Kinship* (1971).
4. In addition to the Latin thesis, his loans reveal work on experimental aesthetics and experimental psychology. These three central themes are worked upon together with Durkheim. Mauss borrows either the same works as Durkheim or the same authors.
5. We have summoned up a geographical metaphor: Durkheim had not yet finished drawing the outlines and reliefs of the map of the new sociological territory when Mauss, in intellectual agreement with him, already began to review the contours and reliefs of this map and to locate its regions, cities, rivers, etc.
6. We deliberately do not take into account the two somewhat special texts that make up the two copies of Durkheim's *agrégation* written in 1882 and discovered by André Chervel in 1993 (again presented without analysis, see Durkheim 1993 [1882]) and the introduction to *The Division of Labour in Society* that was initially deleted and only published in the second edition. Their content and the interpretation we make of them are, however, fully in line with our argument. We wish to thank Anne Warfield Rawls, who has supervised a new edition of the *Division*, with its complete introduction, for drawing our attention to this other form of "hiding."
7. Durkheim wanted to have a monopoly, or at least the most advanced position, on the definition of general sociology, and so did Mauss with and after him; this position lead to an exploitation of general sociology by the two men that has enabled them to maintain both intellectual and political leadership in the group and in the field, however, without reducing the theory to this use.
8. The conclusion foreshadows a possible lecture at the Collège de France, which Mauss eventually wrote in 1931 and which Fournier did not know in 1997 since it was not published until 2012 by Bert (Mauss [1931] 2012).
9. Some sociologists can be seen as personifying this kind of general sociology; in France it was first and foremost Pierre Bourdieu (see, for example, his course on "general sociology" at the Collège de France in the early 1980s), and today others like Bernard Lahire have followed suit.

References

Bert, Jean-François. 2012. *L'atelier de Mauss*. Paris: Éditions du CNRS.
Borlandi, Massimo. 2000. "Lire ce que Durkheim a lu. Enquête sur les sources statistiques et médicales du 'Suicide.'" In *Le Suicide, un siècle après Durkheim*, ed. Massimo Borlandi and Mohamed Cherkaoui, 9–46. Paris: Presses Universitaires France (PUF).

Borlandi, Massimo. 1998. "Durkheim, les durkheimiens et la sociologie Générale: De la première section de 'l'Année' à la reconstruction d'une problématique perdue." *Année sociologique (AS)* 48: 27–65.
Daux, Auguste. 1877. *L'Industrie humaine: ses origines, ses premiers essais et ses légendes depuis les premiers temps jusqu'au déluge*. Paris: Belin.
Durkheim, Émile. [1882] 1993. "Rapports de l'imagination et de la pensée." In *Histoire de l'agrégation: Contribution à l'histoire de la culture scolaire*, ed. André Chervel, 270–74. Paris: Kimé.
———. 1893. *La Division du Travail Sociale*. Paris: Félix Alcan.
———. [1883] 1975. "Le rôle des grands hommes dans l'histoire: Discours aux lycéens de Sens." In Émile Durkheim, *Textes I. Éléments d'une théorie sociale*, ed. Victor Karady, 409–17. Paris: Minuit.
———. [1887] 1975. "Nécrologie de Victor Hommay." In Émile Durkheim, *Textes I. Éléments d'une théorie sociale*, ed. Victor Karady, 418–24. Paris: Minuit.
———. [1899] 1998. "Ce que devrait être la sociologie générale," ed. Massimo Borlandi, *AS* 48: 66–75.
———. 1912. *Les formes élémentaires de la vie religieuse, le système totémique en Australie*. Paris: Félix Alcan. [1995. *The Elementary Forms of Religious Life*, trans. Karen E. Fields. New York: The Free Press.]
Durkheim, Émile, and Marcel Mauss. [1903] 1974. "De quelques formes primitives de classification: Contribution à l'étude des représentations collectives." In Marcel Mauss, *Œuvres II. Représentations collectives et diversité des civilisations*, ed. Victor Karady, 13–89. Paris: Minuit.
———. [1910] 1974. "Compte-rendu de Strehlow." In Marcel Mauss, *Œuvres II. Représentations collectives et diversité des civilisations*, ed. Victor Karady, 434–39. Paris: Minuit.
———. [1913] 1974. "Note sur la notion de civilisation." In Marcel Mauss, *Œuvres II. Représentations collectives et diversité des civilisations*, ed. Victor Karady, 451–55. Paris: Minuit.
Figuier, Louis. 1860–1861. *Histoire du merveilleux* (4 volumes). Paris: Hachette.
Geertz, Clifford. 1973. "Thick Description: Toward an Interpretive Theory of Culture." In *The Interpretation of Cultures*, 3–30. New York: Basic Books.
Ginzburg, Carlo. 1990. *Myths, Emblems, Clues*, trans. John and Anne C. Tedeschi. Santa Fe, NM: Radius Books.
L'Hébreu, Léon. [1551] 2006. *Dialogues d'amour*. Paris: Vrin.
Hartmann, Eduard von. 1884. *Philosophy of the Unconscious: Speculative Results According to the Inductive Method of Physical Science*, trans. William C. Coupland. London: Trübner.
Lévi-Strauss, Claude. 1971. *Elementary Structures of Kinship*, trans. James H. Bell, John R. von Sturmer, and Rodney Needham. Boston: Beacon Press.
Mauss, Marcel. [1909] 1968. *La Prière*. In Marcel Mauss, *Œuvres I. Les fonctions sociales du sacré*, ed. Victor Karady, 357–477. Paris: Minuit.
———. [1930] 1979. "L'œuvre de Marcel Mauss par lui-même," ed. Philippe Besnard, *Revue française de sociologie* 20(1): 209–20.

———. [1927] 1997. "Comme si." In *Actes de la recherche en sciences sociales*, ed. Marcel Fournier, 116–17, 105–6.

———. [1947] 2002. *Manuel d'ethnographie*. Paris: Éditions Payot & Rivages.

———. [1931] 2012. "Leçon d'ouverture au Collège de France." In *L'atelier de Mauss*, ed. Jean-François Bert, 249–64. Paris: Éditions du CNRS.

Sembel, Nicolas. 2013. "Les emprunts de Durkheim à la bibliothèque universitaire de Bordeaux: une 'imagination méthodologique' en acte." *Durkheimian Studies* 19: 5–49.

———. 2015. "Les emprunts de Mauss à la bibliothèque universitaire de Bordeaux: la genèse d'une 'imagination sociologique.'" *Durkheimian Studies* 21: 3–60.

———. 2019a. "Religion, éducation, connaissance: La méthode de Durkheim vers la sociologie générale." In *'Les Formes élémentaires de la vie religieuse', cent ans après. Emile Durkheim et la religion*, ed. Matthieu Béra and Nicolas Sembel, 235–92. Paris: Classiques Garnier.

———. 2019b. "Le plan reconstitué de *La Prière*." In Marcel Mauss, *La Prière*, ed. Florence Weber and Nicolas Sembel, 203–204. Paris: PUF.

Tiryakian, Edward A. 1967. "Le premier message d'Emile Durkheim." *Cahiers internationaux de sociologie* 14: 23–25.

Watts Miller, William. 2005. "'Dynamogénique' and 'élémentaire.'" *Durkheimian Studies* 11: 18–32.

Waquet, Françoise. 2015. *L'ordre matériel du savoir. Comment les savants travaillent (XVIe–XXIe siècles)*. Paris: Éditions du CNRS.

Chapter 3

MANA IN CONTEXT

FROM MAX MÜLLER TO MARCEL MAUSS

Nicolas Meylan

Henri Hubert and Marcel Mauss's "Esquisse d'une théorie générale de la magie" (Hubert and Mauss 1904) is rightly celebrated as a major landmark in the history of the study of magic. The text, published in 1904, proposed a radically new way of understanding magic, reshuffled the received relationship between magic, religion, and science developed by British intellectualist anthropology, and announced a number of key ideas that would be at the heart of Émile Durkheim's *Formes élémentaires de la vie religieuse* (Durkheim 1912), in particular that of *mana* and collective effervescence. Most conspicuously, the two Frenchmen cast *mana* as a general category to address the problem of (magical) causality. At the same time, their formulation of *mana* as a second-order category laid the groundwork for a new paradigm in the study of religion, dynamism, which replaced gods with impersonal power (and would eventually come to be called the "sacred") as the central object/category of study (e.g., Alles 1987). And yet however groundbreaking and original Mauss and Hubert's text may have been, it nevertheless belongs squarely in the context of later *Belle Époque* scholarship. It is to a brief exploration of that context—which saw the transformation of mana from "a glossed item of exotic native terminology" (Smith 2004: 125) into a category of universal application—that this chapter will be devoted,[1] in order to do something rather un-postmodern, to look for points of convergence between the "Esquisse" and other scholarly productions. However, to do so first requires us to turn to the anthropological paradigm against which Hubert and Mauss were positioning their study of magic.

The Frenchmen's quest to demonstrate the social, collective nature of magic and to account for its widespread role in society brought them up against the towering figures of Edward B. Tylor and his successor James G. Frazer. More than these two British anthropologists' exact views on magic, it was their basic assumptions about the nature of magic, religion, and science and their relationships that proved unacceptable to Hubert and Mauss, assumptions that had been dominating the fledgling sciences of religion ever since the publication of Tylor's *Primitive Culture* in 1871 (Tylor 1871). These assumptions, often subsumed under the label "intellectualism" (e.g., Stocking 1996: 79), are closely linked to Tylor's and Frazer's evolutionism and the associated concept of the psychic unity of mankind (see e.g., Stocking 1987). Tylor's intellectualism is nowhere more obvious than in his *Primitive Culture*'s myth of the origin of religion:

> It seems as though thinking men, as yet at a low level of culture, were deeply impressed by two groups of biological problems. In the first place, what is it that makes the difference between a living body and a dead one; what causes waking, sleep, trance, disease, death? Looking at these two groups of phenomena, the ancient savage philosophers practically made each help to account for the other, by combining both in a conception which we may call an apparitional-soul, a ghost-soul ... Far from these world-wide opinions being arbitrary or conventional products, it is seldom even justifiable to consider their uniformity among distant races as proving communication of any sort. They are doctrines answering in the most forcible way to the plain evidence of men's senses, as interpreted by a fairly consistent and rational primitive philosophy. (Tylor 1871: I, 387)

Religion, minimally defined as "belief in spiritual beings"—or rather "animism" as Tylor labeled it (1871: I, 383)—thus represented an individual and rational phenomenon (however marred it might be by ignorance). For Tylor then, animism is nothing but the savage philosopher's explanation of the world, an explanation that would in time give way to its more developed counterpart, science, which according to Tylor shares the same individualistic and rational character, indeed evincing the same basic function: to explain the world. Magic fit neatly into this frame, being represented as yet another, cruder mode of explanation of the world.[2] Moreover, while Tylor insisted on magic's fundamental inefficiency, he nonetheless insisted on its rational nature, describing it as a misapplication, again by individuals, of the psychological law of association of ideas, a law Tylor believed to be a central element of rational thinking.[3]

In *The Golden Bough*, whose first edition came out in 1890, James Frazer maintained this basic evolutionary, intellectualist framework but distinguished more sharply between religion and magic, defining the latter as an activity governed by impersonal laws "in which we may detect a germ of the modern notion of natural law" (Frazer 1894: I, 9). Importantly, while these scholars acknowledged that magic was grounded in rational thinking, they rejected it as fundamentally spurious, as "pseudo-science" and "delusion" (Tylor 1871: I, 101), belonging to an anterior, less-developed stage of human culture.

With "Esquisse," Hubert and Mauss were pursuing two related aims. First, they wished to demonstrate the collective nature of magic and, second, to account for the widespread belief in its efficacy (and in specific conditions its actual efficacy, which Hubert and Mauss explained by means of "collective and traditional suggestion"; Hubert and Mauss 1904: 141). In so doing, they were explicitly breaking with the intellectualist (and especially Frazerian) perspective, which at the time enjoyed a nearly hegemonic status in the study of religion, whether in Great Britain or in France (see, for instance, Marett 1941: 157; Rosa 1996). To do so, the sociologists turned to a cross-cultural examination of the representations of magic. Lying behind the various emic accounts of its workings (classified either as involving sympathy, properties, or demons; Hubert and Mauss 1904: 61–85), they identified the presence of a more fundamental (and seemingly universal), if normally implicit notion of force acting within a specific milieu, a notion they insisted was not rational, at least from the perspective of European adults (Hubert and Mauss 1904: 107). There remained for Hubert and Mauss to flesh out empirically this underlying representation, which amounted to a causal category. To do so, they turned to the writings of Robert Codrington (1830–1922), a British missionary scholar who, after having spent over twenty years in Melanesia, had penned in 1891 an acclaimed and highly influential account of Melanesian life and customs, *The Melanesians: Studies in Their Anthropology and Folk-Lore* (Codrington 1891). In his monograph, Codrington had given an influential description of *mana*, noting that "the Melanesian mind is entirely possessed by the belief in a supernatural power or influence, called almost universally *mana*. This is what works to effect everything which is beyond the ordinary power of men, outside the common processes of natures" adding later that "this again is the active force in all they do and believe to be done in magic" (1891: 118, 191). Codrington's description of Melanesian *mana* proved convenient in a number of ways for Hubert and Mauss. First, Codrington spoke of *mana* in the idiom of causality.[4] Second, insofar as *mana* was at the same time an adverb, a verb, and a noun, the word (and so presumably the category) defied Aristotelian logic. Moreover, it belonged to the realm of the "supernatural" (1891: 119), and thus by extension appeared irrational.[5] Just as importantly, being described as impersonal, *mana* did not fit in with Tylor's animistic theory (which grounded its definition of religion on the notion of personal beings). Finally, Codrington's fieldwork-based discussion suggested that *mana* was not so much about theorizing or explaining the world but rather about doing things in the world.[6] Melanesian *mana* thus represented perfect ethnographic proof of the inadequacy of intellectualist theorizing about magic (and religion).

The Melanesians, however, was not Codrington's first attempt to make sense of *mana*. Some twenty-five years before the publication of "Esquisse," in 1877, the missionary had sent the Oxford-based comparative philologist and mythologist Max Müller (1823–1900) a letter from the field in which he gave a detailed description of *mana*. A year later, Müller was invited to give the prestigious Hibbert lectures (published as Müller 1878). The topic he selected for the lectures was the origin and development of religion, a topic of which he had been the undisputed expert in Great Britain (see van den Bosch 2002).[7] Unfortunately for Müller, his leadership in the field had been abruptly brought to an end by the publication of Edward Tylor's "Primitive Culture" in 1871. Müller thus chose to devote his first lecture to a theoretical explanation and defense of his theory of religion, which may be summarized in the following manner. According to Müller, religion consists in the perception of the Infinite, a perception that has nothing to do with Kantian sense or reason, but rather with what Müller construed as mankind's "faculty for faith" (Müller 1878: 22–23). The Infinite, that which is worshipped under various names by the religions of the world, was initially perceived through the spectacle of nature—the sky and the sun in particular—a perception Müller closely associated with feelings, usually wonder (Müller 1878: 44) but also (Christian) humility. Importantly, Müller noted that at an early stage in the history of humanity, such perceptions were non-personal in nature, the personalization of the Infinite being a later and quite accidental development in the history of religion.[8]

Tylor's theory posed two specific problems for Müller. First, Tylor's definition of religion/animism as "belief in spiritual beings" (Tylor 1871: I, 383) clashed with Müller's understanding of religion as the "perception of the Infinite." But more problematic for Müller was the anthropologist's intellectualism. For Müller, who combined a liberal Protestant outlook with a firm rooting in German Romanticism (van den Bosch 2002), religion had nothing to do with explanation and science. Quite on the contrary, religion was a matter of feeling and of poetry. Worse, Tylor's discussion of religion in terms of rationality clashed directly with Müller's view that religion arises from a human faculty for faith and not from (Kantian) reason. To make his case, Müller dedicated his second lecture to a more pointed refutation of his anthropological opponent. On the one hand, he attacked Tylor's comparative method and its equation of contemporary "savages" with prehistoric man (Müller 1878: 55–127), and on the other hand, he sought to offer empirical proof to support his own theory. Unable to tap his material of choice, the highly personal Indo-European mythology, Müller turned to the letter he had recently received from his informant in the Melanesian field, Robert Codrington. From what appears to have been a lengthy letter, Müller extracted the following passage:[9]

> The religion of the Melanesians consists as far as belief goes, in the persuasion that there is a supernatural power about . . . and as far as practice goes, in the use of means of getting this power turned to their own benefit. The notion of a supreme being is altogether foreign to them, or indeed of any being occupying a very elevated place in their world . . . There is a belief in a force altogether distinct from physical power, which acts in all kinds of ways for good and evil, and which it is of the greatest advantage to possess or control. This is Mana. . . . I think I know what our people mean by it. . . . It is a power or influence, not physical, and, in a way, supernatural; but it shows itself in physical force, or in any kind of power or excellence which a man possesses. (Müller 1878: 53)

Müller, however, did not merely quote Codrington, he also gave directions as to how his letter was to be read. He introduced *mana* as the "Melanesian name for the Infinite" (1878: 53), and stressed—somewhat awkwardly[10]—the impersonality of *mana*, in order to show the defectiveness of Tylor's minimum definition of religion. Müller's discussion of *mana* moreover foregrounded the fact that the Melanesian notion was irrational. Müller—but not Codrington who remained silent on the issue—stated that *mana* is a "vague and hazy form . . . of the idea of the infinite," and "this *mana* is one of the early helpless expressions of what the apprehension of the infinite would be in its incipient stages" (Müller 1878: 53–54; Meylan 2017: 38–39). Here thus was a phenomenon that was at the same time emphatically religious, impersonal, and irrational. As Müller saw it, this was a phenomenon that functioned as the perfect foil to Tylor's theory of religion. It remained, however, a one-off, an ethnographic oddity with no theoretical import.

Müller's efforts had no effect. Tylor, and his intellectualism, remained the foremost authority on religion in British and French study of religion for some two more decades and Müller's work on religion increasingly lost its relevance. This, however, should not be taken to mean that no one challenged Tylor's theory. In the United States, for instance, John King (1843 until after 1905) offered a rival evolutionist theory of religion, centered not around animism but on the concept of the "supernatural." In his two-volume study entitled *The Supernatural: Its Origin, Nature, and Evolution*, published in 1892 (King 1892), King disagreed with Tylor on two counts. First, King broke with Tylor's intellectualism. Religion according to King has nothing to do with rational thinking, far from it, but rather with "the sentiments of wonder, fear, hope, and love" (King 1892: I, 15; Meylan 2017: 53). King thus produced a rather different myth of origin:

> Under the general aspects of things there is a quiet accord between the mind of man and the phenomena of the universe, but should the condition of things lose its accepted normal character then influences of dread fill the mind, and, as in the presence of the eclipse or the meteor, if the dread is more than spasmodic, man doubts the stability of the universe. So it is even with less variation from the normal. It may be a feather, a leaf, a stone, or an animal which presents unknown characteristics and excites first wonder, then dread, and on his failure to recognize their status they become to him uncanny—they are not natural—and excite sentiments of erratic influence, of supernal action. (King 1892: I, 15)

Thus, for King, the central object of all religion and so historical religions—supernatural power—is a notion that arises precisely at the point where reason ceases its action. It follows that King's religion has nothing to do with explaining the world, with science; religion is in fact about power—or humanity's lack of it.

Second, this view led King to reject the privileged position Tylor granted to personal (spiritual) beings in religion. While King accepted animism, he did not grant it the status of *summum genus* for religion, rather it appears in his work as but one stage in the development of religion so that before animism there were less evolved, impersonal forms of religion, for instance those based on the conception of "luck." At this very early stage of religion, individuals perceive events that stand outside of the normal working of nature, which they ascribe to the workings of unknown "occult virtues," that is, supernatural power, "adapt their behavior either to avoid harm or derive advantages therefrom" (e.g., avoiding crossing the path of a black cat or carrying a rabbit's paw to attract good luck; King 1892: I, 100, 94; Meylan 2017: 54). At the next stage of religious development, people actively manipulate this luck by means of charms and spells, which amounts to the practice of magic. It is only at the following stage that belief in personal beings, and thus animism, appears.

King introduces *mana* in the second, magical, stage as he discusses the wizards and medicine men who manipulate supernatural power. At first, Codrington's *mana* represents, in King's discussion, only a circumscribed element alongside other emic representations such as the Iroquois's *orenda* and Australian Aborigines' *boylya*, all of which he glosses as magical power, and thus function as ethnographic examples of King's second-order category of power. King, however, goes further. Abruptly, he begins using the word *mana* as a shorthand for his generic, universal second-order category. Accordingly, King turns to this etic *mana* to account for the doings of wizards, shamans, priests, as well as gods, ghosts, and so forth the world over—including the seventeenth-century English magus Sir Kenelm Digby "who so loved to discourse upon the old sympathetic *mana*" (King 1892: I, 135). By so raising Melanesian *mana* to second-order category status King confers on mana a central role in his theory of religion,[11] in a way anticipating the development, in the study of religion, of the dynamist paradigm, of which Hubert and Mauss's "Esquisse" is a seminal text.

For all the scholarly and personal differences between King and Müller, we find in both a similar use of the Oceanic term *mana* as a means to respond to Tylor's theory of religion, a theory they rejected on identical grounds. First for its focus on personality, which they saw at best as only part of the story, and second for its intellectualism. Although for very different reasons—King was a rabid atheist while Müller has been likened to an esotericist (Josephson-Storm 2017: 107–15)—they understood religion to be a matter not of reason and logical thought but rather of emotions and feelings. For both scholars, Melanesian *mana* as defined by Codrington provided the perfect response, being impersonal and supernatural all the while being explicitly classified as religious.

Other convergent uses of *mana* might be produced at this point, such as those of Andrew Lang (1898) or Léon Marillier (1900), despite the fact that they pursued different ends with different methodologies, but I would like to discuss just one more case, that of another British anthropologist, Robert Ranulph Marett (1866–1943). At the outset, it should be noted that Marett, toward the end of his life, commented on the closeness between his views on magic and those of Hubert and Mauss, writing in his 1941 autobiography that "[b]oth of us had undoubtedly hit the same bird, and theirs was the heavier shot;

but I fired first" (Marett 1941: 161). But what was this bird? Clearly, it was not a sociological analysis of religion and magic. Marett, in 1908, published an article in which he rejected what he called the Durkheimian determinism as well as their explanation of religion in terms of social morphology (Marett 1929: 129–31). To Marett, the queen of the anthropological disciplines remained individual psychology, and Marett is indeed associated with a thoroughly psychological theory of religion he first presented in an 1899 paper entitled "Pre-Animistic Religion" read at the meeting of the British Association and published the next year in the prestigious scholarly journal *Folk-Lore* (Marett 1909: 1–32). As his title suggests, Marett sought to show that Tylor's minimum definition of religion—the belief in spiritual beings—was if not wrong at least insufficiently wide. There are, so Marett argued, classes of phenomena that although not personal should be grouped under the category religion. Marett's argument, however, was tightly linked to the way he understood the category. And although he downplayed his disagreement with Tylor, whose friend he was and who was the one who had introduced him to anthropology (Marett 1941: 117–19), Marett's critique went in fact much further than the amendment of a definition, for at the heart of Marett's article was a fundamental rejection of Tylor's animism as a rational explanation of the world. Marett's religion was precisely about the loss of reason:

> In response to, or at any rate in connection with, the emotion of awe, wonder and the like, wherein feeling would seem for the time being to have outstripped the power of "natural," that is, reasonable, explanation, there arises in the region of human thought a powerful impulse to objectify and even personify the mysterious or "supernatural" something felt, and in the region of will a corresponding impulse to render it innocuous, or better still, propitious, by force of constraint, communion, or conciliation. (Marett 1909: 10–11)

To Marett, then, religion had nothing to do with reflecting coolly about life and the world, but rather with reacting emotionally to some perceived supernatural power—a power that could take either personal or impersonal form (1909: 11). Although he was too polite—or prudent—to state it outright, Marett's theory in fact constituted a major challenge to Tylor's intellectualism, of which animism was but a secondary development.

Very much like Müller and King before him, Marett went on to provide cross-cultural documentation of the validity of his theory by adducing various terms drawn from ethnographic literature representing, according to Marett, a discursive trace of the experience of the supernatural. The terms Marett provides include notions drawn from North America, Madagascar, Eastern Africa, Fiji, and, predictably enough, Melanesia in the form of Codrington's *mana* (1909: 11–12).

In an ulterior text, whose aim was to refute Frazer's intellectualist theory of magic,[12] Marett went a step further, raising Melanesian *mana* to the status of universal and theoretical category:

> The actual *mana* of the Melanesians will on analysis be found to yield a very mixed and self-contradictory set of meanings, and to stand for any kind of power that rests in whatever way upon the divine. I suppose it, however, to have the central and nuclear sense of magical power; and apart from the question of historical fact, let me, for expository purposes at any rate, be allowed to give the term this connotation. (1909: 67)

Mana, together with the awe it irresistibly triggers, thus came to condense Marett's emotionalist theory of religion, incidentally providing the study of religion with a new object—power—that would go on to wield a major influence in the decades that followed.[13] In a later text, Marett spelled out what this new theoretical category could be expected to achieve (Marett 1916). *Mana*, he claimed, would (1) allow the demonstration of the common nature of magic and religion, (2) provide a new "minimum definition of religion," (3) account for the contagious nature of the "sacred," and finally (4) "*mana* is the term best suited to express magico-religious value as realized in and through ritual" (1909: 379).

Mana, presumably, was the bird Marett referred to in his autobiography, but as the present chapter suggests, the bird should more properly be understood as intellectualism, which is the one element that united scholars so different as Müller, King, and the Durkheimians, and accounts for their common resort to Codrington's *mana*. In this sense, it may be desirable to extend Marett's hunting metaphor to a whole range of authors busily firing their guns on the same quarry during the *Belle Époque*. Indeed, the struggle against reason constitutes a significant theme in the study of religion of the period, which is all the more striking in that it united scholars from various disciplines, equipped with very different methods, presuppositions, and aims. Seen in this way, its originality, rigor, and erudition notwithstanding, the "Esquisse" and its construction of *mana* as a general category (which anticipated Durkheim's thoughts on the origins of the category of cause), takes its place among a series of texts that attempted to deal with intellectualism and the specific sets of questions it asked, not the least of which concerned the nature of religion and its origin.

My aim in this chapter has in no way been to diminish Hubert and Mauss's accomplishment with "Esquisse" but rather to suggest that it be read in a different way, that it be set squarely in the sustained discussion with Tylor and British anthropology more generally bearing on the best way to conceptualize religion. In so doing, one is confronted with the fact that their theory of magic is set within a larger intertext that is both extraordinarily wide—as suggest the innumerable book reviews Marcel Mauss wrote—and astonishingly small. At the end of the day, what toppled the intellectualism of British anthropology were the four or five pages Codrington wrote about the *mana* of the Melanesians (Codrington 1891: 118–20, 191–92).

Nicolas Meylan is senior researcher and lecturer at the University of Lausanne's Institute of History and Anthropology of Religions (IHAR). He holds a PhD in History of Religions from the University of Chicago. He specializes in theories and historiography of the history of religions and is the author of *Mana: A History of a Western Category* (2017).

Notes

1. This chapter is based on material published in *Mana: A History of a Western Category* (Meylan 2017: 35–70).
2. While Tylor suggests that magic is linked to "primitive" or backward peoples, he does not specify its place within the linear development of culture. It was Frazer who would remedy this and assign it its place at the beginning of human culture.
3. Tylor thus writes: "The principal key to the understanding of Occult Science is to consider it as based on the Association of Ideas, a faculty which lies at the very foundation of human reason, but in no small degree of human unreason also. Man as yet in a low intellectual condition, having come to associate in thought those things which he found by experience to be connected in fact, proceeded erroneously to invert this action, and to conclude that association in thought must involve similar connection in reality. He thus attempted to discover, to foretell, and to cause events by means of processes which we can *now* see to have only an ideal significance" (Tylor 1871: I, 104). Note the strategic choice to label magic as "Occult *Science*."
4. For instance: "That invisible power which is believed by the natives to cause all such effects as transcend their conception of the regular cause of nature . . . is that generally known as *mana*" (Codrington 1891: 191).

5. Note, however, that Codrington himself did not explicitly label *mana* or the Melanesians as irrational. In a letter to his brother dated 30 September 1872, he writes that Edward Tylor "gives credit most deservedly as most people don't, to savages for having plenty of brains. He quite confirms what I always have said that savages are wonderfully like other people" (quoted by Davidson 2003: 174). Codrington, however, never embraced Tylor's intellectualism and evolutionism, preferring Max Müller's religionist view of religion as the "perception of the Infinite" (see e.g., Müller 1878: 22–23).
6. In addition to placing *mana* within its ritual and pragmatic contexts, Codrington points to its retrospective, rather than systematic nature; see for instance the following: "A man comes by chance upon a stone which takes his fancy; its shape is singular, it is like something, it is certainly not a common stone, there must be *mana* in it" (Codrington 1891: 119).
7. Müller had already presented his theory in a synthetic manner in his celebrated *Introduction to the Science of Religion* (Müller 1873).
8. Personalization of the Infinite presumably occurs at the "mythological stage" of the development of language. To the somewhat prudish Victorian, myths and their sordid features (anthropophagy, rapes, etc.) represented the symptoms of a disease of language (Müller 1909: 12: 70–72). Note that for Müller, religious development goes hand in hand with the development of language (e.g., Müller 1909).
9. In his citation of Codrington's letter, Müller indicates a page number ("in their world (p. 14)"; Müller 1878: 53), that suggests that the letter was quite extensive. I have unfortunately not been able to see the original document, nor has his latest biographer Lourens van den Bosch (personal communication).
10. Codrington indicates that *mana* itself is an impersonal power, "but spirits, whether disembodied souls or supernatural beings, have it, and can impart it; and it essentially belongs to personal beings to originate it" (Müller 1878: 54). Codrington confirmed this idea in 1891, writing that: "this power, though itself impersonal, is always connected with some person who directs it" (Codrington 1891: 119).
11. It should be noted, however, that King is not consistent in his use of the term mana to denote his second-order category, as he regularly reverts to "magical power."
12. Frazer's theory presented a particular threat for Marett as Frazer distinguished (ideal-typically) magic from religion on the basis of the former's impersonality (Frazer 1911: 220). Marett carefully showed that the emotion of awe lay behind both magic and religion and so subsumed the two in the more general category of the "magico-religious," the distinction between the two representing a later "superinduced" moral dimension (Marett 1909: 131–32).
13. Indeed, the early dynamist formulations in terms of *mana* were progressively morphed in the more Western-sounding holy and sacred, which still endure (see e.g., Meylan 2017; Paden 1991).

References

Alles, Gregory. 1987. "Dynamism." In *Encyclopedia of Religion*, ed. Mircea Eliade, 527–32. New York: Macmillan.
Codrington, Robert. 1891. *The Melanesians: Studies in Their Anthropology and Folk-Lore*. Oxford: Clarendon.
Davidson, Allan K. 2003. "The Legacy of Robert Henry Codrington." *International Bulletin of Missionary Research* 27(4): 171–76.
Durkheim, Émile. 1912. *Les formes élémentaires de la vie religieuse: Le système totémique en Australie*. Paris: Félix Alcan.
Frazer, James. 1894. *The Golden Bough: A Study in Comparative Religion*. London: Macmillan.
———. 1911. *The Golden Bough: A Study in Magic and Religion*, 3rd edn. London: Macmillan.
Hubert, Henri, and Marcel Mauss. 1904. "Esquisse d'une théorie générale de la magie." *L'année sociologique* 7: 1–146.
Josephson-Storm, Jason. 2017. *The Myth of Disenchantment: Magic, Modernity, and the Birth of the Human Sciences*. Chicago: The University of Chicago Press.
King, John. 1892. *The Supernatural: Its Origin, Nature, and Evolution*. London: Williams and Norgate.
Lang, Andrew. 1898. *The Making of Religion*. London: Longmans, Green, and Co.
Marett, Robert R. 1909. *The Threshold of Religion*. London: Methuen.
———. 1916. "Mana." In *Encyclopædia of Religion and Ethics*, vol. VIII, ed. James Hastings, 375–80. Edinburgh: T. & T. Clark.
———. 1929. "A Sociological View of Comparative Religion." In Robert R. Marett, *The Threshold of Religion*, 4th edn, 122–44. London: Methuen.
———. 1941. *A Jerseyman at Oxford*. London: Oxford University Press.
Marillier, Léon. 1900. "Religion." In *La grande encyclopédie: Inventaire raisonné des sciences, des lettres et des arts*, ed. Henri Lamirault, 341–64. Paris: Société anonyme de la grande encyclopédie.
Meylan, Nicolas. 2017. *Mana: A History of a Western Category*. Leiden: Brill.
Müller, Max F. 1873. *Introduction to the Science of Religion: Four Lectures Delivered at the Royal Institution in February and May 1870*. London: Longmans, Green and Co.
———. 1878. *Lectures on the Origin and Growth of Religion as Illustrated by the Religions of India*. London: Longmans, Green and Co.
———. 1909. *Comparative Mythology: An Essay*. London: Routledge.
Paden, William. 1991. "Before the 'Sacred' Became Theological: Rereading the Durkheimian Legacy." *Method and Theory in the Study of Religion* 3: 10–23.
Rosa, Frederico. 1996. "Le movement 'anthropologique' et ses représentants français (1884–1912)." *Archives Européennes de Sociologie* 37(2): 375–405.

Smith, Jonathan. 2004. *Relating Religion: Essays in the Study of Religion*. Chicago: University of Chicago Press.
Stocking, George. 1987. *Victorian Anthropology*. New York: The Free Press.
———. 1996. *After Tylor: British Social Anthropology 1888–1951*. London: Athlone.
Tylor, Edward. 1871. *Primitive Culture*. London: Murray.
van den Bosch, Lourens. 2002. *Friedrich Max Müller: A Life Devoted to the Humanities*. Leiden: Brill.

Chapter 4

DURKHEIM, THE QUESTION OF THE CATEGORIES, AND THE CONCEPT OF LABOR

Susan Stedman Jones

Durkheim initiated the idea of a category project with his claim for the social origin of the categories: that the fundamental concepts with which we think are formed socially and historically is a strong argument for the sociology of knowledge. In *Les formes élémentaire de la vie religieuse*, Durkheim claims that the question of the categories is a matter of "history." Categories are "complex." To understand them "it is not sufficient to examine our conscience"; we must look "outside of ourselves" for these are conceptions that we have "not made ourselves"—it is "human groups who have laboriously forged them over centuries" (Durkheim [1912] 1985: 27).[1] And to achieve this, a science must be established—a "complex science" that can only advance slowly through "collective work (*travail*)" (28). This edited volume can be seen to contribute to this complex science and its collective nature. But exactly what is the role of work in the formation of the categories and how does this unfold over history? This is the theme of this chapter.

In my *Année sociologique* article "Forms of Thought and Forms of Society" (2012), I suggested that Durkheim was offering a labor theory of epistemology. By this I meant a theory of knowledge in which labor plays a crucial role in the formation of concepts and in this case in their supreme form—the categories. A number of questions arise. How can he associate labor and knowledge? Does this not sound like a form of historical materialism? Yet he has repudiated this (Durkheim [1912] 1985: 605) together with the labor theory of value (Durkheim

[1899] 1986: 136). He uses the concept of capital to refer to the accumulation of knowledge in the categories (Durkheim [1912] 1985: 27), just as he identifies labor with this process of epistemological formation. Although not a Marxist, there is nonetheless a radical theory of social epistemology here in which labor—human work—is dominant. Rather than Marxism, it is his humanism and his rationalism that are evident here. A second set of questions revolves around the consequences of this for the type of theory Durkheim espouses: How can he identify labor, which is a form of action, without becoming a pragmatist? In his lectures on pragmatism he rejects basing knowledge on the interest of action. Further questions concerning both constructionism and realism arise. He insists again and again on the reality of society and at the same time on the constructive nature of collective representations. How can they both be constructed and be real? Much of this debate involves philosophical considerations that go beyond the scope of this chapter, but in the conclusion I will suggest a way labor can be seen to mediate between these two positions.

Whatever the answers to these complex questions, for him to be able to associate labor with these supreme concepts (that is, the categories), there must be a compatibility between the nature of category and action, for labor is a specific form of human action. What is it about the nature of labor that allows Durkheim to say that categories are "laboriously forged" and how does his definition of category allow him to claim this?

The Nature of the Categories

There are categories and categorizations. There are culturally specific categorizations which were outlined in "Classification primitive" (Durkheim and Mauss [1902] 1969). However, in *Les formes*, Durkheim's concern is also with "fundamental categories" (Durkheim [1912] 1985: 19). Clearly specific categorizations and fundamental categories are on different levels—both in terms of abstraction and of epistemological authority. It is clear that for him the categories have authority within representation: "Among our representations there are some which play a preponderant role, these are the categories" (Durkheim [1909] 1975: 185). So in this 1909 essay, categories are "preponderant representations." Yet their epistemological authority is increased in *Les formes* and is connected with their "irreducible" a priori nature (Durkheim [1912] 1985: 21). Now there must be a connection between the specific and concrete cultural levels of categorization and this higher epistemological level. Unless there is an imprinting by the social and its specific practices onto the formation of the categories at the highest level then his sociological hypothesis cannot get off the ground. Although there are important questions about this, I will suggest a way labor offers a route to the reconciliation of these levels.

So, Durkheim in 1912 ambitiously aims for social explanation of the highest epistemological level. In so doing, he enters philosophical territory with his sociological hypothesis that "[C]ategories are essentially collective representations" (Durkheim [1912] 1985: 22). Durkheim in 1909 dismisses certain aspects of philosophical method as "dialectical and ideological" (Durkheim [1909] 1975: 187), although he stresses the importance of the science of mind here (186). He argues that if categories have a collective origin we must know "of what they are made, which elements enter into them, what determines the fusion of these elements in these complex representations" (187). It is on these assumptions—that categories are made, that there are significant elements in them, and that the fusion of these elements forms them—that his explanation in terms of labor and the collective is made. In so doing, he apparently sweeps aside Aristotelian philosophy, scholasticism, and Kantian transcendentalism as definitive in this most difficult of philosophical questions—what are the categories?

Durkheim insists that *au fond* what they are actually dealing with are collect representations since that is just what categories are. This is a major hypothesis, executed far too briefly with less than glance at this eminent tradition. Elsewhere I have suggested that it was Charles Renouvier who directed him and that Durkheim was developing and putting flesh on an argument known to his contemporary audience (largely philosophers—including his friends Octave Hamelin and Xavier Leon, but now forgotten, see Stedman Jones 2012).

Nevertheless, this sociological hypothesis does not preclude him from adopting characterizations of the nature of categories from this tradition. They are dominant concepts that serve to organize experience—and as such they are fundamental to the possibility of knowledge. He has a deep account of the categories: they are "essential notions which dominate our whole intellectual life" (Durkheim [1912] 1985: 12). They are "the solid framework (*cadres*) which encircles (*enserrent*) thought. They are like the skeleton of (*l'ossature*) of intelligence" (13). They are "inseparable from the normal functioning of the mind (*l'esprit*)" (12). We cannot think without them; we can only think objects as spatial, temporal and as numerable (13). They have a universality and necessity and are irreducible (19). They are central to rationalism and to the authority of reason: "the world has a logical aspect which reason eminently expresses" (20). They have a function of "dominating" and "enveloping" all other concepts (628). In this they express "the fundamental condition of understanding between minds" (627).

There are philosophical influences clearly evident and another seminal one that is not at first sight evident. First, in his account of being and its relation with the categories there are echoes of Aristotle. Social being (*l'être social*) "represents in us . . . the highest reality in the intellectual and moral order" ([1912] 1985: 23). In contradistinction to Aristotle, being is social being for Durkheim. This revolves around his account of collective representations, which he insists are of a different order than purely individual ones. These represent social being, and it is this that explains classic philosophical issues—philosophical dualism, logical necessity, and moral irreducibility.

Like Immanuel Kant, categories are complex and synthetic, that is, they bring together elements that are not analytically connected. And with Kant, the categories are representations for Durkheim. Although there are individual representations, his primary focus is collective representation. The first philosophical formulation of collective representation was introduced by Renouvier who argued both with and against Kant. With Kant, he held that the categories were synthetic, are central to judgement, and thus to the whole structure of representation. Yet he disputed both Kant's list of the categories and their nature, specifically of Kant's account of relation, which for Renouvier is the seminal category. Most importantly for him transcendentalism is not the route to the discovery of the categories. Against Kant, he argued that to discover their nature the whole "human tableau" must be consulted, not merely the table of judgments. The categories as "the skeleton (*la squelette*) of representation" are "a difficult work (*oeuvre difficile*)" and are the result of "prolonged collective work (*travaux collectifs et prolongés*)" (Renouvier [1875] 1912: II:203). The implications thus at the end of his *Logique* is that categories are collective representations, since they are the result of a collective endeavor, and are formed historically and collectively. And significantly he associates work with their formation. There is here a substantial philosophical impulse that points in a different methodological direction to that of Aristotle and Kant—even though it was formulated through Renouvier's philosophical arguments with both of these giants of category theory. Renouvier's influence on Durkheim's account of the nature of the categories is also significant, as we will see.

So Durkheim was directed philosophically to locate the categories within history and collective labor. But to make sense of how Durkheim associates labor with the formation of categories, we must look closely at his account of the nature of the categories and at neglected aspects of this.

First, categories are synthetic: "If the human mind (*l'esprit humain*) is a synthetic expression of the world, the system of the categories is a synthetic expression of the human mind" (Durkheim [1909] 1975: 187). Synthesis is central to the complexity of collective representation for Durkheim: "Synthesis is the work of the whole" (Durkheim [1898] 1974: 40) and the force that drives this is association. Synthesis is not evidence of his false scientism—why else would he associate it with representation and consciousness? The concept of conscience is central to this work of synthesis. The individual conscience synthesizes, but only "imperfectly." It is the conscience collective that fully synthesizes (Durkheim [1909] 1975: 186; [1912] 1985: 633). So for Durkheim what is called "impersonal reason" is really "collective thought" (*la pensée collective*) and this is only possible through the "grouping of individuals" (Durkheim [1912] 1985: 636). If reason is collective thought then synthesis cannot be the result of reason, as it is for Kant, but must be the result of collective thinking. It is the group, through association, that connects representations and forms them into collective representations ([1898] 1974). In *Les formes*, this synthesizing activity is central to "the psychic state of the group" (Durkheim [1912] 1985: 541). Society is central to this epistemological activity precisely because "society is a synthesis of human consciences" (615). And central to conscience is relation: "relation sui generis is central to all combination" (Durkheim [1898] 1974: 27).

Secondly categories express "the fundamental relations which exist between things" (Durkheim [1912] 1985: 25). Relation is central to the concept of the category: it is part of what Durkheim means by category. The relations the categories express are "the most general relations (*rapports*) which exist between things" (23). Indeed "the very function of the categories" is to express "the fundamental relations between things" that "are not fundamentally dissimilar according to the realms" (26). This identification of the very nature of the categories with relation is central to how he can offer a social explanation of them, since society is nothing if not a set of relations. It was Renouvier who held that categories express relation since they are all forms of relation. "To bring together (*unir*) or to separate relations (*rapports*) is the function of thought, common-sense (*usuelle*) or scientific, and such is also the development of the category of categories—relation" (Renouvier [1875] 1912: I:147).

Relation is connected to the enveloping nature of the categories for Durkheim: "the categories envelop all other concepts" and this "is their role" (Durkheim [1912] 1985: 629). The category of time "envelops" our "individual existence and humanity" (14). It was Renouvier who stressed the enveloping quality of the categories: he identified the enveloping nature of the categories with their universality (Renouvier [1875] 1912: I:119). As will become evident, this is an important criterion of the categories for Durkheim and is central to how he offers his social explanation of them. Unfortunately, the concept of enveloping has been translated out of the Fields translation of *Les formes*.[2]

Now, relation is linked to another aspect of the categories for Durkheim: extension. "They express the most general connections (*rapports*) which exist between things—which, in terms of extension, go beyond all other notions (*qui dépassent en extension*)" (Durkheim [1912] 1985: 23). Extension is central to Durkheim's account of the epistemological activity of the group and is an important aspect of the debates of logic, which Durkheim contributes to here. The reference to extension—a crucial philosophical term and problem—is translated out of the text by the Fields 1995 translation.[3] The force of his argument here is undermined.

The argument for the relational nature of the categories is developed by the concept of extension. Categories "express relations," says Durkheim, and their primary location is in the individual consciousness: "The relations which they express exist implicitly in individual consciences" ([1912] 1985: 628). That is, "all these relations are personal to the individual" (629). The group develops these into impersonal forms; the personal relations of each conscience are developed extensively into impersonal relations by the group. The group action extends them; the personal relations of each conscience are developed extensively into impersonal forms.

This claim that relations are extended by group action lies at the core of Durkheim's sociological rationalism and his explanation of the categories. These extended relations can be seen in the category of totality, which is the most important for Durkheim, for "the idea of the whole is at the basis of all classification" ([1912] 1985: 629). Similarly, the category of genus involves extension. Genus, he says, is "an ideal grouping of things between which there are internal links (*liens*)." Durkheim argues that genus, as a logical symbol, requires "a field of extension" (209).[4] The disappearance of this concept through translation is unfortunate since this concept is central to how Durkheim is attempting a sociological explanation of a philosophical problem.[5] This field of extension here, in his science of man, is covered by the plurality of consciences; this allows extension to be established. So it is no accident that for Durkheim the basis for the extension of this is "the association of men" (210).

So we have three features that are crucial—synthesis, relation, and extension. A fourth and final feature central to his account of the nature of the category is the concept of "reference points" (*points de repère*). These are essential to his definition of space ([1912] 1985: 629) and time (14) for him: "The total space . . . contains all the particular extensions (*les étendues particulières*) . . . where they are co-ordinated through connection to impersonal reference points" (629). It is important to note the concept of co-ordination Durkheim uses in his account of space and time (15, 629). For example, spatial representation consists in "a first co-ordination introduced into the given of sensible experience" (15). It is the movement and action of the group by which these become the "impersonal reference points" "common to all individuals" (629). Furthermore, he identifies reference points with differentiation. Space and time are "unthinkable" (*impensable*) without "divisions" and "objective signs." Space and time requires "differentiation" (14). His claim is that the group and its ritual action drive the divisions and differentiation central to space, through the "different affective values" communally ascribed to regions (15–16).

The central features of categories for this case are synthesis, relation, extension, and differentiation. These features facilitate Durkheim's explanation of the formation of the categories by labor. I suggest that only by recognizing these features can we begin to make sense of his claim.

Labor and Collective Representations

Categories are "wise instruments of thought which human groups have laboriously (*laborieusement*) forged over the centuries where they have accumulated the best of their intellectual capital. A whole part of the history of humanity is summed up here (*résumée*) there" ([1912] 1985: 27). Unfortunately, this key term *laborieusement* disappears in the 1995 translation.[6]

I suggest that collective labor, viewed historically, can be seen to contribute to the development of synthesis, differentiation, interrelation, and extension. For example, the group, as a set of human relations, gives the first historical formulation of relational totality, which as we have seen is central to the categories for Durkheim ([1912] 1985: 629). The central idea is that of co-operation, which is central to his account of collective representations. Collective representations are "the product of an immense co-operation which extends not only in space but in time" (22). And labor is central to co-operation. Co-operative labor has a historical axis for Durkheim. The great law of co-operative labor that governs historical development is the central theme of *De la division du travail social* ([1893] 1986). Historically and gradually the symbolic, affective, and ritual dimensions of ancient social action begin to recede and in their place the division of social labor emerges. That is, co-operation develops beyond the symbolic and the rituals of ancient society, and with the progressive differentiation of function in society, the division of labor becomes central to social action and formation.

Labor is central not only to co-operation and but also to exchange—indeed to large scale exchange and thus economic interrelationship. These forms of large scale economic and social interrelationship are sweeping relational structures and indicate a source for the enveloping quality of the categories. There are spheres of social and economic exchange that extend beyond particular economic and social acts and enclose them—indeed they envelop them. Large scale co-operation enables the development of human relational structures. It demonstrates what can be called the relational enveloping nature of these supreme concepts. Further the historical dimension shows that cooperative forms of interrelationship change. Their historical changefulness means they are "subject to becoming (*devenir*)" (Durkheim [1898] 1974: 16). Change and relational structures are central to Durkheim's account of social historical action. Thus we now have at least two candidates for the fundamental categories: relation and becoming.

This great historical shift in forms of social relations has an effect on the nature of consciousness: social and historical change has epistemological consequences for Durkheim. Does he not tell us in *Les règles* that as the social milieu becomes "more complex and more undetermined . . . faculties of reflection develop which are indispensable to societies and individuals" (Durkheim [1895] 1987: 96)? I suggest that the significance of labor for social epistemology is that it forges relations in *le dehors*. This infamous phrase of *Les règles*, which has made Durkheim the bogey man of interpretive sociology, is actually crucial to his sociology of knowledge. To view social facts *du dehors* means to see them not from the inside but in terms of the sphere of logically external relations (Stedman Jones 2001: 143). We can see the importance of the sphere of external relations not just in co-operative labor and in systems of exchange, but it is evident in the outward movement of the group in its search for land and food or in nomadic groups in the following of animals. These are all examples of collective action extending relations.

Labor is central to the co-ordinated action of the group, and it involves the inner force of agency. Labor links the inner force of this to the external force of the group (Durkheim [1912] 1985: 522). Labor goes from inner to outer. The inner force of each conscience, which is a form of power, is developed into the forms of power of the group (522). Group action allows the movement from inner to outer and most importantly from outer to inner. That is, the external social and historical relations affect the inner nature of consciousness. This is the social and historical axis of epistemological development.

Labor through the group is central to the historical development of mind. We can only fully understand this by acknowledging another neglected term of his: "psychic life" (*la vie psychique*). This grows and develops through social change. It is "greater sociability" that leads to "the greater development of psychic life" (Durkheim [1893] 1986: 338). And in particular it is the extension of "psychic life" that is associated with the growth of societies: "Psychic life only extends (*prend de l'extension*) when societies develop" (338).

Labor, Repetition, and Distinction

Central to this whole discussion of labor is a theory of action. A full discussion of Durkheim's account of action must involve the passions, the ends of action and tendencies. The human group, of course, is the theater for both action and consciousness. The group not only extends relational structures but also extends the ends of action. The ends of action pursued by the individual are extended and developed by the group through the constitution and enactment of collective ends. We can see this particularly in his account of ritual action. The claim that labor can affect the fundamental forms of consciousness requires an account of a deep relationship between action and consciousness; indeed, there must be a passage from action to consciousness. We find Durkheim acknowledging this in *Les formes*: "Just as activity cannot do without (*se passer de*) intelligence it follows that this is drawn (*entrainée*) in the same way and adopts, without discussion the theoretical postulates, which practice calls for (*réclame*)" (Durkheim [1912] 1985: 527).

But exactly what is it about the division of labor and its effect on thought that is so significant? We are here concerned with the features of a process that leads to the "crystallization" of thought ([1912] 1985: 618). Two concepts associated with the division of labor and its role in this first repetition and second distinction.

The concept of repetition is central to Durkheim's account of social life. Repetition, we must remember, is central to his definition of social fact "ways of acting and thinking." Repetition gives them a kind of consistence—a body "a reality sui generis" (Durkheim [1895] 1987: 9). Indeed, repetition is central to the formation of a whole. "Every group is a whole formed of parts . . . the ultimate element whose repetition constitutes the whole is the individual" (Durkheim 1950: 53). Labor is also repeated action (Durkheim [1893] 1986: 357). As central to social function, labor is part of "definite ways of acting" that are "repeated" (Durkheim [1893] 1986: 357). Repetition is central to ritual action: the cult is "regularly repeated action" (Durkheim [1912] 1985: 596). Ritual and its repetitions forge connections of the mind. We see this in his account of the formative principles involved in the principle of causality in the Intichiuma rite. The collective repetition of the rite affects the psychic nature of mind. An "association" is formed between the ritual gestures and the expectation of the result. The obligation of regular repetition brings around a connection between action and consequence. Repetition leads to the development of forms of mind—in this case that of causality, which is another candidate for a fundamental category.

So repetition in action is central in the formation of the connections of mind. Repetition forms connections; ritual labor forms connections—with nature and others. That which we repeat significantly forges connections and thus relations. These repetitions and the connections they form sink into the lower unconscious reaches of the mind and form tendencies, both of action and of thought. The concept of the unconscious is identified by the concept of the "obscure." And the unconscious affects action. There are "obscure representations" "linked" to "tendencies" (Durkheim [1893] 1986: 331). The categories for Kant and post-Kantian thinking operate explicitly in the understanding. Durkheim accepts this, but offers a deeper picture of its location and its source: "The understanding is not the seat of psychic life . . . it is the culminating and most superficial part of conscience" ([1893] 1986: 266n4). The understanding has deep unconscious and emotional roots, and it is in these that the connections of thought take place. Repetition leads to the formation of connections in the unconscious and these form relations. Representation is a network of relations (Durkheim [1898] 1974: 39). The unconscious is a source of the structure of relations that can rise up to become the conscious activities of judgment in the understanding. So we see here how repetitions form unconscious connections and thus relational structures that rise up to become forms of judgment operated by the understanding. Here we see the action of what Durkheim describes as "relation sui generis" (Durkheim [1898] 1974: 27). This is central to the operation of judgment (Durkheim 1911). It is in this sense that labor can be seen to be a bridge from concrete social and economic practices and the higher levels of the mind where the fundamental categories operate.

Distinction and Differentiation

The concept of distinction has an unusual role in Durkheim's account of epistemology and its historical dimension. This is clear in his account of the division of labor and the differentiation that this brings about. His discussion of the types of solidarity in *La division* is articulated within terms of representation. He distinguishes between the type of solidarity that confounds and another that distinguishes.

> Undoubtedly there can never be solidarity between the other and ourselves unless the image of the other is united to our own. But when the union results from the resemblance of two images it consists in an agglutination. The two representations become solidary because being indistinct they are confounded; they are only solidary in so far as they are confounded one with the other. On the contrary in the case of the division of labour they are outside each other; they are only linked because they are distinct. (Durkheim [1893] 1986: 26)

The argument of this important passage is that the division of labor allows intellectual differentiation and thus distinction. The division of labor is an important step away from what he elsewhere calls "the state of indistinction from which the human mind began" (Durkheim and Mauss [1902] 1969: 396). The state of indistinction is where things are "confounded" or run together. Confounded does not mean confusion but where there is "a lack of definite concepts" (397). Taken out of philosophical context this sounds less than flattering to the thinking of ancient cultures—it sounds as though he means they are confused. It must be noted this state of indistinction also applies to the Christian rite of transubstantiation (397).

There is an important philosophical background to this argument. Renouvier gives the concept of distinction a central role in propositional logic: a categorical proposition is a synthesis of the same and the other. They can only be associated if they are distinct (Renouvier [1875]1912: I:155). He argues that the "Principle of Identity" should be called the "Principle of Distinction" (156). We must be able to distinguish one thing from another so that first we know what we are talking about and second we can go on to identify them. Durkheim claims that distinction is central to psychic life. "Psychic life is a continuous course of representations, whereby the mind comes to distinguish the parts . . . those distinctions are our work (*notre oeuvre*). It is we who introduce them in the psychic continuum" (Durkheim [1898] 1974: 25). Significantly, Durkheim connects work to the creation of distinctions in this important passage.

In summary, the repetition of labor and forms of co-operation develop a structure of relations that are central to society but also to the nature of the mind. This is initially at the unconscious level, but emerges with the development of philosophy. So Greek philosophy expressed "in philosophical language" what "had pre-existed as obscure feeling" (Durkheim [1912] 1985: 623). And, of course, it was Aristotle who first formulated a theory of the categories. Furthermore, the progressive development of the division of labor brings around philosophy. It also enables a process of differentiation in the mind that gradually introduces a process of distinction at the conceptual level.

Labor and the Question of Realism

Lastly, I can return to the puzzle I raised at the beginning: how is constructionism compatible with realism? For if collective representations make society, how is it real? This is not to suggest that representations and reality are opposite terms. Rather they are philosophically co-extensive (Durkheim [1898] 1974). I suggest that the concept of labor can enable us to see a reconciliation of two apparently opposed concepts. First, labor provides a connection with what is, with being in an Aristotelian sense. Labor is central to social being. It is central to the formation of relations and relational structures. Furthermore, labor is work, which is collective and involves relation with others and the physical world. Again, it makes connections, which are relations. Relations are both internal and external. Labor forges relations in the outside (*le dehors*). These external relations are, for example, class, family, and all structural forms of power. But relations are also internal to the mind. It is the passage from the external to the internal that is formative in the development of the mind. Labor is a pivot for this transformation of the mind. Labor is central to his science of man, it is connected to the outer and to generality and sustains generality through exchange.

Second, labor is not simply co-operative, important though that is. Labor deals with the environment, with animals, with physical things or space. A reality we confront here is not merely believed or imagined; it has to be dealt with successfully, however it is understood. This is the sphere where things must be "practically true." We find here "the test of facts" (*l'epreuve des faits*; Durkheim [1912] 1985: 113). A "system of errors is not viable" (113). Although he raises this concept in his criticism of animism, it also applies to labor and its engagement with the physical world. Thus in the lectures on pragmatism, he argues for a veridical account of reality, and in contradistinction to pragmatism, effective action is only possible if we know the circumstances in which we act (Durkheim 1955: 65). There must be some degree of truth in our apprehension of states of affairs or of things. This is certainly true of labor—for hunting must produce meat for consumption, just as agriculture must produce crops. There is a realism here that goes beyond simple constructivism.

It must be remembered that the sphere of the outer in the Kantian tradition has significance for the categories. In his *Critique of Pure Reason*, Kant argued that the objective reality of the categories is tied up with the outer: "To demonstrate the objective reality (of the categories), we need not merely intuitions, but intuitions which are in all cases outer" (Kant [1781] 1929: 254, B29 1). Labor deals with the sphere of the outer; that is with toiling with the earth, animal husbandry, and so on. These are material forces that must be mastered if human life and society are to continue. The collectivity must be successful in the production of food; Durkheim's analogy of the category with tools carries this meaning. This is part of the "laborious" work central to the development of categories. Kant, in his "Idea for a Universal History with a Cosmopolitan Purpose," says, "[R]eason in a creature, is a faculty which enables that creature to extend far beyond the limits of natural instinct. Reason does not work instinctively it requires trial, practice and instruction" (Kant [1784] 1970: 42).

Conclusion

The categories are aided in their long historical development by the group and by co-operative labor. Durkheim's argument can only be understood by acknowledging the features of synthesis, relation, extension and differentiation, but above all the relational nature of the categories. Durkheim's account of action and consciousness and "psychic life" and particularly the role of repetition in the formation in the structures of consciousness is seminal to this radical epistemology, as is the idea of distinction and its connection to the division of labor. The importance of labor and its contact with the world echoes Kant's argument about the objective reality of the categories.

Susan Stedman Jones is an independent scholar and a member of the British Centre for Durkheimian Studies in the University of Oxford's Institute of Social and Cultural Anthropology. She is the author of *Durkheim Reconsidered* (2001), and has worked on the critical reception of Durkheim's *The Elementary Forms of Religious Life* in British Social Anthropology. Journal articles include "Durkheim, the Question of Violence and the Paris Commune of 1871" (*The International Social Science Journal*, 2009) and "Forms of Thought and Forms of Society: Durkheim and the Question of the Categories" (*L'Année sociologique*, 2012).

Notes

1. The translations are by the author, if not otherwise noted.
2. For example, where Durkheim says that "the categories envelop all other concepts" and this "is their role" (Durkheim [1912] 1985: 629), "envelop" is translated as "contain" (Fields translation *The Elementary Forms of Religious Life* 1995: 441). Also on page 26 of the original where Durkheim talks of "formes plus enveloppées," this is translated as "more shrouded forms" (17). The concept survives only once in Swain's (1915) translation when Durkheim says "the role of categories is to envelop all other concepts" (Durkheim [1912] 1985: 609; 1915: 441). However, Durkheim's phrase "formes plus enveloppées" ([1912] 1985: 26) is translated by Swain as "less pronounced" (Swain translation 1915: 18).
3. "[Q]ui dépassent en extension" (Durkheim [1912] 1985: 23) is rendered as "having broader scope than" (Fields translation 1995: 16).
4. This reference to a "field of extension" (*champ d'extension*) disappears and becomes "potential scope" in the Fields translation (1995: 148).

5. In general, the extension of concept is made up of all those things to which the term applies and is connected to that of class. *La logique, ou l'art de penser* of Antoine Arnauld and Pierre Nicole (1662) introduced a distinction between extension and comprehension. Later in the history of philosophy, extension is contrasted with intension, which broadly is the meaning of a concept. There is an extensionality thesis in modern logic espoused by W. V. O. Quine (1908–2000), who claimed that logical truth can be defined in purely extensional terms.
6. *Laborieusement* is a key term translated as "painstakingly" by Fields (1995: 18). There is, however, a clear association with labor in the original French according to Larousse; it means "qui travaille beaucoup" (Larousse 1996: 596).

References

Note: References are to the French editions as indicated.

Arnauld, Antoine, and Pierre Nicole. 1662. *La logique, ou l'art de penser.* Paris: Imprimeur et libraire du roi.

Durkheim, Émile. [1893] 1986. *De la division du travail social.* Paris: Quadrige/Presses universitaires de France (PUF) [Paris: Félix Alcan].

———. [1895] 1987. *Les règles de la méthode sociologique.* Paris: Quadrige/PUF [Paris: Félix Alcan].

———. [1898] 1974. "Représentations individuelles et réprésentations collectives." *Revue de métaphysique et de morale* 6: 273–302. [Reprinted 1974. In Émile Durkheim, *Sociologie et philosophie,* 1–40. Paris: PUF].

———. [1899] 1986. "Book review 'S. Merlino: Formes et essences du socialism.'" *Revue philosophique* 48: 433–39. [1986. In *Durkheim on Politics and the State,* ed. Anthony Giddens, trans. Wilfred D. Halls, 136–45. Cambridge: Polity Press.]

———. [1909] 1975. "Rapports de la sociologie à la psychologie et à la philosophie." In *Textes I. Éléments d'une théorie sociale,* ed. Victor Karady, 184–88. Paris: Minuit.

———. 1911. "Jugements de valeur et jugements de réalité." *Revue metaphysique et de morale* 29: 437–53.

———. [1912] 1985. *Les formes élémentaires de la vie réligieuse.* Paris: PUF. [Translations: Joseph W. Swain (1915), London: Allen and Unwin; Karen E. Fields (1995), New York: Free Press.]

———. 1950. *Leçons de sociologie.* Paris: PUF.

———. 1955. *Pragmatisme et sociologie.* Paris: Vrin.

Durkheim, Émile, and Marcel Mauss. [1902] 1969. "De quelques formes primitives de classification." In *Journal Sociologique,* ed. Jean Duvignaud, 395–462. Paris: PUF.

Kant, Immanuel. [1781] 1929. *Critique of Pure Reason*, trans. Norman K. Smith. London: Macmillan.
———. [1784] 1970. "Idea for a Universal History with a Cosmopolitan Purpose." In *Kant's Political Writings*, ed. Hans Reiss, trans. Hugh B. Nisbet, 41–53. Cambridge: Cambridge University Press.
Renouvier, Charles. [1875] 1912. *Traité de logique générale et de logique formelle*. Paris: Librairie Armand Colin.
Larousse. 1996. *Dictionnaire de Français (dir. par Jean Dubois)*. Paris: Larousse.
Stedman Jones, Susan. 2001. *Durkheim Reconsidered*. Cambridge: Polity Press.
———. 2012. "Forms of Thought and Forms of Society: Durkheim and the Question of the Categories." *Année sociologique* 62(2): 387–407.

Chapter 5

INEQUALITY IS A SCIENTIFIC ISSUE WHEN THE TECHNOLOGIES OF PRACTICE THAT CREATE SOCIAL CATEGORIES BECOME DEPENDENT ON JUSTICE IN MODERNITY

Anne Warfield Rawls

Émile Durkheim's "category argument" took an innovative social contract position that proposed a novel "constitutive" approach to social facts that conflicts with approaches that aspire to be morally neutral, or "value free," and with the individualism and naturalism that permeates most philosophy and social science.[1] Durkheim was advocating a sociological approach to the study of justice, predicated on different requirements of social fact making that he argued would develop in diverse and specialized modern societies. He rejected August Comte's position, which treated social facts/categories as a kind of durable residue of social processes in consensus-based societies, arguing instead that "categories" or "social facts" only come into being as and when they are created through social practices. Durkheim's conception of social facts was an advance on Comte because it could handle social change and diversity: increasingly important issues. But it ran up against a deeply embedded belief that social facts/categories have an independent existence as concepts that are sustained by a consensus-based symbolic system, which makes them independent of interactional processes. This led to the misperception that Durkheim agreed with Comte, and his innovative approach to social order and justice was lost.

For Durkheim, categories/social facts need to be continually made and remade through "constitutive" technologies of practice in ritual, occupations, sciences, and daily life interaction. Durkheim's approach treats categories as fragile objects, the interactional processes for making which need to be protected, while Comte and most others treat social facts as durable objects whose surrounding cultures are what require protection. Confusing the two positions explains many misunderstandings of Durkheim. Trying to keep cultures from changing in diverse modern contexts—which follows from Comte—is a losing game. But, the situated character of the novel technologies of practice introduced by Durkheim suits them to diverse contexts, and their fragility makes the practices, and the equality and justice they require, what need to be protected, not consensus, or cultural norms. That the practices involved are often considered "sacred" as a consequence, was Durkheim's unique explanation of religion (Rawls 2004).

Durkheim's argument provided a new theoretical foundation for social science that rests on a conception of implicit social contract; a working agreement between participants in social settings about how these fragile categories are to be made in specific situations/locations, which technologies of practice will be used, and how they will be used, that challenges positivism, naturalism, and philosophical individualism; much of which Comte's position had left intact.

Durkheim not only reformulated Comte's durable social facts/categories as fragile, requiring constantly to be remade, he also distinguished two processes—or technologies—for making them, and argued that the social contract and its moral obligations would be different in the two cases.[2] In smaller societies without diversity, change, and specialization, the predominant way constitutive practices are used to make social facts tends to remain essentially the same over time, creating the false impression that categories are durable, and exist and convey meaning as concepts in comprehensive symbolic systems, independently of practices. The second social fact making process is predominate in very early societies (that do not have comprehensive belief systems), and again in late societies characterized by increasing diversity and specialization that erode belief systems. Durkheim called these practices "self-regulating." They are localized—situated in places rather than populations—and function as indexicals that can change rapidly. Mastery of self-regulating practice is displayed in situ; accomplished through attention to the order properties of interaction—to technologies of practice and their preferences—rather than to "meaning" as an attribute of a conceptual system. Criteria are "witnessable" and empirical.

All societies have both forms of practice. But as a society becomes more diverse and specialized, practices that operate as summaries of tradition become untenable—because they assume a consensus that no longer exists—and the proportion tilts toward self-regulation. In such societies, categories and the social processes that create them become more fragile, and increasing levels of equality and justice are required. Durkheim worried that the failure to recognize (1) the dependence of categories on practices, and (2) that there are two quite different technologies of practice had been detrimental to philosophy and social science. In treating meaning as conceptual, scholars were missing the implications of self-regulating practices for moral and social theory—and setting up false dichotomies (mind/body, ideal/material) that were impossible to overcome. The imposition of structure from the top down that these positions assume is also problematic, because meaning and order at the "top" must first be established in local orders of practice. The new role for government and formal institutions, according to Durkheim, will be to support practices by guaranteeing justice and equality, not to order them.

Durkheim's achievement was partially recognized and taken up by Talcott Parsons (1938) as a way of solving problems plaguing US sociology as a result of its heavy indebtedness to Comte. This had left US sociology committed to the idea that consensus is necessary to support a comprehensive system of durable social facts—which is problematic because broad consensus is no longer possible. It also left US sociologists focused on ways of maintaining consensus and stratification, and minimizing deviance, which is the opposite of what modern society needs. The biggest problem, however, is that the assumption that categories and social objects are durable has encouraged social thinkers to ignore how they are made—leading to a kind of positivist counting of social things (Gender, Race,[3] crime)—as if they were natural things. This has enabled ethnocentrism to masquerade as scientific objectivity.

Parsons argued that adopting Durkheim's innovation would solve problems, such as the growing qualitative/quantitative split in US sociology in the 1930s and 1940s. When Parsons passed his interest in Durkheim on to his student Harold Garfinkel in the 1940s (and from there to Erving Goffman and Harvey Sacks in the 1950s and 1960s), Garfinkel picked up on the situated constitutive and self-regulating side of Durkheim's argument and began documenting it through studies of social interaction (Parsons would do the same after 1960, see Garfinkel [1962] 2019; Rawls, Duck, and Turowetz 2018).

In the mid-1940s it seemed that Parsons might succeed in reorienting social theory toward Durkheim's conception of social contract. But there were problems with Parsons's early approach, which left it stuck somewhere between Durkheim and Comte, focusing on deviance and stratification instead of interaction. Then just as Parsons (1949) began arguing that culture is an independent interactional level of social action, US sociology moved sharply against studies of interaction and toward positivism, adopting a scientific narrative that extolled the necessity of a "value free" science with a "unified" theory and statistical methods (Rawls 2018). This narrative, which still reigns, abandoned Parsons's iteration of Durkheim and returned to the individualism and naturalism of Comte. While Parsons struggled to maintain his prestige in the face of this change, Garfinkel was left on his own to articulate situated constitutive practices in something of a vacuum, until Parsons rejoined the effort after 1958 (Garfinkel [1962] 2019; Rawls and Turowetz 2021). Durkheim's own effort to found a social contract approach had already been derailed by World War I, during which Durkheim and most of his students lost their lives.

The result is that Durkheim's two principal arguments about categories/social facts got lost. First, social facts are fragile and need to be constantly remade in social interaction, which makes an implicit social contract about how we make them necessary; and, second, there are two kinds of practices for making social facts/categories, and that diverse societies, and their sciences and specialized occupations, cannot succeed without developing the self-regulating kind, which, in turn, require justice. Durkheim's position, along with those of the later Parsons and Garfinkel, stand in direct conflict with the direction taken by most philosophy and social science (with the exception of the later Ludwig Wittgenstein). Durkheim and Garfinkel were calling attention to social justice issues, while mainstream sociology was obscuring them.

Since World War II it has been popular to aspire to "value free" research and to treat that aspiration as more "objective" than other approaches, particularly if it uses statistics, even though social categories and the technologies of practice that are used to create them are neither natural nor value free. This trend marginalized the work of Durkheim, Garfinkel, and other minorities and women, who called attention to the values built into categories and social facts (Rawls, Whitehead, and Duck 2020; Rawls and Duck 2021; Rawls 2021). A "value free" approach obscures the values embedded in meaningful social processes, and the moral cooperation in the use of valued technologies of practice that the "objectivity" of social categories depends on. Categories that are inherently social are consistently treated as if they are natural, independent, and value free, with the result that the values embedded in them and the processes of creating them are not examined. Many of the big mistakes in modern social science (like treating crime statistics generated by a racist criminal justice system as objective facts—creating the false appearance that Black Americans commit more crime when they do not) come from overlooking how unexamined values and social processes are embedded in categories.

That social categories are morally loaded was a central premise of Durkheim's position, the aim of which was to set sociology on an objective footing by putting the values and practices on which social categories depend back at the center of social science. Garfinkel, and to some extent Parsons, took up the task of examining this moral loading and how it works to create what we consider "social reality" in actual situated social interactions.

Durkheim's Category Project Misunderstood

Durkheim and Marcel Mauss initiated the first phase of what has become known as the "category project" around 1900 and published their initial efforts in *Primitive Classification* (1903). Most discussions of Durkheim's category argument have focused on that publication and other writings that survey social processes of category making in non-European societies. Unfortunately, that book does not contain Durkheim's own earlier discussion of classification, which is situated in the context of European history. Instead, the book presents a survey of classifications without the accompanying theoretical discussion of practices, or the problems of individualism and naturalism that Durkheim's inquiry into classifications was designed to solve. This has obscured the relationship between the constitutive practice argument and the work on classification, making Durkheim's argument appear to be compatible with Comte's earlier position (and its counterparts in anthropology and philosophy) when it rejected those positions.

The foundation for the category project was actually laid in Durkheim's (1893) *Division of Labor*. Unfortunately, there has been a tendency to treat that argument as entirely different from both the argument of *Primitive Classification* and the epistemological argument of Durkheim's (1912) *Elementary Forms of the Religious Life*—as if Durkheim had undergone a radical change in thinking between the publications of the earlier and later work. This mistake was exacerbated by the fact that the later work has been both neglected and misunderstood (Rawls 1996, 2004). The three works are, in fact, consistent and necessary companions, although, as one would expect, the sophistication of Durkheim's argument increased over time.

Durkheim focused on categories because he was interested in problems of social fact making that are specific to the transition to diverse and highly specialized modern societies, not because he was interested in traditional societies per se, a distinction he laid out in *Division*. Overlooking the relevance of his distinction between self-regulating practices and those that act as summaries of tradition to the category argument has had serious implications for approaches indebted to Durkheim, including much of anthropology and social and cultural theory. The tendency has been to treat category issues and social facts in traditional and modern societies as if they were the same (Rawls 2021). In the process, Durkheim's epistemological argument, his distinction between modern differentiated societies and more homogeneous traditional societies, and his insistence that justice is only necessary to support self-regulating technologies of practice as they become increasingly important in modernity, all got lost. His insistence that without justice modern society would fail, also got lost.

The loss of this argument obstructs our ability to understand political and social problems occurring around the world today. People are calling these "culture wars" as if the differences were between alternate but coherent and plausible cultures, and focusing on personality traits (such as "authoritative personality syndrome") rather than social structure. Following Durkheim, we argue that the difference is between traditional consensus-based practices that favor authority, which now find themselves in diverse and specialized surroundings that threaten their coherence, and the self-regulating technologies of practice that have developed—as Durkheim predicted—to handle the diversity and specialization that characterize modernity. It is a clash between two entirely different ways of making categories/social facts—between two different ways of making culture and personality—which have entirely different moral and organizational requirements.

Recovering Durkheim's Lost Argument

In *Division*, Durkheim argued that as communication across groups increases and occupations specialize in modernity, the clash between different cultures will erode shared symbolic frames of reference and make new forms of cooperation—new technologies of practice—necessary to support the creation of social categories. As the forms of practice people use to make social facts change, the underlying moral commitments (or social contract) that ground this creation also need to change. This is an important argument. Most "liberal" scholars have argued that justice is always best. But Durkheim acknowledged that what John Rawls would later call "well ordered comprehensive systems" do not need justice and should be considered moral and "decent" nevertheless (J. Rawls 1999). Durkheim maintained that the need for justice in modern society arises for three reasons: (1) because the parts of the society do not harmonize like they do in a successful comprehensive system (consensus-based system), (2) inequalities begin to multiply as a result, and (3) the self-regulating constitutive practices that become predominant require justice as a prerequisite, or they do not work.

Comprehensive systems—commitment to which supports symbolic and ritual practices in traditional societies—should remain relevant only to a shrinking slice of diverse modern social life. Implicit commitment to technologies of practice that are less constrained by outside influence, more open, and more self-regulating, so that they can work across diverse groups in the absence of shared belief, become necessary. Such practices, Durkheim (1902) argued, had appeared in occupations in Ancient Rome—in guilds or colleges—as its population diversified.

Furthermore, while traditional ritual practices can tolerate inequalities as long as these inequalities are supported by a comprehensive belief system (that is unquestioned), the constitutive practices of modernity require a high degree of equality and open access that Durkheim called justice. This is both because the practices themselves require a high degree of moment-by-moment reciprocity that inequality interferes with (Rawls and Duck 2020), and because a social system based on science and specialization needs everyone participating. Durkheim described the systemic inequality that interferes with this as an "Abnormal Form of society."

This change-over from predominantly traditional to predominantly self-regulating technologies of practice alters the significance and flexibility of categories in modernity, along with their requirements. As the technologies of practice for making categories change they become both more and less important. They are less important as durable media, but more important insofar as the technologies of their production now facilitate the possibility of shared meaning moment-to-moment, even between strangers and across new techniques, as rapidly changing configurations of situated self-regulating practices replace the relatively stable comprehensive beliefs/practices of the past with a new moral foundation of justice (Rawls and Mann 2015).

The Durkheim Category Project was thus, not only an investigation of the form and function of categories in different societies, as presented in 1903, but also a key part of Durkheim's overall effort to demonstrate the changes that the relationship between categories and social functions would undergo as societies passed into a differentiated modern "organic" condition, that requires new forms of cooperation. The new requirements, he argued, make justice a functional prerequisite for a new self-organizing kind of constitutive social cooperation freed from belief and ritual that must come to predominate for modernity to succeed.

Discussion of these important issues is missing from *Primitive Classification*. Those issues were worked out first in *Division* and its "Second Preface," and then in the *Elementary Forms*. In those two books Durkheim dealt with categories in terms of a distinction between two kinds of rule or practice—which he referred to as constitutive versus rules that are a summary of tradition (Rawls 2012). Durkheim's distinction is between summary rule practices (that produce what Comte identified as social facts) and self-regulating practices. In *Division* he also launched a pointed criticism of philosophy—specifically Kantian and Utilitarian moral philosophy—for taking the individual as a given and not recognizing its social fact status; an argument that grounded his claim that justice becomes necessary.

What Durkheim meant by constitutive practices of science and occupations contrasts with what most social thinkers building on Durkheim's category project have focused on. Durkheim was distinguishing a modern "open" form of practice from a more "closed" traditional (ritualized) form of practice. Anthropologists (Claude Lévi-Strauss and Bronisław Malinowski in particular) have tended to treat closed practices as if they were the same as self-regulating practices, and this has negatively impacted the development of cultural theory in sociology and anthropology (Rawls and Turowetz 2021). Increased communication across groups in conjunction with population density in modernity forces the change. The work of making social objects and categories, and the technologies of practice on which that work depends, become differentiated in the new modern form of social practice, producing a "Division of Social Labor" (the proper translation of the title into English). In each part of society, and in each type of social situation, category work would be done independently and differently—thus the need for a local and interactional focus.

No overall top-down societal organization of this category work is necessary (or possible) because the practices self-regulate. All they need from society at large is the guarantee of justice. Aspects of this vision were picked up by Parsons (1949) in his conception of culture as independent from social structure and his theory of "voluntaristic" action. Garfinkel, as Parsons's PhD student from 1946 to 1952, elaborated further on the idea, looking at actual category work in situations of interaction (Garfinkel [1962] 2019; Rawls and Turowetz 2021).

As Durkheim conceived the category project, it was the independence of situated self-regulating practices from the overall social structure and its beliefs and durable cultural practices that made it possible for "immigrants" and "aliens" to contribute to a diverse and specialized modern society, and for science and occupations to develop and specialize. This makes it possible for science and occupations to develop free from belief, as he said in his *Pragmatism and Sociology* ([1913–14] 1983), and in his "Préface de la seconde édition" (1902), Durkheim described the work practices of immigrant technical workers in Ancient Rome in these terms.

The reliance of the overall argument on Durkheim's conception of self-regulating constitutive practices, its connection to his later epistemology, and to the category project as a whole has somehow gotten lost. It is not clear that any of Durkheim's students who worked on the category project with him (with the possible exception of Mauss) understood the broader argument or its unique foundation in implicit social contract. This is unfortunate because Durkheim's overall argument marks an important dividing line between classic and modern social theorizing (in much the same way that Wittgenstein marks a line in philosophy).The resistance by majority thinkers who were wedded to individualism, to Durkheim's novel conception of individualism as itself a social fact also played a role in sidelining the argument (Rawls, Whitehead, and Duck 2020; Rawls and Duck 2021).

Recovering the Missing Epistemology and Justice Arguments

Durkheim's argument with regard to justice—that the new open self-regulating form of practice requires justice as an underlying prerequisite, along with the implications of that argument for social theory—got lost. This happened partly because Durkheim's epistemology was ignored, partly because the work on classification was treated as a separate project, partly because his critique of Comte on consensus and social facts was missed, and partly because the part of the introduction to the *Division* with the critique of philosophy that grounds Durkheim's argument that justice becomes a requirement was removed in 1902. This missing part of the introduction is in a sense another hidden—or forgotten text. In it Durkheim took on moral philosophy and argued that values (and in modernity, equality and justice) are intrinsic to social facts/categories.

The argument that justice is a necessary prerequisite for social fact/object and/or category making processes in diverse and specialized societies that Durkheim laid the groundwork for in the sections cut from the introduction sets the context for all the later work on categories. The argument of the *Elementary Forms* that the social creation of categories of the understanding makes moral rules and complex thinking—makes reason itself—possible, extends the argument of *Division* that the individual and all social meanings are socially created. It follows that in diverse and specialized social contexts that lack comprehensive belief and/or symbol systems, a level of equality and justice must be achieved before (and as a condition of) cooperation in the constitutive technologies of practice—media of cooperation—through which people achieve shared ideas and cooperative work.

The argument that we need justice before we can make sense together, both as Durkheim made it and as elaborated later by Garfinkel (1963), has seemed implausible to many scholars because, as they point out, there is a great deal of inequality and injustice in the world and yet it still seems that we make sense. This is where Durkheim's distinction between traditional ritual practices and self-regulating constitutive practices is so important. Without that distinction, any inequality seems to disprove his argument because people appear to be making sense across inequality. But, if we realize he is arguing that justice is only required in settings that lack a comprehensive belief/symbol system, we can focus on the troubles that plague interaction across inequality in modern contexts of self-regulating practices. In those contexts, people are not able to make sense across inequality.

The marginalization of minority and female voices has been a barrier to achieving this understanding. W. E. B. Du Bois was telling us back in 1903 that communication across inequality does not work well. But minorities are the ones with special awareness of this and no one listened to them. Durkheim was also telling us. Garfinkel was showing us what the problems were—with Black Americans (Garfinkel 1940; 1942; 1949), with Jewish Americans (Turowetz and Rawls 2021), with transsexual Americans (Garfinkel 1967). Goffman was making the argument with regard to mental illness and illness more generally in *Stigma* (1963) and *Asylums* (1961). Overall, minority scholars and women have been telling us about the problem of inequality for a very long time. But, majority thinkers—who are not on the receiving end of these encounters—do not have the experience and have dismissed the evidence.

In this regard, research on social interaction that documents the troubles produced when people are either unequal or not orienting the same constitutive rules in diverse modern interactional contexts is of critical importance (Gayet-Viaud 2015; Rawls 2000; Rawls, Whitehead and Duck 2020; Whitehead 2012). Garfinkel's (1963) "Trust" argument and its specifications about required reciprocities of practice clarifies what Durkheim meant.

Of course there is in some sense always interpretation taking place between people, even across huge power differentials. But conscious interpretation only begins where mutual understanding fails. Most successful interactions do not require conscious interpretation. When there is no equality, the reciprocity and cooperation necessary to create and confirm recognizable social facts and shared ideas—through a back-and-forth sequential interactional process—is not possible. Under such conditions, people are not able to sustain a mutually cooperative, mutually meaningful interaction in which meaning is confirmed turn-by-turn without trouble. As a consequence, they fall back on narrative accounts of the "Other" that invoke divisive stereotypes (Rawls and David 2006; Rawls and Duck 2020).

In traditional societies, by contrast, power differentials within groups should not have this effect because everyone shares a comprehensive belief/symbol system that supports those power differentials. But, in diverse and specialized modern settings, where actual moment-by-moment reciprocities of practice are required, power differentials can make a nonsense of interaction.

The Alleged Clash between the Individual and Society or Social Solidarity

Surprisingly, even among those who are deeply indebted to Durkheim, like Anthony Giddens (1984), the "individual versus society" or "agency versus structure" problem has become a dominant paradigm. As a corollary, a type of formal organizational order and external constraint that is said to oppose the creative development of the individual is identified with modernity. These interpretations conflict with Durkheim's argument that all social objects, including the individual, scientific objects, tools, words, justice, and so forth and individual freedom, are social states of being that must be cooperatively constituted. Individual freedom and the individual are social creations. As such they cannot conflict with society or social solidarity.

What can happen, however, is that a consensus-based form of individualism can find itself increasingly surrounded by self-regulating forms of practice that threaten its authority. As with the false idea of culture wars, the clash is between two forms of social order (their clashing technical and moral requirements) and the conflicting forms of social individual they create, not between "individual" and "society."

Durkheim's big point—that an informal constitutive order of rules will arise spontaneously within practices in diverse social contexts and provide for their coordination through self-regulation while also setting the individual (and science and occupations) free from belief and comprehensive structures—has been lost. At the same time, through the work of scholars like Lévi-Strauss who claim to follow Durkheim, his work became associated with structuralism. The upshot is that the formal models of social institutions (and the "rule of law") we are so fond of, and that are often attributed to Durkheim, are actually contradicted by his position. Durkheim argued that formal organizational rules cannot carry out the required self-regulating constitutive functions and coherence cannot be produced by external constraint in an advanced division of social labor society (Durkheim 1893: III, chap. I). Instead a bottom-up self-organizing/regulating form of practice grounded in justice and social contract is required.

There are many reasons for these misunderstandings. But, the fact that, in contrast to Durkheim, most social thinkers treat the division of labor as a natural phenomenon and its increase as a type of natural selection (between natural objects) plays a large role. That Durkheim was conveying a minority position that majority thinkers do not see, also played a role. As a consequence, the progress of the division of labor has sometimes been seen as setting the social being free from cultural constraints and sometimes as destroying culture. Both of these, however, refer only to consensus-based cultural forms. For Durkheim, as for Parsons, Garfinkel, Goffman, and Harvey Sacks, if we were set free from self-regulation (interaction orders, ethno-methods and their trust conditions) we could not make sense together. It would not be freedom; it would be nonsense.

Durkheim's idea that the increasing division and specialization of labor is a cooperative social phenomenon in a context of implicit social contract that in fundamental ways is both responsive to and creatively changing both the social and moral character of what human life should be was too big a challenge to conventional views for most social thinkers. So, they modified it to fit their own prejudices.

The Moral Duties Entailed by Constitutive Practice

In the part of the introduction to *Division* that was cut in 1902 to make room for the "Second Preface," Durkheim addressed the question of moral duties[4]—what they are, and why and how they can be established. He pointed out that "classical moralists" derived moral duties from their conception of the individual person (or reason) and individual liberty as if they existed independently of social processes. This reified the person in the same way that categories had been reified. Liberty was treated as a quality belonging to individuals as natural objects, rather than as a social/moral fact achieved through cooperative social relations. Durkheim argued that these priorities are backward. If all social facts (including individual liberty and the individual self) are created through cooperative social relations, then we must commit to social relations first in order to create them.

Because cooperating in social processes is necessary to achieve the existence of the human rational being, Durkheim argued that it is a moral duty to maintain these processes. That these social processes can be subjected to rigorous empirical observation was another of Durkheim's innovations. But, the empirical aspects of social duties that can be documented have not been taken into account by classical moralists, he said, because they did not look at empirical social settings. Their considerations were limited to those duties they could derive from abstract notions of the individual or reason. These reifications leave out the social processes through which the individual becomes a rational social being. As such they leave out what we most need to know. In discussing this limitation with regard to Kant, Durkheim (1893: 412) writes that because Kant took for granted the social processes that create the individual, society seemed irrelevant to Kant. But, without society, Durkheim argued, Kant's "end in itself" cannot exist.

Whereas Durkheim considers social practices to come before and generate the individual, moral philosophy in general has considered "the social" to be merely descriptive or normative. But, as Durkheim points out, some social practices are "constitutive" and not merely descriptive. Nor do they just select between what already exists as evolutionary theory supposes. Constitutive processes create new social things, and one of the things they create is the rational individual.

Durkheim's argument in this regard can be confusing, his insistence that the social is a moral duty leading many scholars to think that he subordinated individual liberty to the good of society—as in the structural or structural functional misinterpretation of his position. But this is not the case. According to Durkheim, not all types of society promote individual liberty. Therefore, conforming to most types of society will not produce justice and liberty. But, a highly differentiated society in which self-regulating practices predominate will tend toward individual liberty because the self-regulating constitutive practices of such a society will increasingly need to take place against a foundation of justice and liberty. Only by treating the forms of constitutive practice that can accomplish this as "ends in themselves" can this be achieved; only those forms of social practice require justice and liberty as a moral foundation. The problem with modern society from Durkheim's perspective is that we do not understand this, and consequently do not treat the constitutive requirements of practices as ends in themselves. Therefore, we continue to reproduce an Abnormal Form of society that does not eliminate the inequalities of consensus, and consequently fails to achieve the required individual liberty and justice. This Abnormal Form of society is not a moral imperative—he even argues that it may be a moral imperative to resist it.

Sociology as a New Form of Moral Argument

In meeting the challenge of educating "members" of self-regulating practices about the importance of justice and equality, Durkheim proposed a new type of intellectual inquiry and a new type of argument. He argued that it was necessary for all citizens to understand the new moral requirements, or they would cling to the old consensus and resist their new moral duties. Also, because the division of social labor is a social process in empirical details—not a system of concepts—the study of morality and justice in modernity must be an empirical enterprise.

Classical moralists had explained the inevitable lack of fit between abstract philosophical principles and empirical facts by arguing that actual human relations always fall short of moral ideals. Because Durkheim treats moral imperatives as having their origins in actual empirical social needs, however, he refused to accept this conventional explanation. Instead, Durkheim imposed his own empirical criteria of adequacy on the development of an approach to morality. "Such a formula," he says (1893: 414), "cannot be accepted unless it fits the reality it expresses . . . it must realize all the facts whose moral nature is undisputed." From Durkheim's perspective the relationship between the moral and empirical should be close and demonstrable, and the social needs that give rise to moral obligations should be empirically documentable.

Furthermore, because morality in this social sense needs to be coordinated between participants it must have visible social markers that can be used by members to interpret and coordinate the moral character and shared meaning of their activities and the categories they produce. Garfinkel and Sacks took up the documentation of this argument.

Deriving Morality from the Requirements of Constitutive Practices

This is not a case of "deriving ought from is" in any conventional sense. Durkheim does not expect that social arrangements will be perfectly moral and thereby display their relationship to moral principles. Rather, it is a case of deriving ought from the constitutive requirements of actual social arrangements. If moral obligations relate to social needs, he argues, they must be marked in visible/hearable ways so that others can observe which requirements (rules) have been met and which have not, so that they can coordinate their activities in accord with constitutive rules. In traditional societies the markers are sanctions. In modernity, if the criteria are not met, social fact making fails, and the process self-sanctions—this is part of self-regulation. Different social arrangements impose different requirements. But, none of them can be coordinated between people unless they are marked in obvious ways and sanctioned when they fail. It is the empirical markers of the constitutive requirements that Durkheim proposed the new discipline of sociology should study. These markers of trouble display the orientation of participants toward a constitutive *ought* and exist as both tacit and formal rules/laws and sanctions.

When the rules of practices are constitutive of empirical social realities they cannot be deduced from abstract principles. How basic social needs are fulfilled, however, can be demonstrated with the details of practices. Durkheim writes eloquently about this issue. Moralists, he says (1893: 415), treat the real thing—real people and real society—as a degradation of abstract ethics. Because people and society are imperfect, they believe we degrade the law of ethics whenever we come in contact with it. Durkheim (415) says that the "solidarity of men and time" is blamed for the corruption of moral law. This amounts to saying that if it were not for the "solidarity" of persons over time—that is, human society—moral law could be perfect. For Durkheim this is backward: without human society there would be no issue of morality in the first place, no recognizable human selves, no cooperative action, no meaning.

For classic moral philosophers, society was a problem that stood in the way of achieving human moral perfection. Kant was explicit about this and offered advice on how the individual could resist their social and sentient side. For Durkheim, by contrast, society is the essential moral achievement without which the human individual does not exist as such. The solidarity involved in maintaining society and its categories is not only a moral duty, he says, but the source of morality in the first place.[5] Therefore, to treat actual moral relations, the *is* as less moral than the *ought*, is to treat the source of morality as the corruptor of morality—the source of reason as the corruptor of reason—a fundamental contradiction. Of course actual social arrangements are less than perfect. But, in the case of differentiated societies that is only because constitutive requirements have not yet been met, not because those requirements are not moral.

Because Durkheim has often been interpreted as arguing that if a social norm exists, or is functional for society, it must be moral, it is important to note that he (1893: 416) argues against this position. He is an anti-Utilitarian. Social utility is not the principle behind his analysis, constitutive requirements are, and they are only moral in the sense of "justice" in highly differentiated societies in which self-regulation predominates. In other social forms they are merely normative. Durkheim is explicit in pointing out that there are important moral obligations with no direct social utility, as well as obligations with utility that are not moral. For instance, in *Elementary Forms* Durkheim argues that obligations to the dead, like other religious rituals, have no direct utility: They have a utility only in maintaining beliefs/practices, which only have moral relevance if those social practices are constitutive of the human personality and its ability to reason and communicate through categories of understanding.

Beginning with constitutive rules and the achievement of particular social acts in the quest to discover the transcendent moral character of action was a new approach to moral questions when Durkheim proposed it in 1893. It remains so. Comte, Herbert Spencer (1874–1885), and other nineteenth-century social thinkers had treated evolution as a process of natural selection either between natural objects or between the durable objects of consensus. Given such a view there is no need to continually cooperate to create meaningful objects. Utility is itself a judgment that presupposes the existence of things. For Durkheim (1893: 418), however, things of moral value do not just exist, they need to be created.

Because his approach was empirically based, Durkheim believed that it would not only produce knowledge about the constitutive requirements of particular social practices but also make it possible to achieve general agreement on moral questions. He maintained that it was because philosophers deduce morality from the idea of man (rather than from constitutive moral facts) that their arguments differ as much as their conceptions of man differ: with ethnocentrism being the inevitable result (1893: 421). By contrast, arguments about moral facts that are based on empirical observations of how constitutive practices are used to make categories will differ only insofar as actual constitutive moral requirements differ. In diverse and specialized modern differentiated social contexts these moral facts do not differ much in how they work and in what they require.[6] There may be many different rule/sets for achieving the same social need or purpose. But the underlying constitutive requirements become increasingly similar.

What remained was to establish just what "the social" was needed for—which would in turn set its moral parameters—and this Durkheim did in his later category work. The argument he arrived at was that without the social there can be no rational human thought. The categories of understanding are a social creation, which is the argument he made in *Elementary Forms*.

"Value Neutrality" Contradicts Durkheim's Category Argument

The idea behind value neutrality is that social scientists should not allow an orientation toward "values" to influence their work. This approach dismisses out of hand that the social objects typically the subject of such research are comprised in the first place of an orientation toward a social order of practices and values. Therefore, a commitment to value neutrality explains the continued ethnocentrism in Western social thought. As Durkheim argued, social objects not only depend on value orientations but are themselves moral facts in the strict philosophical sense, because without them (and the cooperative work of making them) we would not be recognizably human. Parsons's (1960) pattern variables and Garfinkel's (1963) "Trust" argument (that social objects and identities depend on reciprocity conditions that are damaged by inequality) follow from Durkheim's argument, not only in drawing an intrinsic relationship between social facts and the value orientations in social practices, but also in being grounded in social contract.

The idea of value neutrality was hotly contested by social thinkers throughout the 1920s and 1930s with Parsons championing Durkheim against the idea of value neutrality. It was only with the advent of World War II that a preference for trying to achieve value neutrality finally gained ascendancy—bolstered by the conviction that value neutral methods would more efficiently deliver "immediate" results to support the war effort (Rawls 2018). There was explicit anti-Semitism and racism involved in this effort to erase the social justice relevance of social theory. Whether the statistical and demographic studies that came to prominence were actually practical or useful was of less importance to disciplinary leaders than the speed with which results could be delivered on topics of relevance to the war. Wartime research was expected to address social questions that would help win the war and at the same time remain value neutral—a deep contradiction. Given this paradox, it is important to ask in what sense any of these studies could have been value neutral. They were often statistical and demographic. But statistics are no more value neutral than the social processes and value orientations that are used to create the categories that statistics count. Demographics are categories. Categories, as Durkheim pointed out, are social in origin, and their creation and maintenance depend on commitments to social processes that involve moral commitments.

It seems obvious that value neutral methods were preferred during the war precisely because they could be aimed at a "value"—the political aim of winning the war—and were not value free. It was their "numerical" form that created the false sense of value neutrality.

Here we come to two intertwined misconceptions that have animated the discussion for a long time: first, the false belief that methods that rely on the statistical measurement of categories have a greater potential to be value free than other approaches to categories; and, second, the false belief that fact and value can be separated in the first place. Believing in the possibility of value neutrality assumes that facts are natural objects, that statistics count natural categories, and that these can exist apart from a set of social criteria for their existence. Believing that statistical and demographic methods have a greater potential to be value free assumes that the categories of persons and actions that statistics count, as well as the counting procedures themselves, are free from value oriented social relationships. This false belief has played a huge role in maintaining both inequality and the status quo. Numbers reassure us that those we punish are really criminals.

Research based on such false assumptions reifies findings in ways that hide inequality and suggest that the status quo is fair. So-called value free research enables racism, sexism, and class inequality. Research on how categories are actually created and used can stop this. Even categories like Male/Female and Black/White that are used to compile apparently straightforward demographic data are social categories with no natural or biological counterpart. Who is male and who is female can vary. Gender and Race are social categories defined differently in different places and times and their definitions embed inequality. Treating the counting of such categories as a value free endeavor is a mistake. There are a wide range of different biological conditions for sex. Societies decide how these correspond with the social categories male and female (or Other). The same is true for Race. A person can be Black in one country and White in another. How societies decide to draw the line is a social matter, determined by social relations; by social orientations toward values, beliefs, and social practices.

It is not just that the categories themselves are social objects but that each social institution develops its own unique categories and its own ways of recording, counting, and processing the social objects within its purview. There are many social processes involved in creating the institutional data sets that "value free" approaches use and these procedures do not hold constant across different institutions. Take crime rates for instance. There is a general misperception that they report the number of crimes committed. They do not. They measure recorded crime that made it onto the "books." Some crime rates measure self-reported crime, some large portion of which never resulted in an arrest and a significant portion of which do not even meet the legal definition of crime. Most local and state crime rates represent the rate at which police officers and courts record and process crimes. All reflect local practices of policing and processing local residents. The police work and prosecutorial decisions involved are not unmotivated or value free. They represent social category work. In a society like the United States with a serious Race problem, there is a higher recorded crime rate for African Americans.

This does not mean that Black Americans commit more crime—they do not—although the crime "rate" is generally treated as though it meant that. It means that Black Americans see more police action. They are "processed" more often—and that processing is more likely to be recorded in the official record. This is, of course, a serious moral issue that has been hidden by the statistics, because the research pretends to be value free. Treating statistical data sets as if they were value free—and pretending to do "value free" research based on them—reifies the prejudices and systemic inequalities that led to the statistical imbalance in the first place, creating even more inequality. The research question becomes "Why do Black Americans commit more crime?" (when they do not—White Americans do), and there is a whole industry devoted to producing explanations that posit the inferiority of Black Americans on one or another measure (poverty, work ethic, intelligence, culture) as an explanation, and advising even more police surveillance, when it seems in actuality that it is White privilege that generates the most crime.

The real question that does not get asked by such so-called value free research is why Black Americans get processed so much more often by the police. How is it that the police are still enforcing a four-hundred-year-old system of racial inequality in the United States, and how are those who do so-called value free research helping to support that racist power structure by naively justifying the inequalities in the social system by hiding the work that creates its categories?

Durkheim's Alternative and Its Elaboration by Parsons and Garfinkel

Is there a better alternative? Yes. Before Max Weber penned the argument that became the anchor of the "value free" movement, Durkheim had already taken the position that all meaningful categories and objects are social facts and that all social facts are moral facts. Durkheim intended by this argument to show that social facts depend on social cooperation and the cooperation involved is an essentially moral enterprise because it creates the ideas, identities, and social relationships without which we would not be recognizably human. Durkheim considered "sacred" the social commitments this creation depends on and therefore considered that the underlying requirements of social processes are also moral.

This is not a functional argument in the usual sense. It is a constitutive argument. If Durkheim is right about this, there is no possibility of value free social science.[7] Durkheim saw this as a plus and argued that the new discipline of sociology that he was founding should become an advocate for social reforms that would better support the needs of constitutive technologies of social fact making in diverse and specialized modern societies.

For Durkheim, this moral advocacy was more scientific than approaches that attempted to be value-free for two reasons: first, social facts are not natural facts, they are moral facts, and therefore treating them as if they were natural is not valid science. Durkheim (1893) laid the major paradoxes of philosophy and social science at the feet of this mistake (for instance, positing a conflict between the individual and society, when individual and human reason would not exist without society, or arguing that social requirements are not properly moral requirements when the highest goods from the human standpoint; the human individual and human reason, would not exist without them). Second, Durkheim argued that the approach that recognizes the moral character of social facts is more scientific because it acknowledges the social processes at work and looks beneath the surface of the facts/categories and our assumptions about them to examine the constitutive social processes and moral relationships that people use to create them.

Durkheim was only the first of many important social thinkers to tread this path. From the late nineteenth through the twentieth centuries, other notable social thinkers began arguing that most of the facts we have to deal with—and every one that achieves shared meaning—is a social fact and not a natural fact. W. E. B. Du Bois made the argument that Race is a social fact. The philosophers Ludwig Wittgenstein (1953) and J. L. Austin made the argument from 1939 to 1955 with regard to language and words. The sociologists C. Wright Mills (1940), Talcott Parsons (1937), Harold Garfinkel and Erving Goffman (1959) elaborated the position in sociology between 1937 and 1960, and Harvey Sacks (1995; Sacks et al. 1974) continued that work in studies of conversation. The economist Herbert Simon (1955) came close to a social fact position in the 1950s with his conception of "bounded rationality" and Joseph Stiglitz (2010) and Thomas Piketty (2014) are elaborating the social costs of inequality in economics in related terms today.

Durkheim argued that his new scientific approach to morality should be taught in public schools so as to firmly ground the moral consciousness of modern citizens on the moral foundation necessary in order to support democratic publics. If Durkheim had studied current crime rates in the United States and found that the high crime rate among Black Americans was the result of differential attention toward the Black community by law enforcement, he would have argued that sociology had a scientific duty to expose those rates as the result of a distorted and unjust/immoral social relationship. Garfinkel (1942; 1949) did exactly that in a study of North Carolina courtrooms in 1942. Parsons (1955) did something similar in his study of the structured strain produced by the US family—an argument that explains the explosion of toxic masculinity among White men in the United States today as the effect of contradictions between inequalities in the structure of the White middle-class family and the equality we are asked to believe in. It is a contradiction that Black American families have largely resolved (Rawls and Duck 2020).

Given the omnipresence of social objects/categories, the almost complete reliance of social persons on them, and the need for a high degree of cooperation and mutuality to create them each next time, the possibility of value neutrality approaches zero. However, it is not desirable to achieve value neutrality if the conditions for making the social facts we rely on are in themselves moral imperatives. As such they cannot be separated from their moral conditions. Hence, scientific studies of the conditions for social fact making will necessarily involve moral issues because moral conditions are requirements for successful social fact making.

Insofar as practices are constitutive of essential human goods, they involve issues of justice. Exclusion of some people from such practices is a moral wrong. Studies of this moral wrong can be scientific. It is when social facts are artificially separated from the moral conditions of their making—as happens in the attempt to be "value free"—that distortion, subjectivity, and ethnocentricity make their way into scientific practice (as they have in conventional social science and philosophy). This works to marginalize the very Black, Brown and female voices we need to hear from. Yet, research in which the distorted values of the status quo go unexamined continues to dominate—going by the name "objective science"—producing false appearances that support distorted and unfair social contexts.

Durkheim's Category Project sought to solve this problem by founding a new discipline to study the conditions for making moral/social facts. The contemporary category project by those ethnomethodologists and conversation analysts inspired by Garfinkel and Sacks has taken up the challenge (Rawls, Whitehead and Duck 2020).

Anne Warfield Rawls is Professor of Sociology at Bentley University (Waltham, Massachusetts) and Director of the Garfinkel Archive. Teaching social and interactional theory for over forty years, she has written extensively on the history of sociology with a focus on Durkheim, Du Bois, Garfinkel, and the implications of their work for coming to terms with racism and social justice. Her *Epistemology and Practice: Durkheim's Elementary Forms of Religious Life* (2004, Cambridge University Press) is a groundbreaking interpretation of

Durkheim's epistemology. *Tacit Racism* (2020, University of Chicago) co-authored with Waverly Duck, brings her conception of Interaction Orders to bear on how racism manifests in social interaction. Rawls has published in journals such as *The American Journal of Sociology, Sociological Theory, The European Journal of Social Theory, Organization Studies,* and *The Information Society.*

Notes

The research of this article was part of the Collaborative Research Centre *1187 Media of Cooperation funded by the German Research Foundation (DFG)— Project number 262513311.*

1. Durkheim's position is indebted to Jean Jacques Rousseau's social contract argument in *Discourse on the Origins of Inequality* (1757) that the requirements of the social condition create the first moral obligations.

    Constitution and constitutive practices do not mean the same thing. For example, Donald Trump's many violations of the US Constitution demonstrate that the constitution is not constitutive of meaningful social action in the United States. The constitution cannot self-regulate. Rather, the constitution acts as a constraint—a limiting condition—marking off what should happen from what Trump is actually doing. Constitutive conditions, by contrast, are criteria that must be met for an action to be recognizable as an action of a particular sort. The susceptibility of formal rules/laws to this kind of manipulation because they are not constitutive is one element of Durkheim's argument that the new role of government in modern societies that do not have consensus practices will be to guarantee justice and not to organize things: because under such conditions practices must self-regulate without constraint. Only such practices can maintain their moral boundaries under diverse modern conditions. What this means for the development of new forms of law and government is something we have, unfortunately, paid almost no attention to (see Rawls 1983).
2. This distinction is often confused with distinctions between traditional and modern societies made by other social theorists, particularly Ferdinand Tönnies. But it is not the same distinction. Durkheim distinguishes between two kinds of practice—not two kinds of society—both of which will be found in all societies in different proportions. One of the main points of his *Elementary Forms* is that the earliest societies had more of the constitutive practices found in modernity than the societies in between. The distinction is between practices that are constrained by belief and practices that self-regulate.
3. These category terms are capitalized to denote their social fact character.

4. Because we are talking about constitutive practices, it is an entailment relation: unless constitutive requirements are met no social object, or category, exists.
5. This does not have the consequences of moral relativity that critics suppose because well-ordered consensus-based comprehensive systems have ways of limiting inequality. It is the societies in transition—like the ones we are living in now—in which inequality goes out of control. In such societies consensus is no longer adequate to limit inequality, but justice and inequality are not yet adequate enough to support self-regulation across the whole society. The postmodern and post-structural critiques do not apply.
6. Sociologists studying constitutive practices of work and interaction are indeed finding that while particular practices vary from site to site, the underlying needs of communication and object coherence that they are responsive to and the constitutive requirements for reciprocity remain sufficiently the same to enable an analysis based on practices oriented toward those constitutive requirements that transcend situations (Lynch 1997).
7. In my view, Max Weber would have agreed with this, his own position having been misinterpreted to serve the "value-free" movement. But for the purposes of this argument, it does not matter.

References

Durkheim, Émile. 1893. *La Division du Travail Sociale*. Paris: Félix Alcan.

———. [1893] 1902. "Préface de la seconde édition." In *La Division du Travail Sociale*, i–xxxvi. 2nd edn. Paris: Félix Alcan,

———. 1912. *Les formes élémentaires de la vie religieuse*. Paris: Félix Alcan.

———. [1913–14] 1983. *Pragmatism and Sociology*. Cambridge: Cambridge University Press.

Durkheim, Émile, and Marcel Mauss. [1903] 1963. *Primitive Classification*. Chicago: University of Chicago Press.

Garfinkel, Harold. 1940. "Color Trouble." In *Best Short Stories of 1941: Yearbook of the American Short Story*, ed. Edward J. O'Brien Boston, 144–52. Boston: Houghton Mifflin.

———. 1942. "A Research Note on Inter and Intra Racial Homicide." MA thesis. Chapel Hill: University of North Carolina.

———. 1949. "Research Note on Inter- and Intra-Racial Homicide." *Social Forces* 27: 370–81.

———. [1962] 2019. *Parsons' Primer*. Edited and introduced by Anne Rawls and Jason Turowetz. New York: Springer.

———. 1963. "A Conception of and Experiments with 'Trust' as a Condition of Stable Concerted Actions." In *Motivation and Social Interaction*, ed. O.J. Harvey, 187–238. New York: Ronald Press.

———. 1967. *Studies in Ethnomethodology*. Englewood-Cliffs, New Jersey: Prentice-Hall.
Gayet-Viaud, Carole. 2015. "Les espaces publics démocratiques à l'épreuve du terrorisme." *métropolitiques*, 20 November. Retrieved 25 February 2019 from https://www.metropolitiques.eu/Les-espaces-publics-democratiques.html.
Giddens, Anthony. 1984. *The Constitution of Society: Outline of the Theory of Structuration*. Cambridge: Polity Press.
Goffman, Erving. 1959. *Presentation of Self in Everyday Life*. New York: Doubleday Anchor.
———. 1961. *Asylums: Essays on the Social Situation of Mental Patients and Other Inmates*. New York: Doubleday Anchor.
———. 1963. *Stigma: Notes on the Management of Spoiled Identity*. Englewood Cliffs, NJ: Prentice-Hall.
Lynch, Michael. 1997. *Scientific Practice and Ordinary Action: Ethnomethodology and Social Studies of Science*. Cambridge: Cambridge University Press.
Mills, C. Wright. 1940. "Situated Action and the Vocabulary of Motives." *American Sociological Review* 5: 904–13.
Parsons, Talcott. 1937. *The Structure of Social Action*. Chicago: Free Press.
———. 1938. "The Role of Theory in Social Research." *American Sociological Review* 3(1): 13–20.
———. 1949. "Presidential Address: 'The Prospects of Sociological Theory.'" *American Sociological Review* 15(1): 3–16.
———. 1955. "The American Family: Its Relations to Personality and to the Social Structure." In *Family, Socialization and Interaction Process*, ed. Talcott Parsons and Robert Bales, 3–33. New York: The Free Press, Macmillan.
———. 1960. *Structure and Process in Modern Societies*. Glencoe: The Free Press.
Piketty, Thomas. 2014. *Capital in the Twenty-First Century*. Cambridge: Harvard University Press.
Rawls, Anne W. 1983. "Constitutive Justice: An Interactionist Contribution to the Understanding of Social Order and Human Value." PhD Thesis. Boston: Boston University.
———. 1996. "Durkheim's Epistemology: The Neglected Argument." *American Journal of Sociology* 102(2): 430–82.
———. 2000. "Race as an Interaction Order Phenomena: W.E.B. DuBois's 'Double Consciousness' Thesis Revisited." *Sociological Theory* 18(2): 239–72.
———. 2004. *Epistemology and Practice: Durkheim's* The Elementary Forms of Religious Life. Cambridge: Cambridge University Press.
———. 2012. "Durkheim's Theory of Modernity: Self-regulating Practices as Constitutive Orders of Social & Moral Facts." *Journal of Classical Sociology* 12(3/4): 479–512.

———. 2018. "The Wartime Narrative in US Sociology 1940–1947: Stigmatizing Qualitative Sociology in the Name of 'Science.'" *European Journal of Social Theory* 21(4): 526–46.

———. 2021. "Durkheim's Self-regulating 'Constitutive' Practices: An Unexplored Critical Relevance to Racial Justice, Consensus Thinking, and the Covid-19 Pandemic." In *Durkheim & Critique*, ed. Nicola Marcucci, 227–63. London: Palgrave Macmillan.

Rawls, Anne W., and Gary David. 2006. "Accountably Other: Trust, Reciprocity and Exclusion in a Context of Situated Practice." *Human Studies* 28(4): 469–97.

Rawls, Anne W. and Waverly Duck. 2020. *Tacit Racism*. University of Chicago Press.

———. 2021. "Developing a White 'Double Consciousness': Implications for Sociology of Qualitative Studies of Systemic Racism Inspired by Du Bois and Garfinkel." Unpublished manuscript.

Rawls, Anne W., Waverly Duck, and Jason Turowetz. 2018. "Problems Establishing Identity/Residency in a City Neighborhood during a Black/White Police/Citizen Encounter: Revisiting Du Bois' Conception of 'The Submissive Man'." *City and Community* 17(4): 1015–50.

Rawls, Anne W., and David Mann. 2015. "Getting Information Systems to Interact: The Social Fact Character of 'Object' Clarity as a Factor in Designing Information Systems." *The Information Society* 31(2):175–92.

Rawls, Anne W., and Jason Turowetz. 2021. "Discovering Culture in Interaction: Solving Problems in Cultural Sociology by Recovering the Interactional Side of Parsons' Conception of Culture." *American Journal of Cultural Sociology* 9 (3): 293–320.

Rawls, Anne W., Kevin Whitehead, and Waverly Duck. 2020. *Black Lives Matter: Ethnomethodological and Conversation Analytic Studies of Race and Systemic Racism in Everyday Interaction*. London: Routledge

Rawls, John. 1999. *Law of Peoples*. Cambridge, MA: Harvard University Press.

Rousseau, Jean Jacques. [1757] 1999. *Discourse on the Origins of Inequality*. Oxford: Oxford University Press.

Sacks, Harvey. 1995. *Lectures in Conversation*. Cambridge: Cambridge University Press.

Sacks, Harvey, Emanuel Schegloff, and Gail Jefferson. 1974. "A Simplest Systematics for the Organization of Turn Taking in Conversation." *Language* 50: 696–735.

Simon, Herbert. 1955. "The Behavioral Model of Rational Choice." *The Quarterly Journal of Economics* 69(1): 99–118.

Spencer, Herbert. 1874–1885. *The Principles of Sociology*. New York: Appleton and Company.

Stiglitz, Joseph. 2010. *Freefall: America, Free Markets, and the Sinking of the World Economy*. New York: W.W. Norton.

Turowetz, Jason and Anne W. Rawls. 2021. "The Development of Garfinkel's 'Trust' Argument from 1947 to 1967: Demonstrating How Inequality

Disrupts Sense and Self-Making." *Journal of Classical Sociology.* 21(1): 3-37.

Whitehead, Kevin. 2012. "Racial Categories as Resources and Constraints in Everyday Interactions: Implications for Non-Racialism in Post-Apartheid South Africa." *Ethnic and Racial Studies* 35: 1248–65.

Wittgenstein, Ludwig. 1953. *Philosophical Investigations.* Oxford: Blackwell.

Chapter 6

EXPERIMENTING WITH SOCIAL MATTER

CLAUDE BERNARD'S INFLUENCE ON THE DURKHEIM SCHOOL'S UNDERSTANDING OF CATEGORIES

Mario Schmidt

> In social facts you have a kind of natural laboratory experiment, abolishing the harmonics and, so to speak, leaving only the pure sound.
> —Marcel Mauss, "Real and Practical Relations between Psychology and Sociology," 1979

In both the German and English versions of Durkheim's *Elementary Forms of Religious Life*, the French term *expérience* is sometimes translated as "experience" and sometimes as "experiment." In their respective translations of the following sentence from the French original, Karen Field, for example, chose to translate *expérience* as "experiment" (Durkheim [1912] 1995: 249) and Ludwig Schmidts as *Erfahrung*, that is, "experience" (Durkheim [1912] 2007: 364): "Les premières nous fourniront l'occasion de faire, en quelque sorte, une expérience dont les résultats, comme ceux de toute expérience bien faite, seront susceptibles d'être généralisés" (Durkheim 1912: 596).[1] Looking at other parts of the German and English versions of *Elementary Forms*, one realizes that an evolutionistic understanding of Durkheim's text guided the decisions to translate the term *expérience* either as "experience" or as "experiment." While "primitive" societies do not conduct experiments, "modern" societies do so frequently. In the following sentence, *expérience* is translated as "experience" when referring to so-called archaic religious beliefs and as "experiment" when referring to modern scientific practice: "religious belief rests on a definite experience [*expérience spécifique*], whose demonstrative value is, in a sense, not inferior to that of scientific experiments [*expériences scientifiques*]... though it is different" (Durkheim [1912] 1995: 420).

The decision to let a wider evolutionary framing of Durkheim's theory guide the translation reflects a modernistic reading of Durkheim. It neglects the specific understanding of "experiments" that circulated in French natural and social sciences at the turn from the nineteenth to the twentieth century. Blinded by contemporary understandings of experiments as being built upon the intentions of scientists and taking place in laboratories, the translators missed out on linking Durkheim's use of the term *expérience* with Claude Bernard's influence on the Durkheim School. I thus argue that the Bernardian impact on Durkheim should not merely be considered an influence of "vocabulaire mais véritablement des concepts" (vocabulary but truly of concepts, Michel 1991: 232).

Instead of drawing a line between primitive and modern ways of knowledge production, Durkheim insisted on the similarities between "modern" and "primitive" forms of knowledge production. In Durkheim's view, both rely on experiments with different types of matter (*matiére*). While the biologist experiments with physical bodies such as frogs or cell tissue, social actors experiment with what Durkheim called the "social matter" (*matiére sociale*, Durkheim [1893] 1926: 237). Both forms of experiment aim to produce verified conclusions about what "the most universal properties of things" are (Durkheim [1912] 1995: 9).

After discussing the influence of the "milieu bernardien" (Michel 1991) on the work of Durkheim, which fills a gap in the otherwise rich discussion of Durkheim's relation to the life sciences (e.g., Barberis 2003; Guillo 2006; Meloni 2016), my contribution argues that taking into account a broader understanding of the term *expérience* can help us to interpret the "category project," that is, the Durkheimians' hypothesis that categorical claims about the world originate and are justified in the sphere of the social (see the introduction to this volume). Interpreting human societies, their rituals, and their classificatory systems as, what Claude Lévi-Strauss has called "ready-made experiments" (2013: 245) leads to an interpretation that in crucial ways differs from Anne Rawls's (2005) practice-theoretical, Warren Schmaus's (2004) functionalistic and Susan Stedman Jones's

(2006; see introduction, this volume) representationalist reading of the Durkheimians' category project.

In contrast to these scholars, I argue that the Durkheim School's category project deals neither with the question of where categories originate (practices or the mind, see the discussion between Rawls 2005 and Stedman Jones 2006; see the introduction to this volume) nor with the question of what their social function is (Schmaus 2004). Rather, Durkheim is interested in finding an answer to the question of how people acquire an experience of categories as universally valid. Comparable to a scientific proof of categories, rituals and moments of effervescence bring forth what Durkheim calls a "demonstrative value" (Durkheim [1912] 1995: 420). It is in this sense that Durkheim's own theory of the social and the rituals of the Australian aborigines can be compared with one another. A focus on their common experimental nature leaves behind simplistic distinctions between Durkheim's allegedly positivist sociology and pre-modern religious, that is, allegedly non-scientific, beliefs.

For Durkheim, actors' experience of categories as universally valid originates in random effects triggered by a uniquely human condition: the necessity to live a "collective life" (*vie collective*, see James, this volume). These effects are ex post interpreted as causes of natural laws whose existence is repeatedly justified under ritualistic, that is, experimental conditions. Comparable to Edward E. Evans-Pritchard's Azande, who transfer scientific questions of cause and effect to areas where they do not belong (1937), Durkheim's Aborigines apply experimental reasoning to a field based on random effects. Durkheim, in other words, argues that the Australian Aborigines chose a well-informed approach to the question of categories, that is, an experimental one, but applied it incorrectly.

Experimenting with Biological and Social Life: Claude Bernard's Influence on Durkheim

The notion of "experiment" in Durkheim's thought and its relation to the work of Claude Bernard remains understudied. Apart from Paul Q. Hirst's laudable *Durkheim, Bernard and Epistemology*, which claims not to be interested in "a relation of 'influences' and manifest historical links between the two thinkers" (Hirst 1975: 13), very few academic works scrutinize the relation between Bernard and Durkheim (see Guillo 2015). This is all the more surprising as Durkheim as early as 1888 referred to a distinction that was crucial for Bernard—the one between observation and experiment—and continued to do so throughout his work.[2] In his "Cours de science sociale," for example, Durkheim writes that "the object are the social facts; the method is observation and indirect experimentation, in other words, the comparative method" (Durkheim 1888: 41).[3]

References to the work of Bernard can also be found in "hidden texts" (Sembel, this volume) such as the list of loans to Durkheim at the University of Bordeaux, which shows that Durkheim borrowed Bernard's two-volume book *Leçons sur la physiologie et la pathologie du système nerveux* (Sembel and Béra 2013: 52). We find additional proof of Bernard's importance in an exam that Mauss took on 22 January 1893. In this exam, Mauss gave an answer to the question of if a single *expérience* could justify the belief in a law (see Mauss and Beuchat [1906] 1979). In his corrections of Mauss's answer Durkheim refers to "C.B.," Claude Bernard. My last example for a Durkheimian reference to the distinction between *observation* and *expérience* occurs in a well-known passage from Durkheim's *The Rules of Sociological Method*:

> A thing is any object of knowledge which is not naturally penetrable by the understanding. It is all that which we cannot conceptualize adequately as an idea by the simple process of intellectual analysis. It is all that which the mind cannot understand without going outside itself, proceeding progressively by way of observation and experimentation from those features which are the most external and the most immediately accessible to those which are the least visible and the most profound. (Durkheim [1895] 1982: 36)

The distinction between *observation* and *expérience* owes a lot to Bernard's epistemology and how he defines the notion of *expérience* in his *Introduction à l'étude de la médecine expérimentale* (Bernard [1865] 1949). According to Bernard, the most important difference between these two epistemological modes of inquiry is that experiments act on bodies, while observations do not: "it is on this very possibility of acting, or not acting, on a body that the distinction will exclusively rest between sciences called sciences of observation and sciences called experimental" ([1865] 1949: 9).

This "acting on a body" does not necessarily have to be an act intentionally performed by the scientist: "But now, let me ask, did Dr. W. Beaumont make an experiment when he came across that young Canadian hunter who had received a point-blank gun-shot in the left hypochondria, and who had a wide fistula of the stomach in the scar, through which one could look inside that organ?" ([1865] 1949: 8). Bernard is quite confident that incidents such as this one "prove that, in verifying the phenomena called experiments, the experimenter's manual activity does not always come in, since it happens that the phenomena, as we have seen, may present themselves as fortuitous or passive observations" (8). Bernard thus concludes that Dr. Beaumont "made a passive experiment" (8). The difference between "active" and "passive," or in the words of Lévi-Strauss (2013: 245), "readymade," experiments makes clear that Bernard's crucial indicator to answer the question if a series of actions should be considered an experiment does not lie in the scientist's intention to perform an experiment, but in his or her intention to interpret them as an experiment.

Even if we agree that the notion of experiment is central for an understanding of Durkheim's work, we thus have to establish what entity, according to Durkheim, is experimented upon by whom. In *The Rules of Sociological Method*, Durkheim writes:

> The horde . . . is a social aggregate which does not include—and never has included—within it any other more elementary aggregate, but which can be split up directly into individuals. These do not form within the main group special sub-groups different from it, but are juxtaposed like atoms. One realizes that there can be no more simple society; it is the protoplasm of the social domain and consequently the natural basis for any classification. (Durkheim [1895] 1982: 113)

I want to emphasize Durkheim's use of the term "protoplasm" here, which, once more, resonates with what Bernard calls the "matière vivante, le protoplasma" that is uniform and does not yet have a concrete definition: "Life resides in this amorphous or rather *monomorphic* matter, but undefined life. This means that one can rediscover therein all the essential properties of which the manifestations of the higher beings are only diversified and defined expressions—higher modalities" (Bernard 1885: 292).[4]

Semantic similarities like these are not coincidental. On the contrary, I suggest that Durkheim considered the ways individuals who change their spatial relations with one another to form new "associations," that is, the ways they change the "social matter" (see Nielsen 1999), are the prime cause not only of new social morphological relations but of ways of thinking as well. What Durkheim and his followers sometimes have called "rhythm of collective life" (Durkheim [1912] 1995: 443), that is, the repetitive change from moments of individualization to effervescence, thus also constitutes a playground for the experimental justification of already existing and the emergence of new categories. Social morphological laws participate in and shape the development of collective representations: "In our opinion, the effects of morphological phenomena are not limited to certain legal phenomena, . . . they extend as well to higher spheres of social physiology" (Mauss and Beuchat [1906] 1979: 90).

The Rhythm of Collective Life:
A Natural Law and Experimental Playground

Durkheim used the notion of effervescence as early as 1897 (e.g., Durkheim [1897] 2005: 336), and the term, initially with rather negative connotations, referred to moments of social tumult, aggressiveness and economic crisis ([1897] 2005). In his lectures on pedagogy and education, held around the turn of the century, Durkheim started to emphasize the creative potential of moments of effervescence (Durkheim 1934; Watts Miller 2017). Given the fascinating and paradoxical nature of effervescence and the concept's crucial role in Durkheim's discussion of ritual (e.g., Crapanzano 1995; Mazzarella 2017; Pickering 1984), it is not surprising that scholars rarely search for effervescence's lost brother: the "monotonous, slack, and humdrum" of everyday life that is characterized by the dispersion of society's members (Durkheim [1912] 1995: 217).

Taking a closer look at both the "Eskimo Essay" (Mauss and Beuchat [1906] 1979) as well as the *Elementary Forms of Religious Life*, one realizes that the Durkheimians understood these two states of social organization as linked by a causal law. They interpreted effervescence as a causal effect of the above-mentioned "dispersed states" of monotony, "languor" and "torpor" ([1906] 1979: 78) and vice versa such "dispersed states" as a causal effect of moments of effervescence:

> All this suggests that we have come upon a law that is probably of considerable generality. Social life does not continue at the same level throughout the year; it goes through regular, successive phases of increased and decreased intensity, of activity and repose, of exertion and recuperation. We might almost say that social life does violence to the minds and bodies of individuals which they can sustain only for a time; and there comes a point when they must slow down and partially withdraw from it. We have seen examples of this rhythm of dispersion and concentration, of individual life and collective life. Instead of being the necessary and determining cause of an entire system, truly seasonal factors may merely mark the most opportune occasions in the year for these two phases to occur. ([1906] 1979: 78–79)

In other words, how individuals form associations is dependent upon contingent as well as necessary factors. Social life necessarily oscillates between "phases of increased and decreased intensity," but the dimension and composition of these effervescent meetings and monotonous periods depend on contingent factors such as, for instance, climatic conditions and social structures, kinship understandings or gender divisions. It depends, in short, upon the natural as well as the social and cultural milieu.[5]

The fact that societies go through the two phases is a natural law, how they go through the two phases and what happens during these phases is culturally contingent. But what is the object of society's law that organizes the shift between "phases of increased and decreased intensity"? Durkheim and Mauss often use the chemical analogy of "substratum" to designate that law's object:

> Society has for its substratum the mass of associated individuals. The system which they form by uniting together, and which varies according to their geographical disposition and the nature and number of their channels of communication, is the base from which social life is raised. The representations which form the network of social life arise from the relations between the individuals thus combined or the secondary groups that are between the individuals and the total society. . . . there is nothing surprising in the fact that collective representations, produced by the action and reaction between individual minds that form the society, do not derive directly from the latter and consequently surpass them. (Durkheim [1898] 2009: 10; alternatively, they talk of "matière sociale" or, as we have seen, of "protoplasme," see Fernandes 2008)

The next section works out the relations between Durkheim's assumption that rituals of effervescence are experiments social actors conduct on themselves, and the bolder claim that categories originate and are justified in these social experiments. Reading rituals of effervescence as experiments helps to understand how Durkheim can argue for the experience of categories as necessary and universally applicable and simultaneously uphold the belief in the relativity of categories. This double movement paves the way for an alternative to both a Kantian transcendental defense and a Humean empiricist denial of the universal validity of categories (see Schrempp, this volume). Durkheim interprets categories as grounded in experimentally justified propositions about the nature of the world. These propositions are invented by incorrectly interpreting movements of the social matter as "readymade experiments" conducted by the world itself on the social matter.

An Aristotelian Approach: How Societies Invent Nature

Before we can understand the way moments of effervescence have to be considered as experiments justifying specific categorical claims about the nature of the world, we must understand what Durkheim means when he talks about categories. Several passages suggest that Durkheim conceptualized categories as fundamental properties of things themselves. This suggests he had a deeply Aristotelian understanding of categories not primarily as innate but external to the human mind: "They [the categories] correspond to the most universal properties of things" (Durkheim [1912] 1995: 8–9). There is hardly an understanding of categories that could be less Kantian.

To substantiate the claim that the category project of the Durkheim School at its core is Aristotelian, let me give a short introduction to Aristotle's theory of categories (Aristotle 1963). We can distinguish at least two different readings of Aristotle's theory of the categories: a linguistic and an ontological one (see Lalande 1926: 125–26). According to the first, Aristotle is interested in classifying the "ultimate types of predicates" (Ryle 2009), that is, the basic ways we can talk about objects. It is an epistemological argument comparable to Kant's theory of the categories, which is not interested in the ways we can talk about objects qua speaking subjects, but in the different ways we can think about objects qua intellectual beings. The second, ontological understanding interprets Aristotle's theory of the categories as targeting "being" itself, that is, by elaborating the diverse ways "beings can be" (Brentano 1862). Here is an apt illustration of the difference: "The first sees the list of the categories as designating kinds of predicates, whereas the second thinks of the items on the list as themselves predicates, designating different kinds of things, more indeed as a list of kinds of subjects than of kinds of predicates" (Kosman 2013: 125; see Collins 1985).

I suggest that Durkheim and Mauss were similarly interested in exploring the diverse ways different societies construct such a "list of kinds of subjects" (see Schmaus 1994: 190–91). They were, in other words, interested in why left and right, *mana* or food, among other things, had acquired categorical status in some societies. But why should the Durkheim School turn to the "rhythm of collective life" in order to answer the question of the categories? In this context it is illuminating that Karen Field's translation of the "Elementary Forms" deletes from the book's introduction a very important paragraph that was incorporated in the translation accomplished by Carol Cosman: "If there is still a consensus that we cannot attribute a social origin to the categories of thought without depriving them of all speculative value, this is because society is still too often regarded as something unnatural; and so it is concluded that representations expressing it express nothing about nature" (Durkheim [1912] 2008: 20–21).

The Durkheim School's point is not that the categories originate exclusively in the social, but that they also originate in the social. The question, which now arises, is: why should the "rhythm of collective life" be a better starting point to construct the "list of kinds of subjects" than philosophical introspection? In fact, I propose it is Aristotle's lack of a systematic principle holding together the table of categories that bothers Durkheim and Mauss just as it troubled Kant. However, Durkheim is equally dissatisfied with Kant's approach, which he considers tautological and unempirical. In contrast to Hume, who plausibly argued that the validity of categories such as causality cannot be observed, Durkheim explores a third option. By suggesting that intersubjectively experienced and interpreted experiments, that is, religious rituals of effervescence, are the origin of categories, Durkheim kills two birds with one stone: He counters Kant's idealism while at the same time avoiding Hume's skeptical solution.

Rituals of Effervescence and the Experimental Invention of Categories

In his famous introduction to Durkheim and Mauss's essay on primitive classification, Rodney Needham dismisses the argument that social classifications are the cause of classifications of the natural world on the ground of its circularity:

> This tendency to argument by petitio principii is more seriously expressed elsewhere in the essay, beginning with the very first example of classification which Durkheim and Mauss consider. They take a four-section scheme of social classification, by which all the members of a society are comprehensively and integrally categorized, and then abruptly assert that the congruent classification of non-social things "reproduces" the classification of people. This single word, that is, immediately assumes that which is to be proved by the subsequent argument, viz. the primacy of society in classification. (Needham [1963] 2009: xiv–xv)

The establishment of a relation between social groups and, for instance, points in space, so the argument goes, already depends on the category of space. It therefore cannot be the origin of the category of space. Needham's accusation of circularity confuses two notions of society that Durkheim and Mauss, unfortunately, do not always properly distinguish. And it is this confusion that prevents Needham from understanding the argument as non-circular: on the one hand, society understood as an innate potential of human beings (*vie sociale*, *protoplasme*) and, on the other, society as a specific agglomeration of individuals who share a common culture, language, territory, and so on (as in the "society of the Eskimo").

While Needham assumes that the social structure of "society x" cannot be the blueprint of the ways "society x" classifies the natural world, because such an argument falls short of making plausible what led to the classification of "society x" itself, Durkheim and Mauss actually conceptualize social life, that is, the necessary rhythm between moments of effervescence and boredom as a part of nature leading to an organization of the social and the natural world into randomly emerging patterns. These patterns are then ex post interpreted as necessary and ordered effects of the way the world is, although they are, first and foremost, effects of the way the social substance is entangled into its own rhythm and the evolvement of this rhythm in accordance with its contingent milieu. Societies thus do not classify the natural world in accordance with their own classification. Rather, they classify themselves and nature simultaneously.

I would like to elaborate this argument by discussing the establishment of what Durkheim calls a society's "emblem" during moments of effervescence:

> By expressing the social unit tangibly, it makes the unit itself more tangible to all. And for that reason, the use of emblematic symbols must have spread quickly, as soon as the idea was born. Furthermore, this idea must have arisen spontaneously from the conditions of life in common, for the emblem is not only a convenient method of clarifying the awareness the society has of itself: it serves to create—and is a constitutive element of—that awareness. (Durkheim [1912] 1995: 231)

The social emblem, in other words, signifies and is signified by the potential totality of the ritual's participants who experience themselves "as one" by means of sharing "social substance" (see Nielsen 1999). Only because they rhythmically link with one another through bodily movements, reciprocal intonation of sounds and other ritual techniques (see Heinskou and Liebst 2016), the participants of a ritual can focus upon an emblem such as a national flag and experience that flag as signifying and even as bringing forth the whole tribe. During this process, the actual cause of the individuals' experience of community and oneness, namely the fact that they are connected to one another by being part of the invisible "social matter," is substituted by an external symbol of that "social matter"—the emblem.

Ritual participants falsely believe that they only meet in order to worship the emblem and not because they are forced to meet one another by way of their nature, that is, by way of the law of the "rhythm of the collective life." The same is true of space. Individuals are randomly distributed in space after a ritual of effervescence and subsequently interpret this distribution as a result of a cosmological order. The ways humans classify space are thus "occasional effects" (compare Mauss and Beuchat's use of the term "opportune occasions," that is, *causes occasionnelles*, [1906] 1979: 79) of the rearrangement of the social "protoplasm" that are subsequently experienced, that is, experimentally interpreted, as necessary causes. Humans thus can, by way of their capacity for experimental reasoning, ex post link a specific social emblem or a social organization of space to a cosmological order and thereby interpret this cosmological order as the cause of the social movement instead of perceiving a specific emblem as a random effect of "collective life."

The random "behavior" of the "social protoplasm," which is at the same time contingent upon natural, geographical as well as social factors, causes patterns that are interpreted as causes of "behavior." In other words, it is not an emblem that establishes social unity. Rather, it is the (natural) social unity that is (naturally and ultimately randomly, i.e., arbitrarily) symbolized by emblems. The accusation of a circular argument is thus not altogether wrong. Humans themselves are trapped in this circularity qua symbolic beings and because the symbolic externalization of their own potential to experience themselves as one helps them to understand this potential as a necessity and establishes rules of conduct that steer this potential in the right, that is, non-violent, direction.

Needham's argument is therefore only partly true. He problematically assumes that the dual organization of the cosmos in societies with a moiety structure is done intentionally by "society x." But during the shift from effervescence to social monotony and vice versa, the movement between two specific spaces is just "felt" as a necessity. People are moved to other places by means of the law of social density, that is, because they are part of nature. This movement is triggered by the "social matter" itself and not by the intention of a mysterious entity called society (understood as in "the society of the Eskimo").

To summarize, I suggest that humans experience themselves as well as the world as spatial and temporal because they experimentally interpret social matter's movement in space (Czarnowski 1925; see Zillinger, this volume) and time (Hubert 1905; see Schick, this volume)—a movement triggered by the "rhythm of collective life" as an effect of a specific constitution of the world itself. Instead of realizing that their bodies are randomly moved by being part of the "social matter" or the "protoplasm," Australian Aborigines, according to

Durkheim, interpret rituals of effervescence as reactions to the ways the world itself is constituted. Instead of realizing that the world is not necessarily split into left and right areas, they assume that this split itself is a fundamental property of the world that has caused their movement to the two sides of the village. Like the results of scientific experiments, this interpretation is then confirmed in subsequent iterations of the ritual.

Hence, Durkheim's understanding of the social origin of categories does not imply that every society needs to have a shared understanding of, for example, space to function properly, as Schmaus suggested (2004: 22). The question Durkheim deals with is rather: How do people acquire an experience of categories that is comparable to a scientific proof of them? What makes societies believe that the world is split into a left and a right side? I have argued that Durkheim is interested in the question of what makes social actors so certain that specific categories correspond to the most universal properties of things. I suggested that they are able to do so because they interpret rituals of effervescence as what Bernard has called "passive experiments" and Lévi-Strauss "readymade experiments," that is, as situations that lend themselves to be interpreted as allowing a glimpse into the fundamental properties of the world itself. The only mistake they make, according to Durkheim, is in interpreting these experiments as taking place outside of themselves while these are actually experiments that the social matter performs on itself. If they limited themselves to the effects the "rhythm of collective life" has on their own bodies, they would, in a truly empirical, repeatable and systematic way, discover and find proof for the universal necessity and validity of the Aristotelian categories. Sociologists and anthropologists should nevertheless take these mistakes seriously and approach the categorical systems of other social actors from a positivist point of view. We should do so not because those categories are related to what we consider "nature," but because they correspond to what the respective society considers to be fundamental properties of the world.

Mario Schmidt is a Postdoctoral Fellow at the a.r.t.e.s. Graduate School of the Humanities at the University of Cologne. He has published in distinguished academic journals such as *Africa*, *Journal of Eastern African Studies*, *Ethnohistory*, and *Journal of Cultural Economy*. Currently, he is editing a German anthology on the Durkheimian category project with Johannes Schick, Ulrich van Loyen, and Martin Zillinger that will be published by Matthes & Seitz.

Notes

The research for this chapter was funded by the Gerda Henkel Foundation (Project number: 49/V/17).

1. "These tribes will provide the occasion to make a sort of experiment, the results of which, like those of any well-made experiment, will be generalized" (Durkheim [1912] 1995: 249).
2. Although Durkheim often does so implicitly, e.g., when discussing John Stuart Mill's logic which equally distinguishes between observation and experiment (see Candea 2019: 56–71).
3. "L'objet, ce sont les faits sociaux; la méthode, c'est l'observation et l'expérimentation indirecte, en d'autres termes la méthode comparative."
4. "Dans cette matière amorphe ou plutôt *monomorphe* réside la vie, mais la vie non définie, ce qui veut dire que l'on y retrouve toutes les propriétés essentielles dont les manifestations des êtres supérieurs ne sont que des expressions diversifiées et définies, des modalités plus hautes."
5. The notion of *milieu* as well as others such as *fait* (fact) are borrowed or at least influenced by Bernard's epistemology as well (see Canguilhem [1965] 2006: 165–98).

References

Aristotle. 1963. *Categories and De Interpretatione*, trans. with notes by John L. Akrill. Oxford: Clarendon Press.

Barberis, Daniela S. 2003. "In Search of an Object: Organicist Sociology and the Reality of Society in fin-de-siècle France." *History of the Human Sciences* 16(3): 51–72.

Bernard, Claude. [1865] 1949. *An Introduction to the Study of Experimental Medicine*. New York: Henry Schuman.

———. 1885. *Leçons sur les phénomènes de la vie, communs aux animaux et aux végétaux. Volume 1*. Paris: Librairie J.-B. Bailliére et Fils.

Brentano, Franz. 1862. *Von der mannigfachen Bedeutung des Seienden nach Aristoteles*. Freiburg im Breisgau: Herder'sche Verlagsbuchhandlung.

Candea, Matei. 2019. *Comparison in Anthropology: The Impossible Method*. Cambridge: Cambridge University Press.

Canguilhem, Georges. [1965] 2006. *La connaissance de la vie*. Paris: Librairie Philosophique.

Collins, Steven. 1985. "Categories, Concepts or Predicaments? Remarks on Mauss's Use of Philosophical Terminology." In *The Category of the Person: Anthropology, Philosophy, History*, ed. Michael Carrithers, Steven Collins, and Steven Lukes, 46–82. Cambridge: Cambridge University Press.

Crapanzano, Vincent. 1995. "The Moment of Prestidigitation: Magic, Illusion, and Mana in the Thought of Émile Durkheim." In *Prehistories of the*

Future: The Primitivist Project and the Culture of Modernism, ed. Elazar Barkan and Ronald Bush, 95–113. Stanford, CA: Stanford University Press.

Czarnowski, Stefan. 1925. "Le morcellement de l'étendue et sa limitation dans la religion et la magie." *Actes du Congrès international d'histoire des religions: Tenu à Paris en octobre 1923*: 341–59.

Durkheim, Émile. 1888. "Cours de science sociale: leçon d'ouverture." *Revue international de l'enseignement* 15: 23–48.

———. [1893] 1926. *De la division du travail social*. Paris: Félix Alcan.

———. [1895] 1982. *The Rules of Sociological Method: And Selected Texts of Sociology and Its Method*, ed. Steven Lukes. London: Macmillan Press.

———. [1897] 2005. *Suicide: A Study in Sociology*, trans. John A. Spaulding and George Simpson. London: Routledge.

———. [1898] 2009. "Individual and Collective Representations." In *Sociology and Philosophy*, 1–16. London: Routledge.

———. 1912. *Les formes élémentaires de la vie religieuse: Le système totémique en Australie*. Paris: Presses universitaires de France (PUF).

———. [1912] 1995. *The Elementary Forms of Religious Life*, trans. Karen E. Field. New York: Free Press.

———. [1912] 2007. *Die elementaren Formen des religiösen Lebens*, trans. Ludwig Schmidts. Frankfurt on the Main: Suhrkamp.

———. [1912] 2008. *The Elementary Forms of Religious Life*, trans. Carol Cosman. Oxford: Oxford University Press.

———. 1934. *L'éducation morale*. Paris: Félix Alcan.

Evans-Pritchard, Edward E. 1937. *Witchcraft, Oracles and Magic among the Azande*. Oxford: Clarendon Press.

Fernandes, T. Sousa. 2008. "Chemical Metaphors in Sociological Discourse. Durkheim through the Imagery of Rousseau." *Journal of Classical Sociology* 8(4): 447–66.

Guillo, Dominique. 2006. "La place de la biologie dans les premiers textes de Durkheim: un paradigme oublié?" *Revue française de sociologie* 47: 507–35.

———. 2015. "Emile Durkheim's Debt to Claude Bernard: Back to the Origins of the Sociology of Generative Mechanisms." In *Theories and Social Mechanisms: Essays in Honour of Mohamed Cherkaoui*, ed. Gianluca Manzo, 47–60. Oxford: Bardwell Press.

Heinskou, Marie B., and Lasse S. Liebst. 2016. "On the Elementary Neural Forms of Micro-Interactional Rituals: Integrating Autonomic Nervous System Functioning into Interaction Ritual Theory." *Sociological Forum* 31(2): 354–76.

Hirst, Paul Q. 1975. *Durkheim, Bernard and Epistemology*. London: Routledge.

Hubert, Henri. 1905. "Étude sommaire de la représentation du temps dans la religion et dans la magie." *Annuaire de l'École pratique des hautes-études, Section des Sciences Religieuses*: 1–39.

Kosman, Aryeh. 2013. *The Activity of Being: An Essay on Aristotle's Ontology*. Cambridge, MA: Harvard University Press.

Lalande, Andre. 1926. *Vocabulaire technique et critique de la philosophie*. Paris: PUF.

Lévi-Strauss, Claude. 2013. "Anthropology and the 'Truth Sciences.'" *HAU: Journal of Ethnographic Theory* 3(1): 241–48.

Mauss, Marcel. 1979. "Real and Practical Relations between Psychology and Sociology." In *Sociology and Psychology*, trans. Ben Brewster, 1–34. London: Routledge & Kegan Paul.

Mauss, Marcel, and Henri Beuchat. 1979 [1906]. *Seasonal Variations of the Eskimo: A Study in Social Morphology*, trans. James J. Fox. London: Routledge & Kegan Paul.

Mazzarella, William. 2017. *The Mana of Mass Society*. Chicago: University of Chicago Press.

Meloni, Maurizio. 2016. "The Transcendence of the Social: Durkheim, Weisman and the Purification of Sociology." *Frontiers in Sociology* 1: 1–11. Retrieved 30 April 2021 from https://www.frontiersin.org/articles/10.3389/fsoc.2016.00011/full.

Michel, Jacques. 1991. "Émile Durkheim et la naissance de la science sociale dans le milieu bernardien." In *La nécessité de Claude Bernard*, ed. Jacques Michel, 229–254. Paris: Méridiens Klincksieck.

Needham, Rodney. [1963] 2009. "Introduction." In Émile Durkheim and Marcel Mauss, *Primitive Classification*, trans. and ed. Rodney Needham, viii–xxxii. London: Routledge.

Nielsen, Donald A. 1999. *Three Faces of God: Society, Religion, and the Category of Totality in the Philosophy of Émile Durkheim*. Albany: State University of New York Press.

Pickering, William S. F. 1984. *Durkheim's Sociology of Religion: Themes and Theories*. London: Routledge & Kegan Paul.

Rawls, Anne W. 2005. *Epistemology and Practice: Durkheim's The Elementary Forms of Religious Life*. Cambridge: Cambridge University Press.

Ryle, Gilbert. 2009. "Categories." In *Collected Essays 1929–1968, Volume 2*, ed. Julia Tanney, 170–84. London Routledge.

Schmaus, Warren. 1994. *Durkheim's Philosophy of Science and the Sociology of Knowledge: Creating an Intellectual Niche*. Chicago: University of Chicago Press.

———. 2004. *Rethinking Durkheim and His Tradition*. Cambridge: Cambridge University Press.

Sembel, Nicolas, and Matthieu Béra. 2013. "Emprunts de Durkheim à la bibliothèque universitaire de Bordeaux/Durkheim's Loans from Bordeaux University Library: 1889–1902." *Durkheimian Studies/Études Durkheimiennes* 19: 49–71.

Stedman Jones, Susan. 2006. "Action and the Question of the Categories: A Critique of Rawls." *Durkheimian Studies/Études Durkheimiennes* 12: 37–67.

Watts Miller, William. 2017. "Creativity: A Key Durkheimian Concern and Problematic." *Revue européene des sciences sociales* 55(2): 17–40.

PART II

Lateral Links and Ambivalent Antagonists

Chapter 7

FREEDOM, FOOD, AND THE TOTAL SOCIAL FACT

SOME TERMINOLOGICAL DETAILS OF THE CATEGORY PROJECT IN "LE DON" BY MARCEL MAUSS

Erhard Schüttpelz

In memory of N. J. Allen

From today's standpoint it is difficult to comprehend the ambition of Émile Durkheim and Marcel Mauss to "replace philosophy" with social anthropology and a social history of the categories of thought: "l'anthropologie complète pourrait remplaçer la philosophie" (Mauss [1939] 2006: 128). For one thing, the philosophical doctrine of neo-Kantian and Hegelian categories was adopted in a period that exhibited an unparalleled disintegration and arbitrariness in its treatment of philosophical categories and their terminological heritage. Second, if reduced to the texts of the Durkheim School itself, their work on the categories has remained a half-finished ruin. Finally, one finds, in Mauss's texts, a series of terminological magic tricks quite similar to those Georges Méliès was developing for film at the time (most notably where Mauss characterizes "magic" itself). Should philosophy become a question of such tricks? We know the terms by which philosophy initially ignores, then condemns, and finally forgets the reasoning of such announcements. And the category project in its integrity seems to have been forgotten, and not even condemned, because most philosophers, with the notable exceptions of Lucien Lévy-Bruhl and Ernst Cassirer, did not even bother to ignore its ambition.

Nevertheless, now more than ever we can recognize the validity of the category project in three different respects, and this recognition will also have an impact on the future of "The Gift"—just as it has hitherto accompanied the anthropological readings and discussions of this text:

Above, all, the category project provides no finished philosophy or doctrine of categories but rather injects a fundamentally unsettling task of elucidating which alien categories of thought are fundamental elsewhere and how they are to be translated, as well as the sociological and ethnographic task of unsettling philosophy by elucidating both the heteronomy from which philosophy emerged and outlining in just which heteronomy it might disappear again. Both these tasks were shared not only by Mauss and the Durkheim School but also by other contemporary philosophers and sociologists, and this cross-disciplinary challenge remains just as relevant today as it was back then.

Furthermore, the category project establishes no definitive list of categories. But Durkheim's *Elementary Forms*, "The Gift," and the corpus of Mauss's writings at least yield a list of "topoi" that (until today) allows us to enumerate everything that might be relevant in reconstructing the categories of thought appertaining to foreign societies. These "topoi" are of immediate help in structuring a shifting reality of possible "modes of thought." The minimal set of categories is a maximal set of categorical questions; places for finding out (*topoi*). And why should one ask for less than the most thorough and at the same time shortest list of philosophical "topoi"?

But perhaps most important is the third point: Because Mauss believed in the category project and its feasibility, the text of "The Gift" is constantly oscillating between "use" and "mention"—that is, between a philologically and ethnographically adequate "usage" of terminology and a perpetual "mentioning" and questioning and re-defining of this terminology, practically in each and every sentence. And what else should be called a mode of "philosophical writing," if not this compulsion or wish to straddle both sides of use and mention (not to mention the *fait social* constituted by such an exercise)? Philosophical writing does not have to be "terminological" writing, but it very often is; and even if philosophical writing tries to avoid the terminologies hitherto used, it will eventually give rise to a new terminology in being read by others (as happened to Ludwig Wittgenstein's later writings once they became part of the philosophical curriculum). "Le don" so far has not been accepted as a regular part of the philosophical curriculum; however, some commentaries on Mauss have been incorporated into it and commenting on "Le don" has indeed become part of philosophy (alas, often without consulting the original). It is no wonder, therefore, that not only Mauss's theoretical challenge but several of the terms "mentioned" and employed by him (for instance, the Chinook word *potlatch*) were adopted into philosophy through readings of Mauss—if under somewhat dubious circumstances. This oblique philosophical success is a consequence of his peculiar way of writing: the mania of "The Gift," wherein each and every "usage" of a term is "mentioned" and discussed and redefined, and every definition has to match a specific ethnographic case exemplifying its crucial point. All this sprang from Mauss's ambition to do justice to the philosophical project of the Durkheim School: the category project. Maybe later philosophical generations will see the reconstruction or even resurrection of the category project as a whole, compelled by the pressing appeal of "The Gift": "Tomorrow to fresh woods, and pastures new!"

In preparation for such a future, I would like to elucidate three categories used and mentioned by Mauss in "The Gift": totality, substance, and force. Other categories will be visited in passing, and the commentary will try to cover the whole range of philosophical reasoning, ethnographic inspiration, whimsical conjecture, and idiosyncratic elegance that make Mauss such a magnificent author. I shall not refrain from esoteric and puzzling details, however obscure they might appear at first. For two reasons: First, the godhead, totality, and society may turn out to be manifestations of one category (said Durkheim). Second, God is in the details (said Aby Warburg). Conclusion: Come to think of it, I would rather stick with God.

First Exercise: The Total Social Fact

What is a *fait social total*? To give a terminological answer first: this term is a fusion of *fait social* and *totalité*, and the fusion itself lies in "reciprocity." I shall try to explain this fusion step by step. In introducing this term (or quasi-term) Mauss cites two chief moments when the "totality" of such a social fact is realized:

> The facts that we have studied are all, if we may be permitted the expression, *total* social facts, or, if we wish—although we do not prefer this word—general ones; that is, they set in motion in certain cases the whole of the society and its institutions (potlatch, clans confronting each other, tribes visiting each other, etc.), and in certain others, only a great number of institutions, particularly when these exchanges and these contracts concern more the individual. (Mauss [1925] 2016: 193)

An entire society with all its institutions is set in motion—is kept going and dynamized—and it becomes particularly conspicuous that it is about "society as a whole" when entire halves or divisions of a society face one another in an exchange of gifts or when the so-to-speak "international relations" of one tribe to another are concerned; even in individual records of gift exchange there is a "whole" that is challenged. Whenever the gift comes from individuals, this "totality" remains in play, pertaining to a multitude of institutions and undermining their division of labor. The second moment can serve as an explanation here: "All these phenomena are at the same time juridical, economic, religious, and even aesthetic, morphological etc." (Mauss [1925] 2016: 193). In Mauss's presentation, the moral, legal, economic and religious sides are emphasized, while the aesthetic side of things is neglected: the dances, songs, parades, dramatizations, the objects with their ornamentation, their performances, festivities, displays of respect, attestations of benevolence—"everything is a cause of aesthetic emotion and not only emotions of a moral order or based in interest" (193).

It is only through recognition of the gift's aesthetic dimension that we arrive at the third hallmark of the gift's holism. It surpasses the modern functional divisions, and it is this surpassing that not only makes for an entire "social system" but also for that fleeting, evanescent, historical, and affective moment when its members recognize one another as social beings:

> So these are more than themes, elements of institutions, complex institutions, even more than systems of institutions divided into religion, law (*droit*), economy, etc. They are 'wholes', complete social systems, whose functioning we have tried to describe . . . It is in considering the whole together that we have been able to perceive what is essential to them, the movement of the whole, the living aspect, the fleeting moment when society, or men, take full sensory consciousness of themselves and their situations vis-à-vis others. (Mauss [1925] 2016: 194)

At a first reading of these assertions—as well as in subsequent ones—they may seem like sociological incantations, and we are left with the impression of a long litany and moral invocation, which drones and tumbles and finally goes into a kind of tailspin, as the recapitulated terms and motifs in the conclusion gradually lose their ethnographic purchase and fixings. Especially the *fait social total* upon closer examination seems to transmogrify entirely into a holistic fog, which transcends everything—unless, that is, we understand it (as most recapitulations of the term do) as entirely heuristic. The archaic exchange of gifts cannot be categorized and structured by concepts framing the modern division of labor. It was just such an unfavorable impression that led Raymond Firth, after his personal encounter with Mauss, to speak of a "social mystic," and it is this impression that likewise necessitates our re-examination of the phrase *fait social total*.

The phrase *fait social total* is ultimately a pairing of two terms from two of Durkheim's major works: *fait social* from *The Rules of Sociological Method* and *totalité* from *The Elementary Forms of Religious Life*. As both terms were already defined by Durkheim—one might even say both books are in fact chiefly devoted to defining these terms—the above descriptions serve less to define the *fait social total* than to draw certain conclusions from a definition that is presupposed by the term (or again, quasi-term) and its shorthand. Mauss does not explain his punchline; its preconditions are simply assumed and therefore one must, at the very least, comprehend both components that have been paired.

Social facts, according to Durkheim, "consist of manners of acting, thinking and feeling external to the individual, which are invested with a coercive power by virtue of which they exercise control over him" (Durkheim [1895] 2013: 21). Or: "Distinctive features of the sociological facts: (1) their external character vis-à-vis individual consciousness, and (2) the coercion which they exercise or are capable of exercising on the consciousness" (21). Such a "social fact" is the compulsion felt by an individual to respond to a gift he or she has received—it comes from an "outside" along with the gift but then impacts one's consciousness. The gift—and in particular the "obligation to reciprocate," which it carries—thus fulfills the two conditions of a *fait social* in prototypical fashion. Moreover, it strikingly illustrates that "fundamental rule" in "consideration of the sociological facts," namely to regard those "sociological facts as things" (29). Finally, the received gifts are either things or are treated as things in the exchange of gifts; their entire description by Mauss stresses the "thingness" of personal obligations manifested in things given and received. Mauss is therefore only consistent when ascribing a (para-)sociological understanding of gifts to alien societies and their religious and legal mavens; and he recovers and interprets a clear awareness of precisely those moments that were enacted in the term *fait social* (e.g., Ranapiri's commentary on the Maori's *hau*): the externality of a social obligation and its tangibility. In taking on gifts, one not only creates this tangibility but also its social consciousness—hence his precise formulation: "where the society *takes*, where humans *take* sentimental consciousness of themselves and their situation vis-à-vis the other" (Mauss [1950] 2013: 275).

And then there is "the whole," *le tout*, and *la totalité*, and here we must go farther afield. Mauss summarized one of the projects of the Durkheim School in the following way:

> We have applied ourselves particularly to the social history of the categories of the human mind. We are trying to explain them one by one, starting quite simply and provisionally from the list of Aristotelian categories. We describe certain of their forms in certain civilizations and through this comparison we try to discover their moving spirit, and the reasons they are as they are. (Mauss [1938] 1979: 59–60)

The kind and number of these categories, which were to be promoted to self-awareness through a sociological derivation ("we are striving to find the moving nature in them"), despite their purported Aristotelian (as opposed to Kantian) template, was just as volatile or "provisional" as the derivation itself. "My uncle and teacher Durkheim discussed the notion of a *whole*, after having dealt with the notion of genus or kind together with me" ([1938] 1979: 60), writes Mauss, and it is in Durkheim's chief work on the derivation of categories that we find the most comprehensive of lists: time, place, space, substance, quantity (number and proportion), quality, relation, activity, and affliction [personality] (Durkheim [1912] 1995: 8), species, strength, person, causality (12). The task of a worldwide comparative sociology was to extrapolate these categories from their social origins:

> Not only do they come from society, but the very things they express are social. It is not only that they are instituted by society but also that their content is various aspects of the social being. The category of genus was at first [indistinguishable] from the concept of human group; the category of time has the rhythm of social life as its basis; the space society occupies provided the raw material for the category of space; collective force was the prototype for the concept of effective force, an essential element in the category of causality. (Durkheim [1912] 1995: 441, translation altered by me)

The concept of "the whole" stood above as well as in this list: "Since the role of the categories is to encompass all the other concepts, the category par excellence would indeed seem to be the very concept of *totality*" ([1912] 1995: 442). The categories constitute and produce "the fundamental conditions of understanding between minds" (441); they encompass all further concepts, which must refer to them and for their part are either accordant or contentious. And what encompasses the categories themselves, the all-encompassing "category of categories," can only be the most encompassing category of all, namely, that of all-encompassment itself: totality. From which social reality can this category be derived? It is worthwhile hearing Durkheim's argument out to the end:

> Since the world expressed by the whole system of concepts is the world society conceives of, only society can provide us with the most general notions in terms of which that world must be conceived. Only a subject that encompasses every individual subject has the capacity to encompass such an object. Since the universe exists only insofar as it is thought of and since it is thought of in its totality only by society, it takes place within the society; it becomes an element of society's inner life, and thus is itself the total genus outside which nothing exists. The concept of totality is but the concept of society in abstract form. It is the whole that includes all things, the supreme class that contains all other classes. Such is the underlying principle on which rest those primitive classifications that situated and classified beings of all the kingdoms, in the same right as men. But if the world is in the society, the space society occupies merges with space as a whole. As we have seen, each thing does indeed have its assigned place in social space. ([1912] 1995: 442–443)

In this passage Durkheim kills two birds with one stone. On the one hand, he offers what is still today a valid explanation of just why in every social system there emerges a cosmology that—through one and the same classification procedures—integrates a "society" into its exterior space (its "world") and integrates this exterior space into social relationships and their division of labor. On the other hand, in a comparison of societies and through an entirely analogous cosmological classification, he can equate the category of categories with society: "In all probability, the concepts of totality, society, and deity are at bottom merely different aspects of the same notion" ([1912] 1995: 443n18).

In view of these Durkheimian definitions, what could be the ultimate point of coining a new *terminus technicus* and call it a *fait social / total*? It is an obligation that obliges individual persons, dyads, groups of every magnitude, and even entire societies; that is to say, it is a *fait social* that particularizes the ostensible totality of one society by acting upon it "from outside." The gift is simultaneously a "total" obligation (in its central imperative of "reciprocity") when it integrates each and every entity (and, as Mauss puts it, every "institution" and adjustment based on the division of labor) into a more comprehensive whole, even the most comprehensive whole: "where the society *takes*, where humans *take* sentimental consciousness of themselves and their situation vis-à-vis the other" (Mauss [1950] 2013: 275). It is therefore no contradiction that Mauss no longer equated "totality" with the holism of a "religion" and its social self-worship but rather with the "international relations" of entangled societies and their magical precautions. The gift's *fait social total* must be effective on all levels of social integration and peaceableness. Outside of its imperative to reciprocate (*fait social*), there exists no sociality (which makes it a total fact). It supposedly undermines the illusion that an individual or a group, even of the highest order, might itself be this "totality" to which one is obliged to reciprocate a (return) gift. Rather, the total social fact itself is this "totality" from which the *fait social* of gift-giving proceeds, subjecting it to the "obligation to reciprocate." As stated above, a *fait social total* particularizes the seeming totality of "one" society and its categories—as the Melanesians undertake it in the *kula*—by entangling different societies in reciprocal obligations. Please allow me to hammer this point home once and for all: The *fait social total* is an anti-totalitarian concept.

Second Exercise: The Coercion to Freedom

Durkheim's most comprehensive execution of the category project was outlined for a particular ethnographic region (Australia) and simultaneously conceived as a prototype for the entire project. The *Elementary Forms* provided one of the main terms in "The Gift"—force—with a genealogy: "collective force became the prototype of the concept of effective force, an essential element of the category of causality" ([1912] 1995: 441). Causality was derived from "effectiveness" (*efficacité*) and this again from collective force: "Individuals die; the generations pass on and are replaced by others; but this force remains always present, alive, and the same" (191). Durkheim gives this underlying "force" the name *mana* and for Australia calls it the "totem principle"; but the same passage also provides the perhaps most famous phrase from the doctrine of corporations, namely that "corporations never die," and, a sentence further on, summons up the Leviathan: "a God without name . . . who is immanent in the world" (191)—or, as Hobbes called him: "this mortal god."

In his book on magic, written together with Henri Hubert, Mauss undertook his own derivation of the concept of collective "force" or *mana*, both notions having migrated into the aforementioned passages of Durkheim and, particularly, into his emphasis on ecstatic mass experience through which collective force becomes efficacious and tangible. Mauss could thus feel like the co-author and authentic interpreter of the category of collective "force." After all, he had developed the Durkheimian perspective of this concept.

In "The Gift" we witness a certain revision of the concept of "force" in at least three respects. The first of these is not as profound as one might think, for Mauss tends to avoid the words *mana* and "totem[-force]," which Durkheim equates with one another. This avoidance most likely is owed to a desire for a correct ethnographic usage that precluded making the word *mana* a surrogate for "force"—except, of course, in those passages where it could be used in its original Polynesian sense. The same desire also restricted the use of the word "totem," which, from an ethnographic standpoint, correlates clans with animal ancestors on the North American northwest coast. On the other hand, Mauss incessantly uses the word "force" as underlying an "obligation to reciprocate": if one is obligated to something it must be by a "force," which, with the unavoidable Durkheimian metalepsis, could only mean a collective force that equals the force of a collective.

Yet in view of the aforementioned sense of "totality" we must revise the corporate foundation of this "force," as (at the lower limit) the dyad of giver and taker is already sufficient to constitute a "collective." Its spontaneous generation permits the co-emergence of such an obligatory "force" while not restricting it to the corporate bodies and the corporateness of a single society (at the upper limit). It transcends any individual entity. The gift originates beneath and outside public bodies and in (other) very specific corporate entities where it becomes a reciprocal obligation.

The third aspect is that the ethnological implementation of a gift's "force" conjures up an image of the relation between freedom and social obligation that differs from the one envisaged in Mauss and Hubert's treatment of magic and from Durkheim's notion pertaining to Australian totemism. Mauss and Hubert's theory defined "magic" as the individual adoption of collective force to one's own purpose and to the possible detriment of others. This definition was applicable to what in most societies is categorized as "sorcery" or stigmatized as "witchcraft" and located in a dubious or even perverse space external to daytime consciousness. However, Mauss and Hubert left the benevolent aspect of "magic," always emphasized by its practitioners, unspecified while making the whole realm of individual "self-interest" appear like a highly suspect "adoption" of collective force. "The Gift" revised both these limitations: it neither denounces self-interest nor ignores the possible shift of magic into (suspicions and accusations of) witchcraft.

All of this came to pass—and how could it be otherwise—by dint of a contribution to the "category project." In 1921, Mauss lent commentary to a philosophical article on "causality and liberty" by suggesting a sociological derivation of these philosophical categories that linked up with the argument in "The Gift" but also in Durkheim's

Elementary Forms: the category of causality was derived from the idea of collective "efficacy," and this efficacy was realized and felt in an ecstatic community's collective festivals and rites. The ritual efficacy of ecstatic communities links the origins of the notion of causality to both the "reciprocity" of collective action and passion and the experience of an external "force" that derives from the reciprocity of rhythmic movements and is experienced as a collective *fait social*, recognized as a "force" of a specific collective but also as the force of any equally passionate collectivity. Looking back into the history of philosophical categories, this does not seem to be the world of Aristotle's or Kant's categories but rather the world of Hegel's logic or *Logik*. In the middle parts of Hegel's system, we encounter exactly those terms that Durkheim and Mauss employ to characterize ritual "effervescence": causality, force, reciprocity (*Wechselwirkung*), and a category whose relevance will be spelled out later, substance.

It is here that Mauss finds the origins of poetry—in rhythm, from the collective rhythms of the dances and songs. One might say that "poetry" was a later name given to the aesthetic form of the emergence of collective force, the force that is able to "make" or break collectives. Both Durkheim and Mauss stress that collective forces and efficacies are experienced and acknowledged as forces from "outside" the individual, as the force of a collective acting upon the individual, even when and especially when this individual is actively contributing to collective practices and their "reciprocity." The notion of individual "freedom," on the other hand, only gradually emerged from the earlier corporate ascriptions of "personhood" and "personality" and, in all likelihood, was initially guaranteed by the modern state. But it is precisely in this sense that "late" categories can be fundamental ones—that is, forming the basis of earlier societies: it is the sociological and especially statistical analysis of the modern category of (civil, political, religious, economic) "freedom" that proves it to be what it is, namely a "synthesis of necessity and contingency" (Mauss [1921] 1974: 124), meaning collective imperatives (which stipulate the category of an "individual" or a "self" who can give and take) and the respective contingency and its distribution as created by the social organization—a form of pre-consciousness: "Both of these forms of the notion of freedom only express the considerable growth in the number of possible actions available for the choice of the individual, the citizen in our nations. It is the reality and the number of contingencies that have given the meaning of contingency" (124).

If instead of applying these explanations to the modern citizen, one were—as Mauss does in "The Gift"—to apply them to the archaic "gift" and its giver, then freedom too emerges as an altogether analog "synthesis of necessity and contingency" where there is place for the feeling of individual "freedom" and the advocacy of self-interest as well as the implementation of social "effectiveness." In the second part of "The Gift" this feeling of a "freedom" to give—as well as of a freedom to refuse or defy—is abundantly emphasized by Mauss. This in turn implies that here too (in the Pacific Rim world from Melanesia to the Northwest Coast) there must be a sufficient "reality and number of contingencies" to enable such freedom. Money is involved here too, but in forms that do not lend themselves to bartering or naked market forces. As in our gifts and favors, contingency in these societies is enabled precisely by their lack of countability and their inability to detach them from persons, resulting in a lack of isometry. This distinguishes these forms from both modern money and ancient cash that originated in the idea of making payments isometrical. The quantity of types of gifts and their efficacies in the *kula* and potlatch—in conjunction with all the contingencies to which they were and had to be subject during their travels, while simultaneously stressing the taker's freedom of choice and the unpredictability of a return gift—were so considerable that one can aptly speak of a "synthesis of necessity and contingency" that may seem superior to any other form of "freedom" and that, instead of being guaranteed by a central political power, was only guaranteed through the exchange of gifts itself and the mutual obligations implied: the force of reciprocating, the efficacy of exchange, and the substance of gifts.

Despite these insights, inspired by his reading of Boas and Malinowski in particular, Mauss could not entirely free himself from the totalitarian image of an "archaic society" and from the idea of *l'homme total*, who is not modern, and his later writings may even be seen as something of a step backward in comparison to "The Gift." In reviewing Mauss's early and later writings and those of the Durkheim School, it is therefore worthwhile to retain the insights of "The Gift" and its ordering of categories. It is only in "The Gift" and the writings related to this text that Mauss acknowledges and even affirms the economic and social benefits of self-interest: "Interest and disinterestedness likewise explain this form of the circulation of wealth and the archaic circulation of the tokens of wealth that follow them around" (Mauss [1925] 2016: 188). Both self-interest and altruism explain the exchange of gifts, for both proceed from a sole necessity with its obligations and contingencies. The self-interest of a giver (speculating on the "credit" the gift will effect) and that of a taker (reciprocating the gift and thus inverting or mitigating the hierarchy between giver and taker) lies in the disinterestedness of the exchange of gifts—the willingness to give and receive and not destroy this relationship by immediate or identical return ("requitability"). And both then and now it is through this coincidence of opposites—self-interest and disinterestedness—that we have a mix of the categories of necessity and freedom: "A considerable part of our ethics and of our lives themselves still exists within this same atmosphere of the gift (*don*), of obligation and of liberty mixed together" (177), which from the standpoint of the individual means that one's self-interest and disinterestedness vis-à-vis the gift remains fundamentally uncertain or indistinguishable, even to the best (or worst) of one's efforts. Both interest and disinterest also hold true for the individual—she or he will not be able to isolate a decision that can divorce them from the other, at least not by giving gifts.

This emphasis on undecidability in "The Gift" is partly a reaction to Mauss and Hubert's earlier concept of "magic." One might even read "The Gift" as a kind of counter-text to that on magic, as a text that describes how societies create and maintain an entire reality or "effectivity" of anti-magic—matching only too well with descriptions of social times of crisis in which one can record both an increase in individual magic and in collective reactions attempting to expel it. But we can also read "The Gift" in a different way: as a recognition of a juridical, economic, categorial reality where both individual magic—as an individual appropriation of collective force—and its de-appropriation are envisaged. In "The Gift" we find both variants: a wholly programmatic stance, concluding with the ability to abnegate magic: "to lay down one's arms and renounce magic . . . [when] men have abandoned their reserve and been able to commit themselves to giving and reciprocating" ([1925] 2016: 196).

Yet in the same breath Mauss (borrowing from Bronisław Malinowski) cites the Trobriand view that explicitly states that for any successful exchange of gifts there must be magical preparations and influences: "[H]e might kill us. But see! I spit the charmed ginger root, their mind turns" ([1925] 2016: 196). It is safe to assume that Mauss saw no contradiction between these two sentences. Placing them back-to-back shows (as much else in the text) that for him magic and anti-magic, appropriation and de-appropriation, self-serving and charitable magic in the gift were meant to fuse. We have here a socialist variation on "The Fable of the Bees"—about the pursuit of one's self-interest in societies that are able to stick to rules supposed to guarantee the promotion of one's own well-being through the facilitation of the other's welfare. The self-interest of individual magic too is neutralized through its pursuit of other people's well-being and of their own "synthesis of necessity and contingency."

Summing up: it seems to be only in "The Gift" that Mauss redefines the category of "force" not only as a coercion by a collective force that acts upon the individual from outside but also as an experience of individual freedom and even self-interest, and he seems to do so not only for societies without a central government but for all societies.

We might add that the external appearance of this coming together is what Mauss all too sketchily (at least compared to Malinowski) describes as the aesthetic and poetic side of gift exchange—"an inextricable network of rites" ([1925] 2016: 62). One of the key or litany words of the text providing its cadences is the aforementioned "rhythm" of dances and festivals, performances and gestures, apparel and jewelry—namely, those phenomena in the category of collective effectivity (*efficacité*) that act upon the individual by way of a celebratory community perceiving itself in its collective "force" and each individual of that community likewise discerning itself in the rhythm and by dint of his or her desire and freedom to delight other individuals and collectives and share in their joy.

Third Exercise: Ambrosia

In 1906, subsequent to and in connection with their theory of magic—as well as initiating the publication strategy of the category project—Mauss and Hubert summarized their concept of *mana*:

> We said that mana is a category. But mana is not only a special category of primitive thought, and today, in the process of reduction, it is still the first form that other categories still working in our minds have taken: those of substance and cause. What we know about it therefore makes it possible to conceive how categories present themselves in the minds of primitives. (Hubert and Mauss [1906] 1968: 29)

As any reader of "The Gift" very soon perceives, the term "force" is one of the work's main words—the "obligation to reciprocate" is a "force" and has also remained a categorial word for the derivation of "cause" from collective effectivity. And as I have tried to show, the "force" that is nourished by the gift is very subtle. We may therefore rightly ask ourselves what—"in the process of reduction"—has become of the category of "substance." An attentive reading of Mauss's writings, as undertaken by Nick J. Allen, demonstrates that Mauss never lost sight of this second appearance of *mana* (and therewith Durkheim's "totem force") and that the entire text of "The Gift" comes to a head with a categorial augmentation and enhancement of "substance" (Allen 1998: 175–91).

A more detailed explication of this assertion requires a statement of the Maussian rules of the game. One of Durkheim's and Mauss's most important ordering schemas was the division of social phenomena into three spheres, which could then intersect or even mix with one another: (a) the sacred aspects of a society, the interaction and communication with supernatural powers ("religion," rites); (b) the impact of a society on itself (from a juridical and moral standpoint); and (c) the impact of a society on its environment ("magic," technology, science, mythology). In the case of both Durkheim and Mauss this tripartition (a, b, c) led to the basic ambiguity and problems of demarcation with which Mauss had to wrestle in all his later attempts at systemization, especially (a/c) his distinction between "religion" (self-influence) and "magic" (handling one's environment) and an analog distinction (a/c) between "rites" and "technologies"; moreover the distinction (a/b) between "sacred" and "profane," as witnessed by Durkheim's and Mauss's emphasis on the indivisibility of law and religion and by their shared secular view on religion (which turned religion into a part of juridical society even where it postulated the inverse for the society being described); also (a/c) in the mobility of institutions, things, persons and "texts" as well as in the impact of societies on alien societies in war and peace, in travel and conquests.

The exciting or disorienting or even dizzying aspect of "The Gift" was, among other things, that this tripartition simultaneously involved a blurring of their boundaries—ultimately it is about both "international" and religious as well as "anti-magic" phenomena. On the one hand, the category of "force" is part of religion and is introduced as such by both Durkheim (with his "totem force") and Mauss (especially with his *hau*); on the other hand, the category of "substance" deals with both social relationships and a person's relationship to the environment. And this category is both the most materialistic and the most mystical of the categories employed by Mauss.

It is particularly in the third chapter where this hidden esoteric aspect (and categorial reordering) occurs or is intended to occur (as another kind of *mana*, that of social anti-magic, of de-appropriation). The relevant key and litany word, as it were, is revealed by Mauss very early on: "Among those with which we are familiar, take for example that of substance, to which I have devoted highly technical attention; how many vicissitudes has it not undergone? For example, among its prototypes there is a different notion, especially in India and Greece, the notion of food" (Mauss [1939] 1974: 32). Yet the relevant studies undertaken by Mauss were never concluded, his last two scholarly lectures were therefore a kind of bequest (cryptically condensed secrets that would have needed a monographic treatment). They deal with the notion of "person" and the category of the self (or "I"), and finally, the genealogy of "matter" and within it the category of "substance." In his last scholarly lecture he so condensed his material that it decomposes into a periodic table comprised of ethnographic and terminological abbreviations and deals with the two main subjects of forest (*silva, hyle, materies*) and food:

> Thus, food connotes subsistence (*subsistance* in French is used as synonym for food) and also substance or matter. For the Romans the notion of subsistence formed the root of substance. . . . The evolution of the notion is analogous in Sanskrit. The meaning of the word has changed along with the changing society. . . . The fine works of Baldwin Spencer and F. J. Gillen on the Arunta of Australia, as well as those of contemporary ethnographers, allow us to extend our theory of the relationship between the notions of matter and of food. In effect, the same complex rites of initiation relating to food can be found among most primitive peoples today. Towards the age of twenty-one, the time when some of us are preparing for the "aggregation" examinations—one of the initiation rites of the "civilized"—the so-called savage for his part is granted the *power to eat*. In other words, he receives his initiation into food, or rather, it is necessary that the owner of a totem *opens his mouth* for him. He will then be able to eat the sacred animal when it will be revealed to him, through images or masks, what the totem is. These images and masks (depending on the tribe) thus grant a power, a new breath in relation to the animal over which they exert power. (Mauss [1939] 2006: 143–44)

This passage is a final and ultimate affirmation of the Durkheim School and its category project. But the text is quite cryptic, and although it refers to studies Mauss undertook before World War I, the immediate context one cannot help detecting between the lines is the end of the interwar years and the threat of another world war (which ended Mauss' scholarly career and writings). As such, it demands a line-by-line commentary that would be as long as some of the early essays of Mauss and Hubert. Here a brief treatment by way of which I will return to "The Gift" must suffice. The passage addresses "rites of passage," "modes of thought," and the totemic ancestry of the Durkheim School, in person and in substance.

The reference is not solely a comment on French academic socialization (a "Persian letter," as it were) and on the initiation of "civilized" man, which Mauss himself had undergone, but it also alludes to the terminology of Van Gennep (whose pursuit of a university career was hindered by the Durkheim School and Mauss in particular) and to his "rites of passage," where the *agrégation* or receipt of the highest teaching diploma (together with the explicit homonym: "admission into a society," "admission into an association," "state exam," "competition among doctors of law and medicine to be appointed as members of their faculty") became a term for one's reincorporation after an initiation. And there is a further meeting in the shafts of this mine, namely between those old friends and opponents—Mauss and Lévy-Bruhl—in the passage on the food initiation. It can be read as a more thorough variant of Mauss's objection to Lévy-Bruhl's "primitive mentality" and indeed the most important and sole riposte (written and discussed in 1923, i.e., in the same year as "The Gift") where Mauss criticizes and redefines Lévy-Bruhl's term of "participation":

> Participation is not only a confusion. It involves an effort to confuse and an effort to make each other resemble the other. It is not a simple resemblance, but a *homoiosis* . . . willingness to bind. For example, the totemic ritual of initiation as a whole is indeed a ritual of "participation" if you will, but above all it is a ritual of revelation; its purpose is to show young initiates that the beings they believe to be animals, for example, are in reality men and spirits. And, on the other hand, the effective rituals of totemism are efforts to show nature, plants and animals that one is what they are. So that, even in these primitive forms of *homoiosis*, there is an act: man identifies himself with things and identifies things with himself, having simultaneously the sense and the differences and the similarities that he establishes. (Mauss [1923] 1974: 130)

This passage from 1923 explains the difference between the Maussian interpretation and that of Lévy-Bruhl concerning alien "modes of thought" (with the categories included): Mauss accepts difference-before-identification and confusion only as a conscious con-*fusion* in explicit (juridical and religious) acts of (secondary) identification. Accordingly, in "The Gift" one finds just one single footnote on Lévy-Bruhl, which analogously states that one might also speak of "participation"—but it is about juridical identifications and their form and ends with an odd truncation: "We are dealing with the principle here, and there is no need to go into the consequences" (Mauss [1925] 2016: 98n54). In other words: the "principle" of the gift is (also) another and better definition of "participation." If one is to seek an answer on the part of Lévy-Bruhl to this Maussian critique, then his later book *Mythologie Primitive* (1935) is unavoidable. It puts the ball back in Mauss's court and deals above all with those mythical metamorphoses (of a confusion-before-identity) upon which any explicit equivalencies in (Australian and other) initiations can be based.

As we now know, in the long run Mauss prevailed; yet he owed a whole line of reasoning to Lucien Lévy-Bruhl, one of the most popular European philosophers of the interwar years, far more popular than any of the Durkheimians could even dream of becoming (then), and a Dreyfusard and socialist like Durkheim and Mauss. A friend, but also a source of misunderstanding, because for instance in Germany, Durkheim's *fait social* and Lévy-Bruhl's *participation mystique* were thought to elucidate each other (even for Ludwik Fleck). But this is not the only correction. From an ethnographic standpoint, Durkheim's *Elementary Forms* did not hold up, as Mauss and Hubert both knew before and became painfully aware after its publication. Read as a monograph on Australian religion, the book was bound to distort the reality of Australian social structure and Aboriginal religion. Mauss nevertheless reiterated Durkheim's "totemism" (from Spencer and Gillen), though not in the form of Durkheim's preferred "sacrificial communion" but as a form of initiation act: of "opening the mouth" (*ouvre la bouche*). And this initiation (into the "totem") is always an initiation with the fundamental equivalence: substance as subsistence. Food is the stuff of which man is made, and if one is to become a particular "new human," then it is through a new eating ability—"the authority to eat" what is forbidden to others or can only be authorized to be eaten by one's own group. Through this insight and practice (which is not restricted to the Australian continent) Mauss was able to en passant deploy a whole slew of colonial attestations of cannibalism so as to explain the notion of (originally) being "made from the same stuff as the other": "Anecdotes abound on this subject, for instance that of the English colonist told by a Maori: 'We are somewhat related; my ancestors ate yours'" (Mauss [1939] 2006: 144).

Looking for this equivalency of substance and sustenance in "The Gift," we find references to food and nutriment on almost every page. Mauss first makes these references in his introduction discussing the quasi-term "potlatch," the Chinook word for their agonistic exchange of gifts ([1925] 2016: 62–63): "'Potlatch' essentially means 'to nourish,' 'to consume'" (62). And somewhat twisting the philological evidence, he adds: "In fact, for the word potlatch, Boas gives—in Kwakiutl, it is true, and not in Chinook—the meaning of 'feeder,' nourisher and literally 'place of being satiated' . . . But the two senses of potlatch, gift (*don*) and food, are not mutually exclusive, the essential form of the prestation here being alimentary, in theory at least" (62n13). Gift and food can be one and the same. Indeed "The Gift" speaks always of food, eating and consumption—that is to say, in the categorial shadow life of the text, it speaks of "substance."

Having drawn this equivalency with its numerous juridical and religious acts—substance has turned into food, and food into the most basic and pervasive gift. And yet the third chapter of "The Gift" intensifies the food motif that one might even call a *leitfmotif*. It is no accident that the chapter concludes on a Wagnerian note with Rhinegold and Hagen's cup; that is to say, one final encoding and decryption of the category substance, which in the book's later condensation (Mauss [1939] 2006) went missing. In light of our discussion hitherto, the following summary of the Hindu doctrine of reincarnation cannot come as a great surprise: "One is reborn in the next world with the nature of those from whom one accepts food, or of those whose food one has in one's belly, or the food itself" (Mauss [1925] 2016: 169n100). In the future life—in the eternal cycle of reincarnation—food is translated into identity and substance into subsistence. And it is in India where Mauss also finds that strongest imperative to give, enunciating in verse the other form of substance, a blessing and a curse that is spoken by the divinity of food himself (i.e., a prosopopoeia of substance):

> He who, without giving me to the gods, to the shades, to his servants and his guests, consumes me when prepared, and in his madness (thus) swallows poison, I consume him, I am his death.
> But for him who offers up the *agnihotra*, accomplishes the *vaishwadeva*, and then eats—contentedly, in purity and faith—what remains after he has fed those that he should feed, for him I become ambrosia, and he has pleasure in me. (quoted in Mauss [1925] 2016: 164)

Mauss comments this old Vedic code as follows: "It is the nature of food to be shared"; not to share it with others is "to kill its essence to destroy it for oneself and for others." And he continues: "This is the interpretation, both materialist and idealist, that Brahminism has given to charity and hospitality" ([1925] 2016: 164). This self-interpretation of "food" (and that of Mauss) is about substance and the category of "substance"; but it is also about that *mélange* of person and thing or "spiritual matter, comprising things and people" (75) that is produced through receiving a gift. The prosopopoeia of food merely encapsulates what the entire text is meant to weave together in a juridical, economic, and categorial exegesis:

> We realize clearly and logically that, in this system of ideas, one must give back to the other what is in reality a part of his own nature and substance, for to accept something from someone is to accept something of his spiritual essence of his soul. To keep this thing would be dangerous and life-threatening, not simply because it would be illicit, but also because this thing comes from the person, not only morally but physically and spiritually too, this essence, this nourishment, these goods, movable or immovable, these women or these descendants, these rites and these communions, create a magical and religious hold over you. ([1925] 2016: 72–73)

What Mauss means by "food" is the material nutriment, any materiality, the cosmological category of substance, the essence or "immaterial substance" of all sociality, namely that it is made by alien persons and societies; and this food protects itself from misuse by a (magic/anti-magic) precautionary measure and inversion. In consuming it one must share it with others, then it will be inexhaustible and delicious; else it turns into poison and one is consumed by it, as a body is consumed by a fire: "I will consume him, I am his death."

An apotropaic curse, spoken by a personification of food and poison. Is this not one of the saddest passages in "The Gift"—the lethality and mortality of the "deathless force"? In opening the *Année sociologique*, series II, and then (sequentially) perusing the frontispiece of the dead master and reading the many obituaries of those members of the Durkheim School who died in World War I, it can also be read as a collective memorial to the Durkheim School falling apart by dying in the trenches, only to survive in British Social Anthropology ever since (after emerging within the German dream of a post-Hegelian sociology that was dreamt for nearly a century but never realized in Germany). Followed by the "Essai sur le don" and the passage on the prosopopoeia of food and the erstwhile "totem force," this Indian quotation marks an extreme, both as a warning and as an apotropaic formula or epitaph. Corporations never die, they say. But in losing their mortal members and not being able to initiate new members, they are mortal too.

The Encore Exercise:
German Beer, or The Poison in the Gift

The food you eat can transform into poison, and this poison will speak from beyond the grave—but it consumes you not in the afterlife (as ordained in the cycle of reincarnation) but in present life—it kills, it eats you. This complement to the gift, this reverse gift quoted by Mauss, seems to cover all gifts in the Germanic section of his Indo-Germanic analysis, especially pertaining to the reception of the gift, which in the juridical and religious formulae was originally expressed as a kind of "being possessed":

> The danger that the thing given or transferred represents is, without doubt, nowhere better sensed than in the very ancient Germanic law (*droit*) and languages. This explains the double meaning of the word *gift* in all these languages: gift (*don*) on the one hand, poison on the other... This theme of the deadly gift (*don*), of the gift (*cadeau*) or the goods that turn into poison, is fundamental in Germanic folklore. (Mauss [1925] 2016: 174)

It is through this double German/Dutch/English meaning that the words *Gift* (= the English word "poison") and *Gabe* (= the English word "gift") converge. In the text of "The Gift," a cycle closes and an advanced philology meets conjectural phantasy. On the one hand, Mauss began "The Gift" with citations from the "Edda" dealing with just this ambiguity and its danger—with the Germanic folklore of amity and enmity, peace and treachery, gifts and revenge; and on the other hand, in 1924, Mauss wrote a piece dealing with German philology for a Strasbourg Festschrift ("Mélanges Charles Andler") that presaged "The Gift" and expressed in a wholly programmatic fashion that succinct summary that concluded not only this Indo-Germanic section but the entire ethnographic and historical examination of the "The Gift." Here he reaffirmed this etymological encapsulation, which on a deeper level of the categories doctrine was intended to replace the expunged term *mana* (having a common root for the categories of "efficacy" and "substance"—"those of substance and cause") by an etymology that, by dint of a comma, separated everything that was to be shared with others as regards food and gifts—the root for which there is no cure, an apotropaic excommunication: "gift, gift" (Mauss [1924] 1969: 46–51).

In his 1924 text "Gift-Gift" Mauss conjectured a different etymology for the homonymy of *Gift* and "gift"—in Dutch, German, and English—than had been proposed in most previous examinations, which simply traced both words back to the Greek-Latin *dosis*. Mauss, for his part, postulated it was the Teutons' drinking of beer, which accompanied and framed every exchange of gifts, that included the possibility of a magical or material "poisoning":

> Indeed, the typical service among the former Germans and Scandinavians is the gift of drink, beer; in German, the present par excellence is that which is poured (Geschenk, Gegengeschenk). There is no need to mention here a very large number of topics of Germanic law and mythology. But one can see: nowhere could the uncertainty about the good or bad nature of gifts be greater than in practices of this kind where donations consisted essentially of drinks drunk together, libations offered or to be given back. The drink gift can be poison; in principle, except in a sinister drama, it is not; but it can always become one. In any case, it is always a charm (the word *gift* has kept this meaning in English) that binds communicators forever and that can always turn against one of them if he or she is trespassing beyond the law. (Mauss [1924] 1969: 49)

From where precisely Mauss drew this conjecture remains unclear, since his evidence is restricted to reference works and Tacitus. The liveliest depiction of the Teutons' beer-drinking, which gives it the status of a true *fait social total* like the potlatch, can be found in Vilhelm Grønbech's *Die Kultur und Religion der Germanen* (Culture and religion of the Teutons). According to him, beer gradually came to saturate all aspects of Germanic life (see especially part II from 1912):

> That it is the ale bowls which dominate in all thought of feasting together shows through the mere names of the banquets. A homecoming was celebrated by a welcoming ale, and when the guest left he was sped on his way with a parting ale, life commenced with a christening ale, and passed by way of betrothing ale and bride ale, drinking one's wedding, to the arvel or burial ale—a series of "ales" to fit each particular occasion. It is with good reason that the frith which embraces the parties at a feast is called ale-frith, and the feast day *mungátstiðir*, i.e., ale days. (Grønbech [1912] 1931: 313)

And every beer was accompanied by gifts. Grønbech writes:

> In the gift, the door is opened to the Germanic will to peace; but at the same time, a host of psychological mysteries pour in ... The gift carries with it an obligation; under whatsoever circumstances it is given, it is binding nevertheless, and that with an obligation the force of which, in justice to itself, demands such strong words as these: the receiver is in the giver's power. ([1912] 1931: 232).

Along with the gift there comes an indissoluble ambiguity: "All that a gift could do, food and drink could also bring about; it could mean honour or dishonour, could bind and loose, give good fortune" and act as a good luck charm (281). Grønbech's vivid descriptions served as an important inspiration and explicit source for a linguistic work on the margins of the Durkheim School, stewarded by Antoine Meillet, and devoted to Germanic beer-drinking (Cahen 1921). Mauss did not mention Grønbech, so Cahen's work, which doubtlessly was known to him, can be seen as indirect evidence for his debt to Grønbech, as Cahen refers both to Mauss and to Grønbech. And so it came about that Mauss, through his reading of Indo-Germanic studies, was prepared to not only discern but recognize the exchange of gifts among the Trobriand peoples:

> The Franks virtually do have their own customs: they "throw" their *festuca*—which correspond with the vadium mentioned above—into the arms of the other party. There is a vestige in this procedure of the olden urgent kind to endorse property in a such way that it completely delivers itself to the receiver ... The Frankish gesture may have had a completely distinct emphasis: the giver hands over the item without touching it on its way and thus entirely dispatches it to the receiver. (Grønbech 1961 [1912]: 344, my translation)

Accordingly, Marcel Mauss found in Bronisław Malinowski's Trobriand peoples the most direct conception of what he had extracted from the Teutons in his conjecture *gift, gift*—namely images about the exchange of gifts, of beer, of the agonal nature of international peace, which cannot be controlled only through pledges, but also through that abrupt gesture that throws down the gauntlet of one's pledges at the recipient's feet:

> The *gage, wage, -wadium, vadi*, which binds the master and the servant, the lender and the debtor, the buyer and the seller, is magical and ambiguous. It is both good and dangerous; it is thrown at the contractor's feet in a gesture of trust and caution, distrust and defiance at the same time. Curiously enough, this is still the most solemn way of exchange among the bold sailors and traders of the Melanesian islands of the Trobriands. (Mauss [1924] 1969: 49)

The footnote appends the illustration credits: Bronisław Malinowski, "Argonauts of the Western Pacific," plates LXI, LXII, and the frontispiece. Watching *ambrosia* or *beer* in action. The *kula* of French Indo-Germanic studies, the most sophisticated sequel to Tacitus and in 1924: an unparalleled declaration of peace.

And One Final German Footnote

Etymology is a tricky business. Looking for the bifurcations and convergences of words and stems, one may be on the wrong track and nevertheless pave the way for others, simultaneously. Mauss's conjecture on the poison in the gift of Germanic beer has so far failed to convince the scholarly community. On the other hand, the convoluted and hyper-compressed summary of his work on the category of "substance" has been vindicated, or could in many respects be vindicated, both linguistically and materially. Mauss could not know that just a few years later, after World War II, a Germanist and Indo-Germanic linguist (and, not to forget the usual nasty surprise: a formerly quite enthusiastic National Socialist party member) would publish a series of books dwelling on quite similar etymologies for "forest" (*nemus*) and "food" and "taking" (*nehmen*)—and called them "etymologies from the coppice" where foliage was the most important food source for animals driven into the woods.

There is even a strong material or materialist argument for the etymological identification of the category of "substance" with "food" and "wood": organisms are those things in the world and, indeed, in the cosmos that require "food," and the vast majority of biomass, the basis of organic matter on this planet, is "wood." From an ecological point of view, both the basis of organic subsistence and the substance of substance may be identified in the equation of "food" and "wood." Thus, this identification or equation may be found in many places of the world, and in historically unrelated languages and cultures.

And speaking of historical German-French relationships between one humiliating encounter at Versailles and the next, the discipline of sociology was built on the foundational category of reciprocity twice, and on both sides of the Rhine: by Durkheim and Mauss on the one hand, and by Georg Simmel on the other: in his "Soziologie" published in 1908, many years after his early exchange with Durkheim and Mauss. Georg Simmel's term was *Wechselwirkung* and translated as *réciprocité* in French and as "interaction" in English; the result being two German sociological terms that nowadays are divorced from their philosophical origins and are called *Interaktion* and *Reziprozität*, respectively, due to Mauss and to US sociology. In Simmel's book, *Wechselwirkung* is declared to be the foundational category, and Simmel goes to great pains to explain the externality and objectivity of social phenomena. It was too early or too late for a sociological "rapprochement," though. Mauss uses the word *réciprocité* only once in "Le don," and in the most entangled and conjectural passage of speculating on the formal mechanisms of early Roman Law (before Roman Law split the rights of persons from the rights of things). The oblique references and deliberate esotericism in the Indo-Germanic part of "Le don" point to a German-French series of philosophical and scholarly rivalry and exchange, of interaction and reciprocity, that began in the eighteenth century and proved to be crucial for the establishment of sociology as a university discipline, and of social anthropology as a theoretical discipline coming to terms with corporate relationships and, in Nick J. Allen's succinct Maussian formula: categories and classifications.

Erhard Schüttpelz is Professor for Media Theory at the University of Siegen. His research focuses on the history of literature and media in the globalized modernity and the history of science in media theory and cultural anthropology. He is the author of, among other monographs and many articles, *Die Moderne im Spiegel des Primitiven. Weltliteratur und Ethnologie 1870–1960* (2005, Munich). He edited, together with Tristan Thielmann, the influential volume *Akteur-Medien-Theorie* (2013, Bielefeld), which includes translations of the most important media investigations of French actor-network theory. He was a Kraut Rock musician in his youth and participated in the Cologne and New York art scenes of the early 1990s, and his last opus is a film on Aby Warburg and Hopi Snake Ritual (with Anselm

Franke): *A Kind of World War* (Haus der Kulturen der Welt, 2021). His next book publication will be *Das Medium vor den Medien* (The Medium before media, 2022).

Note

The research of this article was part of the Collaborative Research Centre *1187 Media of Cooperation funded by the German Research Foundation (DFG) – Project number 262513311.*

References

Allen, Nicholas J. 1998. "The Category of Substance: A Maussian Theme Revisited." In *Marcel Mauss: A Centenary Tribute*, ed. Wendy James and Nicholas J. Allen, 175–91. Oxford: Berghahn.

Cahen, Maurice. 1921. *Études sur le vocabulaire religieux du Vieux-Scandinave: La libation*. Paris: Librarie Ancienne Honoré Champion.

Durkheim, Émile. [1895] 2013. *The Rules of Sociological Method and Selected Texts on Sociology and its Methods*. Basingstoke: Palgrave Macmillan.

———. [1912] 1995. *The Elementary Forms of Religious Life*. New York: The Free Press.

Grønbech, Vilhelm. [1912] 1931. *The Culture of the Teutons*. Oxford: Oxford University Press. Reprint: Liberty Jotun's Bane: Kindred 2010.

———. [1912] 1961. *Die Kultur und Religion der Germanen*. Darmstadt: Wissenschaftliche Buchgesellschaft.

Hubert, Henri, and Marcel Mauss. [1906] 1968. "Introduction à l'analyse de quelques phénomènes religieux." In Marcel Mauss, *Œuvres I. Les fonctions sociales du sacré*, ed. Victor Karady, 3–39. Paris: Minuit.

Lévy-Bruhl, Lucien. 1935. *Mythologie Primitive*. Paris: Librairie Félix Alcan.

Mauss, Marcel. [1921] 1974. "Catégories collectives de pensée et liberté." In Marcel Mauss, *Œuvres II. Représentations collectives et diversité des civilisations*, ed. Victor Karady, 121–25. Paris: Minuit.

———. [1923] 1974. "Mentalité primitive et participation." In Marcel Mauss, *Œuvres II: Représentations collectives et diversité des civilisations*, ed. Victor Karady, 125–31. Paris: Minuits.

———. [1924] 1969. "Gift-Gift." In Marcel Mauss, *Œuvres III: Cohésion sociale et divisions de la sociologie*, ed. Victor Karady, 46–51. Paris: Minuit.

———. [1925] 2016. "Essay on the Gift: The Form and Sense of Exchange in Archaic Societies." In Marcel Mauss, *The Gift: Expanded Edition*, ed. Jane I. Guyer, 55–201. Chicago: Hau Books.

———. [1938] 1979. "A Category of the Human Mind: The Notion of Person, the Notion of 'Self.'" In Marcel Mauss, *Sociology and Psychology. Essays*, trans. Ben Brewster, 57–95. London: Routledge and Kegan Paul.

———. [1939] 1974. "Conceptions *qui ont* précédé la notion *de* matière." In Marcel Mauss, *Œuvres II: Représentations collectives et diversité des civilisations*, ed. Victor Karady, 161–69. Paris: Minuit.

———. [1939] 2006. "Conceptions which Have Preceded the Notion of Matter." In Marcel Mauss, *Techniques, Technology and Civilisation*, ed. Nathan Schlanger, 141–47. Oxford: Berghahn.

———. [1950] 2013. "Une catégorie de l'esprit humain: La notion de personne celle de 'moi.'" In Marcel Mauss, *Sociologie et anthropologie*, 333–62. Paris: Presses Universitaires Paris.

Chapter 8

DURKHEIMIAN THINKING AND THE CATEGORY OF TOTALITY

Nick J. Allen

If the totality of things is conceived as a single system, this is because society itself is seen in the same way.

—Émile Durkheim and Marcel Mauss, *Primitive Classification*, 1963

In referring to Durkheimian thinking rather than Durkheim my title is deliberately ambiguous. Of course Émile Durkheim himself is relevant, but so is his nephew: Marcel Mauss's thinking was probably more Durkheimian than anybody else's has been, though the influence was not only from elder to younger. However, this chapter is mostly a case study of how the category of totality has influenced the thinking of one would-be Durkheimian or Maussian, namely myself; but I hope it will help others to appreciate, and adapt to their own purposes, an underused but versatile mental tool. To follow the terminology of William Watts Miller (2012: x–xiii), the chapter is directed not only to the mythic or historical Durkheim but also to the "living Durkheim."

As many readers will know, Durkheim introduces *Elemental Forms* by emphasizing that the book is not only about the origin and nature of religion, but also about the sociology of knowledge or, more precisely, about the categories, and he lists the following: "time, space, class, number, cause, substance, person, etc." (Durkheim [1912: 13] 1995: 8). It is only at the end of the book that he returns to the topic and fills out the "etc.," adding the category of totality:[1] "There is perhaps no category that is more essential: for since the role of the categories is to envelop all other concepts, it does indeed seem that the category par excellence ought to be the very concept of totality" (442; translation modified by the author). Moreover: "The concept of totality is only the abstract form of the concept of society: it is the whole that embraces all things, the supreme class that includes all other classes" (443; translation modified by the author). And soon afterward a richly suggestive footnote contributes a third abstraction: "basically, the concepts of totality, society, and divinity are probably only different aspects of one single notion" (443).

As Durkheim mentions, and as his nephew recalls when introducing his essay on the category of the person (Mauss [1938] 1985: 2), the idea of the "essential" category of totality goes back to their joint work *Primitive Classification*—to the passage I have used as an epigraph.

When I am asked what I have studied apart from Himalayan ethnography, I list three topics—a world-historical approach to kinship systems; the French tradition in anthropology, especially Mauss and his followers; and Indo-European cultural comparison (for instance, comparison between Homer and the Sanskrit *Mahābhārata*). In all three fields, the category of totality has proved helpful, albeit in the different ways explored in this chapter. By way of rough overview, the three topics can be said to relate respectively to the *Division of Labour* (Durkheim [1893] 1926), to the *Rules of Sociological Method* (Durkheim [1895] 1919) taken together with the *Année sociologique*, and to *Elemental Forms* (Durkheim [1912] 1995). If Watts Miller's (2012) title is *A Durkheimian Quest: Solidarity and the Sacred*, the present effort could be subtitled "Solidarity, Science, and the Sacred." A good deal of what I say can be found in Nicholas Allen (2000), which I am here trying to condense, reorganize, and supplement; however, I shall avoid irritating the reader by referring to it at every point where it is somehow relevant.

Kinship

So what about kinship and the category of totality? As Mauss said in 1927 (Mauss 2005: 37), "In a quarter century of writing, Durkheim never lost sight of the problem of *l'ensemble*, which is basically that of the *Division of Labour* as it is of the *Elemental Forms*." The word *ensemble* here scarcely differs in sense from *totalité*. The very notion of division implies a whole that is divided—in this context then, the totality of work carried out by a society. One recalls the subtitle Durkheim gave to his main thesis in 1893—"A Study of the Organisation of

Higher Societies." The subtitle puts the emphasis squarely on his idea of "organic" solidarity, the phenomenon shown by a society whose component groups are held together by the differentiated and specialized activities they contribute to it. At the same time, it removes emphasis from the "mechanical" solidarity shown by the "lower" or "tribal" societies, which are held together by the similarity of the clans composing them.

While it is easy to criticize the assumptions about tribal societies held by a thesis-writer in the early 1890s, a more relevant issue here is what scope exists for Adam's Smith's phrase "division of labor" to be applied to a society lacking occupational specialisms in the ordinary sense. Clearly some sort of scope exists—being provided by the biology of sex and age, but the point must be taken a little further. The minimum work carried out by any society that endures is its own reproduction, which depends on spouses (or partners) and children—in other words on the rules of marriage and recruitment that constitute what we call "kinship."

Kinship is usually thought of by starting from an individual—an ego, in anthropological jargon. Ego is born with a certain number of relatives scattered across genealogical space—primary relatives in the nuclear family, secondary ones such a parent's siblings, tertiary ones such as first cousins, and so on. As ego grows older, the children of relatives replace the relatives who die, and marriage results in a clutch of new relatives. But in modern or large-scale societies the domain of those counted as relatives fades out after tertiary relatives and never approaches the demographic extent of society. This situation, and the concomitant view of kinship, can be called egocentric.

But kinship can also be approached from the other end, by starting from the totality that is society. For simplicity let us ignore immigration and assume the society to be endogamous, so that all its new members are born from parents who are already members. Now in practice, whether they are large or small, societies are composed of distinct units. Usually such units, for instance, clans or castes, are clearly bounded, but theoretically it makes little difference if they form a continuum divided up by statisticians or popular stereotypes—as applies to classes. Sharply bounded or not, they are normally structured by rules of marriage ("horizontally") and rules of recruitment ("vertically"). It is the combination of these two sorts of rule that governs the reproduction or continuity of the sociostructural units and therefore of society. This view of kinship is sociocentric. Of course ego still has relatives, but their domain becomes secondary. They are distributed within or across the units established by the sociocentric rules.

Even the younger Durkheim knew well that the division of society into units related to kinship, in which he was deeply interested. He opened the first volume of the *Année sociologique* with his article on incest and exogamy (Durkheim 1898); he reviewed books on family and kinship, and wrote specialist articles on Australian kinship. In 1903, he and Mauss open their presentation of Australian material by referring to the four marriage classes typical of a tribe—the sociostructural units nowadays called "sections." Mauss followed up the topic here and there, for instance in his important 1932 article on "Social Cohesion in Polysegmentary Societies" (Mauss 1969: 11–26). But neither of them (let alone Claude Lévi-Strauss) poses the basic question of relating sociocentric and egocentric kinship. We need to ask: under what conditions would the two aspects of kinship come as close to each other as is logically possible?

It is an anthropological commonplace that, in a small-scale society, ego may regard all members of society as relatives, and classify them under the same kinship vocabulary as is applied to close relatives. Such kinship terms are technically called "classificatory." But this formulation leaves the semantics of the terminology entirely obscure. For instance, how many terms are needed in the simplest case?

The answer I proposed in the 1980s was called "tetradic theory."[2] If one starts from society as a whole and asks how it may most simply be divided into units on the basis of marriage and recruitment, the answer is as follows. Split the totality into two endogamous units: all the children born to members of A belong to unit B, and vice versa; all children born to parents in B belong in unit A. So A and B are endogamous "generation moieties." But so far, the only thing said about marriage is that it is within the moiety, and the next step is to split each endogamous moiety into two exogamous sections (say 1 and 2). The result is an ordinary four-section structure for society and a corresponding division of ego's relatives into four categories. Whether individuals are thought of sociocentrically, as members of society and its subgroups, or egocentrically, as relatives of ego, the dividing lines between the units or categories are the same, but the two sorts of entity have different sorts of label. A section can be given a name (e.g., A1 or B2), which is valid throughout the tribe, while the kinship term applied to a category will vary according to the section of ego. If a four-term kinship terminology seems implausibly minimal, one can easily double the number of terms by postulating a gender affix (e.g., one marking opposite sex to ego).

Tetradic theory can be elaborated and explicated in various other directions that need not concern us here. Of course, no perfect tetradic society has ever been reported: the model has been constructed by putting together phenomena suggested by the ethnography—a method that may recall what Durkheim did in *Elemental Forms* to the fieldwork reports from Australia. In any case, the theory offers what is logically the simplest way for a society to achieve a plausible kinship-based social solidarity, and I suppose that its development was a milestone in human evolution. But the theory can hardly be presented without starting from the idea of society as a totality.

A Science of Sociology

As is both obvious and well known, the idea of society as a totality is central to Durkheim's concept of the new discipline that he intended to found, demarcating it both from philosophy and from psychology. The social facts that the discipline was to collect, organize, and analyze presupposed the notion of a society into which individuals were socialized. Furthermore, the category of totality enters into the Durkheimian conception of how social facts can and should be classified. The rubrics used by the *Année sociologique* not only offered a practical division of labor between contributors to the yearbook, but also gave order to what might otherwise have been a chaos of heterogeneous information. The rubrics needed to organize sociology continued to preoccupy Mauss in the 1920s and 1930s, and sometimes he presents them as a set of five. Society consists of people and things, and "social morphology" labels this the most material of the rubrics—it views people as bodies distributed across space and across time. Working upward toward the more ideological, we come next to the three "special sociologies"—economic, juridical, and religious—to end with the crown of the subject, namely, "general sociology." While acknowledging this established label, Mauss preferred to refer to the social facts falling under it by using the adjective "total." As he says at the end of *The Gift*, such phenomena in certain cases "involve the totality of society and its institutions (potlatch, clans confronting one another, tribes visiting one another, etc.), and in other cases only a very large number of institutions, particularly when these exchanges and contracts rather concern the individual" (Mauss [1925] 1990: 100).

Whatever the theoretical value of the rubric "general sociology" in systematic presentations of social phenomena, I find it useful at least for thinking about tetradic theory. Egocentric kinship theorists have to imagine the domain of relatives covered by kinship terms as historically extending outward from the nuclear family and, sometimes, in small-scale societies, reaching the borders of society or its units. Such "extensionism" faces difficulties in modeling the process. By taking the sociocentric starting point, tetradic theory faces instead the deeper problem of imagining the initial division of society.

Here the notion of total social facts suggests a solution. The division of society is most easily imagined as arising when the whole of society, or at least its representatives, are gathered in one place. Although details can only be speculative, one can think of the invention in terms of gift exchange (which is to say, I believe, in terms of the category of relation). Endogamous moiety A gives the children produced in its wombs to endogamous moiety B, which gives back A's grandchildren. But within each endogamous moiety one section exchanges marriage partners with the other. Let us suppose that children are transferred not automatically at birth but ritually at initiation, and that marriage exchanges take place at the same ritual gathering. Effervescent or not, such an assembly would be a total social fact, not only mobilizing the whole society but also creating or recreating it.

In using the notion of totality to think about the field of sociology as a whole we have been led to envisage a purely theoretical ritual. To invent such a ritual is not unprecedented. As Mauss was well aware (Allen 2014; Hubert and Mauss [1898] 1964), Vedic literature includes extraordinarily detailed accounts of rituals that could be and have been performed in India. However, it also contains at least one account of a sacrifice that is "evidently fictitious" (Malamoud 2002: 124)—the *sarvamedha*, the "All-Sacrifice" (Eggeling [1900] 1994: 417–421), which is "supreme amongst all sacrificial performances." But our theoretical ritual also has implications for a Durkheimian view of the whole field of sociology. Early in his efforts to understand religion (in 1899), Durkheim saw it as "*the* primitive social phenomenon, from which others subsequently emerged" (Lukes 1973: 240); similarly, in 1897, he wrote that "in the beginning, all is religious" (232). So the question arises whether his definition of religion (Durkheim [1912] 1995: 44) could accommodate our theoretical primal ritual. What in it exactly is sacred, that is, set apart and forbidden? The answer has to be the rules that govern marriage and recruitment, and the society that is enabled to continue, generation after generation, by obedience to the rules (and prohibition on forms of disobedience—such as incest).

Elsewhere I have proposed that the essentially five-fold classification of social facts in Durkheimian tradition is a remote expression of the pentadic ideology that pervaded the culture of the early Indo-European speakers (Allen 2000: 109–113). Anyway, this ideology is my next topic.

Indo-European Ideology

Though I have often used it before, the late Ṛgvedic hymn 10.90 offers a good starting point, and for many reasons. It is well known, so translations are easily found, for example, in Arthur Macdonell's *Vedic Reader for Students* ([1917] 2002: 195–203). It is important in Indian tradition, above all for providing (concisely—in just two of its sixteen stanzas) a myth of origin for Hindu social structure (as conceived ideologically)—a myth echoed a millennium later in the "law code" of Manu (1.31; Olivelle 2004) and still widely regarded as providing the basis of the caste system. It is important in the history of Indo-European cultural comparison for its place in the thinking of Georges Dumézil whose oeuvre—forty-two years after his death—still dominates the field. Finally, it serves here to demonstrate with particular clarity the value of taking into account the category of totality.

Here is a summary of the hymn.

The first five verses present Puruṣa, the Person (with a capital P, assumed to be male). He is a giant figure, with a thousand heads, eyes, and feet, pervading (or being identified with) the cosmos and all its contents—past, present, and future. Only one quarter of him is on earth, the rest in heaven. He relates by reciprocal parenthood to the female figure called Virāj—each is said to be parent of the other.

The next five verses introduce the theme of sacrifice. Puruṣa is anointed as the victim of a primal sacrifice held by the gods. In it everything is offered and much originates—the world of animals, especially domestic, and the Vedas themselves (words, chants, meters, formulae).

Four verses then describe what originated from the different body parts of Puruṣa when he was dismembered: from his mouth the Brahmins, his arms the Warrior, his thighs the commoner and from his feet the Shudras or serfs. And the list continues: from his mind the moon, from his eye the sun, from his mouth the gods Indra and Agni, from his breath the wind; from his navel the atmosphere, from his head the sky, from his feet the earth, from his ear the cardinal points.

The final two verses return to the ritual: it was the sacrifice *of* Puruṣa the victim *to* Puruṣa the embodiment of Sacrifice, which now has its first rules.

Despite its complexities, this is evidently a text about Creation and Sacrifice. Although it refers only to selected instances of what was created, they stand for the cosmos as a whole. *Puruṣa eva idam sarvam* (Puruṣa is this all)—*sarva* means "all, seen as constituting a whole," as distinct from *viśva* "all, seen as multiple."³ But this emphasis on totality is easily missed in analyses of the sociogony. The hymn does not use what later became the standard term *varṇa* (estate), but it lists the standard set of four varṇas in the standard order, correlating them with Puruṣa's body parts from above downward, from mouth to feet. It also suggests a rough correlation with the cosmic levels, moving from the sky or heaven (*dyaus*) via air or atmosphere to earth. However, the body parts (source of the four varṇas) tend to dominate the picture, hiding the fact that they are parts of a pre-existing whole body. The cutting up of Puruṣa in fact opens the two sociostructural verses (11–12): "When they divided up Puruṣa (*yat Puruṣam viadadhuḥ*), into how many parts did they dispose him?"

As is well known, Dumézil's trifunctional theory of Indo-European ideology builds heavily on the varṇas, but only on the higher-ranking triad, the priests, warriors, and producers—that is, the "Twice-born," those for whom initiation constitutes a second birth. The Shudra were excluded from the analysis, being regarded (unpersuasively, in my view) as being incorporated into the ideology only after the arrival in India of the Indo-Iranian speakers. The idea that Dumézil's theory needed to be expanded to include a fourth function was taken up by Pierre and André Sauzeau (2012), but the two brothers reject the view I hold that the fourth function needs to be dichotomized into valued and devalued aspects. Instead, they argue for a fourth function defined by alterity (otherness) or marginality, but one whose polarization is not common enough to justify postulating five functions or "supercategories." Here I can only touch on a few of the arguments favoring the pentadic theory, noting in passing that all three approaches envisage the ideology as what Durkheim and Mauss called a "primitive form of classification."

The Puruṣa hymn takes into account three ontological levels, the macrocosm or universe, the mesocosm or society, the microcosm or individual (albeit an individual with a thousand heads, eyes, and feet); but it correlates them. The varṇas, the mesocosmic units, arise from the four dismembered body parts of Puruṣa qua microcosm. But the macrocosm too arises from microcosmic bodily components. First of all, luminaries and/or gods come from Puruṣa's mind, eye, mouth, and breath; then the universe is considered spatially. Vertically, heaven, atmosphere and earth come from head, navel, and feet; then, horizontally, the cardinal points come from the ear. Though the mesocosm is only linked with the macrocosm implicitly, via the body parts, it is clear enough that the Brahmins (mentioned first among the varṇas and presumably created first) correlate with heaven and that the Shudra, mentioned last, correlate with the earth.

However, to repeat my basic point, the mesocosm—society—is not just quadripartite. Before the sacrificial victim is dismembered, it is a whole. The Brahmins are the first-born of the varṇas, but before they appeared Puruṣa was entire. Just as the very phrase "division of labor" presupposes a society, so does the mesocosmic division of Puruṣa. And the implied totality is not a mere abstraction. For all its salience, the varṇa schema glosses over a role of the utmost importance in Indian social history, namely that of the king.

Just as the pre-sacrifice Puruṣa transcends the mesocosmic quadripartition, so the king transcends the society over which he reigns. In one sense he is a member of society, in another he is a more or less divine being who stands outside and above it, representing it as a whole. The hymn does not explicitly say this; indeed, in using the older term *rājanya* for the warrior *varṇa* (later called *kṣatriyas*), it implies that the raja is drawn from that estate. But the point of a royal inauguration is to change the ontological status of the king. He ceases to be just a warrior, if that is what he was, and becomes responsible for the whole social order constituted by the division of labor.

A similar argument applies on the macrocosmic level. One quarter of Puruṣa is all beings—that is, all mortal, earthly beings, in all their variety (*viśvāni*)—while three quarters of him are in heaven and immortal. However, all four quarters derive from the undivided whole, the *sarvaṃ*) mentioned in the previous verse.

Puruṣa did not become one of the mainstream Hindu gods; he was replaced by representatives of totality having different names. In the Brāhmaṇas (the Vedic ritual texts as distinct from the Vedic hymns), he is replaced by Prajāpati "Lord of Creatures," a Creator often identified with Sacrifice; and in classical Hinduism Prajāpati in his turn is usually replaced by Brahmā. Brahmā is the Creator in the so-called Hindu Trinity, alongside Vishnu the Maintainer and Shiva the Destroyer, but he is seldom worshipped and is himself sometimes replaced by the much more popular Vishnu.

Here is just one quick illustration from the classical period (Olivelle 2004: 17–18, from *Manu* 1.68–72). Hinduism has an elaborate cyclical doctrine of time, with four ages or *yugas* steadily declining in value and duration. The first yuga represents perfection and lasts (to ignore its "dawn" and "dusk") four thousand years. The last and worst yuga has declined so as to last only one thousand years; it heralds a period of dissolution, after which the cycle restarts. The colors associated with the four yugas—white, red, yellow, black—are the same colors as those of the four varṇas and are presented in the same order; moreover, the two quartets share the theme of declining value. But just as with the varṇas, the salient four-member list leaves out a great deal. First, as is stated explicitly in *Manu* (1.24), it was Brahmā who created time and the divisions of time, and a creator precedes his creation. Second, a thousand yuga cycles constitute a "day of Brahmā"; so Brahmā gives his name to a unit of time that altogether transcends the quartet of yugas.

An account of the world after the thousand cycles is given in the Epic by the sage Mārkaṇḍeya, who experienced it (van Buitenen 1975: 585–593, from *Mahābhārata* 3.186–187). Drought, fire, and flood have destroyed all life, leaving only an ocean. Swimming in it, the solitary sage sees a banyan tree in which there sits a baby—in fact Vishnu, Krishna, or Nārāyaṇa. The sage enters its mouth and finds within the infant the whole universe, including its supernaturals. Releasing him, the deity expounds his own universality, using some of the images familiar from Ṛgveda 10.90. It would be hard to find a deity who more convincingly represents the category of totality.

However, to confine attention to personalized deities is too narrow. Puruṣa's name is used as a metaphysical entity in one of the oldest and most influential and enduring of the Hindu philosophical traditions. Sāṃkhya is a dualistic philosophy that builds on the contrast between Puruṣa, here roughly meaning "consciousness" and the implicitly female Prakṛti, roughly "nature, materiality"—a gendered pairing that recalls Puruṣa and Virāj in the Vedic hymn. Comparably, the monistic philosophical tradition of Vedanta builds on the *brahman-ātman* equation (very roughly macrocosm-microcosm), where *brahman* is a neuter form related to Brahmā. It is "[t]he one self-existent impersonal Spirit, the one universal Soul . . . from which all created things emanate or with which they are identified, and into which they return." Such abstract entities belong under the Durkheimian category of totality no less than do the personalized beings.

The Durkheimian category of totality coincides with the highest-valued component of the pentadic ideology in many contexts, but the two ideas are not identical. First, in principle a concept should only be identified as representing $F4+^4$ when it belongs to a plausible set of representatives of the other supercategories: Puruṣa only represents the king insofar as his undivided body belongs to the set that includes his body parts. Second, the very term "totality" tends to suggest copious contents, like the universe inside the baby Krishna.

But to qualify as F4+, an entity need only combine being supreme inside its pentad with being "qualitatively other, outside or beyond," relative to the core of the pentad; the definition does not require internal multiplicity.

This is a theme that could occupy a whole paper and could be approached in various ways. One way is to return to *Primitive Classification* and its treatment of the category of space, especially among the Zuñi. The sevenfold Zuñi schema is based on the four cardinal points plus zenith, nadir, and center. The center (= middle of space both vertically and horizontally) stands apart from the other components of the schema in having only a single clan (that of the macaw parrot) while the others have three apiece; and in addition, it is linked with all the colors, while the others are linked with only one each. It stands apart from the others in that it can be listed either first or last.

Hindu thought often uses the three-level schema vertically, with or without an explicit center (represented by Puruṣa's navel in stanza 14 of our hymn), and similarly it uses the cardinal point schema horizontally. Now empirically a world center may be occupied by plenty of content (e.g., an F4+ royal palace); but abstractly, the four quarters presuppose a center (as the four body parts presupposed a whole body), and a center must have position but need not have parts. It governs, and provides an origin for, the quarters disposed around it, but it does not need content, let alone content such as the word "totality" seems to suggest. Indeed, it could be so empty as to connote nothingness more than everything, and Hindu theology/philosophy often posits supremely valued abstract conditions like *mokṣa*, *nirvāna* or *kaivalya*. These conditions are the ultimate aim of serious world renouncers, but may appear to Westerners as vacant or empty.[5]

This apparent paradox certainly needs more work, but the idea has been proposed by Sanskritists. Thus Theodore Proferes (2007: 152) suggests that late Vedic and early Hindu spirituality (starting from the Upanishads) reflects the popularization of the ideals of an ambitious king. The king seeks world dominance, the religious virtuoso seeks escape from the world and spiritual freedom, but they both seek forms of completeness and transcendence.

In Conclusion

I have tried to illustrate the range of topics to which the category of totality is relevant, but make no claim to any sort of completeness, even in regard to my own thinking and writing. An omission of which I am particularly aware is the work of Louis Dumont (e.g., 1980). Here is another deeply Maussian anthropologist, who started out as a student of Hindu India and has certainly influenced me. An analysis of his thinking about holism, hierarchy, and transcendence might be able to demonstrate a significant debt to the Durkheimian category. But I hope at least to have called attention to this aspect of the *Année sociologique* tradition.

Nick J. Allen taught social anthropology at the University of Oxford. Building on extensive fieldwork in Nepal, he publishes groundbreaking articles on kinship theory, the ethnography of the Himalayas, the Durkheimian School, and Indo-European comparativism. His work on the Durkheim school is reflected in the publications *Categories and Classifications. Maussian Reflections on the Social* (2000, Berghahn) and *Marcel Mauss: A Centenary Tribute* (1998, Berghahn, with Wendy James). Allen passed away on March 21, 2020.

Notes

1. Though I give the reference to Karen Fields' translation, here, as in some other cases, I retain my own translation, made independently.
2. For an introduction to the theory, see Nicholas Allen (2008).
3. The distinction is neatly expressed by Lillian Silburn (1955: 49): the god Prajāpati is "le Tout sous son double aspect de tout éparpillé (*viśva*) ou issu d'une dispersion et de tout concentré (*sarva*), ou mieux, le tout qui est 'l'un' (*eka*)." In other words, "the Whole under its double aspect of a whole that is scattered or arises from a dispersal and a whole that is concentrated or better, the whole that constitutes 'the One.'"
4. "F4+" is based on the definition of different functions by Georges Dumézil. Nicholas Allen explains in *Categories and Classification* (2000): "As elsewhere, I use the following labels and definitions (abbreviated):
    - F4+ heterogenous and supreme, often transcendent
    - F1 pertaining to the sacred
    - F2 pertaining to the physical force and war
    - F3 pertaining to fecundity, wealth and related ideas
    - F4- heterogenous and excluded or somewhat devalued." (106) [Note of the editors]
5. This "emptiness" recalls a dictum from the penultimate chapter of *Primitive Classification* (Durkheim and Mauss [1903] 1963: 79): "Pan, Brahmán [= Brahmā], Prajāpati, supreme genera, absolute and pure beings, are mythological figures almost as poor in imagery as the transcendental God of the Christians."

References

Allen, Nicholas J. 2000. *Categories and Classifications: Maussian Reflections on the Social.* Oxford: Berghahn.
———. 2008. "Tetradic Theory and the Origin of Human Kinship Systems." In *Early Human Kinship: From Sex to Social Reproduction*, ed. Nicholas J. Allen, Hillary Callan, Robin Dunbar, and Wendy James, 96–112. Oxford: Blackwell.
———. 2014. "Mauss, India and Perspectives from World History." *Journal of Classical Sociology* 14 (1): 22–33.
Dumont, Louis. [1966] 1980. *Homo Hierarchicus: The Caste System and its Implications.* Chicago: University Press.
Durkheim, Émile. 1898. "La prohibition de l'inceste et ses origins." *L'Année sociologique* 1: 1–70.
———. [1895] 1919. *Les règles de la méthode sociologique.* Paris: Félix Alcan.
———. [1893] 1926. *De la division du travail social.* Paris: Félix Alcan.
———. [1912] 1995. *The Elementary Forms of Religious Life*, trans. Karen Fields. New York: Free Press.
Durkheim, Émile, and Marcel Mauss. [1903] 1963. *Primitive Classification*, trans. Rodney Needham. Chicago: University Press.
Eggeling, Julius. [1900] 1994. *The Śatapatha-Brāhmaṇa, Part V*, trans. Julius Eggeling. Delhi: Motilal Banarsidass.
Hubert, Henri, and Marcel Mauss. [1898] 1964. *Sacrifice: Its Nature and Function*, trans. Wilfred D. Halls. London: Cohen and West.
Lukes, Steven. 1973. *Emile Durkheim, His Life and Works: A Historical and Critical Study.* Harmondsworth: Penguin.
Macdonell, Arthur A. [1917] 2002. *Vedic Reader for Students.* Delhi: Motilal Banarsidass.
Malamoud, Charles. 2002. *Le Jumeau Solaire.* Paris: Seuil.
Mauss, Marcel. [1925] 1990. *The Gift: The Form and Reason for Exchange in Archaic Societies*, trans. Wilfred D. Halls. London: Routledge.
———. [1927] 2005. "Sociology: Its Divisions and Their Relative Weightings." In *The Nature of Sociology: Two Essays*, trans. William Jeffrey, 31–89. New York: Durkheim Press/Berghahn.
———. [1932] 1969. "La cohésion sociale dans les sociétés polysegmentaires." In *Œuvres III: Cohésion sociale et divisions de la sociologie*, ed. Victor Karady, 11–26. Paris: Minuit.
———. [1938] 1985. "A Category of the Human Mind: The Notion of Person; the Notion of Self." In *The Category of the Person: Anthropology, Philosophy, History*, ed. Michael Carrithers, Steven Collins, and Steven Lukes, trans. Wilfred D. Halls, 1–25. Cambridge: University Press.
Olivelle, Patrick, ed. and trans. 2004. *The Law Code of Manu.* Oxford: University Press.
Proferes, Theodore N. 2007. *Vedic Ideals of Sovereignty and the Poetics of Power.* New Haven, CT: American Oriental Society.

Sauzeau, Pierre, and André Sauzeau. 2012. *La quatrième fonction: marginalité et altérité dans l'idéologie indo-européenne*. Paris: Belles Lettres.

Silburn, Lilian. 1955. *Instant et cause: le discontinu dans la pensée philosophique de l'Inde*. Paris: J. Vrin.

van Buitenen, Johannes A. B. 1975. *The Mahābhārata, Books 2–3*, trans. Johannes A. B. van Buitenen. Chicago: University Press.

Watts Miller, William. 2012. *A Durkheimian Quest: Solidarity and the Sacred*. Oxford: Berghahn.

Chapter 9

DURKHEIMIAN CREATIVE EFFERVESCENCE, BERGSON, AND THE ETHOLOGY OF ANIMAL AND HUMAN SOCIETIES

William Watts Miller

First, I wish to bring out how Émile Durkheim's last great work, *Les formes élémentaires de la vie religieuse*, came with a new interest in creativity, not least as creative effervescence. Next, since this involves an apparent impasse in his thought, I explore if help is on offer from Henri Bergson's theory of creative evolution. Finally, I consider recent work on animal and early human societies.

A point at stake in my discussion is that it is important to look beyond a conventional list of categories in probing Durkheim's approach to these in *Les formes*. A particular example is that it is all very well to focus on the work's interest in the category of causation. But a limitation of commentaries on this is their neglect of the work's related interest in the idea of creativity, and how it is part of Durkheim's central concern with notions of a vast protean energy and power. Or again, it is essential to link his effort to sociologize philosophical categories with his approach to the sui generis and with his radical distinction between the animal and human. More specifically, *Les formes* looked for the origins of the categories in a sui generis, humanly creative realm of the socioreligious.

Durkheimian Creative Effervescence

Talk of *créativité* did not become current in French until the 1940s and 1950s.[1] Yet although the term never appears in *Les formes*, the idea is clearly at stake in it.[2] In the work's conclusion, "a society can neither create nor recreate itself without, in the very action, creating an ideal" (Durkheim 1912: 603).[3] Next, a contemporary moral malaise is contrasted with the French Revolution's energies, in looking to another great moment of renewal through "creative effervescence" (611). Finally, an overall message bypasses appeals to God to reveal society as a "creative power" unequalled by anything else in the observable world (637). But also, an underlying development in all this offers a new key to an old concern, the creation of a sui generis realm of the social itself, irreducible to either biology or psychology.

A Brief History

An early, sympathetic discussion of "hyperexcitement" can be found in Durkheim's thesis on the division of labor (1893: 106). But it is the work's single allusion to effervescence, and no link is made with creativity—indeed, there are only a few references to this, and they are all hostile (30, 157, 216, 288, 309). Later on, there is increasing concern with effervescence, but above all in a negative way, as in *Suicide*'s critique of anomie and the "hyperexcited forces" of an "unhealthy effervescence" (Durkheim 1897: 408, 422).

Things began to change when, not long afterward, a couple of reviews noticed cases of societies in which the energies of special sacred festive times contrasted with the dullness of ordinary life (Durkheim 1899: 309; 1900: 336). A further development came in lectures given around 1905, as well as in a review of the same date. The French Revolution's "effervescence was immensely creative of new ideas" (Durkheim 1938: 2:169), while the "effervescence and collective enthusiasm that characterized this creative era necessarily came to take on, thanks to its very intensity, a religious character" (Durkheim 1905: 382). However, it was only when Durkheim got round to writing up *Les formes* itself that creativity and creative effervescence became theoretically central in his work.

A Problematic

Throughout his career, Durkheim attacked theories that he thought assumed a magical creation out of nothing. Thus, just as he had dismissed the very idea of a "creation *ex nihilo*" in his thesis (Durkheim 1893: 216, 309), so he continued to dismiss it in *Les formes* (Durkheim 1912: 123). But, in contrast with his thesis and its negative references to creativity, his approach in *Les formes* now included more positive views, as in a discussion of "creation properly so-called," which is "the creation of something entirely new" (509–510). This accordingly helps to set up a core problematic of the work. How, without assuming a creation from nothing, is it possible to identify a creation of the wholly new?

The passage concerned with society's immense creative power explains that creation, far from being a merely mystical operation, is the product of a "synthesis" (Durkheim 1912: 637). Elsewhere in the work, it is also discussed as a "fusion" of various elements. But whether in a "synthesis" or a "fusion" of these, Durkheim's underlying idea is how, without a conjuring from nothing, there can arise something new in that it is irreducible and categorially distinct.

This idea clearly has origins in his essay on individual and collective representations, above all in its final section (Durkheim 1898a: 293–302). Here, "synthesis" and "fusion" are equivalent terms, in an argument about interlinkage and categorial difference in which, just as material embodiment forms a substratum of individual psychic life, a mass of associated individuals constitutes a substratum of society. In one case, individual representations have roots in a "synthesis" in physiological elements that are transformed by the very fact of their "fusion"; in the other, collective representations have roots in a "synthesis" and "fusion" of individualistic psychic elements that are transformed in the very process itself (295–96).

This substratum of the social is in no way just an affair of isolated atoms, but instead consists of an *ensemble* of associated individuals. There is nonetheless an ambiguity in how it is additionally characterized. On the one hand, it is described as a morphological affair of how individuals are organized; on the other, it is also described in terms of the actions and reactions between the particular individual minds that make up society. It remains the case, either way, that in the ongoing dynamics of interlinkage, the "autonomy" of a sui generis realm can only be "relative" (Durkheim 1898a: 293). But this is also why, either way, such a realm entails a break in mechanistic chains of causation. It becomes "free," up to a point, from its continuing roots in a substratum, as, not least, in the case of religion and a "luxuriant growth of myths and legends" that, far from just being a product of social structure, take on "a life of their own" (299).

Oddly, perhaps, the essay has only a passing reference to creativity and makes no mention of effervescence. It was not until *Les formes* that processes of synthesis/fusion became explicitly understood in terms of the extraordinary energies of collective creative effervescence, and indeed involving, through a "surplus" of such energies, "free creations of the mind," "free combinations of thought and action," and "a whole world of feelings, ideas and images" with a far-reaching "independence" (Durkheim 1912: 544–46, 605). So this still very much implies a break in chains of causation. But, even in the case of the far-reaching independence of a whole religious world of feelings, ideas, and images, it also still implies continuing roots in society.

A basic Durkheimian message, after all, is that religion is ineliminably social. Indeed, in the centerpiece of *Les formes* and its account of the work's star case of effervescent assembly, it is suggested that such "effervescent social milieux" helped to give birth to "the religious idea" (Durkheim 1912: 313). Yet what helped to give birth to the social realm itself? Durkheim's account of effervescence entails key roles for the power of assembly, the power of ritual and symbolism, and the power of art. Yet the assemblies he describes not only involve an already constituted social organization, but, together with their ritual, symbolism, and art come laden with a pre-existing sense of the sacred. Accordingly, a central idea of *Les formes* can appear dependent on a circularity in which the social is already part of the dynamics that create and recreate the social itself—or in which, to be more exact, it is the socioreligious that creates and recreates itself in this way.

Rhythms, Revolutions, and Origins

It is essential to notice Durkheim's different concerns with effervescence. It is not just about events that are part of the rhythms of an established social calendar, and that help to renew society in the sense of periodically revitalizing an existing system. Crucially, it is also about times such as the French Revolution and renewal through movements for radical change. Even so, a fundamental similarity between these cases is that there is already a social context within which they arise and should be understood. Worries about a circularity in Durkheim's appeal to creative effervescence above all apply to the question of the birth of the social realm itself.

Durkheim's concern with origins was fundamental to his sociology, including his theory of collective representations, especially as concepts, but also, not least, his category project. Instead of abandoning this concern, one possibility is to imagine the equivalent of a cosmological "big bang," kicking off human social history through a whole explosive, interrelational dynamic. However, a difficulty with this is that it runs into his own general opposition to a creation ex nihilo, as well as into his view that the idea of an "absolute beginning" is unscientific and that religion and other human institutions did not suddenly appear at a particular, dramatic "instant" (Durkheim 1912:

10–11). So an alternative is to picture, with pre-existing animal societies in mind, a gradual evolutionary emergence of human social life. Yet this, too, runs into the opposition of Durkheim himself.

His early work contained favorable mentions of Alfred Espinas, author of *Sociétés animales* (1877).[4] But they were brief, vague references that in no way committed him to Espinas's project for a unified comparative science of animal and human social life. Indeed, in discussing a new article by Espinas on this project, he made clear his disagreement with it. Animal societies lacked "institutions," and so this involved a categorial difference with humans (Durkheim 1902: 129)—a view held until the end of his life (Durkheim 1917: 57), although in *Les formes* it was on the basis that animals lacked "ideas" (Durkheim 1912: 602).

In sum, there is an apparent impasse in his thought. A question, then, is how to get round it. The suggestion of a "big bang" has been considered elsewhere (Watts Miller 2012: 128–29), and other possibilities are instead taken up here.

Bergson

Durkheim's growing interest in creative effervescence coincided with Bergson's study of creative evolution (1907). So perhaps a way of assisting Durkheim is to draw on a basic idea in Bergson's last great work, *Les deux sources de la religion et de la morale* (1932). This is the idea of a development of animal and human social life along many different pathways, but involving, along with continuities, creative, categorial discontinuities.

True, an attack on Durkheim has long been seen as part of the agenda of *Les sources*. Moreover, whether a commentary is pro-Durkheimian (see Pinto 2004), pro-Bergsonian (see Keck 2002), or neutral (see Prélorentzos 2006), it is generally in emphasizing differences between the two writers, even in also pointing to similarities. So, before examining differences, I wish to bring out a neglected similarity—a problematic, in both *Les formes* and *Les sources*, of how to combine causation with a key role for creativity.

Creative Evolution, a Society of Persons, and Dynamogenic Religion

Bergson's two sources of morality and religion set up a fundamental distinction between a closed and an open society. Closed societies confine fellow-feeling to their own members, run on an ethic of duty and constraint, and depend on a "static" religion's mythologies. A crucial concern, then, is with movements toward an open society that "in principle embraces all of humanity" (Bergson 1932: 288). At the same time as linking with a "dynamic" religion, these movements necessarily involve the discontinuities and ontological leaps of a qualitative, sui generis transformation, rather than any merely gradual, continuous, quantitative change. In other words, they help to bring about the new in generating categorial differences that break free from merely mechanistic chains of causation. So, just as Durkheim invokes creative effervescence in a concern with the sui generis social, Bergson's approach to evolution similarly invokes creative energies, creative efforts, creative emotions and indeed, like a Durkheimian "surplus," an "overflowing of vitality" (Bergson 1932: 97).

True, where Durkheim emphasizes a collective dynamic, Bergson emphasizes the role of pioneering, charismatic individuals. What still needs to be recognized is how Durkheim had his own distinctive vision of an open society and the individualism it entails. His commitment to such a vision is already evident in his thesis on the division of labor and was then taken further in subsequent work. His most impassioned expression of this ideal, however, is in his essay on individualism and the intellectuals. Written against the background of the waves of racist, antisemitic hatred that swept through France during the Dreyfus Affair, it defended aspirations to an open, inclusive society centered round belief—indeed, a secular religious belief—in every individual's sacredness as a human person (Durkheim 1898b).

But let us now turn from similarities to differences, above all over an early socioreligious world. A basic message of *Les formes* is that religion, in its stimulation of energies, is above all "dynamogenic."[5] A basic implication, it then seems to me, is the dubiousness of any idea of religion as merely static. Accordingly, what is at stake in Bergson's critique of Durkheim on religion? Far from attacking him as a theorist of a closed, primitive socioreligious world, his account of early religion is seen as mistaken since it is about something more advanced.

In *Les sources*, evolution toward a dynamic religion culminates in a desire to enter into contact and communion with "the creative effort of which life is a manifestation" (Bergson 1932: 235). In early religion there is also creativity, but it is "the creativity of the imagination" and its "phantasmagorical representations" (111). As part of this story, there is a discussion of Durkheim's account, in *Les formes*, of notions such as *mana*, which for Bergson cannot be "primitive." The idea of a power, energy, or force, which *mana* involves, is something the mind encounters in following more elementary and "natural" pathways (141). These include magic, which originated as a practice that did not just assume religion's already constituted idea of a power, as argued by the Durkheimian school, but on the contrary helped to generate it (174–75). Or again, religion did not get going with belief in an impersonal force; instead, in the beginning, intentions were simply projected on to things and events, "as if nature had eyes everywhere and trained them on man" (186). All this prepared the way for a discussion of totemism, and so of an issue central to Les formes. How, then, did the two accounts compare?

Durkheim's Australia involved an early elementary religion that did not yet have an explicit idea of a power such as *mana*. It could nonetheless be inferred that it operated with an underlying belief in a "totemic principle," as a protean life-force at work in humans, animals, plants, things, and indeed the whole of the cosmos (Durkheim 1912: 269). More specifically, it operated in a form that united particular human and animal groups as kindred beings, descended from the same ancestor, belonging to the same stock and sharing the same inner life-energy or "essence" (338). Bergson, however, hesitated to accept talk of such kinship as a literal belief. Instead, he rooted totemism in the use of animals as symbols, reinforcing a biological need to keep intermarrying, exogamous "clans" different and distinct, but then gradually converting into some sort of notion of an actual kinship (Bergson 1932: 194–96).

A perhaps surprising common feature of the two accounts is that both of them appear to start their story of human social evolution, not by conjecturing a primal "horde," but with evidence of an already quite complex organization of "clans." In any case, Bergson's concern with how an early social organization is reinforced by symbolism has affinities with the Durkheimian interest in such an organization as the origin of the category of genre or type—an interest first articulated in an article (Durkheim and Mauss 1903), then repeated in Les formes (Durkheim 1912: 203–5). But this introduced a basic incoherence into the work, since there was little or no attempt to reconcile it with all the new emphasis on a "totemic principle," at once grouping particular humans and animals together as beings with the same underlying socioreligious identity. However, it also entangled Bergson in a basic incoherence, in which his story of totemism's social symbolic beginnings took little or no notice of his concern with the power and energy of primitive religion's "creativity of the imagination" and "phantasmagorical representations"—an energy and power quite capable, in a Durkheimian creative effervescence, of transgressing apparently "natural," commonsense boundaries and generating an early "phantasmagorical" idea of a fundamental animal-human kinship. Indeed, in contrast with Bergson's coolness toward the "phantasmagorical," the author of *Les formes* rooted science in religion and the imaginative rupture with a commonsense world brought about by a creative effervescence that "transfigured the real" (Durkheim 1912: 337). But there were even more fundamental differences of approach.

Social Science and "Virtual" Biology

A claim made in the opening chapter of *Les sources* is that all morality "is in essence biological," albeit in a wide sense of "biology" (Bergson 1932: 103), and it is evident from recently discovered notes that the claim was intended as an attack on Durkheim's sociology (Bergson 2002: 133). What is not so evident is the actual meaning of the claim, not least in the attempt, in the final chapter of *Les sources*, to picture human society as newly sprung "from the hands of nature" (Bergson 1932: 287). This, it is explained, is in an effort to dig down through the long build-up of deposit after deposit of the culturally "acquired" that "overlays the natural" (296). So it could easily seem an effort to excavate a society based, not on acquired, but on genetically programmed characteristics. Yet even in the work's search for the beginnings of human social life, perhaps its key concern is with something theorized as "virtual" rather than actual instinct.

It was no doubt with a touch of irony that Bergson, a well-known critic of Kantian rationalism, introduced his account of morality with appeal to a stripped-down version of a "categorical imperative" (Bergson 1932: 19). Moral rules are habitually followed and obeyed, not thanks to any judgment based on a rational calculation of their pros and cons, and so inherently conditional, but because they involve an almost unthinking sense of their absolute, categorical imperativeness. Accordingly, at the very foundations of morality, it is not any particular, first-order obligation, but a second-order habit of acquiring moral, rule-following habits—"obligation as a whole"—that functions like an instinct. Or, in a word, it is a "virtual instinct," and, to understand the foundations of morality, "we must always get back to what obligation *would have been* if human society had been instinctive instead of intelligent" (23).

True enough, there is not just a general appeal to thought-experiments about life as it "would have been" if based on instinct instead of intelligence. There is also a more concrete guide to these. This is a repeated analogy between the world of human social life and the world of ants and anthills—an analogy that amounts to one of the most original and significant arguments of *Les sources*, according to its author's notes (Bergson 2002: 133). Even so, it might seem a somewhat shaky "virtual biology." It might also be wondered why, instead of rethinking human society in terms of a "virtual instinct," we should not rethink anthills in terms of a "virtual intelligence."

An answer is that a "more natural" type of society is "obviously the instinctive type" (Bergson 1932: 21). Yet intelligence is surely no less "natural" in that it is not only fundamental to human social life, in all its cultural variation, but also has a genetic basis. A source of the problem, however, involves Bergson's appeal to a different sense of the "natural," in which, compared with human society, the link uniting the ants of an anthill more closely resembles the link uniting "the cells of an organism" (21). In turn, this expression of a biologically inspired organic functionalism is part of a wider issue, to do with the interrelation of different types of explanation.

At bottom, an elementary point is at stake in the analogy of insect and human societies. This is that polar extremes of instinct and intelligence might generate similar social functions. Yet although Bergson was anxious to find alternatives both to mechanistic and to teleological explanation, it is hardly the case that his approach could or did end up just as a version of functionalism. Instead, and however mystically, he invoked the energies of an *élan vital* at work in the overall dynamics—with the continuities but also discontinuities—of a creative evolution. Moreover, although Durkheim had spent Book I of his thesis on the functions of an increasing division of labor, he then spent Book II on its causes. In fact, despite the way he has often been caricatured, he always regarded functionalist accounts as inadequate on their own. Thus, much of the significance of *Les formes* is that it combines functionalism, not just with a continuing attachment to causation, but with a new interest in creativity. At the same time, it also comes with an impasse that Bergson's theory of creative evolution is unfortunately unable to overcome, at least as developed in *Les sources*. Whatever the insights that might be gained from a functionalist comparison between insect and human life, it remains the case that they have a different operational basis. A fundamental flaw of *Les sources* is its lack of any serious interest in evolutionary pathways from primate to human societies.

New Research and Debate

There has been a rapid growth, over the last few decades, in research and debate on primates, hominins, and early humans. Here, it possible to consider only a few salient points from all this and their relevance to concerns with "creative effervescence" and "creative evolution" as a way to understand the origins of human society.

Pioneering fieldwork on chimpanzees in the wild got going in the 1960s, and a number of key figures in this research went on to collaborate on a synthesis of information from the longest running studies. As well as revealing extensive cultural differences between groups in regard to particular behaviors, this also showed that the combined repertoire of such behaviors within each chimpanzee community "is itself highly distinctive, a phenomenon characteristic of human cultures but previously unrecognized in non-human species" (Whiten et al. 1999: 682). But whatever the role of genetic, environmental, and cultural factors, a study collating fieldwork on different primate species—again in the wild—has brought out a basic common aspect of their social life. This is the importance of "cooperative and associative behaviors," given that these are far more prevalent than "agonistic behaviors," and indeed that "rates of agonistic behaviors are extremely low, normally less than 1 percent of the activity budget" (Sussman et al. 2005: 84). The cooperative nature of primate social life is also emphasized by Frans de Waal, in arguing that morality is a product of social evolution. As he insists, in talking about humans, "there never was a point at which we became social: descended from highly social ancestors—a long line of monkeys and apes—we have been group-living forever," so that "the building blocks of morality are evolutionarily ancient" (de Waal 2006: 4, 6). In his account, human morality consists of three successive evolutionary layers, beginning with a set of "moral sentiments" as the most basic, followed by concerns and constraints at stake in "social pressure," and culminating in "judgment and reasoning," which he considers "uniquely human": but since it cannot exist without the other levels, "all of human morality is continuous with primate sociality" (166–75). This nonetheless leaves quite a gap in his evolutionary story, and it is necessary to go on from chimpanzees, the genetically closest relatives of humans, to ask about early humans themselves.

A recent guide to human evolution emphasizes straightaway the rapid pace of new discoveries, which "shows no sign of slowing down" (Humphrey and Stringer 2018: 7). For the moment, however, a basic timeframe dates the split of chimpanzee and human lineages to around 7 million years ago, resulting in the appearance over the next few million years of many varieties of hominins, each with at least one anatomical feature identifying them as human ancestors (21–33). A later period, from around 4 to 2 million years ago, involves a type of small-bodied and small-brained bipedal hominin known as *Australopithicus*, made famous by the discovery, in 1974, of a female baptized "Lucy," although a whole spate of discoveries over the last two decades is even more significant (35–69). Fast-forwarding, then, to the first "true" humans themselves, the picture is complex and controversial, thanks to the sheer diversity of hominin fossils from around 2 million years ago on (94). It remains complex and controversial, even in just sticking with the last million years in an attempt to trace the lineages of the three main large-brained, genetically interlinked, recognizably human groups that still coexisted with one another as late as 40,000 years ago, Neanderthals, Denisovans, and Homo Sapiens (142–43).

Another recent work, principally authored by Sang-Hee Lee (2015), provides a highly accessible account of issues involved in all this, and a key general point is concerned with an interaction in which sociocultural change helps to drive genetic change, rather than only the other way round. Here, however, it is particularly relevant to focus on her discussion of things at stake in the emergence of large-brained hominins/humans, including, not least, the impact on childbirth (2015: 60–65). This became both inherently painful and inherently social, requiring the help of others to bring about a child's safe passage into the world, and so linking with the survival of older women who had the experience and skill to assist young mothers, although no longer capable of motherhood themselves. At the same time, there are many other factors making for the linkage of large brains with the need not only to store vast amounts of complex social information but also to access it at appropriate moments, and in examining such factors (171–76), she especially supports the "social brain hypothesis" developed by Robin Dunbar (2003).

The ground is now ready to turn to discussions that specifically draw on Durkheim's evolutionary concern with the social, and one of the most important of these is by Nick Allen (1998). Starting from an interest, as in *Les formes*, in the "origins" of human social life, he sets out to consider "the simplest ways of organizing a primitive, small-scale society," then to ask "how such an organization might itself arise" (149, 151). The ideal-typical organization suggested involves a "tetradic" system that divides an overall society into four sections structured round kinship and marriage. All individuals belong to one of two descent lineages that each exchange spouses but keep offspring, while also belonging to one of two generational classes that each marry within their own ranks and transfer offspring to the next generational cohort. Such an organization simultaneously excludes incestuous brother-sister and parent-child unions (154). Not least, however, it promotes the solidarity of the overall society through a circulation of individuals both within and between groups, in a structure that amounts to a Maussian system of total prestations par excellence (160).

The account of how such a system might have arisen focuses on Durkheim's concern, in *Les formes*, with effervescent assemblies. It is nonetheless emphasized that, far from being a distinctively human innovation, these might "go back many millions of years" (Allen 1998: 158), and long-standing evidence of effervescence among chimpanzees is cited from a work by Vernon Reynolds (1967). Another key point is that the suggestion about a tetradic system's origins in human life relates to effervescent assemblies of a tribal people as a whole, while a review of their various possible core activities pays particular attention to initiation, and how it is a passage, publicly witnessed and ritually dramatized, of a new generational cohort's members into the overall adult community (159–60).

A comment, here, is that the star case of effervescence in *Les formes* does in fact relate to an assembly of a people as a whole, involving both the "phratries" that divide the Warramunga by lineage, while also mobilizing different generational cohorts through the role of "recently initiated young men" (Durkheim 1912: 311). But also and more generally, the emergence of institutionalized generational cohorts—or, as among many Australian peoples, alternating generational marriage-classes—can readily be seen as an internal development, within an already constituted society. In contrast, a long-running debate in Durkheim's time concerned the emergence of descent groups such as "clans," and whether these originated in a merger of separate "hordes" or instead involved an internal process within pre-existing societies. Durkheim drew on a review of the issue provided by Alfred Howitt, who supported an internalist line in his account of a process of "segmentation" within what he preferred to theorize as an "undivided commune" rather than a "horde" (Fison and Howitt 1880: 317–66). Although Durkheim's thesis stuck with old talk of a "horde," it is highly likely that his account of its transformation into a "segmental" society borrowed, without acknowledgement, from Howitt's new terminology (see Durkheim 1893: 189–90). The controversy was also reviewed some years later in a work by Andrew Lang (1903), which argued for an externalist merger of separate groups and included a critique of Durkheim. This prompted a swift response from him, but was also the last occasion, to my knowledge, in which he ever referred to the idea of a horde (Durkheim 1903: 423). Certainly, he never referred to it in *Les formes*, and his account of early elementary Australia got going with a discussion of societies already composed of descent groups and marriage-classes (Durkheim 1912: 142–55). Yet the fundamental and continuing importance of the horde for Durkheim's theory has been stressed in a recent work by Alexandra Maryanski (2018), and so in my view this helps to bring out what, crucially, is at stake in Nick Allen's ideal-type of an early tetradic human society. Could it not be that, in their ideas and institutions, early humans had long left behind primal hordes and already possessed a segmental social organization?

Allen's tetradic model is simpler than any of the main Australian kinship systems listed and described by Howitt (1904: 88–155). It is nonetheless quite complex, and entails a need to store and access vast amounts of social information that makes it highly relevant to the social brain hypothesis. Thus, it could have emerged as far back as 500,000 years ago, in line with one set of calculations by Dunbar (2003: 173–77). Or it might not have emerged until later, if inseparable from religion, and given the different set of calculations of what this requires (177–79). Either way, what is involved is a "theory of mind" (ToM), distinguishing animals/hominins/humans in terms of four increasingly powerful levels of "social cognition" (169–72), a point linking with another key discussion.

This is by Clive Gamble (2013), who quickly brings out Durkheim's insistence that "man is man and distinct from animals" (127). He nonetheless goes on to identify social life as the operative dynamic in all hominin evolution. But while drawing on the concept of the social brain, he combines it with his own interest in a model of "the distributed mind," in which "humans are constituted by their environment and, crucially, the materials and objects they interact with, as much as by their minds" (133). Perhaps it is more of a Maussian than a Durkheimian move, emphasizing that sociability has always been the distinctive hominin means of knowing and imaginative access to relations with others and the natural world, but which "has always been implicated in technology . . . and the experiences of the body, rather than just the reason of the mind" (135). So, where de Waal has three layers of morality and Dunbar four levels of cognition, Gamble outlines a social evolution of technology covering 2.6 million to 6,000 years ago, and running in three stages. An implication, it seems to me, is that a segmental kinship system would have begun to get going in the second stage, from 100,000 to 21,000 years ago. But the implication concentrated on by Gamble himself is that the social conditions of religion were laid during this second stage, without having to wait for Dunbar's highest ToM level of cognition. This does not mean that the hominins/humans of the time "got religion," but that they possessed "the more fundamental Durkheimian property of social imagination" on which religion depends (137).

Put another way, they stood at the threshold of religion. So if we return to Maryanski, her focus on solidarity is through Durkheim's interest, not just in religion but in a vast ritual-symbolic repertoire of materials, techniques and practices, such as churingas, corroborees, circumcision, menstrual blood, and other sacred things. However, these were also a key to his interest in the humanly creative realm of ideas. As he argued, we are all the more persons, "the more we are capable of thinking and acting through concepts" (Durkheim 1912: 389). Yet as he also argued, concrete symbols not only help to form ideas but remain an "integral part" of them (330–31). In effect, and as in the various explorations of time undertaken by Durkheim and his group,[6] there are no such things as purely abstract concepts or categories.

Conclusion

Durkheim's effort to sociologize categories and rescue them from philosophers was part of his wider concern with a humanly creative realm not only of religion and other social institutions but of collective representations and concepts. Yet his account of this realm, and its sui juris irreducibility to biology or psychology, can involve an apparent circularity and impasse in his thought. However, a route out of this is on offer from investigations that, whether in identifying many kinds of hominins, different layers of morality, various levels of cognition or several stages of technology, all point in the same direction. The evolutionary pathways from primate to human society are complex but also creative, in involving a long series of multilinear, qualitative transformations—physiological, moral, cognitive, cultural, technical—rather than any single dramatic leap across a categorial Rubicon. In turn, effervescence can be seen as a vital component of this evolution, not least during the various critical stages of the formation of a social life that Durkheim regarded as distinctively human.

William Watts Miller was for many years editor of the journal *Durkheimian Studies / Études Durkheimiennes*, is author of various books and articles on Durkheim as well as of translations of his writings. Watts Miller is the author of *A Durkheimian Quest: Solidarity and the Sacred* (2012). He is furthermore a member of the British Centre for Durkheimian Studies based in the University of Oxford, and was a close colleague of its founder, the late W. S. F. Pickering.

Notes

Thanks are due to the late Nick Allen and to Vernon Reynolds for their help in reading an earlier version of this discussion.

1. See the entry on *créativité* in the online "Trésor de la langue française."
2. The following account draws on William Watts Miller (2012; 2017).
3. The translations are made by the author, if not otherwise referenced.
4. On Alfred Espinas, see Wolf Feuerhahn (2011).
5. On Durkheim and *dynamogénie*, see Nicholas Sembel (2015).
6. See, e.g., "Durkheimian Time," Watts Miller (2000).

References

Allen, Nicholas J. 1998. "Effervescence and the Origins of Human Society." In *On Durkheim's Elementary Forms of Religious Life*, ed. Nicholas J. Allen, William S. F. Pickering, and William Watts Miller, 149–61. London: Routledge.

Bergson, Henri. 1907. *L'Évolution créatrice*. Paris: Félix Alcan.

———. 1932. *Les deux sources de la morale et de la religion*. Paris: Félix Alcan.

———. 2002. "Une mise au point de Bergson sur 'Les deux sources.'" *Annales Bergsoniennes* 1: 131–42.

de Waal, Frans. 2006. *Primates and Philosophers: How Morality Evolved*. Princeton, NJ: Princeton University Press.

Dunbar, Robin. 2003. "The Social Brain: Mind, Language and Society in Evolutionary Perspective." *Annual Review of Anthropology* 32: 163–81.

Durkheim, Émile. 1893. *De la division du travail social*. Paris: Félix Alcan.

———. 1897. *Le suicide: étude de sociologie*. Paris: Félix Alcan.

———. 1898a. "Représentations individuelles et représentations collectives." *Revue de métaphysique et de morale* 6: 273–302.

———. 1898b. "L'individualisme et les intellectuels." *Revue bleue* 10: 7–13.

———. 1899. "Review of Hagelstange 'Süddeutsches Bauernleben im Mittelalter.'" *Année sociologique (AS)* 2: 306–9.

———. 1900. "Review of Boas 'The Social Organisation in the Secret Societies of the Kwakiutl Indians.'" *AS* 3: 336–40.

———. 1902. "Review of Espinas 'Être ou ne pas être' ou du postulat de la sociologie.'" *AS* 5: 128–29.

———. 1903. "Review of Lang 'Social Origins.'" *Folklore* 15: 420–5.

———. 1905. "Review of Pellison 'La sécularisation de la morale au XVIIIe siècle.'" *AS* 8: 381–82.

———. 1912. *Les formes élémentaires de la vie religieuse; le système totémique en Australie*. Paris: Félix Alcan.

———. 1917. "Société." *Bulletin de la société française de philosophie* 15: 51.

———. 1938. *L'Évolution pédagogique en France*. Paris: Félix Alcan.

Durkheim, Émile, and Marcel Mauss. 1903. "De quelques formes primitives de classification: contribution à l'étude des représentations collectives." *AS* 6: 1–72.

Espinas, Alfred. 1877. *Des sociétés animales: étude de psychologie comparée.* Paris: Germer-Baillière.

Feuerhahn, Wolf. 2011. "Les 'sociétés animales': un défi à l'ordre savant." *Romantisme* 154: 35–51.

Fison, Lorimer, and Alfred Howitt. 1880. *Kamilaroi and Kurnai.* Melbourne: George Robinson.

Gamble, Clive. 2013. "Durkheim and the Primitive Mind: An Archaeological Retrospective." In *Durkheim in Dialogue: A Centenary Celebration of 'The Elementary Forms of Religious Life,'* ed. Sondra L. Hausner, 124–42. New York: Berghahn.

Howitt, Alfred. 1904. *The Native Tribes of South-East Australia.* London: Macmillan.

Humphrey, Louise, and Chris Stringer. 2018. *Our Human Story.* London: Natural History Museum.

Keck, Frederic. 2002. "Bergson et l'anthropologie: Le problème de l'humanité dans 'Les deux sources de la morale et de la religion.'" *Annales bergsoniennes* 1: 195–214.

Lang, Andrew. 1903. *Social Origins.* London: Longmans, Green.

Lee, Sang-Hee, with Shin-Young Yoon. 2015. *Close Encounters with Humankind: A Palaeontologist Investigates Our Evolving Species.* New York: Norton & Co.

Maryanski, Alexandra. 2018. *Émile Durkheim and the Birth of the Gods: Clans, Incest, Totems, Phratries, Hordes, Mana, Taboos, Corroborees, Sodalities, Menstrual Blood, Apes, Churingas, Cairns and Other Mysterious Things.* New York: Routledge.

Pinto, Louis. 2004. "Le débat sur les sources de la morale et de la religion." *Actes de la recherche en sciences sociales* 153 (3): 41–47.

Prélorentzos, Yannis. 2006. "Bergson est-il durkheimien dans 'Les Deux Sources de la morale et de la religion'?" *Philosophy: Academy of Athens* 36: 230–53.

Reynolds, Vernon. 1967. *The Apes: The Gorilla, Chimpanzee, Orangutan and Gibbon: Their History and Their World.* London: Cassell.

Sembel, Nicolas. 2015. "Durkheim, Mauss et la dynamogénie. Le lien Gley." *Durkheimian Studies* 21: 96–133.

Sussman, Robert W., Paul A. Garber, and Jim M. Cheverud. 2005. "Importance of Cooperation and Affiliation in the Evolution of Primate Sociality." *American Journal of Physical Anthropology* 128 (1): 84–97.

Watts Miller, William. 2000. "Durkheimian Time." *Time & Society* 9 (1): 5–20.

———. 2012. *A Durkheimian Quest: Solidarity and the Sacred.* New York: Berghahn.

———. 2017. "Creativity: A Key Durkheimian Concern and Problematic." *Revue européenne des sciences sociales* 55 (2): 17–40.

Whiten, Andrew, Jane Goodall, William C. McGrew, Toshisada Nishida, Vernon Reynolds, Yukimaru Sugiyama, Caroline E.G. Tutin, Richard W. Wrangham, and Christophe A. Boesch. 1999. "Cultures in Chimpanzees." *Nature* 399: 682–685.

Chapter 10

"IT IS NOT MY TIME THAT IS THUS ARRANGED..."

BERGSON, THE "CATEGORY PROJECT," AND THE STRUCTURALIST TURN

Heike Delitz

Émile Durkheim, Marcel Mauss, Henri Hubert, Marcel Granet, and other representatives of the *école française de sociologie* invented a specific and highly original approach to the sociology of knowledge: the search for the origins of human thought, or, the "category project." As a preliminary consideration, the following chapter is interested in the "social origin" of the category project itself. Indeed, the category project arose in parallel with a broader polemical attitude at a particular moment in the history of French philosophy. According to Frédéric Worms, the "philosophical moment" the category project was invented (in fact, the only moment it could have been invented) was the moment of the "problem of spirit" and the "problem of thought" or of knowledge—that of the relation between knowledge and reality, or the problem of the relativity of all thought, scientific thought included (Worms 2009: 36–38, 96–103). Confronted with this contemporary problem, the Durkheimians found their own unique solution: a sociology of thought. Such an idea could only have been developed by assuming a polemical stance with respect to other proposed solutions to the same problem. In particular, the Durkheimians invoked polemics against Henri Bergson and his thought.[1] Given Bergson's contemporary *gloire* (Azouvi 2007) and Durkheim's struggle against "mysticism" and "irrationalism," Bergson can be regarded as a counterpole, in opposition to which Durkheimian sociology emerges. Hence, this article's interest in the "social origin" of the category project itself. At the same time, we will also consider the "legacy" of the Durkheimian sociology of knowledge. Here again, Bergson was probably a key figure. Not only did he provide a polemical counterpoint, against which a thoroughly sociological theory of thought could be elaborated, but in *The Two Sources of Morality and Religion* ([1932] 1935), Bergson (inspired by Durkheim, Mauss, and Lucien Lévy-Bruhl) developed a sociological theory of his own. It was, in fact, Bergson's theory of society—and of classifications of nature—that Claude Lévi-Strauss demonstratively used to arrive at his idea of the symbolic origin of society (as opposed to the social origin of thought and its symbolic expressions). While Durkheimians regard society as the "subject" of all individual actions, feelings, affects, and thoughts, Bergson takes life as the subject of all social and individual facts. Thus, the legacy of the Durkheimian approach and of the category project (or sociology of thought) cannot only be noticed in Bergson's social theory (and in the theories of his followers like Gilbert Simondon or Georges Canguilhem; see Delitz 2015), but in structuralism in general and in all related sociological theories. Structuralism was, of course, developed by Lévi-Strauss in close relation to the work of Durkheim and Mauss. But, as Lévi-Strauss himself writes, he was also informed by Bergson. It was Bergson, not Durkheim, who was "able to make the category of class and the notion of opposition into immediate data of the understanding, which are utilized by the social order in its formation" (Lévi-Strauss [1962] 1991: 97). Structuralism, as a cultural (or symbolic) theory of society, is very familiar to us today. It is therefore easy to locate similar sentences in the work of Durkheim, particularly in *The Elementary Forms of Religious Life*, where Durkheim states that "in all its aspects and at every moment of its history, social life is only possible thanks to a vast symbolism" ([1912] 1995: 233). The notion that society has a cultural origin was introduced by Lévi-Strauss and further developed by Gilles Deleuze, Cornelius Castoriadis, Louis Althusser, Michel Foucault, and others. Although structuralism—as a turn from "constitutive to constituted subjectivity" (Balibar 2003: 10)—was anticipated by Durkheim, it was also something new: while Durkheim and Mauss still thought it "possible to develop a sociological theory of symbolism," for structuralism it was "obvious that what is needed is a symbolic origin of society" (Lévi-Strauss [1950] 1987: 21).

The first part of this article briefly considers Durkheim's sociology of knowledge as a theory of society. The second part analyzes the relation between Durkheimian sociology and Bergson's philosophy. After some introductory remarks, the discussion centers on the polemical origins of the Durkheimian sociology of knowledge, with particular focus on the notions of time (Henri Hubert) and memory (Maurice Halbwachs). Both notions are core concepts in Bergson's philosophy. In each case, Durkheim's project seems to unfold both with and against Bergson: even while employing Bergson's concepts, Durkheim accuses Bergson of being metaphysical, irrational, and psychological. In the third part, our emphasis lies squarely on Bergson. There, our focus is on Bergson's sociological theory—particularly the manner in which he responds to French sociology, thereby paving the way for structuralism and, more generally, other post-foundational schools of sociological thought. The article's overall aim is to reveal structural (and other cultural or symbolic) theories of society as legacies of the Durkheimian category project, legacies that were deeply informed, or altered, by Bergson's philosophy and sociology.

"Socio-centrism": The Originality of the Durkheimian Sociology of Knowledge

> It has quite often been said that man began to conceive things by relating them to himself. The above allows us to see more precisely what this anthropocentrism, which might better be called sociocentrism, consists of. The center of the first schemes of nature is not the individual; it is society. It is this that is objectified, not man. (Durkheim and Mauss [1903] 2009: 51)

This quote reveals the central argument of the Durkheimian sociology of knowledge: society is the source of classifications of nature, space, individuals, and so on. Society—that is, social life as classified and hierarchically ordered—is the subject of all meaning, thought and signification. It expresses itself within symbolic systems. For Durkheim social life exists only as societal life. It is always already structured, for society "is possible only if the individuals and things that make it up are divided among different groups" and "if those groups themselves are classified in relation to one another" (Durkheim [1912] 1995: 444). Furthermore, individuals are, by definition, classified in unequal groups or hierarchical classes. Although such social structures must be expressed symbolically (in order to become objects for thought), they are already given or pre-existent. On several pages, Durkheim and Mauss stress this "socio-centric" view, which takes society as given: social structures (between totemic clans within a tribe, between exogamic kinship groups, or between classes) are the given base of cognitive classifications or the categories of human thought. If human thought classifies animals and plants in species or families, such classifications have their origins in society. All "logical notions have an extra-logical origin," and no "scheme of classification" is the "spontaneous product of abstract understanding." Rather, any classification "results from a process" into which "foreign elements enter" (Durkheim and Mauss [1903] 2009: 5). These foreign elements are social, or better still, societal. Forms of classification of nature, for instance, "merely express . . . the very societies within which they were elaborated"; if they differ from one another, it is because the forms of social organization on which they are based differ—for some categories of thought the "family, the clan, and the moiety" have been "starting point[s]"; others begin with "the spatial relations which people maintained within their society" (38). As Durkheim later formulates: The "model" of the classification of nature is "the panorama of collective life." A "genus," as a defined group of things, is "analogous to the bonds of kinship"; and "we would never have thought of gathering the beings of the universe into homogeneous groups . . . if we had not had the example of human societies before our eyes" (Durkheim [1912] 1995: 148). The same is true for hierarchical classifications. Man "would not even have thought of ordering his knowledge in that way if he had not already known what a hierarchy is." Nothing other "could possibly give us the idea of it. Hierarchy is exclusively a social thing." In sum: "Society furnished the canvas on which logical thought has worked" (149); society is "the basis of the corresponding categories" (445).

Such a sociology of thought undoubtedly represents a great idea and research program, particularly in its anthropological scope—that is, in its interest in non-European concepts and ways of thinking. It has almost no parallel in other traditions of sociology of knowledge, except possibly in the project of Karl Mannheim. There, the interest lies in the social origin of political notions and affects, or their "connectedness to social existence" (Mannheim [1924] 1986). Within French theory, Michel Foucault's "sociology" of knowledge should also be mentioned, notably how he uses historical analysis in order to show, for instance, the political stakes within the definition of "madness" (Foucault [1961] 1964). In Foucault's "history of systems of thought" one also finds a legacy of the category project, which was already present in Lévi-Strauss' analyses—particularly in the latter's examination of the social function of zoological classifications in totemic societies (Lévi-Strauss [1962] 1966). The same is true of Philippe Descola's interest in the different divisions of culture and nature (Descola 2013). And yet, when compared to these more recent sociologies of knowledge, a significant difference emerges: The Durkheimian approach regards cognitive structures as expressions of existing social structures without explicitly analyzing the latter's constitution. "Solely because society exists, there also exists beyond sensations and images a whole system of representations that possess marvelous properties," writes Durkheim ([1912] 1995: 438). While Durkheimian sociology is, therefore, a sociology of the social origins of thought (that is, a social theory of symbolism), its legacy lies in all theories of the symbolic constitution of society and the subject.[2]

A Social Origin of the Category Project: The Philosophy of Henri Bergson

What is Henri Bergson's role in this project and its transformation? To begin with, the relation between the two authors (both of whom were famous in their lifetime) was always antithetical or polemic. This is particularly true for Durkheim (Delitz 2015: 51–82; Durkheim [1914] 1975b; Lukes [1973] 1985: 75), whose anti-Bergsonian positions were obvious to his students (Agathon 1911; 1913). Such polemical and affective aversions were productive: Durkheim could only have invented the new discipline of sociology in opposition to existing approaches and disciplines—particularly to philosophy and psychology. Within French philosophy, one of the most famous schools of thought was that of Bergson. Given Bergson's contemporary *gloire*, the dualistic history of French philosophy—that is, its characteristic split between "rationalism" and "spiritualism" (Foucault [1985] 1998; Pinto 2004; Worms 2009)—and, finally, Durkheim's aversion to the "mystic tendencies" of his time (Durkheim [1895] 1975a; Durkheim [1894] 1982: 33, 74, 159), it is telling that the latter never mentions Bergson by name. Durkheimian sociology was founded as a thoroughly rationalist, a-subjectivist, positivist discipline—that is, as a discipline opposed to all positions to which Bergson's name had been attached ("irrational," "individualistic," "mystic," etc.). Thus, Durkheim's methodological orientation from the outset implied a rejection of Bergson's philosophy: For Durkheim and other rationalist French philosophers, the name "Bergson" stood for all the irrational tendencies of modern thought. By painting Bergson as an "enemy" of science, such thinkers strove to turn sociology into a (positive) science. The Durkheimian sociology of knowledge was conceived as a rational discipline. If the Durkheimian approach consists of sociologizing all philosophical questions (including epistemological ones), thereby satisfying Durkheim's desire to invent a "crown discipline" (Durkheim 1909), then Bergson's philosophy too needed to be sociologized. Sociology, and in particular the sociology of knowledge, is

> destined, we believe, to provide philosophy with the foundations that are indispensable to it and that it is presently lacking. One can even say that sociological reflection is bound to extend by itself and by its natural progress in the form of philosophical reflection; and everything suggests that ... the problems the philosopher addresses will present more than one unexpected aspect. (Durkheim 1909: 758; my translation)[3]

Such is the modus operandi of the category project: sociologizing philosophical notions in order to show their social (but nonetheless rational) origins. In Bergson's philosophy, the notion of time is central. Not surprisingly, the social origin of time is a main theme of the category project. Whereas Bergson understood time as duration (*durée*), as becoming-another, or process, the Durkheimian idea of time is that of a divided time, that is, of time structures. In its attempt to demonstrate the social origins of time, Henri Hubert's *Essay on Time* is illustrative in this regard. It is a masterpiece of the "category project" and was crucial for Durkheim himself, who elaborated his sociology of knowledge vis-à-vis Bergson by asserting the "static" and "already differentiated" character of all reality. In a similar way, Maurice Halbwachs used Bergson to develop a sociology of knowledge in opposition to him, transferring Bergson's notion of "memory" into the domain of the social origin of memory. The category project itself thus had its social origin in its aversion to Bergson.

> The category of time is not simply a partial or complete commemoration of our lived life. It is an abstract and impersonal framework that contains not only our individual existence but also that of humanity. It is like an endless canvas on which all duration is spread out before the mind's eye and on which all possible events are located in relation to points of reference that are fixed and specified. It is not my time that is organized in this way; it is time that is conceived of objectively by all men of the same civilization. This by itself is enough to make us begin to see that any such organization would have to be collective. (Durkheim 1995: 10; for the French original, see Durkheim 1909: 744)

In this passage from the introduction to *The Elementary Forms*, Durkheim summarizes the category project for the first time since *Primitive Classification* (Durkheim and Mauss [1903] 2009). Although Durkheim refers only indirectly to Bergson (via Hubert[4]), the nature of contemporary philosophical discussions allows us to appreciate the obvious sociologization of Bergson's notion of time. Hubert's 1905 *Essay on Time* is a rigorous discussion of Bergson's two first main works—the French dissertation *Time and Free Will* (Bergson [1889] 1910), and Bergson's first major work, *Matter and Memory* (Bergson 1991 [1896]).

A brief sketch of the core of Bergson's philosophy (of time) will permit us to understand the discussion, and sociologization, in Hubert's *Essay on Time*. Bergson's leading idea is to take time seriously. Whereas all "through the history of philosophy time and space have been placed on the same level and treated as things of a kind," Bergson wants to consider "real duration" (Bergson 2012a [1903]: 12; see 2012b [1911]: 131[5]). Time is not a homogenous medium in which things occur. It is not equal to space. Rather, "we must admit two kinds of multiplicity," the "one qualitative and the other quantitative" (Bergson [1889] 1910: 85). Time is a qualitative or intensive multiplicity; it is instantly duration or becoming. Time is "change itself" (Bergson [1903] 2012a: 12); it is "transition" (13). As it is unforeseeable, time is the "new" (18); or, it is a "free act" (19). Space, conversely, is a homogenous multiplicity; it is division and simultaneity; it is already given. Of these two kinds of multiplicity, becoming is the real character of every ontological domain, particularly that of the human social sphere. Bergson's entire philosophy takes recourse to this differentiation between time and space in order to pose all philosophical questions anew, in terms of becoming, duration and time. The questions under consideration are: (1) the relation between mind and body, or between cognition and matter (*Matter and Memory*); (2) questions of organic life and living forms (*Creative Evolution*); and (3) questions of social life and societal forms (*The Two Sources*). In opposition to all philosophies of identity or representation, Bergson elaborates a philosophy of continuous differentiation with the aim of rehabilitating human "freedom"; as he writes, by "introducing space into our perception of duration, it corrupts at its very source our feeling of outer and inner change, of movement and of freedom" (Bergson 1910: 74). In the words of the Bergsonian Gilles Deleuze: Bergson's method consists of replacing problems posed in terms of space with "terms of time" (Deleuze 1991: 31), that is, replacing spatial differences with temporal ones. In this sense, Bergson "has put difference... into time" (Deleuze [1956] 2004b: 43), and Bergsonism is a "philosophy of difference." In Bergson's work, "we meet difference in person, which actualizes itself as the new" (Deleuze [1956] 2004b: 51, see [1956] 2004a).

Hubert (and Durkheim): It Is Not My Time . . .

How does Hubert read Bergson? In his discussion of the latter's first two works, Hubert elaborates a sociological notion of time taking a keen interest in religious time divisions, that is, conventional rhythms of religious and magical life. Indeed, he employs Bergson's notion of time to stress the qualitative, non-homogenous character of social (religious) time. The sociologist's "investigation parallels philosophical analyses" first in Bergson's "Données immediates de la conscience." In considering "the representation of the duration in the individual consciousness," Bergson concludes (according to Hubert) "that the notion of time does not only involve that of quantity, but that it is also qualitative." Second, in the "subtle arabesques of 'Matière et Mémoire,'" Hubert finds the "ideas of length, position and succession" replaced by "the idea of an active tension through which . . . the harmony . . . of different rhythms is realised." From those starting points, and considering "the qualities which constitute the notion of time for magic and religion," the sociologist must now "come even closer to a theory of time as a scale of tensions" (Hubert [1905] 1999: 63). On the one hand, Hubert shares the idea of a qualitative time—of time *qualities*. On the other hand, he at the same time rejects Bergson's central idea: time as becoming, or, more precisely, becoming-another. Instead, Hubert only considers "the different qualities of the parts of time" (64). He is interested both in the "critical dates" at which a duration "begin[s] and end[s]" as well as in the "linkage of multiple series, cycles and orders of durations" (78) in social and natural life. Hubert's sociology of time focuses on the arbitrary connection between a signifying fact on the one hand, and religious time spans on the other. He is interested in the "system of signatures" on which religious time spans are based (64). Such "durations" (or better, time spans) have a social origin, for they entail "the maximum of convention and the minimum of experience" (70). In sum, for Hubert religious time is qualitative but nevertheless divided, whereas Bergson defines real time as a continuous undivided becoming-another. And if Bergson understands all ontological domains as becoming (not only the domain of human thought), Hubert regards this philosophy as "individualistic." For the later Durkheimian interpreter of Hubert, François-André Isambert, Bergson "destructures time in order to make the duration the indefinitely varied and fluid course of the consciousness" (Isambert 1999: 20; see Isambert 1979).

Durkheim: Sub Specie Aeternitatis ...

In Durkheim one finds several critical discussions of Bergson, including arguments against any subjective notion (i.e., of time, of space, etc.), as well as criticisms of any philosophy of process as one of inner life (as Bergson's philosophy was notoriously understood by the Durkheimians and others). On the first point, Durkheim follows Hubert's discovery of the divisions of time and their "social origin."[6] After Hubert one "cannot conceive of time, except on condition of distinguishing its different moments" (Durkheim [1912] 1995: 10). Moreover, there is no subjective or individual time: It "is not *my time* that is thus arranged; it is time in general, such as it is objectively thought of by everybody in a single civilization" (10, original emphasis). In contrast to any idea of an "inner" life (as Durkheim understands Bergson's philosophy), "the notion or category of time is an abstract and impersonal frame which embraces not only our individual existence but that of humanity" (10). Only impersonal, non-individual notions are rational and logical; therefore, society alone is "the origin of logical thought" (437). To "think logically ... is always ... to think impersonally." And furthermore, logical thoughts are thoughts of existence, of states, and of identity; a logical or rational view is a view *sub specie aeternitatis* (as obviously opposed to *sub specie durationis*). "Impersonality and stability: Such are the two characteristics of truth" (10).

By concluding the category project with the assertion that human thought is one of society (and not the subject), Durkheim forcefully, yet implicitly opposes Bergson's philosophy in general. In his "Pragmatism" lectures, again, he revisits the category project, applying the same reasoning, while now explicitly discussing Bergson. The only rational philosophy, he argues here, is a philosophy of identity—not a philosophy that takes becoming as the prior character of all reality. Contradicting Bergson's view, Durkheim claims that the "need for distinction and separation ... lies in things themselves"; it is "not simply a mental need" (Durkheim [1913/14] 1983: 95); life "cannot be defined by mobility alone"; and even "in change itself there must be a static aspect." States are "real elements of becoming"—the "most important" ones, in fact. We "can only represent what is" (96). Once again Durkheim addresses the category project: Truth "is a product of that higher form of life," which is social life, and social life is "the condition for its existence." Truth and the categories of thought are "diverse, because that form of life presents itself in multiple and diverse forms." Regardless of what "pragmatism says" (Bergson included), truth and the categories are "by no means arbitrary," for they are "modelled on ... the realities of social life" (97). "[T]hese indispensable points, in reference to which all things are arranged temporally, are taken from social life. The division into days, weeks, months, years, etc., corresponds to the recurrence of rites, festivals, and public ceremonies at regular intervals. A calendar expresses the rhythm of collective activity while ensuring that regularity" (Durkheim [1912] 1995: 10).

However, despite this epistemological controversy—which lies at the core of the category project and underpins the idea of sociology as rational and positive knowledge—there may yet be a hidden Bergsonian influence, as Dominique La Capra ([1972] 2001: 254–55), Steven Lukes ([1973] 1985: 505–6), William Pickering (1984: 404–5), and Gérard Namer (1994: 305) have all argued. These commentators refer to Durkheim's idea of collective effervescence (Durkheim [1912] 1995: 213, 429) that signals a certain similarity between the two vocabularies of Bergson, and of Durkheim—a similarity further evinced by phrases such as *élan à croire* ("leap," 365) and *élan à agir* ("spur," 432). Others have further argued that not only Bergson, but also Durkheim speaks of social life, becoming, and creativity (see Riley, Pickering, and Watts Miller 2013).

Halbwachs: It Is Not My Memory ...

Let us now turn to how the notion of "memory" might be treated as part of the category project. How can it be conceived as having a social origin? Maurice Halbwachs, one of Bergson's pupils, waged a lifelong "epistemological war" against Bergson (Namer 1997: 261),[7] accusing him of being subjectivist and of advancing a psychological theory (particularly with respect to memory, but also with regard to all other philosophical questions). If Durkheim stated, "it is not my time," Halbwachs added, "it is not my memory." For Halbwachs, memory always is a group phenomenon; any individual memory is socially conditioned. Furthermore, any society or group requires a shared imagination of its history—that is, a collective memory. To arrive at this influential concept, Halbwachs considered Bergson's philosophy of memory in both *La mémoire collective* (Halbwachs 1997; see Halbwachs 1980) and *Les cadres sociaux de la mémoire collective* (Halbwachs 1994; see Halbwachs 1992). According to him "we speak of collective time, as opposed to individual duration" (Halbwachs 1997: 156; my translation). With every argument he counters what he refers to as Bergson's "hypothesis of purely individual and mutually inaccessible durations" (Halbwachs 1980: 90). Consciousness, or individuality, is an "illusion"; the individual is merely the "point of intersection" of groups (97). The "individual conscience is only the point of passage." It is the "meeting point of collective times" (Halbwachs 1997: 190; my translation). In strict keeping with Durkheim, Halbwachs insists that any notion of time, memory or duration must have social origins; all such notions are founded "in a collective time" (Halbwachs 1980: 98). Bergson, by contrast, seems to assume the existence of "as many durations as individuals, and an abstract time that comprehends them all" (Halbwachs 1997: 190; my translation). Moreover, Bergson seems to assume that

> our past in its entirety remains in memory . . . fully formed in the unconscious mind like so many printed pages of books that could be opened, even though they no longer are. In my view, by contrast, what remains are not ready-made images in some subterranean gallery of our thought. Rather, we can find in society all the necessary information for reconstructing certain parts of our past, represented in an incomplete and indefinite manner or even considered completely gone from memory. (Halbwachs 1980: 75)

In short, memory has social origins; time has a social origin; durations have social origins. Since every individual belongs to several groups, "participates in several social thoughts," and is "immersed in several collective times," all "those psychologists who believe that each individual consciousness has a distinctive duration" stand in need of correction (Halbwachs 2011: 148). In all of the above, however, Halbwachs distorts Bergson's philosophy or, to put it more sharply, wants to reduce it to "nothing" (Namer 1997: 261). In fact, Bergson is not so much concerned with the individual or subjective consciousness. Rather, Bergsonism is a new "monism" (Deleuze [1966] 1991: 29). More than a philosophy of process, Bergson's philosophy is an ontology of immanence. In other words, Bergson develops a non-Cartesian way of thinking. For him there is no inner life at all. In stressing the selective activity of memory Halbwachs actually shares a core conviction with this ontology of immanence, duration, and becoming (a conviction that Bergson elucidates precisely in *Matter and Memory*): that is, "virtual" or pure "memory can only become actual by means of the perception which attracts it" (Bergson [1896] 1991: 163).

Bergson: The "Foundations of a Genuine Sociological Logic"

"Societies are just so many islands consolidated here and there in the ocean of becoming," writes Bergson in *The Two Sources of Morality and Religion* (Bergson [1932] 1935: 95). As the author himself stressed in a letter to Halbwachs, *The Two Sources* is a "book of sociology" (not philosophy), for sociology is a "whole discipline and not only one school" (Bergson 2002: 1387; my translation).[8] Our interest now turns to understanding Bergson's sociological theory as a "legacy" of the Durkheimian approach (and more specifically—but not solely—as a legacy of the category project). We are also interested in the ways in which Bergsonian sociology paved the way for structuralism as a turn from the search for the social origins of categories to the constitution of society within classificatory systems. On the one hand, Bergson follows Durkheim closely, while on the other hand criticizing him for being an "enemy of freedom" (quoted in Benrubi 1942: 63). He accepts Durkheim's need to integrate the moral and the cognitive and yet, unlike Durkheim, is always interested in new social ideas and the emergence of society. Rather than taking society as a given, Bergson's sociology is a sociology of the institution of society. It is in this context that Lévi-Strauss states: If Durkheim "affirms the primacy of the social over the intellect," it "is precisely to the degree that Bergson intends the opposite of the sociologist, in the Durkheimian sense of the word, that he is able to make the category of class and the notion of opposition into immediate data of the understanding, which are utilized by the social order in its formation" (Lévi-Strauss [1962] 1991: 97). Because Durkheimians' interest lies in the social origin of thought, they only implicitly address the constitution of society. However, they do address it nonetheless. In retrospect one must correct Lévi-Strauss: while he claims to find only "vague ideas such as contagion or contamination" in Durkheim (97), Durkheim does, in fact, have a clear idea of the constitution of society. For Durkheim society is constituted within affective situations of collective effervescence (see Durkheim [1912] 1995: 217–21) but not by means of systems of classification. It is only from this standpoint that Bergson seems to be "in a better position than Durkheim to lay the foundations of a genuine sociological logic" (Lévi-Strauss [1962] 1991: 97); indeed, Bergson is wholly focused on totemism as a classificatory system. Bergson thereby questions Durkheim's thesis of personal identification with the totem and of its merely emblematic function—eventually settling on a middle way. The clan member "does not identify himself with his totem," since he has an idea of his existence as human; neither does he "simply take it as an emblem." The totem

> occupies too large a place in their existence for us to see in it merely a means of designating the clan. The truth must lie somewhere half-way.... To express the fact that two clans constitute two different species, the name of one animal will be given to one, that of another to the other.

> Each of these designations, taken singly, is no more than a label: taken together they are equivalent to an affirmation. They indicate in fact that the two clans are of different blood. (Bergson [1932] 1935: 156)

Different clans are constituted via totemic classifications. Societies integrate themselves via difference or by introducing discontinuities into continuous nature. So, if the clan members "declare that they constitute two animal species, it is not on the animality, but on the duality that they lay the stress" (157). Again, Durkheim not only recognized this aspect of totemism ("Between two beings that are classified in two different phratries, there is not only separation but also antagonism," Durkheim [1912] 1995: 240), but also, as mentioned above, regarded society as symbolically constituted. Nonetheless, for Lévi-Strauss it was Bergson who saw "what lay behind totemism" (Lévi-Strauss [1962] 1991: 98–99), that is, the cultural necessity of introducing the discontinuous into the continuous in order to constitute collective life, which, by definition, is differentiated or classified into a plurality of collectives. In following Durkheim, Bergson exhibits the imagination of collective unity, of identity over time, and of the foundation of society, while simultaneously inventing a theory of difference. Bergson calls this the "myth-making function" or societal "fiction" that brings something into existence rather than merely expressing an extant collective (Bergson [1932] 1935: 88). In other words, societies are imaginary institutions (Castoriadis [1975] 1998).

One can go even further: for Bergson it is life that is existent or real. Life is the subject of all social facts, including both "the subject" and society. Life is instituting; it is therefore "tendency," as Bergson says, or bifurcation. Life creates "divergent directions among which its impetus is divided" (Bergson [1907] 1944: 110). Social life, too, is a constant becoming-another (differentiation); to live in collectives, social bodies must differentiate themselves from one another. In other words, social life is only real or existent in "closed" societies. As a "real and effective duration" (Bergson 1935: 95), social life implies differentiated societies. Therefore, societies only possess unity and identity as imaginations. While Bergson speaks of *natura naturata* and *natura naturans* or of the relation between "closed society" and "open society" (Bergson [1932] 1935: 44–45),[9] for Castoriadis it is the instituting society (i.e., social life, becoming or *natura naturans*) that permanently creates instituted societies (i.e., societal life, institutions or *natura naturata*):[10]

> The social-historical is the anonymous collective whole . . . that fills every given social formation but which also engulfs it, setting each society in the midst of others, inscribing them all within a continuity

in which those who are no longer, those who are elsewhere and even those yet to be born are in a certain sense present. It is, on the one hand, given structures, "materialized" institutions and works, whether these be material or not; and, on the other hand, *that which* structures, institutes, materializes. In short, it is the union *and* the tension of instituting society and of instituted society, of history made and of history in the making. (Castoriadis [1975] 1998: 108)

Implicitly, and contrary to his own understanding (Castoriadis 1985: 9–10), Castoriadis draws the conclusions from Bergson's theory: a society is an imaginary institution; it always implies the idea of living in this or that society; it requires fixation and identification. Thus, society must deny its "radical otherness," its "novelty" and its "incessant transformation" (Castoriadis [1975] 1998: 114) "by providing itself with 'stable' figures" (126). The symbolic constitution of society becomes obvious here: as an imaginary institution a given society only exists symbolically. In positing the imagined and symbolic character of society Bergson occupies a key position between the category project and structuralism (or cultural theories of society).

At this point further developments in the theory of society beyond Bergson, Lévi-Strauss, and Castoriadis need to be briefly sketched. Claude Lefort, Chantal Mouffe, and Ernesto Laclau emphasize not only the imaginative character of a given society's unity and identity, but also the hegemonic character of any such imagination. For the incessant becoming-another is real; and conflicts over the determination of society and the plurality of constitutive differences are real too. The constitutive "outside" always "impedes" the closed character, or the "full realization" of society's unity (Laclau and Mouffe [1985] 2001: xviii).

> The limit of the social cannot be traced [simply] as a frontier separating two territories—for the perception of a frontier supposes the perception of something beyond . . . that is, a new difference. The limit of the social [is] subverting it, destroying its ambition to constitute a full presence. Society never manages fully to be society, because everything in it is penetrated by its limits, which prevent it from constituting itself as an objective reality. ([1985] 2001 126–27)

Conclusion

Bergson served two different functions at two different times for Durkheimian sociology of knowledge and its theory of society. Initially he played a negative role. At the outset of the "category project," Bergson was useful both as an inspiration and as an adversary.

Later—after Durkheim's death and at the moment of structuralism's invention—Bergson played a more inspiring or positive role. First, his own book on sociology was built on the conceptual legacy of the category project, transforming Durkheim's and Mauss's sociology of knowledge into the (proto)structural concept of the symbolic constitution of society. If Lévi-Strauss rightly recognized Bergson as having invented "a genuine social logic," we must concede that Bergson's work precipitated a veritable turn in sociological theory. Second, both structural and post-foundational social thought (Delitz and Maneval 2017; Marchart 2007) share the following idea with Bergson: society has no fixed base; it is never given and therefore it must constantly be imagined and symbolized. In other words, society is as impossible as it is necessary (see Laclau and Mouffe [1985] 2001: 112–15). Seen in this light, structuralism is a legacy of the Durkheimian project—a project simultaneously determined by a second movement of thought: an understanding of society as something imagined, something that must be symbolized, if it is to exist, and that, therefore, can never be identical to itself.

Heike Delitz is a private lecturer at the Chair of Sociological Theory at the University of Bamberg. Her research focuses on sociological theory, political and religious sociology, and the sociology of architecture. She researches, among other things, imaginaries of society or collective identity as well as societal effects of architectures. Delitz has published an introductory work on Durkheim (2013), and her habilitation focused on "Bergson Effects. Aversions and Attractions in French Sociological Thought" (2015).

Notes

1. Delitz (2015, chap. 1). For the polemical nature of Durkheim's work see Terry Clark (1968), Philippe Besnard (1979), Victor Karady (1979), and Bertrand Müller (1993).
2. Durkheim founds society on collective feelings or affects. Although Lévi-Strauss regarded this as a mistake, current sociological theories once again find the Durkheim of affects to be of high topicality. See, for instance, Randall Collins (2004), Christian von Scheve (2009), or Robert Seyfert (2013).
3. "destinée, croyons-nous, à fournir à la philosophie les bases qui lui sont indispensables et qui lui manquent présentement. On peut même dire que la réflexion sociologique est appelée à se prolonger d'elle-même et par son progrès naturel sous la forme de réflexion philosophique; et tout

permet de présumer que ... les problèmes que traite le philosophe présenteront plus d'un aspect inattendu" (Durkheim 1909: 758).
4. Durkheim only mentions Bergson, explicitly, in the lectures on *Pragmatism and Sociology* (Durkheim [1913/14] 1983).
5. "A philosopher worthy of the name has never said more than a single thing: and even then it is something he has tried to say, rather than actually said."
6. Both Isambert and Watts Miller stress the fact that "the essay does not fall in with Durkheimian 'orthodoxy'" (Watts Miller 2000: 6) in that it offers "a theory of sacred time, rather than of social time." For Durkheim (and Mauss), conversely, the social and the religious are interconnected; religious ideas, rites, and symbols are constitutive of society, collective life, and collective identity. See the famous conclusion in Durkheim: "the god of the clan, the totemic principle, can be none other than the clan itself, but the clan transfigured and imagined in the physical form of the plant or animal which serves as totem" ([1912] 1995: 208). "The gods are only the symbolic expression" of society (351).
7. "The sociology of memory in 'Les cadres sociaux' was a political as well as an epistemological war, bringing to bear against Bergson a new rationalism, a new sociology and a new theory of progress" (Namer 1997: 239, my translation).
8. In Mauss's view ([1933] 1969: 436), *The Two Sources* is only a "literary view of social facts." For another take on *The Two Sources*, see Célestin Bouglé (1935: 28–29), who writes that Bergson "invites us to break the ice of the concepts of social origins in order to rediscover the stream of inner life."
9. In this quote from *The Two Sources*, Bergson indicates a free use of Baruch Spinoza's formula "*nature viewed* as *active (natura naturans)* and *nature viewed* as *passive (natura naturata)*" ([1677] 1981: 51): "[I]n passing from social solidarity to the brotherhood of man, we break with one particular nature, but not with all nature. It might be said, by slightly distorting the terms of Spinoza, that it is to get back to *natura naturans* that we break away from *natura naturata*" (Bergson [1932] 1935: 44). In a certain sense, Bergson could be called a Spinozist. This is particularly true for the notion of affect and the immanentism in *Matter and Memory*. In 1927 Bergson famously wrote: "[E]very *philosopher* has *two philosophies*: his own and *Spinoza's*." For Spinoza in Bergson, see, for instance, Gregory Adamson (2000); for the relation between Bergson, Deleuze, and Spinoza, see Keith Ansell-Pearson (2012: 11–13). Durkheim, too, had an intense relation to Spinoza—both in his work in general (Lazzeri 2008) and its category of "totality" (Nielsen 1999) as well as in his theory of affect in particular (Barnwell 2018).
10. In the work of Castoriadis, the reference to Spinoza is more implicit than with Bergson. Nevertheless, the affinity is obvious here too: "For all those who have read Spinoza, ... notions like 'the imaginary institution of

society' can't be meaningless: one feels immediately on a familiar terrain," writes Frédéric Lordon (2018: 94; my translation; for the relation between Castoriadis and Spinoza, see also Saar 2015).

References

Adamson, Gregory D. 2000. "Bergson's Spinozist Tendencies." *Philosophy Today* 44(1): 73–85.
Agathon. 1911. *L'esprit de la nouvelle Sorbonne*. Paris: Mercure de France.
———. 1913. *Les jeunes gens d'aujourd'hui*. Paris: Mercure de France.
Ansell-Pearson, Keith. 2012. *Germinal Life: The Difference and Repetition of Deleuze*. London: Routledge.
Azouvi, François. 2007. *La Gloire de Bergson: Essai sur le magistère philosophique*. Paris: Gallimard.
Balibar, Étienne. 2003. "Structuralism: A Destitution of the Subject?" *differences: A Journal of Feminist Cultural Studies* 14(1): 1–21.
Barnwell, Ashley. 2018. "Durkheim as Affect Theorist." *Journal of Classical Sociology* 18(1): 21–35.
Benrubi, Isaak. 1942. *Souvenirs sur Bergson*. Neuchâtel: Delachaux et Niestle.
Bergson, Henri. [1889] 1910. *Time and Free Will: An Essay on the Immediate Data of Consciousness*. London: Allen & Unwin.
———. 1927. "Letter to Léon Brunschvicg, February 22, 1927." *Journal des Débats*, 28 February.
———. [1932] 1935. *The Two Sources of Morality and Religion*. London: Macmillan.
———. [1907] 1944. *Creative Evolution*. London: Macmillan.
———. [1896] 1991. *Matter and Memory*. New York: Zone Books.
———. 2002. *Correspondances*. Paris: Presses universitaires de France (PUF).
———. [1903] 2012a. "Introduction, Part I." In *The Creative Mind: An Introduction to Metaphysics*, trans. Mabelle L. Andison, 1–17. New York: Dover.
———. [1911] 2012b. "Philosophical Intuition." In *The Creative Mind: An Introduction to Metaphysics*, trans. Mabelle L. Andison, 87–106. New York: Dover.
Besnard, Philippe. 1979. "La formation de l'équipe de 'L'Année sociologique.'" *Revue française de sociologie* 20: 7–31.
Bouglé, Célestin. 1935. *Bilan de la sociologie française contemporaine*. Paris: Félix Alcan.
Castoriadis, Cornelius. 1985. *Domaines de l'homme. Les carrefours du labyrinthe 2*. Paris: Seuil.
———. [1975] 1998. *The Imaginary Institution of Society*. Cambridge, MA: MIT.
Clark, Terry. 1968. "Émile Durkheim and the Institutionalization of Sociology." *Archives européennes de sociologie* 9: 36–71.

Collins, Randall. 2004. *Interaction Ritual Chains*. Princeton, NJ: Princeton University Press.

Deleuze, Gilles. [1966] 1991. *Bergsonism*. New York: Zone Books.

———. [1956] 2004a. "Bergson, 1859–1941." In *Desert Islands and Other Texts 1953–1974*, ed. David Lapoujade, trans. Michael Taormina, 22–31. Los Angeles: Semiotext(e).

———. [1956] 2004b. "Bergson's Conception of Difference." In *Desert Islands and Other Texts 1953–1974*, ed. David Lapoujade, trans. Michael Taormina, 32–51. Los Angeles: Semiotext(e).

Delitz, Heike. 2015. *Bergson-Effekte. Aversionen und Attraktionen im französischen soziologischen Denken*. Weilerswist: Velbrück.

Delitz, Heike, and Stefan Maneval. 2017. "The 'Hidden Kings,' or Hegemonic Imaginaries. Analytical Perspectives of Postfoundational Social Thought." *Im@go: Journal of the Social Imaginary* 10: 33–49.

Descola, Philippe. 2013. *Beyond Nature and Culture*. Chicago: University of Chicago Press.

Durkheim, Émile. 1909. "Sociologie religieuse et théorie de la connaissance." *Revue de Métaphysique et de la Morale* 17(6): 733–58.

———. [1894] 1982. *The Rules of Sociological Method*. New York: Free Press.

———. [1895] 1975a. "L'enseignement philosophique et l'agrégation de philosophie." In *Textes 3. Fonctions sociales et institutions*, ed. Victor Karady, 403–34. Paris: Minuit.

———. [1914] 1975b. "Une confrontation entre bergsonisme et sociologisme: le progrès moral et la dynamique sociale." In *Textes 1: Éléments d'une théorie sociale*, ed. Victor Karady, 64–70. Paris: Minuit.

———. [1894] 1982. *The Rules of Sociological Method*. New York: Free Press.

———. [1913/14] 1983. *Pragmatism and Sociology*. Cambridge: Cambridge University Press.

———. [1912] 1995. *The Elementary Forms of Religious Life*, trans. Karen E. Fields. New York: Free Press.

Durkheim, Émile, and Marcel Mauss. [1903] 2009. *Primitive Classification*. Chicago: University of Chicago Press.

Foucault, Michel. [1961] 1964. *Madness and Civilization: A History of Insanity in the Age of Reason*. New York: Pantheon Books.

———. [1985] 1998. "Life: Experience and Science." In *Michel Foucault: Aesthetics, Method, and Epistemology*, ed. James D. Faubion, 465–78. New York: The New Press.

Halbwachs, Maurice. 1980. *The Collective Memory*. New York: Harper & Row.

———. 1992. "The Social Frameworks of Memory." In *On Collective Memory*, ed. Lewis A. Coser, 37–190. Chicago: University of Chicago Press.

———. 1994. *Les cadres sociaux de la mémoire collective*. Ed. Critique. Paris: Gallimard.

———. 1997. *La mémoire collective*. Ed. Critique. Paris: Gallimard.

———. 2011. "From 'The Collective Memory.'" In *The Collective Memory Reader*, ed. Jeffrey K. Olick, Vered Vinitzky-Seroussi, and Daniel Levy, 139–49. Oxford: Oxford University Press.

Hubert, Henri. [1905] 1999. *Essay on Time: A Brief Study of the Representation of Time in Religion and Magic.* London: Berghahn.

Isambert, François-André. 1979. "Henri Hubert et la sociologie du temps." *Revue française de sociologie* 20(1): 183–204.

———. 1999. "Introduction." In Henri Hubert, *Essay on Time: A Brief Study of the Representation of Time in Religion and Magic*, ed. Robert Parkin, 3–42. London: Berghahn.

Karady, Victor. 1979. "Stratégies de réussite et modes de faire-valoir de la sociologie chez les durkheimiens." *Revue française de sociologie* 20: 49–82.

Laclau, Ernesto, and Chantal Mouffe. [1985] 2001. *Hegemony and Socialist Strategy: Towards a Radical Democratic Politics.* New York: Zone Books.

La Capra, Dominick. [1972] 2001. *Emile Durkheim: Sociologist and Philosopher.* Aurora: The Davies Group.

Lazzeri, Christian. 2008. "Spinoza et Durkheim." In *Spinoza au XIXe siècle: Actes des journées d'études organisées à la Sorbonne (9 et 16 mars, 23 et 30 novembre 1997)*, ed. André Tosel, Pierre-François Morau, and Jean Salem, 269–280. Paris: Éditions de la Sorbonne.

Lévi-Strauss, Claude. [1962] 1966. *The Savage Mind.* London: Weidenfeld & Nicholson.

———. [1950] 1987. *Introduction to the Work of Marcel Mauss.* London: Routledge.

———. [1962] 1991. *Totemism.* London: Merlin Press.

Lordon, Frédéric. 2018. "Sens, valeur, et puissance du collectif—entre Castoriadis et Spinoza." In *Actualité d'une pensée radicale—Hommage à Cornelius Castoriadis*, ed. Vincent Descombes, Florence Giust-Desprairies and Mats Rosengren, 94–105. Uppsala: Uppsala Rhetorical Studies.

Lukes, Steven. [1973] 1985. *Emile Durkheim: His Life and Work: A Historical and Critical Study.* Stanford, CA: Stanford University Press.

Mannheim, Karl. [1924] 1986. *Conservatism: A Contribution to the Sociology of Knowledge.* London: Routledge.

Marchart, Oliver. 2007. *Post-Foundational Political Thought: Political Difference in Nancy, Lefort, Badiou and Laclau.* Edinburgh: Edinburgh University Press.

Mauss, Marcel. [1933] 1969. "La sociologie en France depuis 1914." In *Œuvres III. Cohésion sociale et division de la sociologie*, ed. Victor Karady, 436–59. Paris: Minuit.

Müller, Bertrand. 1993. "Critique bibliographique et stratégie disciplinaire dans la sociologie durkheimienne." *Regards sociologiques* 5: 9–23.

Namer, Gérard. 1994. "Postface." In Maurice Halbwachs, *Les cadres sociaux de la mémoire*, 297–367. Paris: Gallimard.

———. 1997. "Postface." In Maurice Halbwachs, *La Mémoire collective*, 239–95. Paris: Gallimard.

Nielsen, Donald A. 1999. *Three Faces of God: Society, Religion, and the Categories of Totality in the Philosophy of Émile Durkheim.* Albany, NY: Suny Press.

Pickering, William. 1984. *Durkheim's Sociology of Religion: Themes and Theories.* London: Routledge & Kegan Paul.

Pinto, Louis. 2004. "Le débat sur les sources de la morale et de la religion." *Actes de la recherche en sciences sociales* 153: 41–47.

Riley, Alexander, William S.F. Pickering, and William Watts Miller, eds. 2013. *Durkheim, the Durkheimians, and the Arts.* London: Berghahn Books.

Saar, Martin. 2015. "Spinoza and the Political Imaginary," trans. William Callison and Anne Gräfe. *Qui Parle* 23(2): 115–33.

Seyfert, Robert. 2013. "Identifikation—Imitation—Imagination: Transformative Mechanismen in Durkheims Religionssoziologie." In *Émile Durkheim—Soziologie und Ethnologie*, ed. Tanja Bogusz and Heike Delitz, 503–27. Frankfurt am Main: Campus.

Spinoza, Baruch. 1981 [1677]. *Ethics.* Ann Arbor, MI: J. Simon Publisher.

von Scheve, Christian. 2009. *Emotionen und soziale Strukturen: Die affektiven Grundlagen sozialer Ordnung.* Frankfurt am Main: Campus.

Watts Miller, William. 2000. "Durkheimian Time." *Time & Society* 9(1): 5–20.

Worms, Frédéric. 2009. *La philosophie en France au XXe siècle: Moments.* Paris: Gallimard.

Chapter 11

"LET US DARE A LITTLE BIT OF METAPHYSICS"

MARCEL MAUSS, HENRI HUBERT, AND LOUIS WEBER ON THE CATEGORIES OF CAUSALITY, TIME, AND TECHNOLOGY

Johannes F. M. Schick

Managing time has always been a central task of human beings. The calendar, sacred periods, festivals, as well as the scientific notion of time are products of the desire to manage, to predict, and to manipulate what cannot be fully managed: the course of time and the encompassing nature that goes beyond the reach of human beings.

Time's ontological force is managed by techniques that allow the repetition of the same action with always the same outcome: from present causes future effects are induced. Thus, if one considers *technology*[1] as a category, as Émile Durkheim and his *équipe* did,[2] the categories of causality and of time are necessarily implied.

Technology is therefore within the framework of the "category project" a relational, hybrid category, which intrinsically links time, space, substance, and causality. Techniques refer to and channel a fundamental, ontological force (*mana*, *physis* or *nature*) in creating socio-technical structures and institutions. Yet, the question arises whether the categories of space and time are prior to the technical activity or if techniques—be they social or material—generate the categories of space and time. This fundamental, metaphysical quest to search for the first cause of these categories is at the heart of the philosophical project of the Durkheim School and subject of critique on the part of philosophers.

One of these philosophers was the now forgotten Louis Weber, who, according to René König, gave one of the most pertinent critiques of Durkheim (König 1978: 57). He was at center stage of the discussions at the turn of the century on the status of sociology as a science and its relationship with philosophy. The discussion started in 1914 after Weber had published *Le Rythme du Progrès* (1913) and presented his work at the Societé Française de Philosophie (SFP; Weber 1914). While Marcel Mauss was not present at the session in 1914, he was in 1921, when Weber presented his views concerning the question of free will and its relation to language at the SFP (Weber 1921). Mauss used this occasion to dare Weber and the audience to "a little bit of metaphysics" (Weber 1921: 103).[3]

This discussion between Mauss and Weber provides the background against which technology can appear clear and distinct as a category. One can interpret Louis Weber as critique of Durkheim's disregard of technology. While Durkheim, as Nathan Schlanger points out, deemed it necessary to argue against historical materialism in favor of religion rather than technology as the primary source of social evolution (Schlanger 2006: 8), Weber held that the origins of human intelligence are technical. This opposition between technical origin and social origin crystallized in Bergson's notion of the *homo faber*, which led to controversial discussions in France in the first half of the twentieth century (Sigaut 2013). Weber argued against Durkheim's fundamental thesis that the social, or rather the experience of the social force, is the primary source of the category of causality. He also defended a radically dualistic position proposing two concepts of causality: a primary one derived from technical activity and a secondary one derived from language (Weber 1914: 62–63).

In this chapter I will follow the genesis of the categories of causality, time, and technology, starting with Weber's criticism of Émile Durkheim, Henri Hubert, and Marcel Mauss. His insistence on the independence of technical intelligence had its foundation in the engagement of the individual human being with matter. The dualistic conception of Weber will be contrasted in the second part of this chapter with Mauss's and Hubert's holistic ontology. They argued for the interpenetration of the social and the technical. The concomitance of the social and the technical generates differences, categories, and concepts that are in a recursive relationship with the human body and its sociotechnical practices. This argument will be illustrated in the third part of this chapter, where I will focus on the genesis of the category of time, which Hubert conceives, as we will see, as "symbolic and an operating system" of society (Isambert 1999: 31). The category of time is thus a product of "rhythm techniques." I situate the discussion of time and technology within the debate concerning Bergson's notion of the *homo faber*. Instead of opposing Hubert's theory of time to Bergson's (see Delitz, this volume), this will allow us to read both theories as complementary to each other. I argue that Hubert "socializes" Bergson's theory of duration via technical practices. Technical developments—from the invention of the first calendar to the invention of the smartphone—participate in the creation of the category and thus influence the social experience of time. This means that the implementation of the abstract, quantitative notion of time has consequences for the qualitative experience of time. In this interplay of theory and praxis, the human body serves as the medium in which the operating system "time" runs.

Two Forms of Causality

In order to search for the origin of human intelligence, Louis Weber goes back to the most fundamental practices of man. This point of departure differs significantly from the project of the Durkheim School. While Durkheim, in the *Elementary Forms of Religious Life*, researches Australian tribes as purportedly offering the "most primitive" and thus elemental form of social life (Durkheim 1995: 1), Weber searches for the origins of progress and finds distinct phases of development of significant social or technical types. Although Weber is very well aware of the fact that the social activity and the technical activity constantly interpenetrate each other, he nevertheless claims that one can "discern and affirm their distinct existence" (Weber 1913: XII). These distinct modes of existence are, according to him, linked to two different notions and faculties of man: the technical faculty of the *homo faber* is equally valid and essential as is the social faculty of the human being (XII). The most elementary form of human existence is therefore an individual using tools to survive and to structure its environment.

It follows that the technical activity is logically possible prior to any social activity. Weber develops this argument against the background of Mauss and Hubert's *A General Theory of Magic* (1904) and Durkheim and Mauss's "Essay on Classification" (Durkheim and Mauss 1903). In general, he argues that a social force can only be efficient, if the "instrument of language" (Weber 1913: 140) already exists. Thus, magic and classification presuppose language. Language is a tool that instantiates a form of causality that allows magic to be efficient, since "gesture and speech are agents whose effectiveness expresses itself in its sole result, without sensitive vehicle" (141). Thus, the social force can only be efficient, because it already employs language.

Weber does not deny that society has causal effects on the individual mind, but rather questions how collective representations are formed and what kind of primordial experiences are needed in order to create the categories of understanding.

In an extensive commentary on a passage from *A General Theory of Magic*, where Hubert and Mauss introduce the notion of *mana* and argue that "magic is the most childish of skills (*techniques*)" and "possibly the oldest" (Mauss 1904: 175), Weber disagrees "with the animistic conception or rather animist feeling of nature" (Weber 1913: 155). Weber does not deny the existence of *mana* as a social force, but rather argues for the independence and primacy of the technical faculty of intelligence:

> In short, it [*mana*] is a "category," but not a category of individual understanding; it is "a category of collective thought" ... it results only from the functioning of living as a group. Taking this analysis and conclusion as being accurate, it follows that the institution of magic presupposes an earlier work of social forces in individual consciences, a prior organization of life in society, an already quite advanced integration of individuals into groups. There is no evidence that these conditions were necessary for the invention of the first techniques, because they do not require any collective belief to be transmitted; their effectiveness is the subject of immediate individual perception; their functioning can be repeated by imitation, from one individual to another. It is perfectly possible that they are anterior to language. (Weber 1913: 156)

The argument of Weber against the Durkheimians is developed in three steps: First, he argues against a primordial animistic notion of matter. Matter, according to Weber, is not primarily perceived as an animated entity (Weber 1913: 132) but rather by means of the technical activity of man, which provides the primitive with an "unconscious direct sentiment of the relations of cause and effect" (140). This "sentiment" provides the basis to form a mechanical conception of the material world (140). Furthermore, the primitive human being needs, "1st, a purely empirical, but already fairly objective representation of the material world" and, "2nd, an exact perception of causality" (138) in order to create tools.

Second, Weber turns from the general notion of matter to the more specific and already "social" notion of *mana* and asks for its origin. *Mana* belongs to the distinct form of social intelligence that is performed by collectives and groups. Grasping the effectiveness of techniques does not require a collective representation nor does it presuppose society. Individuals can experience the efficacy of techniques without any link to a group or a collective.

Third, language is necessary to form collective representations. Weber points out that conceptual thought is very different from practical thought. We are, however, so used to thinking in words and concepts that we are unable to conceive of thought other as in terms of language (Weber 1913: 123–24).[4] Gestures and words are the "instruments of social practice" (165). They are performed according to a specific rhythm and cause effects without any sensual vehicle, as we have seen above.

The distinction between prelinguistic, technical thought on the one hand and linguistic, social thought on the other is derived from an ontogenetic argument. Primitive individuals hunt, gather, and create tools alone to accomplish tasks. They have only representations that are bound to technical activity: "The ideation is enveloped in sensations or emotions or is welded to motor representations" (Weber 1913: 188). This technical reasoning and its accompanying representations follow the laws of causality and identity naturally; they have an immediate practical goal and are linked to the gestures and acts that have to be performed to achieve it (188). According to Weber, "the hunter, who represents the bow and the arrow, does not separate the image of the movements that he executes. . . . Thought and action are welded together, precisely because thought is effective, exactly adapted to reality and immediately translated by effective gestures" (188).

This technical intelligence, however, does not generate conceptual thought by itself, since the formation of concepts already presupposes a form of thought that is detached from action (1913: 188). This leads to Weber's paradoxical argument that reflexive thinking began in the illogical, namely religious, social thought, where the importance of ideation is reversed: as soon as man entertains "immaterial relations with things, beings and gods, . . . ideation is no longer accidental, but becomes essential" (189). Implicitly referring to Bergson's theory of attention in *Matter and Memory* (Bergson 1991: 101–103), Weber explains that when establishing immaterial relations, all movements and muscular efforts are reduced to a minimum. A Durkheimian might immediately object that within rituals of effervescence it is precisely the body that is affected and involved in the ritual.

However, Weber does not deny the involvement of the body in the ritual. The social function of language entails not only speech, but also a system of gestures, which is crystallized in dance and in facial expressions (Weber 1913: 178). Both, dance and facial expression are, according to Weber, powerful tools to convey and express collective feelings (178). Language with the help of gestures, among other things, introduces an immaterial, foggy conception of causality by habitually acting upon immaterial things. Accordingly, first ideal classifications are created, that is, classifications independent of raw sensations that are seemingly random and heterogeneous (179).

Language is conceived of as an instrument, a tool that is used by the body of an individual. These bodily movements are directed by a collective representation and have a goal that is different from their technical representation: the goal of the ritual is not the representation of organized movements directed at a material, technical outcome. Language instantiates, according to Weber, a process of differentiation and detachment (1913: 189).[5]

The genesis of human intelligence, according to Weber, begins with the technical activity of man. As soon as others are involved, a different form of activity is performed, allowing individuals to act at a distance without any material medium being involved. With language, human beings have an instrument that can be either applied to something else or used upon itself: "With language not only the objects are put in relation to one another, but also their names and the ideas they signify" (1913: 192). Human beings have thus gained power over the whole of nature, be it material or immaterial. Religion and its rituals, are for Weber as for the Durkheimians a technique sui generis (Weber 1914: 62), but this technique relies upon a different conception of intelligence and a different set of representations. The genesis of the concept of causality is an example of Weber's argument:

> The concept of cause is much later. But it might never have been formed without this first contribution that comes from our contact with matter and the first attempts to use matter to overcome matter itself. It may seem paradoxical to put at the origin of a "category," of the category of cause, experiences that do not require any use of concepts as such. But the paradox diminishes, if we think that in this first state the feeling of causality cannot be dissociated and separated from the practices themselves.... The notion of causality, with all that it signifies, implies that the consequent is determined and always the same, whenever ... a certain antecedent is given. Such regularity can only be implanted in the spirit through the exercise of the technical faculty.... Indeed, the effects of mass, weight and shock were the first whose immutable irregularity manifested itself in the very practice of material techniques. (1914: 72)

Weber distinguishes between the sentiment of causality and the concept of causality to point out that the very notion of causal relations is derived from the bodily, technical practice. Concepts, as we have seen above, have their roots in concrete experiences, but are no longer involved in them. The advantage of these detached, ideal entities is that one can work with them and vary the relations among them freely.[6] The disadvantage is that this association of ideas, according to Weber, is random and does not necessarily comply with natural causes.

The primacy of technical causality and technology does not mean that technology does not need language, that is, social intelligence, in order to be effective over time. On its own, the technical faculty cannot survive. It needs the social milieu, where the practices and tools are transformed into and replaced by words and thus be guaranteed to be transported through time (1914: 62).

Weber's argument might seem byzantine or, at the very least, copious, but his goal is to establish symmetry between primitive and modern thought (since both the modern and the primitive apply and understand in their respective technical activity the laws of causality and identity) by pointing out a seemingly weak spot in Mauss and Hubert's theory: magic and technology follow very different forms of reasoning, according to Weber. He seems to reproach Mauss, Hubert, and especially Lucien Lévy-Bruhl that the effort to symmetrize the primitives with the moderns has to account for the difference between magical and technical thought, rather than to blur and dissolve it.

Another reason for Weber's insistence on the primacy of technical intelligence was to retain an intellectual basis for the sciences. If technical intelligence has direct access to matter, then objective science is possible, whereas the primacy of the social might lead to relativism and social constructivism. Weber is thus not refuting the Durkheimian argument as such (see also the introduction to this volume). As we have seen, he does not argue against the functional description of religion. Religion and magic for him are techniques sui generis as well, but this new genus is the expression of an inherent dualism of human intelligence, as Weber concludes in his essay "Civilisation et Technique" criticizing the Durkheimians: "*Duplex in humanitate* says Maine de Biran. I myself would say: *duplex in intellectu*, seeking to mark the original dualism that we have to admit" (Weber 1930: 139).

Mauss and Hubert on Causality

Mauss and Hubert advocate, however, a completely different ontology. The *homo duplex* marks a dualism of a different nature. Human beings can experience themselves as duplex, according to the Durkheimians, since they are social and individual beings. The dualism is therefore not interior to human intelligence, as Weber claims, but rather produced by the ability of self-understanding. The dualism is the object of human intelligence and creates tensions between individualistic drives and social requirements.

It is thus not surprising that Mauss reacts quite polemically to Louis Weber:

> Let us dare a little bit of metaphysics. It is quite possible that there are, down to the roots of being, the same quantities of determinism and no more than in the social phenomena that we study. Without a doubt the other sciences are not better placed than ours. But then you have to believe, like Mr. Weber, a statistician, that there is a certain kind of freedom everywhere, otherwise it is nowhere. In no case, from our point of view, can metaphysical freedom be the privilege of man. It is to be determined everywhere in statistical qualities, or it does not exist. (Mauss in Weber 1921: 103)

Mauss alludes here to central topics of the Durkheim School: sociology has the same value as the other sciences; its method, statistics, can provide the means to determine the validity of particular claims; and freedom, if it exists at all, cannot be limited to human beings alone, but rather has to be found on each and every level of being.

This ontological claim is at the heart of the category of causality. It shows that Mauss thought social phenomena to have the same ontological status as physical and biological phenomena.[7]

Accordingly, causality does not differ on the technical or the social level. Human beings are part of nature and the social force is therefore also a natural force. This implies that categories have not only social functions, but express the relations of human beings with their different milieus. Religion, science, and technology share common roots and express a spectrum of different actions in and with the world. Science, technology, and religion are all effective and traditional techniques, yet they differ in their domain: "traditional techniques ... are felt by the author as *actions of a mechanical, physical or physicochemical order* and they are pursued with that aim in view" (Mauss 2006: 83, original emphasis).

Although the body as center and starting point for the different techniques of the body—be they social or material—was developed by Mauss as late as 1935, Mauss and Hubert had started the discussion on the differences and the common ground of techniques already in *A General Theory of Magic*. They point out that the efficacy of magic and techniques are often perceived as equal, even though magic cannot be controlled by experience and the effects of magic do not follow immediately from the coordination of actions (*gestes*), tools, and physical agents (Mauss 1904: 24). Rites are defined as "*traditional actions whose efficacy (efficacité)* [modification of the translation by the author] *is sui generis*" (24, original emphasis).

This "efficacy *sui generis*," however, has a different ontological status than in Weber's dualistic theory. Mauss does not distinguish between intentionality and causality, that is, ascribing causality merely to material operations and intentionality only to operations of the mind (Sigaut 2003), as Weber's dualistic account suggests, where linguistic intentionality is distinguished from material causal relations.[8]

Mauss rather employs the notion of efficacy (*efficacité*), not worrying about the aforementioned distinction and aiming to show that the modern distinction between science, technology and myth does not apply to the genesis of our most basic categories such as time, causality or space. As an example for this interpenetration of science, technology, and religion, Mauss points to the development of the calendar:

> The scientific-technical complex is a single bloc. For example, the oldest calendars are as much the work of farmers as of religious minds or of astrologers; technique, science and myth are there blended. In the same way, pigeons had been selectively bred before Darwin found the notion of natural selection. The same is true for pure and experimental science—which in our days replaces mythologies, metaphysics and pure action, even action based on reflection; it is not in the least disengaged from the action which it directs, even when it detaches itself most clearly or most deliberately. (Mauss 2005: 49)

In this quote one can fathom how easily Mauss relates the work of farmers and astrologers of ancient times to Darwin's theory of evolution and modern attempts in physics to develop stable and reliable methods. All of these scientific and technical inventions are the result of socio-technical processes and have a common origin. Mauss even suggests that it might be helpful to follow Espinas and Plato, who did "not . . . distinguish *techné* and *episteme*" as did Durkheim, who "separate[s] them profoundly" (2005: 50). Even the measurement of time is not a pure, abstract act, but stems from socio-technical practices that are increasingly "purified."

Time: Symbolic Structure and Operating System

This necessity to rely on techniques provides freedom—since human beings are no longer bound to their instincts—and creates a new perception of the future as something to be anticipated. The management of time, especially the manipulation of the future, becomes an essential task for human beings. Hubert thus conceives of time, as Isambert points out, as a "symbolic structure . . . with rules," which makes it an "operating system" (Isambert 1999: 30–31). It is precisely this role as an "operating system" that allows for considering time itself as a specific technique to make the future predictable. Time and techniques are in a recursive relationship: on the one hand, time employs techniques in order to operate; on the other, the cultural variations of the category of time show that techniques participate in its creation.

The first "calendars served essentially to predict the return of events" and the "authority of the convention that created the calendar gives it a reality equal to that of the phenomena which, it is claimed, regulate it" (Hubert 1999: 81). As the quote of Mauss already showed, calendars result first and foremost out of a socio-technical operation and are in a recursive relationship with natural phenomena, that is, the phenomena that are supposedly regulating the calendar. According to Hubert, "[t]he division of time entails the maximum of convention and the minimum of experience" (70). Experience confers authority on the abstract concept of time, but the quantitative, scientific notion of time is based upon a qualitative notion of time (82).

This argument is in accordance with Bergson's theory of time. Hubert, as François-André Isambert has already pointed out on numerous occasions, socializes Bergson's notion of time: analogous to Bergson's work, quality is preferred over quantity, discontinuity over continuity, indivisibility over infinite subdivision, interpenetration over exteriority, in short: lived, experienced time over scientific time (Hubert 1999: 63–64; Isambert 1999: 20).

The interesting aspect of Hubert's interpretation of Bergson is his synthesis of Durkheim's insistence of the priority of the social with Bergson's rather individualistic account of time as duration. The result is a dynamic conception of the individual's relation with society that Hubert, in a very dense and subtle commentary on Bergson's *Matter and Memory* ([1896] 1991), relates to the notion of *tension*:

> In the subtle arabesques of "Matière et mémoire," he replaces ideas of length, position and succession as the generating element of the representation of time with the idea of an active tension through which, on the one hand, the harmony of independent durations of different rhythms is realized in the consciousness, and on the other, images are distributed and circulated among the different planes of this same consciousness. (Hubert 1999: 63–64)

Hubert praises Bergson for stressing the essential qualitative aspect of time. However, Bergson is merely interested in the duration of a singular living being and does not mention the idea of harmony between different independent durations and different rhythms in one consciousness. Duration consists of the simultaneity of virtual memories (i.e., they lie in the past) and actual sensations (i.e., the present moment). The tension of individuals depend on their activity: If individuals are performing bodily actions that require their attention, only those memories are actualized that are needed by individuals to perform their tasks (Bergson [1896] 1991: 100–1).[9]

The tension Hubert points to is for Bergson interior to the individual and constitutes its ability to act in the world. The medium of the tension is the body, as Bergson explains, which is an "instrument of choice": "Now let us turn to memory. The function of the body is not to store up recollections, but simply to choose, in order to bring back to distinct consciousness, by the real efficacy thus conferred on it, the useful memory, that which may complete and illuminate the present situation with a view to ultimate action" (Bergson [1896] 1991: 179–80). Yet, although Hubert principally agrees with Bergson's theory, he quickly asks "whether it is necessary to invoke some other principle, which is not completely represented in the consciousness of the individual but develops and operates in the course of collective life" (Hubert 1999: 66). Hubert challenges Bergson by introducing another series of representations, which is not internally produced by efforts of synthesizing different degrees of tension, but rather shows that it is the social force that generates the notion of time. The individual thus not only has to integrate the various different images and impressions of physiological origin, but also social representations.

Hubert multiplies the duration of the individual and thus "socializes" time: religious rites and periods of time have their own duration, that is, they have their own quality and are forced upon the individual. The individual is therefore constantly trying to harmonize individual duration with social life:

> One is constant and periodic, that is, the calendar and chronology with their points of reference and all the details which they record: the other is perpetually being constructed through the contribution of new representations. The mind works constantly to associate certain elements of these two series within the same tension. The whole is dominated by general ideas of duration, period and date, which are endowed with a certain objectivity and which, with this objectivity, enter as essential elements into the mental operations in question. (Hubert 1999: 65)

Subjects experience in this act of integration the force of the "social." They are no longer bound to their solitary existence as abstract subjects but are rather exposed to the milieu they inhabit with other subjects.[10] The body serves as a medium, but now the "operating system" time employs the body, whereas for Bergson it is the mind of the individual. Hubert points to the "states of collective excitement" (ibid.: 77), which Durkheim calls *effervescence* (Durkheim 1995: 424). In these states, where the "idea of the sacred was formed," society modifies the consciousness of the individual and transports the content of these modifications through time via categories and concepts:

> In fact, it is necessary to take account of those states of collective excitement in which, formerly, we supposed the idea of the sacred to be formed. The profound modifications, which our own emotions bring to our consciousness, of the duration help us to imagine how the multiple emotions of a society could have affected the consciousness of all its members in the same way, but with greater intensity and for a longer period. These primitive emotions, exceptional and momentary, have left behind them a residue of belief, which renews or maintains certain of their effects when their cause has largely disappeared. They are perpetuated and continue to condition thought through the logical force of categories and concepts. (Hubert 1999: 77)

The body is integral in a double sense in these states of collective excitement. It is the social body and the individual body that interpenetrate each other in these effervescent phenomena. Emotional states are modified and the modifications are perpetuated over time, since they are crystallized not only in the individual body, but also in concepts and categories. The social is felt as an exterior force the individual participates in.

Although not every state is collective or effervescent, all collective rhythmic activities modify the experience of their participants. The body in these activities plays the role of a dynamic medium that can adapt to the social rhythm, learn rhythmic behaviors, and execute technical operations. It is this rhythm of human activities that creates the representation of time, rather than natural periodicities:

> The representation of time is essentially rhythmic. But has it not already been demonstrated that, in work, poetry and song, rhythm was the sign of collective activity, becoming more strongly marked as social collaboration spread and intensified? If this is true, it is legitimate to suppose that the rhythm of time does not necessarily model itself on the natural periodicities established by experience, but that societies contain within themselves the need and the means of instituting it. (Hubert 1999: 71–72)

Societies institute a rhythm and have the need to do so. This social rhythm is the basis for the representation of time and its symbolic structures such as the calendar. The category of time results from a rhythmic technique, which is the basis of social activity. The general notion of time was developed, as was the notion of *mana*, from particular experiences, which consist in such rhythmic activity (Hubert 1999: 79).

Mechanical arts, techniques, manual labor, and the operations in modern technological objects, such as smart phones, demonstrate this process. The most primitive of arts share with the most advanced microprocessors essential aspects: all of these operations are cadenced—they need a specific rhythm[11]—the same action can theoretically be repeated ad infinitum, and they institute a relationship that is supposed to have the same outcome every time it is performed. However, the representation of time created via these techniques depends on these techniques. Time, techniques, and causality are thus intrinsically related to each other.[12]

The body is the medium where this relationship is played out in rituals, in concrete technical practices as well as in abstract technical operations. In his reply to Louis Weber, shortly before daring his audience to do metaphysics, Marcel Mauss elaborates on this relationship:

> [T]he gesture, in these religions, is conceived as a language; the rite is generally a mimed dance or a mime; in any case, at least, it is a symbol.... One makes a gesture not only to act, but also for other men and spirits to see and understand it. Furthermore, from another point of view, the unity of the manual and oral rituals is still apparent: formulas and gestures are rhythmic, cadenced. They are not just words and deeds, they are poems and songs and mimes. In both of them there is the same collective element: rhythm, unison, repetition often pushed to levels unthinkable for us. The notion of effectiveness therefore has to be linked to the existence of these beliefs in the effectiveness of rhythms, that is to say, the existence of not raw but formal words and gestures. Thus it is in the origin of symbolism of all kinds and not only in that of language, that the origin of the notion of cause must be sought. (Mauss in Weber 1921:101)

A gesture is simultaneously an action and a symbol. This combination allows information to be conveyed. Rhythm is fundamental for the effectiveness and existence of words. It is the efficacy of the rhythm that provides the spoken word with value. The contrast between Weber and the Durkheimians is evident: Mauss and Hubert start from the simultaneity of language and of action. While for Weber, social intelligence and technical intelligence are distinct from one another, Mauss and Hubert affirm that only the simultaneity and inseparability of the social and the technical can produce the notion of cause and the category of causality.

Once Upon a Time in the Future

If we think of the image that Sergio Leone paints in the famous opening sequence of his film *Once Upon a Time in the West*, where a group of gangsters is waiting for a train to arrive, we may note that the flow of time is cadenced by technical objects and body techniques: the squeaking of a windmill, the singing of the telegraph (eventually stopped by a man violently ripping out the cables), water dropping from a ceiling onto the head of a gangster, a fly annoying another, who captures it with his gun. The passing of time is structured in socio-technical operations. As soon as the train arrives, the rhythm changes, people are disembarking, seemingly operating in a different rhythm, which the gangsters at the station attempt to ignore and resist. The arrival of the train sets the motive for the whole film. The train is a symbol for and the operating system of a new time (even though, as soon as it has left the station, the old time returns, which for the waiting men spells their death at the hands of "Harmonica"). The development and implementation of the new technological object and its supporting infrastructure leads to fundamental societal changes and a reorganization of the social body as a whole. The social role of the old Wild West characters, portrayed by Charles Bronson, Henry Fonda, and Jason Robards, becomes obsolete and is replaced by engineers, managers, and turbo-capitalists. This does not, however, mean that there is a qualitative difference between the old and the new practices. It is still possible to envisage a situation "once upon a time," if we can grasp the techniques that were then used by human beings.

Time and techniques are intrinsically linked, since technological objects are never completely out of date (Simondon 2005: 340). They are accompanied by practices that actualize these objects and provide them with a new rhythm, which in turn structures the relationship of humans, signs, and things. While there are significant differences in the experience of time in modern and premodern societies, the mode of production of the category of time remains the same. It is based upon this rhythmic technique, which institutes a recursive causality between practices and categories, between theory and praxis. The operating system "time" is constantly updated and modified. The social is thus a natural, ontological force. Techniques, be they magical and/or technological, illustrate how this force instantiates causal relations.

Technology has, therefore, to be literally understood as *logos* of *techné*. Consequently, as a hybrid category linking time, cause and substance, it can provide the epistemological basis to create new modes of being human. The essential socio-technical and scientific abilities of humans remain diachronically the same, while humans are constantly "drawn out of [them]sel[ves] towards nature" with the goal to have "control over things" (Mauss 2005: 50). The temporal dimension of technology is always twofold: human beings turn to their past to create the future. The future, however, does not play a passive part. As an unknown, virtual force it acts upon the present (Simondon 2017: 156–157) while remaining out of reach. Being human—in its fullest sense—requires technology as category-practice, and thus "human science" (Haudricourt 1987). To understand our technological present and future thus means to go back in time and to understand its "primitive" beginnings (42).[13]

Johannes F. M. Schick is scientific coordinator of the CRC 1187 Media of Cooperation since January 2022. He was head of the research project "Action, Operation, Gesture: Technology as Interdisciplinary Anthropology" at the a.r.t.e.s. Graduate School for the Humanities (University of Cologne) from October 2017 to February 2021His research focuses on interdisciplinary (techno-)anthropology (from Bergson, Espinas, and Mauss to Simondon, Bergson's philosophy of life), French epistemology, and the relation of anthropology to philosophy. He has published in journals such as *Parrhesia: A Journal of Critical Philosophy* and most recently in *Techné: Research in Philosophy and Technology*.

Notes

1. Techniques and technology differ in their scope. Within the tradition of French techno-anthropology, starting with Alfred Espinas up to André-Georges Haudricourt, technology is understood literally as the science of techniques. This conception of technology renders it "integral to the social sciences" (Schlanger 2006: 1).
2. *Technology* was introduced as a section in the *Année sociologique* (Durkheim [1901] 2006), but, as Nathan Schlanger (2006:10) remarks, this may have been more for strategic reasons rather than out of genuine theoretical interest. Mauss and Hubert, however, thought more highly of the role of techniques than Durkheim (Mauss 2005: 39), which, in the case of Mauss, had to do with an "engagement with modernity" that Durkheim lacked (Schlanger 2006: 14).
3. Weber and Mauss must have had further encounters as members of the "Revue de la synthèse." At least one is documented: Mauss discussed Weber's intervention on "Civilisation et techniques" (Weber 1930) at the "Première semaine internationale de synthèse" organized by Henri Berr.
4. The argument that "we think with words" refers to the beginning of Bergson's *Time and Free Will* (Bergson [1889] 1950: xxiii). For Bergson,

however, this aptitude of human intelligence to "think with words" is already an expression of the technical faculty of the *homo faber*, who constructs intellectual tools, thus inhibiting us from expressing time as duration (Bergson [1907] 1998: 139). For Weber, techniques create a specific kind of perception and reasoning, which can be simultaneously intuitive and intellectual, that is, in Bergsonian terms, temporal (as duration) and spatial. Although Bergson in his last work *The Two Sources of Morality and Religion* introduces a theory that accounts for the temporal aspects of technology, he does not provide as detailed an analysis of technology as Weber does.

5. "Il y a bien, dans la parole, des représentations motrices, qui la produisent physiquement, mais elles ont un caractère spécial. Elles se détachent peu à peu des autres images motrices qui correspondent aux mouvements du corps; elles forment dans l'esprit un groupe à part, et, leur différenciations s'accentuent à mesure que leur importance s'affirme, elles finissent par accaparer pour elles seules une région étendue du cerveau, qui devient leur territoire d'élection. Désormais, soit qu'il parle à haute voix, soit qu'il parle intérieurement, l'homme accomplit une fonction bien différente de toute fonction technique matérielle. Sa conscience intellectuelle n'est plus uniquement constituée soit par les images de ses perceptions extérieures, soit par les images de ses membres en mouvement ou en tension" (Weber 1913: 189).

6. This alludes to the definition of Bergson's *homo faber*: "intelligence, considered in what seems to be its original feature, is the faculty of manufacturing artificial objects, especially tools to make tools, and of indefinitely varying the manufacture" (Bergson [1907] 1998: 139).

7. Mario Schmidt makes a similar argument in his chapter in this volume with regard to *expérience*. Durkheim famously describes effervescence in analogy to electricity (Durkheim 1995: 217).

8. François Sigaut suggests to disconnect *efficacité* from utility in order to understand how Mauss conceived of causality (Sigaut 2003). Mauss' notion of *efficacité*—as well as that of Hubert and Durkheim—does not distinguish between causality and intentionality.

9. Bergson's example is to learn something by heart, for example, a poem. In order to recite the poem, one does not need the memories of each instance one has read the poem in its entirety, but only its material markers, that is, the words that constitute the poem. Once memorized, one can start reciting it and add the appropriate rhythm to recite the poem. Each recitation contains virtually all the memories in their fullness, every instance with all its contextual elements ("where did I read the poem for the first time," "how did I feel when reading it," etc.), but to remember every little detail would hinder the individual from reciting the poem. The task "to recite the poem" therefore requires to extract aspects of the memories that are virtually present (Bergson 1991: 79–81).

10. Thomas Hirsch points out that Hubert's conception of social time presupposes a new distribution of duration and abstract time according to

the time of society (Hirsch 2016: 59). Hubert's interpretation of Bergson is therefore closely linked to Durkheim's principles of sociology (59).
11. This is especially true for the synchronization of hardware and software in modern computers. The rhythm of the processor has to be in sync with the software that runs on it, otherwise the output on the screen may be flawed or there may be no visual representation at all.
12. This also implies that in our "modern times," where smartphones are able to make 4.2 billion times the binary distinction between 1 and 0, we are shaping new experiences of time that might even cause ruptures in the relation between human beings and their techniques and their technological objects, as Guillaum Carnino argues. Carnino claims that digital technologies are no longer within the phenomenal horizon of human beings—as analog technologies have been. While traditional techniques were transductive in the sense that there was continuity between human beings, their actions, and the technical objects they were involved with (e.g., hand axes, steam engines, electric motors), the digital has transcended time and space as forms of intuitions: the computational power of smartphones goes beyond the boundaries of the temporal experience of human subjects and the practices performed with smartphones rely on a infrastructure of satellites surrounding the globe and eroding the spatial relations formerly needed for communication (e.g., one can have a face-to-face conversation and chat with somebody on the other side of the planet almost in real time) (Carnino 2018).
13. "Quelle est la méthode de la technologie? Partir du présent pour remonter au passé. Le présent sera étudié partout, aussi bien chez les peuples les plus 'primitifs' que chez les artisans et les ouvriers de nos sociétés" (Haudricourt 1987: 42).

References

Bergson, Henri. [1889] 1950. *Time and Free Will: An Essay on the Immediate Data of Consciousness*, trans. Frank L. Pogson, 6th edn. London: George Allen & Unwin Ltd.

———. [1896] 1991. *Matter and Memory*, trans. Nancy M. Paul and W. Scott Palmer. New York: Zone Books.

———. [1907] 1998. *Creative Evolution*, trans. Arthur Mitchell. Mineola, NY: Dover.

Carnino, Guillaume. 2018. "Unbehagen in der Transduktion: Technik und Technologie im digitalen Zeitalter." *Zeitschrift für Kulturwissenschaften* 2/2018: 67–82.

Durkheim, Émile. 1995. *The Elementary Forms of Religious Life*, trans. Karen E. Fields. New York: Free Press.

Durkheim, Émile. [1901] 2006. "Technology." In *Techniques, Technology and Civilisation*, by Marcel Mauss, 31–32. Translated and edited by Nathan Schlanger. New York: Berghahn Books.

Durkheim, Émile, and Marcel Mauss. 1903. "De quelques formes primitives de classification—contribution à l'étude des représentations collectives." *L'Année sociologique* 6: 1–72.

Haudricourt, André-Georges. 1987. *La Technologie Science Humaine: Recherches d'histoire et d'ethnologie des techniques*. Paris: Éditions de la Maison des Sciences de l'Homme.

Hirsch, Thomas. 2016. *Le temps des sociétés: D'Émile Durkheim à Marc Bloch*. Paris: Éditions de l'École des Hautes Études en Sciences Sociales (EHESS).

Hubert, Henri. 1999. *Essay on Time: A Brief Study of the Representation of Time in Religion and Magic*, trans. Robert Parkin and Jacqueline Redding. Oxford: Durkheim Press.

Isambert, François-André. 1999. Introduction to *Essay on Time: A Brief Study of the Representation of Time in Religion and Magic* by Henri Hubert, 3–42. Trans. Robert Parkin and Jacqueline Redding. Oxford: Durkheim Press.

König, René. 1978. *Emile Durkheim zur Diskussion: Jenseits von Dogmatismus u. Skepsis*. Munich: Hanser.

Mauss, Marcel. 1904. "Esquisse d'une théorie générale de la magie." *AS* 7: 1–146. [2005. *A General Theory of Magic*, trans. Robert Brain. London: Routledge.]

———. 2005. "Sociology: Its Divisions and Their Relative Weightings." In *The Nature of Sociology: Two Essays*, trans. William Jeffrey, 31–85. New York: Durkheim Press.

———. 2006. "Techniques of the Body." In *Techniques, Technology and Civilisation*, trans. and ed. Nathan Schlanger, 77–95. New York: Durkheim Press/Berghahn Books.

Schlanger, Nathan. 2006. "Introduction. Technological Commitments: Marcel Mauss and the Study of Techniques in the French Social Sciences." In *Techniques, Technology and Civilisation* by Marcel Mauss, 1–29. Trans. and ed. Nathan Schlanger. New York: Durkheim Press/Berghahn Books.

Sigaut, François. 2003. "La Formule de Mauss." *Technique & Culture* 40. https://doi.org/10.4000/tc.1538.

Simondon, Gilbert. 2005. *L'individuation à la lumière des notions de forme et d'information*. Grenoble: Millon.

———. 2017. *On the Mode of Existence of Technical Objects*. Minneapolis, MN: Univocal Publ.

Weber, Louis. 1913. *Le Rythme du Progrès*. Paris: Félix Alcan.

———. 1914. "Y a-t-il un rythme dans le progrès intellecutel? (Séances du 29 Janvier et 5 Février 1914 à la Société Française de Philosophie, avec la participation de Parodi, Meyerson, Le Roy, Belot, Darlu, Leclère)." *Bulletin de la société française de philosophie* 14: 61–140.

———. 1921. "Liberté et Langage (Séance du 23 Juin 1921 à la Société Française de Philosophie, avec la participation de Roustan, Parodi, Lalande, Berthod, Belot, Mauss)." *Bulletin de la société française de philosophie* 21: 75–106.

———. 1930. "Civilisation et Technique." In *Civilisation. Le mot et l'idée: Première semaine internationale des synthèses*, ed. Lucien Febvre, 131–43. Paris: La Renaissance du Livre.

PART III

Forgotten Allies and Secret Students

Chapter 12

THE RHYTHM OF SPACE

STEFAN CZARNOWSKI'S RELATIONAL THEORY OF THE SACRED

Martin Zillinger

In a letter from 21 April 1922, Stefan Czarnowski announced to his former teacher Henri Hubert that, together with Jan Marian Krassowski, he had started research on astronomical knowledge and representations of space among the ancient Greeks. In particular, they were interested in "the representation made by each Greek, the mass of citizens, of the world and its organization" (Kończal and Wawrzyniak 2015: 244). Czarnowski hoped this research would bring him a little closer to the bigger question he was preoccupied with—the representations [*sic*] of space. "On my side," he wrote, "I have started digging into the question of God-Terminus [*dieux termes*]," that is, the gods of boundary markers in Roman religion, "which, I think," he continued, will "allow me to grasp the representation of the rhythm of space (and the measures of extension)" (*représentation du rythme de l'espace (et des mesures de l'étendue)*, 2015: 244). Only a few days later he writes in another letter: "I think I see, judging by certain indicators, that the notion of *extension* has formed in human consciousness along a path similar to that of the notion of time. It is a collective representation, and such it was before it became a philosophical notion. *Extension* began to be represented as concrete—before it became a form of perception" (247).

Obviously Czarnowski takes up a concern that Hubert has already formulated in the *Année sociologique* in 1901: "Time," he writes there, "is an object of collective representation to the same extent as space" (Hubert 1901: 234). A year later, in 1902, when the student Czarnowski joined him in Paris after being expelled from Berlin as a Polish nationalist,[1] Hubert dug deeper into time and space as collective representations by studying ritual: "Given that in fact religious acts take place in space and time," Hubert writes in the *Année*, "one of the enigmas of ritual is the reconciliation of the inescapable conditions with the infinite extension and the theoretical immutability of the sacred. Ritual must consequently bring into play representations and figurations of space and time necessary to resolve this antinomy" (Hubert 1902: 248; see Isambert 1999: 18–19). Hubert sets out to solve this antinomy in his essay on time, published in 1905, and continues to work on it together with Mauss in the years after. Czarnowski, without doubt, was well acquainted with this endeavor and while preparing the manuscript on space discussed here, he asked Hubert to send him a copy of the "Introduction à l'analyse de quelques phenomènes religieux" to Warsaw, in particular the part on the question of space in religion and magic (10 February 1923). In this text, Mauss and Hubert summarize the findings of their work on space and time as follows:

> For the one who deals with magic and religion, the categories that attract the most attention are those of space and time. The rites take place according to certain rules in space and time: right and left, north and south, before and after, favorable and unfavorable, etc. are essential considerations in the actions of religion and myths, because by means of the rites that describe the myths and the celebrations to their memory, they settle in space and occur in time. But the sacred time and the sacred space in which the rites and myths are *realized* are capable of receiving them. The rooms are always real temples. The times are festive. (Hubert and Mauss 1908: 192)

Czarnowski seems to refer to this work when he explains to his teachers: "I would like to get to grips with this question of space [by exploring the notion of extension] . . . and to identify the 'extended' representation in the facts of religion and magic, where it seems to me to have a much more concrete aspect than anywhere else. It is more easily graspable" (Kończal and Wawrzyniak 2015: 247–48; 24 February 1922). In October 1923, Czarnowski traveled to Paris and presented the results of his work by speaking about "Fragmentation and Limitations of Extension in Religion and Magic" (Le morcellement de l'étendue et sa limitation dans la religion et la magie) at the International Congress for the History of Religions. "This," he announced in a letter beforehand, "is the substance of the results I arrived at by studying the question of space, starting with the limits" (2015: 273;

5 September 1923). In this lecture, which is largely forgotten today, Stefan Czarnowski presented the key to rethink Durkheim's notion of "the sacred" in non-essentialist, relational terms. Unrecognized by many of his contemporaries and rarely acknowledged until today Czarnowski here offered a re-reading of Durkheim's central theoretical concept that could have informed the work of the Collège de Sociologie a decade later in important ways—if they had only taken note of his work.

The text, published in 1925, is one of the hidden or rather neglected texts of the Durkheim School, which elaborates on topics that had already been discussed prior to the canonical presentation of the category project in *Elementary Forms* in 1912. It belongs to the dispersed but interconnected efforts to revive the work on the category project after World War I.[2] Czarnowski followed Hubert and Mauss in their attempts to overcome the Kantian notion of time and space, which Durkheim summarized later as too vague and indeterminate (see Godlove 1996: 446). In his *Elementary Forms,* he objected to Kant that space, "if purely and absolutely homogeneous, would be of no use and would offer nothing for us to hold on to. Spatial representation essentially consists in a primary coordination of a given sense experience. But this coordination would be impossible if the parts of space were qualitatively equivalent, if they really were mutually interchangeable" (Durkheim 1995: 10). Taking up this line of argument in the 1920s, Czarnowski appears to develop a theory of boundaries and thresholds, which define, delimit and connect spaces in and as collective representations of extension. In doing so, he takes up several concerns of his teachers regarding not only the notion of space, but also the notion of the sacred, and offers a compelling re-reading of both. In particular, Mauss's response to Granet, to which Nick Allen has offered several compelling paragraphs in his work on Mauss's reflections on the social, puts forward several systematic thoughts on space that seem to be informed by Czarnowski's work (see Allen 2000: 120, 142f).

In order to foreground "Le morcellement de l'étendue" in the study of space, Czarnowski turns to the history of religion and analyzes the religious topography of the city of Rome. As the focal point of his relational notion of space he introduces a distinction of a "centralized sacred" from a "relieved sacred." What he calls *sacré concentré* reveals itself in all its efficacy and relevance at the center of a social space, while across its borders a different, "free sacred," the *sacré libre,* would reign. More strictly speaking, this distinction is a transformation: once the *sacré concentré* crosses the boundaries to an outer space and competes there with other powers and spirits, it turns into a "free" *sacré* facing dangerous and competing forces from the outside, which likewise transgress the boundaries in the opposite direction and need to be presented in the center. Czarnowski thinks of the sacred moving out from a sacred center and across concentrically arranged boundaries around it. It is most interesting that these boundaries are thought of as crossings and thresholds in a graduated space. The crossings and thresholds are the points in space where different claims and powers clash, merge, and compete.

For students of the Durkheim School, it is quite apparent that this text takes up work on boundaries and thresholds pursued by other members (and outcasts) of the Durkheimian *équipe*—notably by van Gennep in his famous work on ritual and spatial passages (1909) and by Robert Hertz in his study of the cult of Saint Besse in the Alpes (1913). Czarnowski significantly develops this work as an ethnological theory of central and peripheral cults *avant la lettre* and presents a bold attempt to rethink the Durkheimian dualism of sacred and profane in important, relational ways.[3] According to the dominant reading of Durkheim, the division of things into sacred and profane structures the real into two distinct regions. One includes the sacred things and makes up the social world providing the symbols for the identity of a group, the other includes everything opposed to the sacred and is defined by its opposition to it—all the profane things that lie in front of and outside the temple (pro-fanum). As we will see, by conceiving of the *sacré concentré*, which is manifest in all its power in the center of a social space, as turning into a *sacré libre* at and beyond the margins, and even integrating the relieved sacred at the center, he provides an important revision of Durkheim's theory of the sacred.

It is quite apparent that Czarnowski takes up Mauss's interest in spatial rhythms of concentration and dispersal as developed in his Eskimo essay. As Allen points out, much in line with Durkheimian thought in *Elementary Forms*, Mauss and Hubert early on emphasized the identity of the sacred and the social, not, however, without giving it a dynamic twist: "When society concentrates so as to manifest itself as a whole, it also generates the idea of the sacred, and when it disperses into its parts it reverts to the profane. [To them, the] sacred is, as it were, the concentrated social" (Allen 2000: 143). Czarnowski comes up with a twofold argument to complicate this view. To begin with, he thinks of the sacred as relational. In his example of the city of Rome, the ancestral deities, as described by the highly influential book by Fustel de Coulange *La cité antique* (1864), turn into spirits of wilderness for neighboring groups and vice versa. But he does not stop there; rather he provides a theory that accounts for the co-existence of both in social and religious centers. Questioning the absolute identity of the social and the sacred as contained in space, he overcomes binary approaches to space that characterized much of the work of the Durkheimian *équipe*. It is not far-fetched to argue that he very likely informed Mauss's change in perspective on space as laid out in the latter's comment on Granet and Hertz in 1933. Mauss arrives here at an understanding of a "variety of positionings, powers and purities" that extends the basic binary classification developed by Robert Hertz (Mauss 1933: 112–13). To quote an important paragraph in Nick Allen's work on Mauss and classification, Mauss makes it very clear that "notions of taboo and correlations such as right:sacred::left:profane were too absolute, took too little account of relativity in their application (what is right or left depends on which way you are facing). Moreover . . . [in] Hertz's time the notion of religion had been extremely restricted, being confined to the notion of the sacred, but for many purposes one needed much richer models" (Allen 2000: 120), for example, in order to make sense of religious life in Rome.

Until today many scholars of ancient Rome have noted a tension that consists in simultaneously rejecting and incorporating foreign gods and cults at the religious center. Czarnowski's article must be read in line with much later arguments that tried to account for the persistence of foreign, orgiastic cults in the center of Rome, which were performed by or close to Roman elites. As Mary Beard has plausibly shown for the cult of *Magna Mater*, any linear narrative of a gradual incorporation of the foreign into the mainstream of Roman religion is unconvincing. The sacred incorporated the foreign in an economy of power that aimed at integrating defeated peoples into the Roman Empire. However, the persistence of competing sacred forces testifies to the "unending process of defining the ruling power" (Beard 1996: 187) and negotiating proper relations with the divine.

The Duality of the Sacred and the Fragmentation of Space: Roman Insights

In his lecture and in the subsequent publication, Czarnowski focuses on the Roman god Terminus, the god of bordermarkers, and thus zooms in on a topic Arnold van Gennep (1909) had devoted parts of his *Les rites de passage* a decade earlier. Czarnowski writes to Hubert (24 April 1922) that, by reading Ovid and comparing two passages, he got the idea that Terminus was "a god not only because he is the guard and

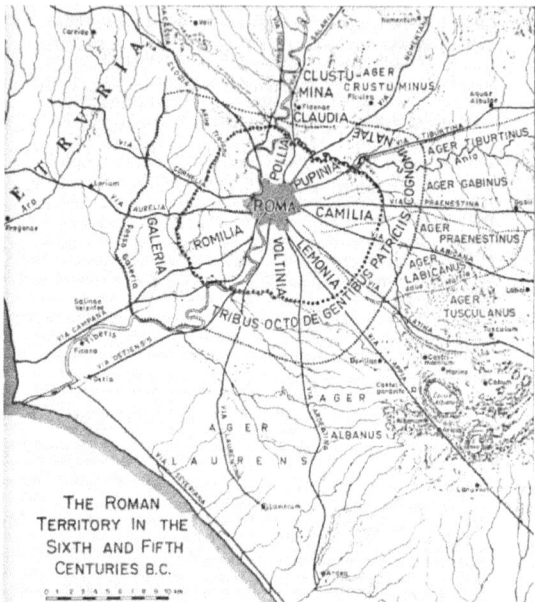

Figure 12.1. *Ager Romanus Antiquus* (after Alföldi 1965: 297, in Ziółkowski 2009: 99).

guarantor of the boundary, but also because the boundary is sacred in itself and a number of measures of extension (*mésures de l'étendue*) end in such a place" (see Kończal and Wawrzyniak 2015: 248).

But what does Ovid actually say here? In the first passage Czarnowski alludes to, he states that for building the central temple of the Roman state, Jupiter Capitolinus, older altars and temples were cleared away, however, "an old boundary stone, which was found on the spot, was allowed to remain" (Ovid, Book II, 509: 229). In conjunction with another passage in Ovid, which recounts a sacrifice at the sixth milestone on the *Via Laurentia* separating Roman territory from the territory of the Laurentes, Czarnowski infers that the cult of the god Terminus at the Capitol represented the spiritual powers of the different boundary markers at the very center of the capital. This cult in the center of Rome thus needed to be related to the different cults at the side of the roads and, ultimately, to all rites that have "delimitation" as their object.[4]

In "Le morcellement" Czarnowski sums up:

> The gods of the sacred place, the patron saints of the respective area, are particularly present in two places: in their sanctuary and at the

border itself. The saints and gods who protect the city remain in their temple or cathedral. But at the same time they also appear on the city walls.... They protect the border of the town's territorial property and receive the admiration from the traveller arriving from abroad. Conversely, the gods of the borders also remain in the central shrine and receive their cult there. (1925: 349)

In order to understand the significance of this ritual correspondence between center and periphery for Czarnowski's relational theory of space, it is important to recall its Durkheimian base and what Robert Hertz called *la polarité religieuse*, the fundamental opposition between the sacred and the profane, that allegedly reigned over the life of the "primitives."
Czarnowski writes:

From a religious point of view, the world appears clearly divided into two opposing parts. On one side there is the area where you live normally. The sacred can also be felt there, but only mediated through the channel of rituals. It is realized through actions, organized in a system, that makes it possible to recognize the sacred, to renew it periodically and to make it useful for human life. On the other side there is an undefined area, that of the unorganized sacred. The spiritual powers rule there unleashed, fearsome and sinisterly over the one who invades without being adequately prepared. (1925: 341)

Czarnowski's notion of the "other," "unorganized sacred" as opposed to the "organized sacred" is interesting here. At first glance, he seems to take up the notion of the "Impure Sacred," but, as mentioned above, he gives this move an interesting twist. Let me develop Czarnowski's new position among the Durkheimians step by step.

Hertz was already well aware that the clear-cut opposition between sacred and profane is complicated through the ambiguity of the sacred. This *sacré ambigu* had already been discussed by his teacher Durkheim and of course by William Robertson Smith. Durkheim followed Robertson Smith in claiming that religious forces are of two sorts: some—connected to the places, persons, and things consecrated to the cult and its rituals—are beneficial, some are evil and impure powers, producing disorder. Even though Durkheim emphasized a most radical antagonism between these two kinds of powers (see Durkheim 1995: 409), he also saw them as clearly connected by having the same relation to the profane, that is, from the perspective of the profane they are "two varieties of the same class" (415). However, while this might be true, Hertz (1960), in "The Pre-eminence of the Right Hand," argued that from the sacred point of view the impure joins the profane to a point where impure and profane become one and together they form the negative pole of the spiritual world (188). Neither Hertz nor Durkheim developed this threefold differentiation into sacred, impure sacred, and profane beyond the basic dualistic scheme of an opposition between sacred and profane.

Czarnowski's exploration of the Roman religious topography invites a somewhat different concept of the sacred. In line with his teachers and colleagues, Czarnowski territorializes the duality of the sacred in a fragmentation of space. "The power of the gods ends at the territorial border, beyond which the power of the neighboring god [or the spirits of the wilderness] begins" (Czarnowski 1925: 342). At the center of this parceled space is the *templum*: the sacred in all its powerful manifestations is concentrated in religious units and at cardinal places, from which it extends through space. "The *mana*," he explains to Hubert in a letter from 24 April 1922, "is not only of varying intensity according to the various places—but . . . it manifests itself, so to speak, according to the qualities of the *étendue*. In a word, the extension as such is endowed with *mana* manifesting itself at the beginning and at the end of the measures of the extension" (Kończal and Wawrzyniak 2015: 248).[5]

Space as Practice

The collective representation of an extended, fragmented space endowed with spiritual power is processed and inscribed into the landscape by the Roman land-conveyers and augurs, Czarnowski argues.

> The drawing of limits takes the division of space into two times two parts by two lines as a starting point that intersect at the central point of the measured area. One of these lines runs from north to south. This is the *cardo*. The other runs from east to west and is called *decimanus*, or *decumanus*. Parallel to the main axes of the *cardo* and the *decimanus* . . . more lines are drawn at equal distances, so that the entire room is divided into square plots of equal size. (1925: 353)

In the practice of the official diviners, space thus practiced is differentiated insofar as it is differently endowed with spiritual powers. The division of the different qualities in the aligned spatial areas revolves around a central sacred point, around which the limited areas are arranged. "This point is simply the one where I am, where my gods live and where I hold my cult. Space has a value only in relation to this" (Czarnowski 1925: 355). Outside of the religious territorial unit there exists only the wide world from which it is excluded and to which it opposes itself as a whole: "Beyond the border of my field or city, there

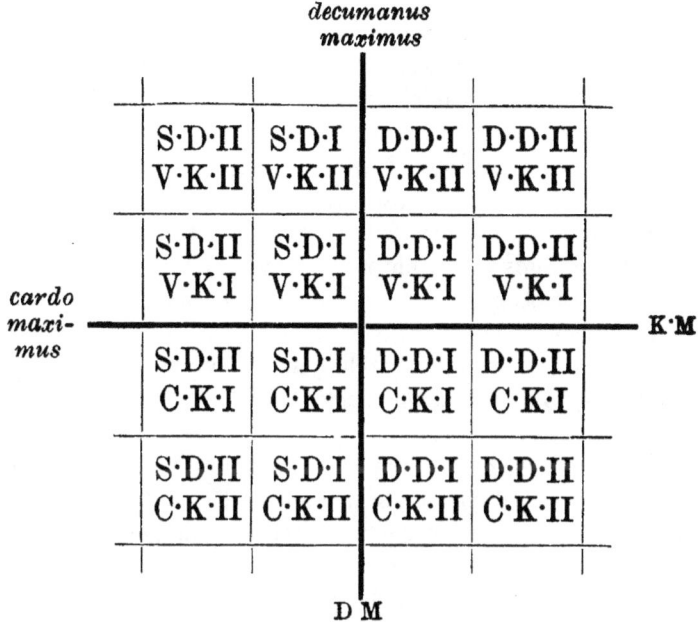

Figure 12.2. Ager. In Paulys Realencyclopädie der classischen Altertumswissenschaft (1893), 788.

immediately begins the area in which the differently organized sacred merges with the unorganized sacred. The one and the other are *de jure* strangers. From a religious point of view, they form the sphere of the untamed powers that must be fended off or appropriated by actions carried out within my borders" (1925: 344).

This relational categorization of pure and impure goes beyond the complementarity of the sacred and the profane in Durkheim's thought. Inside and Outside, Sacred and Profane become relational categories, which are subject to change. Czarnowksi proposes a form of perspectivism introducing a qualitative definition of the sacred and of space that lacks in the work of his teachers. In Mauss's Eskimo text, according to which people change from one setting to the next and rearrange their social order in an annual cycle, the rhythm of space remains within a fixed classification system within a society. In Rome, however, spatial centralization becomes a task for every citizen—and their defeated enemies and neighbors alike. Clearly, Czarnowski seems to allude to the practice of *evocatio* here, that is, a ritual by which, in the course of a war, Romans would attempt to deprive the enemy of divine protection and persuade foreign powers to surrender by formally offering the protecting deity a new home and cult at Rome. The differently organized sacred is thus represented in the sacred center and the *sacré concentré* of one's own territorial unit. It is crucial for Czarnowski that the foreign power is worshipped in the center of one's own cult.

Furthermore, in this model, what is inside/outside and sacred/profane changes with the person who defines it, who inscribes these classifications in space, and who worships his particular gods and ancestors. This remains a dynamic process: Czarnowski lays a concentrically arranged space like a foil over the geometrically arranged space of land surveyors. "These two systems overlap (*chevauche*)" (1925: 353), he writes, to recursively relate mutually opposed *sacrés concentrés*. Instead of being neatly divided in a dualistic space, they get nested, so to speak.

He writes: "Space does not appear like a chessboard arranged of adjacent squares, but consists of a central cell and an environment that encompasses the rest of the world. We are dealing with an image that corresponds to the representation of a water surface into which a stone has been thrown" (1925: 345).

Now, remember how Czarnowksi explained his notion of *l'étendue* to Hubert as being endowed with *mana*, which manifests itself along the measures of the extension and varies according the quality of the *étendue*, thus constituting the rhythm of space. He thinks of a system of correspondences as well as a system of waves and distances that regulates the intensity of the manifestations of the sacred:

> Every central place of worship corresponds to the universe. Each strip of terrain that serves as a boundary corresponds to the outer space. The manifestations of the sacred occur at the sacred place and at each of the concentric borders that surround it, the city border, the border of its property, its administrative district, the state—up to the undefined space, which has no other border than that of the universe itself and beyond which the dwellings of the gods . . . as well as the land of the dead can be found. (1925: 350–51)

The relation between outer and inner spaces is not only one of correspondence, if with reversed signs, but also canalized through the borders that delimit them. These borders are pathways along which sacred powers travel: they are pathways of influences, Czarnowski says, along which men, spiritual beings, demons, benevolent or malevolent powers move. The sacred—and the efficacy of religious acts—extend through space in waves and reaches its maximum intensity at the different sacred places and, again, at the borders. The sacred flows across the territorial units and into the sacralized spaces, and

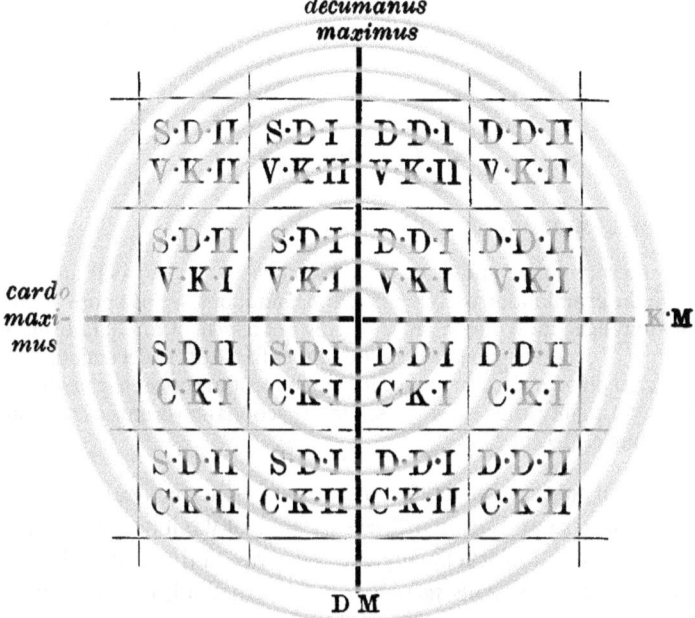

Figure 12.3. Ager. Paulys Realencyclopädie der classischen Altertumswissenschaft (1893), 788 (concentric circles added by the author).

there manifests itself with all its power, which means "that *all* the gods and *all* the spirits flow together in the closed area of the holy place just as one sees them squeeze into the circle that the wizard's staff has drawn. The macrocosm returns to the microcosm" (1925: 346)—and needs to be ritually ordered, for example, by inviting the foreign gods to be worshipped at one's own shrine. Borders become thresholds that connect territorial units and the wider world. Powers go back and forth across these borders connecting different human and spiritual realms and competing for their realization—as much as the concentrated sacred of a cardinal place seeks to be represented at the borders, but also invades the space beyond the boundaries and, there, ultimately transforms into a liberated sacred among other spiritual forces in the realm of the wilderness. Czarnowski makes explicit what remains implicit in Mauss's later work on the same topic, as Nick Allen points out. In his 1933 reply to Granet, he only insinuated "that the center transcends the rest of space ... by referring to its special quality and envisaging it as the starting point for relations" (Allen

2000: 142), which includes the center as an embodied point in space, from which "le morcellement de l'étendue" (the fragmentation of the extension) and the categorization of space departs.

Conclusion

Czarnowski sums up:

> Let me summarize and draw a few conclusions. Space, as it appears from the examination of its division and limitations, is not a pure quantity in religion and magic, and certainly not a form of mind. It forms a system of concrete and irreducible qualities that exist in dependence on a sacred place and are arranged in relation to it in concentric areas ... Space as quality intervenes by itself in the actions and events of religion and magic. (1925: 357)

The focal point of his relational notion of space is the distinction of a "centralized sacred" from a "free sacred"—of what he calls *sacré concentré*, manifest in all its efficacy and relevance at the center of a social space, from what he calls *sacré libre* at the other side of the social and religious border. More strictly speaking, this distinction is a transformation: once the *sacré concentré* crosses the boundaries to an external space and competes there with other powers and spirits, it turns into a *free sacred* and faces dangerous and competing forces from the outside, which likewise transgress the boundaries in the opposite direction and need to be presented in the center, transforming gradually into a *sacré concentrée*. Czarnowski thinks of the sacred moving between sacred centers and across the concentrically arranged boundaries. Please note, that the forces of the wilderness are thus recursively represented at all units of this graduated social space. The forces of the social are found not only in different intensities within, but also without, in the outer space of nature. *La polarité religieuse* is therefore translated, suspended into a third notion of a sacred that envelops the concentrated and the liberated sacred, the sacred of the inner and the sacred of the outer space—*le sacré droit et le sacré gauche*. Czarnowski did not live long enough to see his ideas elaborated among the next generation at the Collège de Sociologie. But already in this paper culture—as it develops at the *ager cultura*—becomes the machine that puts every single individual in the center of his or her world.

Martin Zillinger is Professor of Social and Cultural Anthropology at the University of Cologne. His major field research has been in Morocco on trance, ritual, and new media. In his publications he addresses issues at the intersection of anthropology, media studies and practice theory. His works on the history of anthropology and the Durkheim school are published in journals such as *Durkheimian Studies*, *HAU—Journal of Ethnographic Theory*, the *Zeitschrift für Ethnologie*, as well as the *Zeitschrift für Kulturwissenschaften*.

Notes

Research for this chapter has taken place over several years as part of a cooperative project between the a.r.t.e.s. Graduate School, University of Cologne, and the CRC 1187 Media of Co-operation, University of Siegen, Project number 26251331, which provided more than only funding. I thank Johannes Schick, Mario Schmidt, and Erhard Schüttpelz for companionship and extensive discussions on Czarnowski and the Durkheim School, and Ole Reichhardt for his tireless work in organizing enormous amounts of literature as well as for his invaluable assistance in administrating the project and its international networks. Also, I would like to express my gratitude to Robin Cackett, whose poignant comments and meticulous copy-editing helped to improve the text and made it more accessible. All translations from French into English are mine, if not otherwise indicated.

1. See Kończal and Wawrzyniak (2015: 371).
2. See Wawrzyniak (2018) for a more comprehensive view of Czarnowski's intellectual biography. Her article is among the few to recognize Czarnowski's "return to Durkheimian categories in order to work on the social construction of space" (2018: 12) as part of dispersed efforts to tie in with the prewar work of the Durkheim School. It is therefore doubtful that Czarnowski's works were not "in line with the general theory of categories outlined by Durkheim in 1912," as Thomas Hirsch has recently argued in his fine book *Le temps des societés* (2016: 107).
3. He thus anticipates the famous work of Ioan M. Lewis (1971) in *Ecstatic Religion* and provides us with a theory of religious space that entails a notion of flux and reflux of competing social and religious orders, as we learned from Ernest Gellner (and Ibn Khaldoun, see Gellner 1981). See also, for more recent work on space and the sacred inspired by Czarnowski, Danouta Liberski-Bagnoud (2002), see also Zillinger (2021).
4. In Ovid it reads: "Terminus speaks to the one landlord, then to the other. Tuus est hic ager, ille suus" (Book II: 520) – the god Terminus thus separates territories, it delimits space."
5. Czarnowski confesses to Hubert that he finds the topic of limits "infinitely more confused . . . than assumed . . . [All the] questions related to it, like [divination], the cults of the limits and the folklore of border markers like the orientation and the cardinal points, [so far have] remained almost entirely outside research."

References

Allen, Nicholas J. 2000. *Categories and Classifications: Maussian Reflections on the Social.* Methodology and History in Anthropology. New York: Berghahn Books.

Aföldi, A. 1965. *Early Rome and the Latins (Jerome Lectures, Seventh Series).* Ann Arbor: University of Michigan Press.

Beard, Mary. 1996. "The Roman and the Foreign: The Cult of the 'Great Mother' in Imperial Rome." In *Shamanism, History and the State,* ed. Nicholas Thomas and Caroline Humphrey, 164–190. Ann Arbor: The University of Michigan Press.

Czarnowski, Stefan. 1925. "Le morcellement de l'étendue et sa limitation dans la religion et la magie." *Actes du Congrès international d'histoire des religions. 1923 1,* 339–359.

Durkheim, Émile. 1995. *The Elementary Forms of Religious Life,* trans. Karen E. Fields. New York: The Free Press.

Fustel de Coulange, Numa Denis. 1864. *La cité antique. Étude sur le culte, le droit, les institutions de la Grèce et de Rome.* Paris: Durand.

Gellner, Ernest. 1981. *Muslim Society.* Cambridge: Cambridge University Press.

Godlove, Terry F. Jr. 1996. *Religion, Interpretation, and Diversity of Belief: The Framework Model. From Kant to Durkheim to Davidson.* Cambridge: Cambridge University Press.

Hertz, Robert. 1913. "Saint Besse: Étude d'un culte alpestre." *Revue de l'histoire des religions* 67: 115–80.

———. 1960. "The Pre-Eminence of the Right Hand: A Study in Religious Polarity." In *Death and the Right Hand,* trans. Rodney and Claudia Needham, 89–116. London: Cohen & West.

Hirsch, Thomas. 2016. *Le temps des sociétés: D'Émile Durkheim à Marc Bloch.* Paris: Éditions EHESS.

Hubert, Henri. 1901. "Review of Fowler (1899): 'The Roman Festivals of the Period of the Republic.'" *L'Année sociologique* 4: 234–39.

———. 1902. "Review of Kellner (1901): 'Heortologie oder das Kirchenjahr und die Heiligenfeste in ihrer geschichtlichen Entwickelung.'" *L'Année sociologique* 5: 252–56(i).

Hubert, Henri, and Marcel Mauss. 1908. "Introduction a l'analyse de quelque phènomènes religieux." *Revue de l'histoire des religions* 58: 163–203.

Isambert, François-André. 1999. Introduction to *Essay on Time: A Brief Study of the Representation of Time in Religion and Magic,* by Henri Hubert, 3–42. Trans. Robert Parkin and Jacqueline Redding. Oxford: Durkheim Press.

Kończal, Kornelia, and Joanna Wawrzyniak, eds. 2015. *Stefan Czarnowski: Listy do Henri Huberta i Marcela Maussa (1905–1937). Lettres à Henri Hubert et à Marcel Mauss (1905–1937).* Warsaw: Oficyna Naukowa.

Lewis, Ioan M. 1971. *Ecstatic Religion. An Anthropological Study of Spirit Possession and Shamanism.* London: Penguin Books.

Liberski-Bagnoud, Danouta. 2002. *Les dieux du territoire: Penser autrement la généalogie*, Paris: CNRS Éditions.
Mauss, Marcel. 1933. "Discussion of M. Granet: 'La droite et la gauche, en Chine,' 9. Juin 1933." *Bulletin de l'institut francaise de sociologie* 3/3.
Paulys Realencyclopädie der classischen Altertumswissenschaft. 1893. Stuttgart: Metzler.
Schüttpelz, Erhard, and Martin Zillinger. 2017. "The Bodily Efficacy of the Categories: Durkheim and Mauss's Intervention into the History of Philosophy." *Durkheimian Studies* 23(1): 106–27.
van Gennep, Arnold. 1909. *Les rites de passage*. Paris: Émile Nourry.
Wawrzyniak, Joanna. 2018. "From Durkheim to Czarnowski: Sociological Universalism and Polish Politics in the Interwar Period." *Contemporary European History*: 1–16.
Zillinger, Martin. 2021. "Hamid's Travelogue. Mimetic Transformations and Spiritual Connectivities across Mediterranean Topographies of Grace." *Zeitschrift für Ethnologie/Journal of Social and Cultural Anthropology* 2020/2: 237–254.
Ziółkowski, Adam. 2009. "Frontier Sanctuaries of the Ager Romanus Antiquus: Did They Exist?," *Palamedes* (4): 91–130.

Chapter 13

LA PENSÉE CATÉGORIQUE

MARCEL GRANET'S GRAND SINOLOGICAL PROJECT AT THE HEART OF THE *L'ANNÉE SOCIOLOGIQUE* TRADITION

Robert André LaFleur

Marcel Granet (1884–1940) published his first book-length study in 1919. Entitled *Fêtes et chansons de la Chine Ancienne* ([1919] 1982), he dedicated it to his two mentors, Émile Durkheim (1858–1917) and Edouard Chavannes (1865–1918). The former, of course, was the founder of the *Année sociologique* school of social thought; the latter was one of the leading sinologists in France, whose studies of Chinese sacred mountains and many translations made him a global influence in the fledgling field of Chinese studies. The combination of social thought and sinology that formed the dedication to his first book would follow Marcel Granet throughout his career. Granet's entire *oeuvre* seeks to articulate the key features of the *Année sociologique* tradition—especially those of classification and categorization in society and thought—within the context of Chinese civilization.

Born in 1884 in the Rhône-Alpes region, Granet studied in Aix-en-Provence, and soon found his way to Paris. He was *agrégé* in history at the École Normale Supérieure in 1907, studying with Durkheim during his time there.[1] Soon thereafter, he received a grant to study at the Fondation Thiers, where he established himself as a factor in early-twentieth century French intellectual life. He began his studies with Edouard Chavannes during that period, and followed his research at Thiers with a two-year stint in China from 1911–1913 (see Goudineau 1982: 18–43),[2] during which he studied Chinese classical texts and volumes of the *Année sociologique* that he had carried with him from Paris.

A sociologist by training, Granet turned his formidable energies toward interpreting early Chinese society, focusing his most intensive efforts on key Chinese texts of that period, including the *Book of Songs* (詩經), the *Book of Rites* (禮記), and the formative historical text, the *Zuozhuan* (左傳, *Tradition of Zuo*) (see the following English translations: Allen and Waley 1996; Watson 1992; Legge 2003). His early writings constituted a kind of imaginative ethnography of early China based on textual sources. Narrowly sinological readings of Granet's works often miss the point entirely of Granet's Durkheimian sociological foundations. At every step in his career, Granet blended both.

A Durkheimian First

Marcel Granet participated in Émile Durkheim's 1904–1905 seminar on education—a required component of his studies at the École Normal Supérieur—several years before he initially committed to the study of Japan, and then, upon the persuasion of Edouard Chavannes, of China (Goudineau 1982: 18–43). He formed alliances within the *Année sociologique* school in those early years, and committed himself to the study of kinship dynamics and "feudalism" in the European, and eventually the Chinese, tradition. That sociological groundwork would never leave Granet, even as his examples—always meant to be generalized beyond the specifics of Chinese culture—became more and more deeply sinological.

Granet's first two works show his social-analytical approach most clearly. *Fêtes et chansons* represents an analysis of the poems of the *Book of Songs* and the text of the *Book of Rites*, combined with a resonantly ethnographic focus. His second book, *La religion des Chinois* ([1922] 1989) is a brilliantly resourceful study of religion and society in early China. The text is as audacious as it is enterprising, and distinguished Granet as a scholar to be reckoned with—but clearly not one who could easily be placed within this-or-that intellectual tradition.

Consider the manner in which Granet begins his descriptions in *La Religion des Chinois*—the book that also most clearly shows his own engagement with Chinese life. The opening passages of his chapter on peasant religion are straightforward, appearing to be a standard monograph by an ethnographer and historian laying out the basic framework of his study.

> The peasants lived in villages set upon high ground and enclosed by thick hedges. Certain among them were troglodytes, and perhaps all of them were so in ancient times. Most often, they built their houses of mud and clay, shaped in the manner of an oven. The walls and the roofs were so frail that even a rat or sparrow could pierce through them. At the center of the roof was a square opening to let out the smoke from the hearth and to collect the rainfall that came through. (Granet [1922] 1989: 23)

In fact, however, Granet is already bending the assumptions, even for his early twentieth-century era, of history and ethnography. An abundance of detail in even this brief paragraph comes straight from the *Book of Songs* (Allen and Waley 1996), establishing only for those acquainted with Chinese classics the deeply literary ethnographic picture to follow.

The social-analytical perspective begins soon thereafter, as Granet—echoing Durkheim—notes the division of labor and the alternating rhythms of social life in the wet and dry seasons. From there, his focus turns squarely to social analysis, peppered with precise details from the Chinese classics.

> Throughout the year, in the fields cultivated in common, just as in their enclosed villages, the peasants dealt only with members of their kinship groups. A village contained a large, homogeneous, and unified family. Blood ties and natural filiation did not introduce true divisions into this large community: a nephew was not less than a son nor a father more than an uncle. The life of the household scarcely led to exclusive sentiments. (Granet [1922] 1989: 24)

The closed domestic unit soon opens up further—whole families and communities, laden with food and gifts, moving in concert toward local holy places (*lieux saints*) every spring and autumn to commune with other "closed" kinship groups, opening themselves to something larger than they ever experienced in day-to-day life. In Granet's telling, these were China's most powerful and elemental forms of effervescent sociality, and the foundation of what would become an exceedingly complex social order and an elaborate set of intellectual categories. With the following lines, Granet channels the lessons of Durkheim's ([1912] 1960) *Les formes elémentaires de la vie religieuse*; closed kinship gives way to fervent meetings, and society is recreated in the process (Granet [1922] 1989: 299–304).

> The individual, from day to day, belonged entirely to his family, and the awareness of that belonging implied a habitual sentiment of opposition with regard to neighbors. It was only on exceptional occasions that familial egoism could come to be dominated by the vision—sudden and

radiant—of higher interests that could not ordinarily be clearly seen. These occasions were furnished in their rhythmic life on two moments during the year [in the spring, before planting, and autumn, after harvest]. The penetration between these different groups was even more tempestuous, more moving, more intimate, and more absolute because of their isolation and narrowness being, in normal times, more complete. (Granet [1922] 1989: 27)

From that opening, Granet paints a detailed picture in subsequent pages of the holy places, festivals, their mythology, and the rhythms of social life and the calendar, creating full, rich scenes that give readers a palpable sense of "being there."[3]

Even the casual reader of the *Année sociologique* tradition will quickly see the persistent themes of Durkheim and his followers in Granet's descriptions of peasant life in early China. With every subsequent publication, that clear line to the *Année* would become more and more obscure, laden with Chinese cultural and linguistic detail. And yet, the social analysis with which Granet began his career works its way through every page he wrote until his death.

A Sino-Sociological Oeuvre

Near the beginning of his chapter on *rivalités de confréries* (rival brotherhoods) in *La civilisation chinoise* (Granet [1929] 1994b), Granet describes the winter season ceremonies that formed reunions of the brotherhoods and the development of the first "male authorities" in early China.

> It seems that the first masculine authorities were constituted—in the course of ceremonies of the winter season—during meetings of brotherhoods. In the course of wintering, in the common house, the plowmen, by dint of jousts, expenses, and orgies, gained confidence in their virile virtues. Their prestige grew as their clearings extended. But the Founding Heroes do not draw their glory solely from the fact that they managed the soil and conquered the scrubland with fire. In another manner, they are the Masters of Fire. They are potters or smiths. They know, with the aid of sacred and tragic unions, how to fabricate divine utensils. In the magic cauldrons cast by Yu the Great, all of the dynastic virtue was incorporated, exactly as it could be in a sacred Mountain or River. (Granet [1922] 1994b: 219)

Granet explains that Yu the Great, the third sage-king in a mythical line that began with Yao and Shun, was an ironsmith. Before them all, the Yellow Emperor was also a smith who gained his power in a victory over the apical agricultural spirit, Shennong. Shennong had been said to preside over festivals of the forge and became the god of burning winds, the god of fires of the clearing, indeed, the god of husbandmen. "He is the forge, the forge deified—and yet the resemblance between him and the god of field-labor is complete" (Granet [1929] 1994b: 220). For Granet, there is little surprise that these figures and their very occupations would meet with approbation on the part of the assembled males during the winter season ceremonies, when they came together in ritual feasting and celebration of community.

Already, the weight of Chinese history and culture presses against the non-sinologist, yet Chinese details are simply part of a larger analysis of social dynamics fueled by the intellectual life of the *Année sociologique*.

> The comparison of these facts suggests a hypothesis. Within the large group of the plowmen, brotherhoods of technicians, possessors of magical information and masters of the secrets of the primeval powers, were recruited. The existence of rival brotherhoods supposes a milieu whose organization is no longer founded upon simple bipartition. Now, according to the most ancient Chinese conceptions currently known, the Universe—the Universe is not distinguished from society—is formed of sectors whose Virtues oppose each other and alternate. These virtues are realized under the aspect of directional *Winds*. The Eight Winds correspond not only to departments of the human and natural world, but further to magical powers. Everything is distributed in the domain of the *Eight Winds*, but the latter preside together over music and dance. Dance and music have as their function to manage the world and tame nature for the benefit of men. (Granet [1929] 1994b: 220)

Granet makes a serious sociological point about Chinese cultural categorization based upon his understanding of early societies, both through his Chinese texts and his wide reading of ethnography and social theory. He clearly links the ideal of field-labor and legendary ironsmiths with the growth of rival brotherhoods. For all of his practicality, however, Granet is intent on explicating the magical center of such social practices, and the manner in which beliefs and social practices are intertwined.

Toward that end, he combines the fundamental ideas of opposition and alternation in early Chinese thought with the divine winds, all of which are brought together in singing and dancing, whose function it was "to manage the world and tame nature for the benefit of men." Seemingly static categories are suddenly set into motion, much as were those narrowly focused domestic communities when they came together in social celebration in the sacred places of early China.

> In most of the mythical dramas in which the legend of a foundation of power is commemorated, we see represented, under the traits of dy-

nastic Ancestors or heraldic Beasts, beings that command a sector of the world and that, in numerous cases, appear under the aspects of directional Winds. We have the right then to suppose that, in place of the bipartite organization of society, a division into oriented groups is substituted, or rather superimposed, each one being appointed to a department of the Universe with all working in concert—by dancing, jousting, rivaling for prestige—in the maintenance of a single order. Emerging from these rivalries and these jousts came a new order of society, a hierarchical order founded upon prestige. (Granet [1929] 1994b: 220)

Marcel Granet, in just the first few pages of a chapter analyzing the central theme of brotherhoods in China (so important that they have figured prominently in even recent Chinese history),[4] mixes a set of unapologetically mythical themes with sociological analysis that weaves a blend of Durkheimian social theory with Granet's own study of Chinese kinship. Patiently explaining the mythological themes and articulating the sociological issues relevant to his case, Granet mixes them with dancing, music, wind—*et voilà*, we see rival brotherhoods where a simple kind of social solidarity once stood.

Classification and Embodied Wholes

Marcel Granet shows, in the example above, progression from simple social bipartition to a much more complex classification and categorization of the elements of society. He was not alone in this interest and was intrigued by the writings of his mentor, Émile Durkheim, and close friend, Marcel Mauss (1872–1950). Several studies published in the *Année sociologique* while Granet was still a student cast a long shadow of influence over his career, two of the most significant being Emile Durkheim and Marcel Mauss's (1903) "De quelques formes primitives de classification" and Mauss and Beuchat's (1906) "Essai sur les variations saisonnières des sociétés eskimo".

The influence of "De quelques formes primitives de classification" on Granet's work is enormous. The question that Durkheim and Mauss sought to answer in that text was distinctive in the sociology of the era, for it addressed squarely "why people classify things as they classify themselves" (Needham 1963: xl).

> Not only the outward form of classes, but also the relationships that unite them to each other—all are of social origin. It is because human groups fit together (the sub-clan into the clan, the clan into the phratry, the phratry into the tribe) that groups of things come to be ordered in a similar manner. Their decreasing extension in passing from genus to species, from species to variety, and so forth, results from the equally

decreasing extension presented by social divisions as we move away from the larger and older to get closer to the more recent and most derivative of them. And if the totality of things is conceived as a single and unitary system, it is because society itself is conceived in the same manner. It is in itself a whole, or, rather, the unique whole to which everything else is related. Thus, the social hierarchy and the very unity of knowledge is nothing other than the very unity of the social collectivity, extended to the universe itself. (Durkheim and Mauss 1903: 68).

Granet immediately saw the potential for the study of Chinese society and thought—especially the core ideas of yin-yang 陰陽 alternation, as well as far more complex categories based upon the five phases 五行, the eight trigrams 八卦 (and "winds"), and the twelve zodiacal forms 十二生肖.

In a note contained in the introduction to his 1934 masterwork, *La pensée chinoise* ([1934] 1994c), Granet cites the pages on China in "De quelques formes primitives de classification" as a significant date in Chinese studies:

> As long as there have been sociologists, their premier object, when they work, is it not to discover facts? Perhaps I have signaled several that have not attracted previous attention. The principle of their discovery is found in the memory of *Les classifications primitives*, published by Émile Durkheim and Marcel Mauss; I have the pleasure of saying ... that the few pages of their work relating to China will be marked as a date in the history of sinological study. I will add, as well, that, if I have conducted the analysis of Chinese categories with the sole concern to draw from the Chinese facts only a correct interpretation, the better reason that I have to believe this analysis to be accurate is that it highlights the rule of the category of totality upon which, after an extensive investigation, Emile Durkheim (*Les formes élémentaires de la vie réligieuse*, 630) has strongly insisted. (Granet [1934] 1994c: 485)

While it is difficult to see any direct relevance to Granet's own arguments in the account of Chinese classification found in *Les classifications primitives*, the theoretical orientation—indeed, the "problem" of classification itself—was of great and continued interest to him. One can see very clearly the overall, perspectival, impact of the essay upon Granet's studies of language, matrimonial customs, and left-right distinctions in his collected essays, as well as in his later work (see Granet 1953).

To the conceptual power of Durkheim and Mauss's classificatory schemes, Granet added movement. Chinese categories are always in motion, and correlative thought dominates. Far from being static, platonic forms, yin and yang are always moving—yin is always becoming yang and yang is always becoming yin. And so it goes for every category in Chinese thought. The five phases, in turn proceed from earth to metal to water to wood and to fire, beginning over again in an endless cycle throughout time.[5] In a significant sense, Marcel Granet's powerful response to "Les classifications primitives" establishes the overwhelming theme of *mouvement*.

To that classificatory complexity, Granet added the social and calendrical cyclicality that can be seen in Marcel Mauss's (1906) "Essai sur les variations saisonnières des sociétés eskimo." Mauss's essay focuses upon the social fact of human gathering and dispersal. The core question is deceptively simple. Why do Eskimo groups winter in one place and summer in another? No good Durkheimian would expect anything but a social answer. As Durkheim himself maintained, there is a perpetual need for renewal in social groups. Marcel Mauss makes the point that there is a powerful need for integration and dispersal that goes to the very core of human society.

> Social life is not maintained at the same level of exertion during different periods of the year. Instead, it passes through successive and regular phases of increasing and decreasing intensity, of rest and activity, of social energy and recuperation. It truly appears to do violence to the bodies and to the consciousness of individuals—something they can only endure for a brief period—and that a moment comes when they are forced to slow it and at least partially to avoid it. (Mauss 1906: 127)

This perspective can best be seen in Granet's almost forgotten blend of sociological insight and sinological depth, *Danses et légendes de la Chine ancienne* ([1926] 1994a), which he dedicated to Marcel Mauss. The spirit of the work can best be summarized by Granet's student, Rolf Stein, who has done as much as anyone—even while producing a formidable scholarly reputation of his own—to preserve the memory of Granet's work.

> In order to work as Granet did, a student would have to have complete knowledge of ancient Chinese literature. He had set forth this general principle: no single detail about any civilization can be understood and explained except as part of the entire civilization, in the manner of a puzzle in which the value of any individual piece can only be perceived as part of the complete image . . . But he did, in fact, have one preconceived and overarching idea, that of the value of his work method. He accepted only explanations that clarified facts by placing them side-by-side, putting them into discussion among the others, and, finally, grouping them together as a whole. (Stein 1987: 14–15)

It is this "grouping of wholes" that lies at the heart of Granet's method and his publications; his own body of work needs to be understood in the same spirit. They constitute their own jigsaw puzzle of sociological and sinological analysis, and it is not possible to experience the full thrust of Granet's scholarship without it.

I turn briefly to a key argument in *Danses et legends*, for an example. As part of the book's final section on "Heroic Sacrifice and Dynastic Dance," Granet analyzes another kind of movement, the *Yubu* 禹步—the Step of Yu. Beginning memorably with the phrase: "He knew how to dance" (Granet [1926] 1994a: 549), Yu, the great sage king and founder of the Xia,[6] "dragged a leg as he walked," the result of his toil on behalf of the fledgling empire as he worked without respite to quell the flood waters ravaging all under heaven. The Step of Yu is a Daoist dance and ritual that celebrates, in precise motions—left foot trailing, right foot in front—the toils of the mythical sage king Yu.

> Yu the Great, apparently, knew his craft as King of Blacksmiths . . . he knew how to use a drum; he knew how to dance . . . The Step of Yu remains celebrated. "Being in the correct position, the right foot is in front and the left to the rear. Now, carry the right foot forward; follow the right foot with the left, and place them along the same line: this is the first step. Again, carry the right foot forward. Then, carry forward the left foot; follow the left foot with the right, placing them along the same line: this is the second step. Finally, carry the right foot forward again; follow the right foot with the left; place them along the same line: that is the third step." These are the principles of the Step of Yu, formulated by the Daoist savant Ge Hong. It sufficed to do the dance in order to penetrate with impunity the forests of the mountains. (Granet [1926] 1994a: 549–551)

The "Step of Yu" is precisely the kind of ritual that fascinated Granet, and, in a complex argument, he connects the Step of Yu to shamanistic trance states. Combining classificatory schemes and cyclical movement, it forms a mimetic representation and encapsulation of powerful political and historical processes. For many readers, however, it is read in isolation, and becomes nothing more than part of a catalog of interesting rituals that give "flavor" to Chinese civilization and culture.

But Granet precedes and follows this passage with dozens of pages dealing with the context of Chinese history and political dynamics in early China. Indeed, it grows directly out of a chapter that begins with an analysis of agnatic and uterine kinship as they connect to sacrificial ritual in early China. Unlike many other sinologists of his era—or even some of his own students—Marcel Granet showed little interest in the scholarly "trinkets" of Chinese texts (see Freedman 1974: 10).[7] For Granet, the "Step of Yu" was instead part of a great riddle of Chinese society that must be understood—indeed, could only be understood—as part of a complete and embodied social whole, emphasizing the overarching themes of cyclicality and *mouvement*.

Chinese Civilization, Chinese Thought

Granet's final two works create their own social and intellectual cyclicality, and form a fitting ending to his relatively brief, fifteen-year, publishing career. In Granet's culminating publications, *La civilisation chinoise* and *La pensée chinoise*, it is sometimes difficult to remember that Granet's focus was social theory and a kind of global humanism that only happened—as a result of contingency and serendipity in his early education—to be grounded in Chinese society. And yet, Granet's admiration for Chinese tradition is also clear; he devotes an entire, 100-page, chapter in *La pensée chinoise* to an analysis of Chinese numbers alone. That chapter takes the classificatory concepts found in Durkheim and Mauss (as well as Granet's earlier works) and, in effect, supercharges them.

Marcel Granet wrote *La civilisation chinoise* and *La pensée chinoise* to be read as a pair. When read separately, they lack the solidity Granet planned for these works.[8] Indeed, there is significant overlap in the two books, and they form two sides of a single research question—one that dominated Granet's own thought throughout his career. His crowning texts about early China would show the profoundly social influences upon intellectual life. Just as importantly, however, they show the intellectual influences upon social life.

It is here that we see the problem with reading *La pensée chinoise* in isolation, as is common among China scholars to this day. It forms both an embracing of and a significant step beyond both the sociology of Emile Durkheim and the sinology of Edouard Chavannes. If *La pensée chinoise* is read alone, it might appear that, for example, Granet's descriptions of the numerical values of various notes on the Chinese musical scale are truly ingenious baubles. It might well appear to readers of *Pensée* that the impact of the *Année sociologique* had been lost in the density of early Chinese musical notations, as his analysis of "tube production" in the "Numbers" chapter of *La pensée chinoise* suggests.

> This does not prevent considering all the tubes of *odd* rank as male tubes [= Yang = *Odd* = Heaven = Round = 3 (value of the circumference inscribed in a square on side 1)] and all the tubes of even rank as female

> [= Yin = *Even* = Terre = Square = 2 (value of the demi-perimeter of the square circumscribing the circumference of value 3)]. To conclude in this way, the Chinese had good reasons. If the first three odd tubes are equal to 3/2 of the first three even tubes, the three last odd tubes are equal to, respectively, 3/4 of the last three even tubes; 3/2 expresses the rapport of the circumference (= Heaven) to the demi-perimeter of the square (= Earth) that it circumscribes; 3/4 expresses the rapport of the circumference to the perimeter: similarly, 3/2 and, even better, 3/4 can thus express the relation of Yang to Yin. (Granet [1934] 1994c: 181).

What the careful reader will see in these detailed explanations is that cyclical movement (of peasant festivals as well as musical notes) is embedded in Chinese thought, and each has profoundly social origins. Sociality is everywhere—intellectual categories, musical tubes, yin and yang, and the five phases.

One can see in the diagram an articulation of something that is deeply social in its origins—recalling, in distant fashion, rural families gathering in holy places every spring and autumn to punctuate their ordinary lives, just as the notes on the scale do the same by creating melody. The sinologist sees something equally significant—profound connections to the details of Chinese thought found in the works of early China that linked ruling philosophy and the calendar to the movements of the universe. For Granet, the perspectives are inextricably linked, and he sought to show just how the pieces fit together. For that, we must begin with *La civilisation chinoise*, which launches a two-work, 1,000-page argument[9] for a sociological and sinological whole.

Chinese Civilization

From the opening pages of *La civilisation chinoise*, we see a world in rhythm, a world in which powerful sovereigns radiate virtue outward and unify all under heaven.

> A Sovereign is a sage who, possessing a virtue fitting heroes, civilizes the world by the direct effect of his efficacy and reign, in accordance with Heaven, for the happiness of the people. He is, essentially, the author of an exact and benevolent calendar. His ministers act, inspired by his Virtue. As for him, he reigns without thinking about governing. He strives to create or, rather, to secrete, order. This order is, above all, moral, but it embraces all things. (Granet [1929] 1994b: 23)

Marcel Granet does more in *La civilisation chinoise* than shape the background for his study of Chinese thought. He forges new arguments and sets his older ones—those concerning rural festivals and social life, as well as marriage customs and polygyny—in the broader historical and philosophical context of early China. Above all, we can see a subtle change in Granet's writings that would not come fully to the fore until *La pensée chinoise*. He shows great fascination with the way that people think and move, move and think, and in *La civilisation chinoise* he shows the ways that those thoughts and movements have been rendered in early Chinese literature.

> This is the spirit in which I have conceived the present work—to try to determine the social system of the Chinese; to try to indicate its specific features (in political life, in manners, in thought, and in the history of thought and manners); to try to indicate what lies hidden in larger human experience, by making clear that, from civilization to civilization, only the symbols often differ; to try, finally, to make apparent this system of conduct in the setting and in the movement proper to it. (Granet [1929] 1994b: 11–12)

La civilisation chinoise summarizes the key elements of Marcel Granet's research before 1929, provides far fuller historical and philosophical context than any of his works before *Danses et légendes*, and sets the stage for *La pensée chinoise*, a book that mirrors it in every sense. The mirror image is significant, and not only because of the centrality of bronze mirrors in early Chinese civilization (several of which appear as plates in *La civilisation chinoise*). Right becomes left, and left right. So it is with *La civilisation chinoise* and *La pensée chinoise*. The very force of the earlier book shows a rich social context for key Chinese ideas. Those very same ideas would come to the fore in *La pensée chinoise*, but their social power, articulated powerfully in *La civilisation chinoise*, can be overwhelmed by the sheer detail of intellectual operations and schemes detailed in *Pensée*. Yet the force of sociality remains, even in that work, as Marcel Granet articulates the deep cycles of Chinese intellectual life.

Chinese Thought

In *La pensée chinoise*, Marcel Granet begins with the world of language in China, maintaining that it is an extension of both individual and collective thought. Chinese characters were heaven-issued, yet were brought to life as *mots vivantes* (living words). It is as though, in their formulation in speech and writing—even at the level of the sentence—the living words circulate to connect social interaction with the heavenly order. Speech is, then, a way of putting social life and shared sentiments into motion. Writing goes even beyond that to transmit an equally cyclical quality, connecting readers across space and through time. Indeed, it gives living reality to mere ideas. Words are brought to life in the very act of setting them into motion in an utterance or text.

> The Chinese term that signifies life and destiny (*ming* 命) is hardly distinguished from the one (*ming* 名) that is used to designate the vocal (or graphic) symbols. It matters little that the names of two beings resemble each other to the point that there is a chance one can be taken for the other: each one of these nouns fully expresses an individual essence. It is an understatement to say that it expresses it: it calls it, it leads it to reality. To know the word, to say the word is to possess the being or create the thing. (Granet [1934] 1994c: 40)

Granet goes on in *La pensée chinoise* to articulate the divisions of time and space through yin and yang, as well as the five phases. The work proceeds to ever-larger themes, including the dao, macrocosm, and microcosm, concluding with a 138-page section focusing on the "Sects and Schools" that codified, categorized, and—in significant ways that Granet articulates in detail—ossified the vibrant intellectual exchanges of early Chinese thought.

The argument becomes more detailed—and ever more sinological—with each passing page of Luo River Charts and divination boards, as Granet builds a picture of the universe through Chinese classificatory schemes. It is, indeed, difficult to imagine how sociologists untrained in Chinese texts could follow the arguments adequately, but the text is no less sociological for that. All of the text's themes are grounded in the division of labor in Chinese society, in the very division of work among men and women in and beyond the fields.

That scholarship is then set into motion, showing the manner in which poetic couplets balanced, musical notes harmonized, and odd numbers combined with even ones to build auspicious numerical units with the power to influence all under heaven. Every one of these intellectual pairings flows from the seasonal festival chants that celebrated the most basic division in traditional social life, the focus of Granet's initial research, published fifteen years earlier—with rival groups of young men and women chanting across valleys at spring festivals, bringing the very universe into motion after a winter slumber. These alternating songs, twin couplets, harmonic notes, and odd-even numbers would connect space and time, extension and duration, under the categories of yin and yang and five phase correlative thought.

The categories themselves are never static. Like human society itself, they are always in motion. Work after work, and chapter after chapter, every page of Granet's oeuvre is imbued with the theoretical—or, better put, conceptual and classificatory—focus that Granet found in the issues of *L'Année sociologique* that he carried with him to China a quarter century earlier.

Robert André LaFleur is Professor of History and Anthropology, and holds the George Russell Corlis Chair in History, at Beloit College in Beloit, Wisconsin. LaFleur received his doctorate from the University of Chicago's Committee on Social Thought, where he combined study in three distinct fields—anthropology, history, and Chinese literature. LaFleur's ongoing work comprises historical and literary research using Chinese, Japanese, and Korean sources with ethnographic fieldwork on each of China's five sacred mountains. He is currently completing a translation of Marcel Granet's final two books (*Chinese Civilization* and *Chinese Thought*), as well as doing research for an intellectual biography of Granet.

Notes

All translations from French or Chinese are mine.

1. For context about French education in the early twentieth century, see Terry Clark (1973).
2. Granet lived in China from August 1911 until March 1913; he made a brief trip there after World War I, as well.
3. Clifford Geertz notes, in his first chapter of his *Works and Lives* that creating a sense of "being there" was an integral aspect of early ethnographic writing (see Geertz 1988).
4. In just the past two centuries brotherhoods have figured prominently in the White Lotus Rebellion (1796–1804), the Taiping Rebellion (1856–1864), the Boxer Rebellion (1898–1900), and numerous uprisings between the fall of the Qing dynasty (1911) and the advent of the People's Republic of China in 1949.
5. There are several patterns of the five phases, debated over the ages. This example is called the 生 *sheng* pattern, in which each phase gives rise to the other.
6. The traditional dates of the 夏 Xia era are c. 2100–c.1600 BCE.
7. Even Granet's own students struggled with these matters, becoming bored with Granet's kinship details.
8. Granet writes, "I have already attempted, by analyzing the system of attitudes and comportments that govern the public and private life of the Chinese, to give an idea of their civilization. To make the outline more precise, I will attempt to describe the system of conceptions, symbols,

and preconceptions that in China govern the life of the mind. I claim to offer to the reader of this book only a complement to *Chinese Civilization*" (Granet [1934] 1994c: 9).

9. The page number reference refers to the 1929 and 1934 original editions.

References

Allen, Joseph, and Arthur Waley, eds. 1996. *The Book of Songs*, trans. Joseph Allen and Arthur Waley. New York: Grove Press.
Clark, Terry N. 1973. *Prophets and Patrons: The French University and the Emergence of the Social Sciences*. Cambridge, MA: Harvard University Press.
Durkheim, Émile. [1912] 1960. *Les formes élémentaires de la vie religieuse*. Paris: Presses universitaires de France (PUF).
Durkheim, Émile, and Marcel Mauss. 1903. "De quelques formes primitives de classification." *Année sociologique (AS)* 6: 1–72.
Freedman, Maurice. 1974. *The Religion of the Chinese People*. New York: Harper & Row.
Geertz, Clifford. 1988. *Works and Lives*. Chicago: University of Chicago Press.
Granet, Marcel. 1953. *Études sociologiques sur la Chine*. Paris: PUF.
———. [1919] 1982. *Fêtes et chansons de la Chine ancienne*. Paris: Albin Michel.
———. [1922] 1989. *La religion des Chinois*. Paris: Albin Michel.
———. [1926] 1994a. *Danses et legends de la Chine ancienne*. Paris: PUF.
———. [1929] 1994b. *La civilisation chinoise*. Paris: Albin Michel.
———. [1934] 1994c. *La pensée chinoise*. Paris: Albin Michel.
Goudineau, Yves. 1982. "Introduction à la sociologie de Marcel Granet." Ph.D. diss. Nanterre: Laboratoire d'ethnologie et de sociologie comparative, Université de Paris X.
Legge, James. 2003. *The Book of Rites*. New York: Kessinger Publishing.
Mauss, Marcel, with Henri Beuchat. 1906. "Essai sur les variations saisonnières des sociétés eskimos: étude de morphologie sociale." *AS* 9: 39–132.
Needham, Rodney. [1963] 2009. Introduction to *Primitive Classification* by Émile Durkheim and Marcel Mauss, viii–xxxii. London: Routledge.
Stein, Rolf. 1987. *Le monde en petit*. Paris: Flammarion.
Watson, Burton. 1992. *The Tso Chuan*. New York: Columbia University Press.

Chapter 14

DRAWING A LINE

ON HERTZ'S HANDS

Ulrich van Loyen

Handedness: What Makes a Right Hand "Right"?

"Right" and "left" are going through difficult times. Politicians of the recent populist movements claim for themselves to be neither right nor left, while sociologists confirm that these terms do not identify or even describe any political approach any longer. We are living in an era of confusion, whose agents like to put on the masks of "practical constraint" and "pure objectivity," as if the ways of handling a problem would not derive from one's worldview and character, but rather be a short-sighted reaction to what is considered the obstacle of the moment.

In 1907, the young sociologist Robert Hertz wrote an essay on the "Pre-Eminence of the Right Hand," which soon became a classic in his field and until now has inspired countless anthropologists, scholars of religion, and even philosophers of Italian *postoperaismo*. Albeit not at first glance, it has become recognized as a politically relevant essay itself influenced by a contemporary political question. But foremost, it is a lasting attempt to explain how human beings themselves should be considered "natural symbols," or rather, to what extent cosmology has already to be embedded in order to become "handleable"—in the sense that humans are part of the cosmos and at the same time can take a distance from it. Hertz's essay also offers an approach to the praxeology of classification, to classification as experience, and to the way classification can be learned.

Hertz asks where the widely observed supremacy of the right hand comes from. Regardless of what scholarly literature at the time and until today prescribe, he was sure that such a supremacy was not a natural fact; if it were, training people to use their hands would make no sense. His text is strictly Durkheimian, in that it does not explain the pre-eminence of the right hand as a result of the human neurophysiological or anatomical structure, but rather regards the neurophysiological structure as shaped by the signifier, which is attributed comparatively arbitrarily, and by the cultural task of establishing solid routines. In other words, the left side of our brain is well developed because we exercise our right hand according to the positive connotations the society has attributed to its use. Our physical makeup is both socially formed and informed. Up to a certain point, the development could have been different, but starting from a certain moment the solidity of the right hand's world became almost unquestionable.[1]

Most readers agree that the primary justification for organic asymmetry and the pre-eminence of the right ultimately derives from a religious distinction so fundamental that it has embodied itself in human beings and especially at the center of their action—in their hands. Taking into account Hertz' conviction (the supremacy of the social and of religion as its expression), the majority of scholars follow his assumption by connecting the distinction of right and left to the (not less incongruent) distinction between the sacred and the profane.[2] While the latter is the basis for the classification of values, the former is something humans inevitably have to do—they have no choice but to choose. So why should they not be both "primordially" connected? Does not the distinction between right and left, or left and right, form not only the basis for drawing any distinction, but also for making it look evident, natural, and to a certain extent, offering interchangeability between the various polarities? And does not the dichotomy of sacred and profane provide a coherent and continuous framing of human actions, not only with regard to what is performed, but also with regard to the way in which it is performed (and by doing so offering a rather methodological device to make ordered action predictable)? Also, in the eyes of some biologists, the dichotomy of sacred and profane—and with it, religion in a broader sense—was a helpful tool to transform the notion of a slight asymmetry between right and left in something evolutionary useful.[3]

But is this the only promising way to read Hertz's essay?

At the beginning of his text Hertz evokes a short phenomenological description of the two hands highlighting the astonishing contrast between their obvious similarity and the different ranks and honors ascribed to them. This can be read as a document of surprise, as well as of critique. Superiority and inferiority as objective and quite unchangeable characteristics of the two hands derive from what they continually do and not from what they look like. From this perspective, the essay puts its emphasis on the continuity and persistence of a distinction that is not a priori justified by an inherent characteristic. "Nobility" on the one hand, "servitude" on the other, are the key words of Hertz's introduction, and they may allow us to shift the attention from "religious polarity" to his interest in "the justification of inequality." But even as such a shift may invite us to see a causal connection between the two terms, the question remains: how does it operate? From the very beginning of the text, it is "inequality" that has to be explained. I would therefore like to unfold the tentative idea that by inviting one hand to do the same all the time one enables a regime of stability as the basis for cosmological distinctions that otherwise would collapse, and that this is the hidden core of the argument. Ritual—as the way how "sacred" and "profane" acquire evidence—has to be accompanied at least by socially relevant production (as an entity whose practices can be criticized and/or justified by rituals and religion). In other words, it is the regime of labor that "naturalizes" that distinction and thus shapes the two hands. As the following chapter suggests with regard to Hertz's ground-breaking work, cosmological stability is based on human labor.[4]

Labor: Assimilation and Subordination

Hertz's socialist background, or rather, his socialist perspective, has been highlighted on many occasions.[5] As one of the founders of a socialist student movement, he was actively involved in discussions concerning the political perspectives and emancipatory endeavors of his generation. At the same time, some scholars claim that there is also a dark and discriminatory aspect of the civilizing process to be traced inherent in Hertz's writings. Robert Parkin (1996: 20–21), who has published extensively on Hertz and shed light on various aspects and interconnections between his life and his work, pointed out how his undertaking was informed by the "dark side of humanity." According to Mauss, the dark side was at stake in Hertz's studies on religion and morals, for example, in his work on sin and second burial rites (Mauss 1925: 24). While Mauss links this rather generally to Hertz's supposedly pessimistic character, others hint to his concern with the social breakdown of contemporary France and the urge to find a convincing collective answer (Moebius 2007: 16–18). However, his political activism seems far away from the obscure aspects to which he dedicated his scholarly work. Although Hertz's work on the rites of the Dayak ("Contribution à une étude sur la représentation collective de la mort," 1907), the embodied differentiation between the sacred and the profane ("La prééminence de la main droite," 1909), the alpine cult of Saint Besse ("Saint Besse: Étude d'un culte alpestre," 1913), and finally the problem of the social reintegration of the sinner ("Le péché et l'expiation dans les sociétés primitives," 1922) can be only partially seen in the light of his political commitment, ultimately his continual attempts to transcend the internal "division of labor" has left an indelible mark on contemporary French anthropology (see Charuty 2010: 31). At any rate, Parkin recalls his wife's statement that Hertz's interest in the right and the left was first caused by a problem in education, the encouragement of ambidexterity (which would have meant the suspension of a fixed regime of labor). Even if this were considered a noble "socialist task," in the sense that it may have meant to be a statement against any kind of imposed preferences that might eventually lead to alienation, its difficulty, as explained by the argument of this essay, still has much in common with the difficulty of turning the deceased into good ancestors or cancelling a single man's transgression that has been stigmatized by his whole community. The fact that almost all people have chosen one hand as their "right" one demonstrates that the cosmos is not complete. Thus, one could say that Hertz is interested in both rupture and reintegration and that this interest may have caused a tragic worldview: rupture can be necessary, and reintegration can cost one's life. An echo of this tragic undertaking has been noticed in Hertz's sacrifice as a soldier: while volunteering in active service during World War I, he was killed in action on 13 April 1915. Tradition has it that in a seemingly hopeless situation he tried to make a breach for those who came after him.[6]

Generally speaking, from a socialist perspective, mankind regenerates itself by (non-alienated) labor.[7] Strongly inspired by Georg W. H. Hegel's *Phenomenology of the Spirit* (1807), traditional socialism puts its accent on the transformative and mediating aspect of labor, that is, on the humanization of nature as well as on the self-objectification and self-representation (*Selbstvergegenständlichung*) of the working person.[8] Once labor enters into capitalistic logic, particularly into the division between "productive forces" (*Produktivkräfte*), "means of production" (*Produktionsmittel*) and "capital," the moment of alienation begins. In spite of much evidence, the classical socialism of Marx and Engels only recognizes this alienating moment in the case of productive labor, that is, when the relation between the working hand and the result of this work is affected (Neilson 2010). In his *Foundations of the Critique of Political Economy* Marx writes:

> Productive labor is only that which produces capital. Is it not crazy ... that the piano maker is a productive worker, but not the piano player, although obviously the piano would be absurd without the piano player? But this is exactly the case. The piano maker reproduces capital, the pianist only exchanges his labor for revenue. ([1858] 1973: 232)

Thus, productive labor is labor in the sense that an artisan tells his or her hand what to do. It is based on a complex interaction between physical skills, materials, the supply of materials, the training of workers, their recreation, and it is never free of hierarchies. Productive labor means "mastering," and a result of "mastering" is the "opus" in which human beings ideally recognize themselves, at least, if it is not taken away from them without reward. To master something, one has to bring sacrifices and experience pain, but usually one is more than rewarded by the end since these sacrifices serve as a means. Accordingly, it is within the realm of "productive labor" that the Weberian idea of the "bourgeois" and of cultural Protestantism has found its highest expression. Traditional socialism, to make it short, only wants its just share.

Productive labor adheres to the late nineteenth-century Western transition of the "sacred," indicated by the preeminent use of the right hand. It follows that productive labor is an activity that at best reproduces the cosmological order. It is "valuable" work because it produces something that ultimately belongs to a sphere independent of the action by which it was created; and it can last. Because it can be separated, the means of the action can gain a higher quality: The right hand that swings the hammer and the right hand that touches the holy cross express righteousness and virtue. This hand has acquired skills and competences and sacrificed itself; it therefore needs blessing or expresses humility. But what about the piano player? He or she is an extraordinary example of ambidexterity, a single-handed piano player would not be worth listening to. However, in Marx's perspective the piano player is not completely involved in the experience of alienation because he has no "opus." Action and product cannot be separated from each other, so, at least until the first half of the twentieth century, it remains difficult to make profit from the action—rather than from the person as a whole (as in slavery). Non-productive work is therefore considered a key-issue in the criticism of post-Fordist capitalism. As Giorgio Agamben or Luc Boltanski explain, this is because it is connected to the alienation of "world making" as well as of "innovative action." Non-productive work, like the work of a piano player or the work of a nurse, who cares for the suffering, or, again, the creative work of those using existing means and platforms to perform something no one has performed on those instruments before, is work on whose constant "being in action" society relies; moreover, it is work that, instead of singling out, includes and invites and opens up for participation (here one might even think of sports in its age of innocence). It is work that the reproduction of society relies on, that teaches to withstand a crisis and to keep things in one's "own hands"; it is, in one word, "subsistential work" because it produces the means (and symbols) for social subsistence—that what is common. And, besides being ambidextrous, this labor is very often female, invisible, marginalized, or even considered to be impure. Whenever it entered the market, suspicions were raised: something, which had to be a free gift or at least belonged to the regeneration of the family as the smallest economic unit, was perverted by being turned into something everybody could participate in (and this exactly is the scandal of "prostitution").[9]

If one agrees with this analysis of (in a broader sense: manual) labor, one may conclude that, with today's automation and digitalization, the pre-eminence of exercising one's right within the context of opus-producing labor has come to an end, while non-productive labor has become exploitable and "alienable" by similar techniques and technologies and therefore become normalized and free of both sacred or "impure" connotations. The symbolic value of the right hand thus has become less "embedded" and claiming ambidexterity in an emancipatory perspective makes less sense.

As Robert Parkin has already pointed out, it would be more than incorrect to ignore the differences between Marxist socialism and the one of Jaurès to which Hertz seemed to be inclined. And even Marx's view on non-productive labor itself underwent various changes. According to Hubert Bourgin, who reported that Hertz "understood Socialism as a method for studying and resolving social problems" ([1938] 1970: 481–82), as well as to Judith Zimmermann's (2016: 326–28) meticulous analysis of his letters, Hertz understood "socialism" in this context as a kind of applied sociology or "perspective" that included a kind of moral commitment to being a sociologist, as becoming a sociologist ultimately stemmed from the choice of being a socialist. Be that as it may, the question of labor is a prominent socialist topic, and the question to which degree one is involved in one's labor, to which extent labor is an expression of being or becoming human, and in what way society is made up of labor (as, for example, stated by the Italian constitution of 1946) remains a crucial one. Making use of the association of (productive) labor and the two hands, it becomes clear that the polarity in labor as a process concerned with the transformation of goods—from the formless and ambivalent to the formed and definite—is inscribed in the use of the hands itself, so that each hand is closer to one of the two poles in this process. As obviously the "left" hand is less involved in shaping and applying something new to a given object than the "right"—the left hand usually holding, maintaining, pressing—it enters into a strange relationship with the present past of labor's object, making it passive and at the same time becoming passive too (a passivity enhanced by the pressure of the capitalist to reproduce again and again the same object with less effort and cost). However, it seems as if the polarity of the two hands at least partly is a result of the way they assimilate to the objects they deal with. It seems quite logical that the left hand is more inclined to this experience of corresponding than the right one, which imposes a pattern on the object kept by the left hand. The object in between those hands becomes the medium through which the violence of changing a form is transmitted from the right to the left, and so it seems that this ongoing process of disciplining or human self-domestication is nothing else but the inevitable process of becoming single-handed, of learning to face the socially demanded subordination of the left hand. The gap between productive labor and non-productive labor is permanently increasing, because it becomes less and less clear how non-productive labor (piano playing, for instance) should be possible for people growing up in a world where ever more productive labor requires single-handedness (the sacrifice of one hand) or ultimately automation. Non-productive labor very often acquires the aspect of veiling the devastating effect of productive labor, it becomes more ideological than therapeutic. In effect, the symbolism of right and left itself turns into an instrument in the hands of the hegemonic power, helping to keep the one on the A-side (the side of productive labor and of increasing "handlessness" on the part of those who are told: keep your right hand, even if it is not operating now) and the other on the B-side (where righteousness as well as ambidexterity are supposed to be only "imitated"). In other words, there is confusion about keeping up a distinction, and it is in this situation that for Hertz the following question arises: Would it not be better to have two right hands—instead of a right and a left one or ultimately none at all? And be it only to stop the dirty work of our exploiters: "Alle Räder stehen still / Wenn dein starker Arm es will" ("All wheels will stand still, / if your strong arm so will," Bundeslied für den allgemeinen deutschen Arbeiterverein).

Gender: Inversion and Complementarity

Concentrating on the regime of labor alone, there are not sufficient arguments for the pre-eminence of the right hand as "the right," that is, for the connection of the single elements of the embedded cosmology. We would be dealing only with the stability of one regime, while the questions of its plausibility are resolved elsewhere, where the interconnectivity, including the coherence, of symbols is treated. In this respect Hertz's article offers a lot of material. His findings and conclusions, particularly those concerning Maori customs, have later been generalized, especially with regard to the archaeological reconstructions of burial sites. From such burial sites, the idea was born that people were placed in their tombs facing the rising sun (east) and following the sun's movement along their right side (southwards), while north (their left side) was associated with the realm of death. Attempts to naturalize the left/right distinction in terms of light and dark or life and death have tried to establish logical connections between complementary and contrasting pairs. Although consistent up to a certain degree,[10] they are no longer sufficient when it comes to the introduction of distinctions that are social and natural at the same time, such as "male" and "female."[11] They reduce the question of the hands' nobility to their belonging to the right or wrong side (the side of life, the side of darkness), regardless of what they do.[12]

Like many others, Robert Hertz has pointed out that the "female" side is usually the left one. Maybe it would be more accurate to speak of the "non-male" side, as this would encompass even more, for example the "past" of masculinity (including, to some extent, the edge between "nature" and "culture"). Regarding Maori customs, Hertz writes:

> In general, man is sacred, woman is profane: excluded from ceremonies, she is admitted only for a function characteristic of a status, when a taboo is to be lifted, i.e., to bring about an intended profanation. But if woman is powerless and passive in the religious order, she has her revenge in the domain of magic: she is particularly fitted for the work of sorcery. (Hertz 1960: 93)

The attempt to project one polarity onto another is obvious here, as is the kind of labor addressed in these lines: instead of veneration, representation (including the representation of what cannot be represented), and especially instead of the public, on the female side we find the privatization of the religious, its subversion and manipulation, and, foremost, the complete ignorance of the male-held division between human and non-human (even as Hertz's passage unconsciously points to the complementarity of "religion" and "magic," that is to religion as purified and *clair et distinct*, which at the same time implies a preceding unification). The many negative associations of the female "left" in fact derive from their transgressive character, and their transgressive character can be interpreted in light of their relation to "world-making" actions, that is to say: to non-productive labor.

Thus, if we wish to follow the initial argument of this chapter (and of Robert Hertz), the division of labor according to gender must be taken into account. For it is the solidity and stability of a regime of labor that imposes the analogous relation of oppositions such as left and right, female and male, and, at least associated with it, of sacred and profane. Often this conjuncture becomes most obvious, when it seems broken. For instance, Rodney Needham, who, among others, translated and edited Robert Hertz works in English, in his essay about "Right and Left in Nyoro Symbolic Classification" (1967) points out the following case: "The puzzle is that left-handed people in Bunyoro are 'hated,' and nothing may be given with the left hand (Roscoe 1923: 50), yet that in divination by the casting of cowrie shells, which is by far the commonest technique resorted to whenever Nyoro are in trouble, the diviner holds the shells in his left hand" (Needham 1967: 426). As in other cultures, male affirmative symbolism is tied to the right, while female is tied to the left. Nevertheless, whenever it is not gender that counts (in status-related contexts other than reproduction, division of labor, etc.), even "natural" women participate in the "righteousness," indicating that "left" and "right" are understood as a distinction to foster social values rather than as a "given" nature. However, the opposition of right and left, usually mirrored in the relation of the sexes, becomes more stable in the relation between the living and the dead. The world of the dead is the world of total subversion. And, of course, it is also the realm one has to get in contact with for divinatory purposes. According to Needham, in Nyoro symbolism we find the two basic relations of "opposition" and "analogy" (the first as a logical one, the latter as a mode to organize experience) creating a continuous association of the various polarities and giving meaning to their various members. So female "biological" vicinity to the subversive world of the dead can become a mask for the diviner, who enters the dangerous realm. The female left, of course, is usually not the same as the male left, just as the man who becomes a woman (or a non-man) has to undergo several *rites de passage*, during which he becomes a purified member of the other group, even more pure than the "natural" members of the group itself. But his "liminal competence" is acquired only by turning the perspectives and experiences of the other group into his own.

So men do female work in ritual form. Does this mean that, whenever men do female work, they perform a ritual or they can only accomplish it ritually?[13] The rite offers the horizon not only of a beginning but also of an end; it is a way to organize reversibility against the contingency and non-reversibility of nature. By suspending the natural course of the time arrow, the rite creates a double, twofold reality. So to some extent, female work done by men in a ritual context is different from female work as such: it is the pure essence of it and therefore gains a higher status. From which follows, that without the possibility of the other ritually performing the proper work (or the proper characteristic), the pure essence of it would remain unknown. It is by ritual change that the female and the male world, which seen separately are destined to remain "parts," become a whole. Only by separation are the conditions induced that make them "meaningful" at all.

When "meaning" requires differentiation, and as such is derived from a "duality," the process of making a distinction is simultaneously imbued with "symbolical" (or cognitive) and physical (or spatial) parameters. Therefore, the underlying level of "meaning" is not merely spatially "represented," it is itself spatial. In other words, whenever human action in the world is spatially hindered and the capacity of making a distinction fails, the "presence" collapses (de Martino 1977: 202). In the once so-called primitive cultures this foundational level is only more prominent, but we find evidence of it in modern Western cultures as well; for instance, through Ernesto de Martino's studies on spatial distinction and the "end of the world" ("La fine del mondo," 1977), which can be read as an essay on right and left. The underlying level of meaning is twofold, complementary and, above all, the expression of an irreducible duality (you *cannot not* make the difference), while space is only where divisions can be made ("left" and "right" for instance). This is exactly what the social philosopher, Jesuit, and anthropologist Ivan Illich had in mind when he looked for a starting point of his much acclaimed and much discussed book on *Gender: A Historical Critique of Equality* (Illich 1982). Illich here detects a profound relation between gender as an asymmetrical but complementary duality and the ancient production mode of a world prior to industrialization. By "complementary gender" or "vernacular gender," as Illich calls it, he means

> the eminently local and time-bound duality that sets off men and women under circumstances that prevent them from saying, doing, desiring, or perceiving "the same thing." Together they create a whole,

which cannot be reduced to the sum of equal, merely interchangeable parts; a whole *made of two hands, each of a different nature*. Gender implies a complementarity within the world that is fundamental and closes the world in on "us," however ambiguous or fragile this closure might be. The domains of activity inside that closure—be it child rearing, cooking, sewing, plowing, the use of a hammer or a pot—have a dignity and meaning, often ritually expressed or mythologically represented, and valued solely by its contribution to the subsistence of a community. (Illich 1982: 23; my emphasis)

For Illich, the experience of gender is a necessary condition to experience oneself as a part of a social unity, the intriguing sameness of the other and the intriguing otherness of the same. (The way in which this coincides with a Durkheimian notion of "effervescence" we do not have to discuss here.) It is only by the introduction of a "regime of scarcity" (1982: 10–12) and the privatization of an accessible space to fulfill substantial needs—the "commons"—that the complementary duality of gender gets replaced by two competing sexes and, in consequence, by the capitalist inclusion of their respective ways of "labor," which are made more and more interchangeable in the course of capitalist history: so-called productive and creative work. Their biological difference in some way becomes prevalent over the cultural one, because within the industrial era they are both forced to take part in the struggle of the fittest, and it is only in this context that speaking of gender "discrimination" makes sense.

Today this point of view, which is a prerequisite to any gender theory, reappears in the discussions about the limits of economic growth vis-à-vis climate change and the destruction of multiple life worlds. The "dream of humanity gifted with two right hands," as Hertz calls it, compared to Illich's "two hands, each of a different nature," looks rather doubtful, as if it was one of the inherent causes for the failure of socialism. It certainly fades out the notion of limits (and of reciprocal limitation). Contrary to the frequent assumption that limitlessness is characteristic of a regime of scarcity, societies of commons or of gendered activities, both being embedded in a cosmological whole, survive thanks to their imposed limits. Looking back to the recent history of labor, one is tempted to say: Two right hands are no hands, or if they are, they do no longer belong to anybody. They are a capitalist fetish.

Nevertheless, in an interesting footnote, Ivan Illich (1982: 73) pays tribute to Robert Hertz. He acknowledges that the latter had recognized asymmetry and ambiguity as characteristics of the fundamental polarity in social sciences. Asymmetrical is the "relative position" in a relation, "ambiguity" means that the two do "not fit congruously" by following the same principle. From this perspective, the use Marcel Mauss made of Hertz's duality as the condition of reciprocal exchange in his "Essay on the Gift" (Mauss [1925] 2016) mirrors the reduction from gender to sex. At the same time, Illich and any new critical left could fully agree to Hertz's dictum: "If organic asymmetry would not have existed, it would have had to be invented" (Hertz 1960: 98).

Coda: The Golden Age

We may conclude that Hertz's utopian outlook regarding ambidexterity, or even the educational achievement his wife reported to his biographer (Parkin 1996: 3–4), may seem more questionable than at the beginning, all the more so if we recall that Hertz himself remained somewhat ambivalent: "[F]rom the fact that ambidexterity seems possible it does not follow that it is desirable" (Hertz 1960: 113). Does this short hesitation imply that it had become clear for Hertz and his first readers that an ambidextrous world would, at best, mark a cosmological shift, while, at worst, it proved the crack within the chain of polarities that, thanks to the condition of the homo duplex, can be conceptualized as belonging to the same human world? As Hertz stated in the last part of his essay:

> For centuries the systematic paralyzation of the left arm has, like other mutilations, expressed the will animating man to make the sacred predominate over the profane, to sacrifice the desires and the interest of the individual to the demands felt by the collective consciousness, and to spiritualize the body itself by marking upon it the opposition of values and the violent contrasts of the world of morality. It is because man is a double being—homo duplex—that he possesses a right and a left that are profoundly differentiated. (Hertz 1960: 112)

The end of this mutilation is presented as the end of exploitation by labor: by the introduction of (not only technologically) improved means of production and by the liberation of the human body from social constraints. Today's readers know that history took a different path. "A more harmonious development of the organism" in Hertz' view might have required a more harmonious synchronization between individual and society, between morals and law. As Hertz makes clear, this would not abolish polarities and their perception; the fading out of the antithesis of left and right would not result in the cancellation of "good" and "evil." But how would it survive if not embodied? Did Hertz expect a new revival of classical values—the harmonious as good, the incongruent as evil? Did he hope for aesthetic completeness substituting the ancient "natural symbols"? And did he not, by sharing this dream, unwillingly and unconsciously participate in the emergence of a new world order that turned out more totalitarian and inhumane than any other before? Finally, does this have anything to do with the way he got himself killed in action, betting on a future that did not belong to him but that he was eager to belong to?

Times have changed, and at least in Western societies the harmonious body has merely been a prelude to a radically individualized body—a prelude less to a liberation of nature (leading to non-alienated relationships between man and his kin, man and work) but rather to endless modifications based in an ever-multiplying homo duplex (and their physical appearances and digital presentations). Still, it seems as if homo duplex were constantly in need of re-establishing polar orders: even if queer, they want a marriage, and also a wedding ceremony; even if they want to step out of traditional role models, they welcome the dichotomous symbolism associated with them. In view of the worldwide symbolism of polarities it becomes less relevant if a special opposition is officially repudiated. In this sense, the ongoing translation and connection of oppositions and analogies seems to be a tangible necessity, and as such situates itself at the core of any culture and any person embedded in it. At this core, where one ponders examining the emergence of a completely new future, one actually finds shared strategies of world making, which render us not only very similar to the people who lived before us, but also to contemporaries, to our fellow human beings near and far.

Ulrich van Loyen, PhD in both German Literature and Social Anthropology, is a scholar of the Anthropology of Religion and its history. He is working at the Department of Media Studies at the University of Siegen. Recent publications include: *Neapels Unterwelt: Über die Möglichkeit einer Stadt* (Berlin 2018, Italian translation Milan 2020); *Der Pate und sein Schatten: Die Literatur der Mafia* (Berlin 2021).

Notes

1. This view is confirmed by the ongoing debate in the neurosciences, which I cannot expand on here. More than a hundred years after Hertz's essay neither neurologists nor evolutionary theorists have brought forth convincing evidence to the contrary (amid growing doubts about the supposition that handedness and the hemispheric dominance of speech processing are somehow connected, etc.). In view of the fact that the brain activities we study are the result of a choice preceding the single individual, one might even argue that no scientific proof at all could refute

Hertz's argument. Be that as it may, the difficulty to give an epistemologically sound answer poses more than a minor problem for the question itself (see Corballis 2014).

2. Both dichotomies deal with incongruent elements, although in a reverse way: the range of activities covered by right-handedness is wider than the extension of the sacred when compared to the profane. Hertz attributes the impure sacred to the side of the profane, thus highlighting the purity of the sacred and the ambivalence of the profane. This prioritization is reproduced in the distinction between "religion" and "magic" and their respective ascription to male and female and the right and the left hand or side.

3. For a while it was suggested that the asymmetry between right and left was uniquely human, however, neurobiologists today claim it is widespread among vertebrates and non-vertebrates. From this point of view, it might be a condition for evolution itself. If so, these results could be used as an argument against the Durkheimian position according to which "the distinction between right and left . . . is very probably the product of representations which are religious and therefore social" (Durkheim [1912] 1915: 12) or they could enhance a far wider notion of "society."

4. Hertz mentions labor in three contexts: first, in the context of gender division; second, in the context of ritual labor (worshipping the sacred); third, and quite abruptly, as a perspective of overcoming mystical ideas associated with left and right.

5. For further reading see Robert Parkin (1996: 51–57), and Stefan Moebius (2007: 21–23).

6. For Robert Walter Hertz's biography, see Parkin (1996).

7. Although in his *Economic and Philosophical Manuscripts* from 1844 Marx describes roughly four types of alienated labor, he is far less specific about the notions of non-alienated and non-estranged activity proper to the conscious "species-being" (Marx [1844] 1988: 82–83).

8. In Hegel's footsteps Marx emphasizes the strictly human aspect of labor. Human beings bring a human form to the objects they work upon and thus duplicate themselves in the world; see Marx ([1894] 1971: 28–29).

9. It is, of course, especially impure labor that is related to the sacred, and the labor of a revenue artist as well as that of a sex worker in various cultures finds itself associated to both. Nevertheless, one should remark that it does so because the sacred itself as the expression of wholeness has to take impurity into account. In other words: the idea of the sacred can only be incorporated in somebody (or something) that comprises all the possibilities of being as they present themselves under the living conditions of a given society. This does not mean that the impure are more sacred than others, but only that they are closer to it; they invoke it by their very existence and express it symbolically. But this awareness of their sanctity and sacredness is almost always embedded in certain contexts, rituals, or other kinds of framing, that is in moments when their laborious aspect is obscured or does not appear at all.

10. For an adaptation by modern popular science, see Chris McManus, *Right Hand, Left Hand* (2004: 36–41). Naturalistic explanations for the asym-

metry are rather common in this kind of literature, while Hertz himself dismisses the universality of, for example, the influence of the sun or other stimuli. As he points out for Hindus and Romans, the south belongs to the dead and is therefore inauspicious. Moreover, the suggested association of the positive right does not change among people in the southern hemisphere where the sun shines from the north (see Parkin 1996: 61).

11. In many respects the polarity of right and left helps translate "given" distinctions into culturalized ones by reducing the number of elements involved and by ordering them analogically. Analogy and opposition seem to be primary relations organized by "right" and "left," and they are neither exclusive nor do they entail each other (opposed elements are organized analogically).

12. Durkheimians themselves critically discussed the binary distinction revealed by Hertz. In his long comment on Granet's explorations of "La droite e la gauche, en Chine" (1933), Marcel Mauss explicitly recognized Hertz's merits in having elucidated the division of things into "two sides, two hands" while at the same time admitting to have simplified the problem by focusing on the "charactèristique impérative du tabou e du sacré" (the imperative character of the taboo and of the sacred; Mauss 1933: 109). With regard to Granet's analysis of the right/left distinction within Chinese social life—a life ordered by "etiquette"—Mauss declares that "cette notion de 'pre-eminence' . . . doit faire place à la notion de positions e qualités corrélatifs" (this notion of pre-eminence has to give way to the notion of correlative positions and qualities; Mauss 1933: 111).

13. In many cultures the diviner can be both female and male. Usually the female role is more prepared and of a culturally stabilizing character—think of the various female trance mediums and their actively induced passivity. Male trance mediums, especially in southern Italy and the Mediterranean, are regarded as somehow effeminate but no less effective (De Martino 1961: 62; Apolito 2006). Nevertheless, beyond professionality, crises, initiation rites, and so forth, are required for them to acquire credibility. In this way men are singled out, while female diviners or mediums describe themselves as becoming included, or more "profoundly female," by such experiences (see van Loyen 2018: 121–22).

References

Apolito, Paolo. 2006. *Con la voce di un altro: Storia di possessione, di parole e di violenza*. Naples: L'ancora del mediterraneo.

Bourgin, Hubert. [1938] 1970. *De Jaurès à Léon Blum: L'École normale et la politique*. Paris: Gordon & Breach.

Charuty, Giordano. 2010. "'Keeping Your Eyes Open': Arnold van Gennep and the Autonomy of the Folkloristic." In *Out of the Study and into the Field: Ethnographic Theory and Practice in French Anthropology*, ed. Robert Parkin and Anne de Sales, 25–43. New York: Berghahn.

Corballis, Michael C. 2014. "Left Brain, Right Brain: Facts and Fantasies." PLoS Biology 12(1): e1001767. https://doi.org/10.1371/journal.pbio.1001767

De Martino, Ernesto. 1961. *Terra del rimorso: Contributo a una storia religiosa del sud*. Milan: Il Saggiatore.

———. 1977. *La fine del mondo: Contributo all'analisi delle apocalissi culturali*. Turin: Einaudi.

Durkheim, Émile. [1912] 1915. *The Elementary Forms of Religious Life*. London: Allen & Unwin.

Granet, Marcel. 1933. "La droite et la gauche, en Chine." *Bulletin de l'institut français de sociologie* 3(3): 87–116.

Hertz, Robert. 1907. "Contribution à une étude sur la représentation collective de la mort." *L'Année sociologique* 10: 48–137.

———. 1909. "La prééminence de la main droite: Étude sur la polarité religieuse." *Revue philosophique* 68: 553–580.

———. 1913. "Saint Besse: Étude d'un culte alpestre." *Revue de l'histoire des religions* 67: 115–80.

———. 1922. "Le péché et l'expiation dans les sociétés primitives." *Revue de l'histoire des religions* 86: 1–60.

———. 1960. "The Pre-Eminence of the Right Hand: A Study in Religious Polarity." In Robert Hertz, *Death and the Right Hand*, trans. Rodney and Claudia Needham, 89–116. London: Cohen & West.

Illich, Ivan. 1982. *Gender: A Critical History of Equality*. New York: Pantheon.

Marx, Karl. [1894] 1971. *The Capital. Vol III. The Process of Capitalist Production as a Whole*. Moscow: Progress Publishing.

———. [1844] 1988. *Economic and Philosophical Manuscripts of 1844*. Unabridged Edition. New York: Prometheus.

———. [1858] 1973. *Foundations of the Critique of Political Economy*, trans. Martin Nicolaus. London: Penguin Books.

Mauss, Marcel. 1925. "In memoriam: L'œuvre inédite de Durkheim et de ses collaborateurs." *L'Année sociologique, nouvelle série* 1: 7–29.

———. [1925] 2016. "Essay on the Gift: The Form and Sense of Exchange in Archaic Societies." In *The Gift: Expanded Edition*, trans. and ed. Jane I. Guyer, 55–200. Chicago: HAU Books.

———. 1933. "Discussion of M. Granet: 'La droite et la gauche, en Chine,' 9. Juin 1933." *Bulletin de l'institut francaise de sociologie* 3/3.

McManus, Chris. 2004. *Right Hand, Left Hand: The Origins of Asymmetry in Brains, Bodies, Atoms and Cultures*. Cambridge, MA: Harvard University Press.

Moebius, Stefan. 2007. "Einleitung." In *Das Sakrale, die Sünde und der Tod. Religions-, kultur- und wissenssoziologische Untersuchungen* by Robert Hertz, ed. Stephan Moebius and Christian Papilloud, 15–65. Konstanz: UVK.

Needham, Rodney. 1967. "Right and Left in Nyoro Symbolic Classification." In *Right and Left: Essays on Dual Symbolic Classification*, ed. Rodney Needham, 425–52. Chicago: Chicago University Press.

Neilson, Brett. 2010. "On Ambidextrousness, or, What Is an Innovative Action?" *Comparative Literature and Culture* 12(4). https://doi.org/10.7771/1481-4374.1674.

Parkin, Robert. 1996. *The Dark Side of Humanity: The Work of Robert Hertz and its Legacy.* Amsterdam: Harwood Academic Publishers.

Roscoe, John. 1923. *The Bakitara or Banyoro.* Cambridge: Cambridge University Press.

van Loyen, Ulrich. 2018. *Neapels Unterwelt: Über die Möglichkeit einer Stadt.* Berlin: Matthes & Seitz Berlin.

Zimmermann, Judith. 2016. *'Sozialismus ist aktive Soziologie': Religion, Politik und Gesellschaft im Leben und Werk von Robert Hertz.* Leipzig: Universität Leipzig.

Chapter 15

BETWEEN CLAUDE LÉVI-STRAUSS, PIERRE BOURDIEU, AND MICHEL FOUCAULT, OR

WHAT IS THE MEANING OF MAUSS'S "TOTAL SOCIAL FACT"?

Jean-François Bert

I would like to "recompose" the different ways three major readers of Marcel Mauss belonging to a generation emerging in the 1950s have read his "total social fact project." A small shift, or rather a change in focus, will allow me to show how this idea has been subjected to quite contradictory, reductive, rigidifying or, conversely, totalizing readings.

To be exhaustive, these three names should be supplemented with many other readers and commentators—most of them unfortunately forgotten today, despite their importance in the postwar humanities and social sciences. I am thinking here of Georges Gurvitch, Claude Lefort, Jean Cazeneuve as well as Roland Barthes or André Leroi Gourhan and his notion of a total social object (Athané 2011). However, focusing on Claude Lévi-Strauss, Pierre Bourdieu, and Michel Foucault will allow me (a) to "recompose" the different ways these three readers, belonging to a new generation of scholars emerging in France at the beginning of the 1950s, understood Mauss's "total social facts"; (b) to show how they transformed the idea in order to (c) insert it at the heart of their own methodological approach.

Lévi-Strauss's Introduction to "Sociologie et Anthropologie"

It is in his introduction to *Sociologie et anthropologie* that Lévi-Strauss (1950) comments, utilizes, but also critiques Mauss's perspective. He especially insists on the principle of the "total social fact" as a means to avoid simplistic functionalist interpretations by revealing the mutual dependency between the individual and the social, which is always actualized within the context of a set of interrelated structures.

Mauss understood that it was necessary to link techniques of production to ritual practices, to the economic, the legal, the religious. Social reality could only be understood as a system. But if we read closely what the anthropologist is saying, we can also see how careful he is in protecting the total social fact from the functionalist tendency to provide a totalizing and global reading of social phenomena. Indeed, such a reading would deprive Mauss's principle of its main objective, that is, the return to concreteness.

Lévi-Strauss makes a second observation in his preface: Mauss saw all social reality as subjectively lived, as experienced by the individual. To account for a social fact, one must look to objective realities as well as subjective experiences sustained by individual actors. As Lévi-Strauss summed it up: "For the first time in the history of ethnological thinking, effort was made to transcend empirical observation in order to reach deeper realities" (1950: XXXIII).

On this point Lévi-Strauss seeks to establish a clear-cut difference between Marcel Mauss and Émile Durkheim, at least the Durkheim of the *Elementary Forms*. Mauss's totality, which belongs to the realm of experience, can only be seized through observation at specific points in social life.

The preface did not sit well with numerous Mauss experts, such as Pierre Métais, a specialist of New Caledonia, and Georges Gurvitch, the editor of *Sociologie et anthropologie*, who, unlike Lévi-Strauss, felt that Mauss was a radical empiricist and pluralist anthropologist who certainly did not seek to oppose individual and society in a dualist way (Jeanpierre 2004), a point Lévi-Strauss either did not see or chose to neglect in his rather personal interpretation of the Maussian text.

The conflict between these two is important, even crucial to understand the genesis of structural anthropology in France. Gurvitch took a more ambivalent position. He criticized Durkheim's sociology for its idealism and, based on the approach of Mauss, whom he admired for his realism and relativism, he proposed a division of social life according to different levels of reality, following a sociological distinction between morphology, institution and regular conduct, symbol, values and ideas, and states of consciousness. For Gurvitch, a fervent reader of Marx as well, this was the only way to give an accurate idea of the dynamics that agitate the social world. However, the sociologist was not satisfied with the idea of the total social fact and intended to complement Mauss by indicating how total social phenomena were in fact, and always, multidimensional. Each particular grouping of facts could be studied as a total phenomenon, but only on condition that each of these groupings was seen as integrated into more diverse global societies (Marcel 2001).

Mention might be made here of the philosopher Claude Lefort, who likewise disagreed with Lévi-Strauss's propositions and decided to link Mauss's perspective with a phenomenological anthropology that did not aim at sketching a system but rather tried to reflect on the experience of rivalry. Claude Lefort charged Lévi-Strauss with seeking to inordinately reduce Mauss's transhistorical reading of the gift—that distinguished between various forms of gifts (agonistic, non-agonistic, magical, ordinary)—to a regular and mechanical model (Lefort [1951] 1978a; [1952] 1978b). For Lefort, this amounted to nothing less than a misrepresentation of Mauss's initial aim and intention to understand the effective relationships human beings create among themselves by means of gifts. Lefort's position was rather more complex. It was a question of taking Mauss for what he was, oscillating between a Mauss dogmatically close to Durkheim (and thus a functionalist and positivist sociology) and a proto-structuralist Mauss who, as Lévi-Strauss argued, came to consider practices of reciprocity to be a result of an unconscious that necessarily controlled them. For Lefort, it was about continuing Mauss's questioning of the apparent freedom of giving when in reality it was constrained and obligatory. Contrary to Lévi-Strauss, this consideration for Lefort was enough to make the gift an act that amounted to a decision in a relationship with an other.

Bourdieu and the Case of Kabylia

In his work on Kabylia, Bourdieu was confronted with the issue of the gift in Mauss's sense. An agonistic gift constitutes a challenge. It is a gift that speaks of honor and prestige, of the acknowledgment of the other and of the possibility, granted through the gift, of asserting oneself against that other. The relationship acquires its meaning through violence and the challenge. It is on this point that Bourdieu was to distance himself from Lévi-Strauss's reading and application of Mauss's work.

Bourdieu's response to Lévi-Strauss's reading of Mauss, rebuking him for not having grasped Mauss's thesis in its entirety and, above all, for having neglected the question of time in his discussion of the process of reciprocity, is to be found in his ethnography of Kabylia (Bourdieu 1972; 2017). There he accuses Lévi-Strauss of proceeding reductively and seeing reciprocity as an irreversible cycle—when in fact, Bourdieu intimates, reversibility belongs squarely to the cycle: "a gift can stay without counter-gift." For the sociologist, at the time devoted to defending a phenomenological approach and to develop a renewed conception of the "subject," there is more than one possibility of responding to the gift.

The recipient, moreover, may not have the means to respond—a situation that can lead to dishonor. Counter-giving is no automatic sequel to donation, on the contrary (as Lefort too kept stressing) there is always a choice. It is in the same text that Bourdieu for the first time mentions "social facts" in relationship with sexual relations, a total social fact literally imprinted on schemes of perception and bodies themselves.

In a later text, Bourdieu returned to this Maussian principle, opening his discussion with the following quotation from Mauss, which he found to be extraordinary: "Everything in society is relationships. Everything in society, even the most special things, is function and functioning. Nothing can be understood outside of its relationship to the whole" (Mauss [1909] 1968: 401, cited in Bourdieu 2004: 16). In his commentary, Bourdieu added: "There is no need for me to underline the modernity and the rigor of this formulation. 'An institution is not an indivisible unit separate from the facts that manifest it, it is nothing but their system'" (Mauss [1909] 1968: 401, cited in Bourdieu 2004: 16).

Mauss's phrasing allows for two inferences. First, it avoids mistaking the structure for the basis of the organization of society. Rather, structure appears as a constantly challenged and precarious balance within the total social phenomenon. Second, it stresses the relational aspect that Bourdieu sought to bring to the fore in his own work by showing—contrary to common wisdom—that social facts do not impose themselves on individuals as a matter of pure coercion. Ways of acting, thinking, and feeling are not compulsory, they are the result of a choice, of a modality.

Total social facts allow Bourdieu—and this explains their significance for the development of his own sociology—to draw attention to the complexity of social situations. They provide a means to avoid a priori replicating distinctions such as the one between history and sociology or between understanding and explaining (Bourdieu 1987).

Foucault and the Mauss Alternative

Foucault ventured into Mauss's thought with the publication of *Sociologie et anthropologie*, in the form of a probationary lecture given at the École Normale Supérieure (ENS) at the very beginning of the 1950s (Bert 2017; Foucault 2017). This unpublished lecture deals with magic and the fault line between rationality and irrationality. In the last part of his lecture Foucault returns to the notion of total social facts, introducing it as an alternative to Durkheimian dualism. Unlike Lévi-Strauss and Bourdieu, Foucault remains very faithful to Mauss's text. He analyzes the way Mauss came to develop, ever since his 1904 text (with Hubert) on magic, this idea of complexity. It indeed allowed Mauss two things: (a) making possible a generalization of institutions and phenomena; (b) rethinking the relation to reality, because total social facts enable us to deal with humans and groups rather than ideas and rules. Here are the first lines of the Foucaultian explanation:

> 1. The dimensions of the total social fact
> "They are wholes, complete social systems, whose functioning we have tried to describe" (Mauss 1950: 275)
> Advantages: [Generality]: the abstract institutions are [illegible]
> Reality: people, groups, not ideas and rules are captured
> This has several meanings:
> Rule of observation:
> Do as historians do: "Observe what is given. So, the given is Rome, it is the average Frenchman, it is the Melanesian of this or that island, and not prayer or law as such" (Mauss 1950: 276).
>
> Conception of the relations between the social and the other dimensions of the individual, relations that must be grouped into an inseparable unity: "We describe what people are within their organisms and their psyche, at the same time as describing the sentiments, the ideas, the volitions of the crowd or of organized societies and their subgroups" (ibid.: 276). Hence, the importance of phenomena such as the behavior of the body or incited deaths.
> But such a conception of the human whole necessarily leads to a denial of the anthropological dualism: there is no longer any need to conceive the anti-social manifestations of magic as an expression of the anti-social/individual polarity of the human situation.
> Unity of the subjective and the objective: not only is the dualistic anthropology of social man outdated, but this conception of the social fact surpasses the opposition between the objective and the subjective.
> Cf. e.g. for expectation: the law, the gift, the promise are all phenomena of expectation (Lehmann's work)
> We can say that between
> the Durkheimian conception of the society as an objective spirit
> the Blondélian conception of the individual as a subjective spirit

Mauss sees the social human being as an objective subject. (Foucault 2017: 315–317)

Foucault then goes on to discuss the consequences of the Maussian innovation, which the philosopher would later develop as a way of grounding his own analytical work, "archaeological" first, then "genealogical," without, however, referring explicitly to Mauss's notion of total social facts.

Changing the Rules of Observation

From a historical point of view, total social facts do not orient the analysis toward a center or an origin; much less do they establish strict relationships of causality between observed elements. Quite the opposite: it is only due to causalism that we are invariably led—as Foucault repeatedly notes in a Maussian vein—to "a sort of multiplication of causes," or to the observation of "thousands of various processes."

In the notes to his lecture Foucault adds the following comment regarding the ways Mauss decided to explore magic:

> Magic, far from being this form of diffraction in the unity of the social human being, for Mauss and his school is a behavior in which this unity asserts itself, exalts itself and fulfills itself; far from being a spontaneous dissociation, magic is a synthetic affirmation. Synthesis of behaviors that one might call intero- and extero-ceptive; of behaviors by the magician towards the environment in which he operates; and of those oriented towards the magician from the environment in which he operates. (Foucault 2017: 317)

The aim in destabilizing the status quo, by questioning hierarchies, is to interrogate chains of succession and to foreground the important discontinuity between cause and effect in a social context. This idea had long been defended by Mauss: "the sociologist does not look for some sort of law of development, of general evolution that dominates the past and determines the future. There is no one, universal law of social phenomena. There is a multitude of laws of unequal generality" (Mauss and Fauconnet 1968: 29).

Conceiving the Relationships between Social and Other Dimensions of the Individual in a Different Way

An implication of total social facts is that the various levels of analysis need to be constantly brought together—in particular the level of the actual content of practices and that of the meaning given to them.

This is still the case in his lecture about the difficult question of the belief in magic, which Foucault raises in the following terms:

> [T]he public does neither seek to know that the boy is not a magician nor to punish him for being one, but to coordinate in a coherent whole, in a magical universe—as stable as it can be—the various unusual signs that seem to announce magic: centripetal constitution of magic.
>
> From the subject's belief in his own: the boy does not seek to exonerate himself but, on the contrary, to specify the accusations, to constitute himself as a person [*personnage*]. . . .
>
> Therefore, it is not the announcement of mystification that dispels the mystery of magic; rather it is the thickening of mystification—forgetting its origin—that synthetically constitutes magic and its mystery.
>
> Synthesis of the implicit and the explicit, of the conscious and the unconscious.
>
> Magic is always a presumption of several latent meanings on which it is based. (Foucault 2017: 318–319)

The point is to relinquish dualist thinking and its oppositions such as individual/society, feeling/intellect, true/false, sacred/profane, individual consciousness/collective consciousness. In this perspective, Foucault acknowledges that Mauss has opened the way to another way of thinking about things, thinking about them from the joints or the margins. Here again Mauss's approach overlaps with a significant part of Foucault's research program. As he puts it himself, the purpose of his genealogy is to bring together numerous levels of analysis, in particular those of the real content of practices and of the meaning human beings give them.

An "Archaeological" Attempt

By introducing total social facts Mauss was not trying to reconstruct a historical period but rather wanted to trace the permanence of a way of thinking, or of a practice, up to the present, in order to show the processes that have made us into who we are and that continue to determine us. Once again we are dealing with modality, which Mauss—and Foucault after him—regards as a central aim of total social facts. This is what Foucault tries to summarize in the very last lines of his lecture, returning to the question of symbolism:

> The symbolism of a culture cannot be unique and pure; each culture has its history; each culture has its own internal cultural space; it therefore has to bear the weight of the past, the menace of the stranger, of the unusual; it has a time and a space; there are also different classes in it, diversifications of the symbolic system. (Foucault 2017: 324)

That is, all social phenomena are by nature arbitrary; they proceed from collective decisions. The choices made vary with every society. This was an attempt that proved particularly valid in the case of "The Gift" (Mauss in fact used the term "archaeology" to describe his approach), since, as the anthropologist reminds his readers, its aim is to understand the extent to which our contemporary morals remain steeped in this "atmosphere" of the gift.

Conclusion

Lévi-Strauss used total social facts to construct a system, thereby reducing gift giving to a formula comprising giving—receiving—returning. In so doing, he obscured the fact that Mauss, above all, had sought to find an original means to emphasize affectivity and intersubjectivity, uncertainty and modality. These are essential elements upon which all societies build their permanence. Bourdieu resorted to the notion as an analytical tool allowing him to access the complexity of the social world and jettison the idea of a strictly structural determination. Total social facts also allowed him to push to its limits the historicization of his object of study and to develop a deep interest for action, practice and the experience of their contingency. Foucault, finally, chose to develop a framework that allowed him to move beyond causalism and to bring to the fore the question of choice and arbitrariness, leaving behind the classical dichotomy between liberty and determinism.

The "truth" of total social facts lies undoubtedly at the crossroads of these three readings. Juxtaposing them in this way allows us to give a picture of Mauss more in keeping with the way he saw himself, that is as a scholar free from disciplinary constraints who would not let himself be caught within the bounds of instituted knowledge. In rejecting disciplines, he was joined by Foucault, Lévi-Strauss, and Bourdieu. It is tempting to see this as a consequence of mobilizing total social facts.

Jean-François Bert is a sociologist and historian of social sciences. He is senior researcher and lecturer at the University of Lausanne's Institute of History and Anthropology of Religions (IHAR). Bert is interested in the political sociology of knowledge, the history of science and the anthropology of cultural practices. He has published in *Revue des sciences sociales*, *Ethnologie français*, and *Revue européene de sciences sociales*. His latest publication *Le courage de comparer: L'anthropologie subversive de Marcel Mauss* (Labor et Fides, Geneva) studies the development of the Marcel Mauss method.

References

Athané, François. 2011. *Pour une histoire naturelle du don*. Paris: Presses Universitaires de France (PUF).

Bert, Jean-François. 2017. "Michel Foucault défenseur de l'ethnologie: 'La magie—le fait social total,' une leçon inédite des années 1950." *Zilsel* 2(2): 281–303.

Bourdieu, Pierre. 1972. *Esquisse d'une théorie de la pratique*. Genève: Droz.

———. 1987. "*Fieldwork in philosophy.*" In *Choses dites*, 13–46. Paris: Éditions de Minuit.

———. 2004. "Marcel Mauss, aujourd'hui." *Sociologie et sociétés* 36(2): 15–22.

———. 2017. *Anthropologie economique: Cours au Collège de France 1992–1993*. Paris: Seuil.

Foucault, Michel. 2017. "La magie—le fait social total." *Zilsel* 2(2): 305–26.

Jeanpierre, Laurent. 2004. "Une opposition structurante pour l'anthropologie structurale: Lévi-Strauss contre Gurvitch, la guerre de deux exilés français aux Etats-Unis." *Revue d'histoire des sciences humaines* 2(11): 13–44.

Lefort, Claude. [1951] 1978a. "L'*échange* ou la *lutte des hommes*." In *Les formes de l'histoire*, 15–29. Paris: Gallimard.

———. [1952] 1978b. "Société 'sans histoire' et historicité." In *Les formes de l'histoire*, 46–78. Paris: Gallimard.

Lévi-Strauss, Claude. 1950. "Introduction à l'œuvre de Marcel Mauss." In Marcel Mauss, *Sociologie et anthropologie*, ed. Claude Lévi-Strauss. Paris: PUF, ix–lii.

Marcel, Jean-Christophe. 2001. "Georges Gurvitch: les raisons d'un succès." *Cahiers internationaux de sociologie* 110: 97–119.

Mauss, Marcel. [1909]1968. "La Prière." In Marcel Mauss, *Œuvres I. Les fonctions sociales du sacré*, ed. Victor Karady, 357–477. Paris: Minuit.

———. 1950. *Sociologie et anthropologie*. Paris: PUF.

Mauss, Marcel, and Paul Fauconnet. 1968. "La sociologie: objet et méthode" In *Essais de sociologie*, 6–41. Paris: Minuit.

Chapter 16

FROM DURKHEIM TO HALBWACHS

REBUILDING THE THEORY OF COLLECTIVE REPRESENTATIONS

Jean-Christophe Marcel

This chapter aims to demonstrate how Maurice Halbwachs's work between the two world wars can be seen as an extension of the program Émile Durkheim began to sketch out in his conclusion to *Elementary Forms*. More than Marcel Mauss—who strangely only rarely quotes and uses *Elementary Forms* in his texts after 1918 (Marcel 2012, 2019)—Halbwachs can be considered to be the successor of Durkheim's sociology of knowledge program, all the more so as Mauss, in some ways, did not really want to assume Durkheim's legacy (Marcel 2001).

Halbwachs can be seen as the true continuation of Durkheim, especially if we keep in mind how both Durkheim's as well as Halbwachs's sociology of religion are embedded within a theory of collective representations and classifications. Symptomatically, it is Halbwachs who, in 1918, satisfies Lucien Lévy-Bruhl's request to write an article about "Durkheim's Doctrine" for the *Revue philosophique* (Halbwachs 1918) and who, in 1925, writes a book titled *The Origins of Religious Sentiment according to Durkheim* (Halbwachs 1925a). In a letter to Mauss in 1924 he also states that he considers the book he is working on, *The Social Frameworks of Memory* (Halbwachs 1925b), to be "bound to Durkheim's and Mauss's theory of intelligence and categories" (Hirsch 2012: 226). At that time, memory was already a privileged object of investigation for him[1] and constituted his main contribution to the sociology of mental functions, as previously clarified by Durkheim and Mauss in their text about classifications (Durkheim and Mauss 1903) and in the *Elementary Forms*. All good history of sociology must endeavor to link the contents of writings to the conditions of their production, and so, by looking more closely at the content of his works, we must consider Halbwachs's theory of knowledge a continuation of Durkheim's former results, especially as spatial representations and collective memory were the two main topics that Halbwachs explored. First of all, however, it is necessary to remember that Durkheim had previously established some of the results of Halbwachs's theory.

Collective Representations according to Durkheim (and Mauss)

To build a clear explanation of the world and oneself, everyone has to think with the others; meaning has to be shared through collective representations with others. Collective representations can be defined as the common forms of perception that contain "knowledge surpassing that of the average individual" (Durkheim [1912] 1995: 436). And Durkheim thinks that a collective representation is all the stronger as it is imperative to consciousness—that is to say, shared by the largest number of a group. At the same time, for these representations to be shared by the greatest number, it is necessary that the social link in the group—what Durkheim calls "solidarity"—is strong. Notably religion shows how shared collective representations have dynamogenic effects, creating collective effervescence. Under these conditions, the effects of society on individuals are less of a constraint, as has too often been emphasized, but rather serve the "well-being" of the individual.

> This stimulating action of society is not felt in exceptional circumstances alone. There is virtually no instant of our lives in which a certain rush of energy fails to come to us from outside ourselves. In all kinds of acts that express the understanding, esteem, and affection of his fellows, there is a lift that the man who does his duty feels, usually without being aware of it.... Because he is in moral harmony with his fellows, he gains new confidence, courage, and boldness in action ... Thus is produced what amounts to a perpetual uplift of our moral being. (Durkheim [1912] 1995: 213)

In this way, the more individuals are conscious of sharing the same representations of the world and of themselves, the more opportunities they receive to feel it, and the stronger the social bond between them is, the more they feel integrated. To maintain the strength of the social link, it is necessary to arrange moments of gathering and commemorations during which these representations are activated in some way. This conception allowed Durkheim to postulate that collective representations create in individuals particular psychological states, a "higher" spiritual and mental life, which makes it possible for them to become proper human beings (Durkheim 1898). Regarding this topic, Halbwachs's contribution consists, first, in specifying the cognitive power of collective representations, and second, in describing how they are built and combined in collective consciousness. These questions appear to be crucial in order to lay the groundwork for a "collective psychology" to which, as we know, Halbwachs wanted to devote a course at the Collège de France, although he never had the opportunity to teach it.

The Primacy of the Spatial Representations: First Extension of Durkheim

The first of Halbwachs's repercussions draws on the postulate that the cognitive power of a collective representation comes from its stability. But what is stable in social life is what refers to space, Halbwachs writes in "Social Morphology" (1938). Just as an individual needs to know how his or her body is to define him- or herself, so too must a group clearly know how its body is, that is to say, how its population is distributed in space.

> In other words, just as a living body is partly subjected to the conditions of inert matter, because, by one aspect of itself, it is a material thing, a society, as a psychological reality, a set of collective thoughts and tendencies, it nevertheless has an organic body, and also participates in the nature of physical things. That is why, in certain respects, it encapsulates itself, fixes itself in forms, in material arrangements that it imposes on the groups from which it is made. (Halbwachs [1938] 1970: 168; my translation)[2]

In order to exist, society, that is to say every group, must fit into the material and arrange space at its convenience. Leaving its marks in space is the way society concretely proves its existence to its members. So, the layouts of streets, houses, roads, the location of monuments, squares in the city and so on, are the privileged materials people use to read collective life, building themselves representations of these marks. In other words, spatial collective representations establish the "first representations" in the construction of knowledge, because they provide an original principle of stability to communities. It is a kind of "ballast" (*lest*), which gives more weight (that is, using the French metaphor, more power) to the knowledge so produced. This is why people most forcefully resist the destruction of the areas they live in, for example; or why totalitarian regimes affect monuments and all the material traces of the past. The mark a society leaves on space is a privileged means to make that society last and to impose itself on individuals. Knowledge includes successive coats of collective representations, which come to lie on this first base of spatial collective representations. The latter are thus privileged categories in the constitution of collective thought. I propose to read this result as complementary to Durkheim's early sketch on collective mental life in his article "Individual Representations and Collective Representations" from 1898, and to what he had outlined in the famous text, written with Mauss in 1903, about primitive classifications. Durkheim and Mauss asserted that knowledge is a set of classifications, whose origin is not only social, but also expresses how society thinks of itself (Durkheim and Mauss 1903). By being imprinted on individuals' consciousness, these collective representations create particular psychic states, which stand for themselves within collective life. In this way, we can explain effervescence and religious trance during rituals, for example. The milestones of a collective psychology are thus set. Halbwachs's contribution consists in saying that what we in fact find behind the moral capacities and aspirations of individuals is the material form of society.

For example, revisiting the "Causes of Suicide" in 1930, Halbwachs emphasizes the real variable explaining the vulnerability to the suicide, that is, whether the person lived in an urban or rural environment. So why do urban people more often commit suicide? It is because urban life is more complicated as in a city everyone meets more people of diverse backgrounds in many different places. The different sections of social life (private and professional) are also divided and located in different places. In terms of knowledge, various spatial representations are mixed and less stable because human encounters are briefer. Moments of collective effervescence with similar people alternate with moments of loneliness and a variety of other moments. So, the opportunities to become aware of one's poverty and misery are multiplied (Halbwachs 1930). People are more likely to develop mortiferous psychological states and kill themselves. In short, the sociologist discovers the strength and coherence of collective representations behind the psychological states people show during collective life. While Durkheim emphasized it is collective representations' lack of strength, due to a greater distance between individual and group, that leads to suicide (Durkheim 1897), Halbwachs sees psychological fragility as a result of more complicated and less coherent collective representations. This is one possible way to understand the relation between individuals and society: the structure of interactions (using current terminology) as founded in the spatial conditions of life. Taking back the expression of the famous philosopher Bergson, Halbwachs ([1938] 1970) speaks about the "immediate datum of social consciousness":

> We have to understand ... that the material forms of society act on it not by virtue of physical constraint, as a body would act on another body, but by becoming conscious of it as members of a group who perceive its volume, its physical structure, its movements in space. There is a kind of collective thought or perception, which one could call an immediate data of social consciousness that stands out from all the others. ([1938] 1970: 182–183; my translation)[3]

Because of a back-and-forth motion, society becomes aware of what it is: space has an effect on how people build collective representations, and in turn those representations have an influence on how people think about the places they live and finally themselves.

According to Halbwachs, we have to consider the way individuals organize their lives together, so as to feel their existence, and the way they feel in doing so; enjoyment, punishment, enthusiasm, and so on thus become reducible in an approach in which society—understood as the gathered individuals—decides to work on its preservation. Not only does group life regulate the expression of feelings and emotions (see Marcel 2004; Mauss [1921] 1969), it is at the root of their formation and the intensity with which they are felt. These feelings, impelled and regulated by collective life, are the expression of a kind of social instinct of survival by which humans, while leading their lives, at the same time work to preserve the group. Smaller families in modern urban life, for example, are the best way to raise children and protect them, because this way they can better be prepared for their struggle in a more complicated social life. Halbwachs speaks of an "instinct collectif qui équivaut à une sagesse supérieure," or a "sens intuitif et profond" ("a collective instinct equivalent to a superior wisdom" and an "intuitive and profound sense"; Halbwachs [1938] 1970: 176). From this perspective, suicide is also to be understood as one of the aspects of society's approach to subsistence by ruthlessly eliminating the weakest: "les vaincus de la vie forment ainsi une longue cohorte de captifs que la société traîne derrière son char" (the defeated thus form a long cohort of captives that society drags behind its cart; Halbwachs 1930: 461). No need to distinguish, as Durkheim did, an anomic suicide.[4] Whatever the circumstances that lead people to kill themselves, a suicide is always the result of the active influence of the group. Engaging in this matter is one of the privileged means by which society becomes conscious of itself, an indispensable prerequisite for its continuation in time and space, an impulse of its collective instinct of survival.

Collective Representations as Recollections: Second Extension of Durkheim

As Durkheim (1912) previously stated, collective representations are accumulated knowledge, the legacy of previous generations. Accordingly, they are also memories because while being constantly used by people they blend images, that have been constructed and reconstructed many times over and returned to the history of the group, so as to prove to itself that it keeps existing. In brief, to think collectively is, in the end, to remember. As such, writes Halbwachs (1938a), the memory, as far as it is collective, is the higher function of the spirit by which the collective life organizes knowledge. This is also why when we remember, we always do so within a social framework, that is to say, by referring in one way or another to the other members of the group (Halbwachs 1925b).

In *Collective Memory* (Halbwachs 1950), Halbwachs explains collective life relies on "social time," a category Durkheim (and almost Hubert 1905) had already emphasized. Durkheim in fact supposed that the category of time is based on a consciousness of duration, which stems from the rhythm of social life. Collective life alternates between moments of intense activity and others when life is much slower, as during holidays. These different rhythms have an influence on the social bond insofar as collective activities give the individuals more or less the opportunity to feel a sense of belonging to their community (Durkheim 1912). Mauss, for his part, had already illustrated this idea in his masterly study on the Eskimos, written together with Beuchat, in which he shows how the life of these people changes fundamentally according to the summer or winter season. In winter, the Eskimos live a more communal life, full of religious rites and sacrality, with dozens of people gathering in a big house, whereas during the summer families only consist of mother, father, and children living in a single igloo and isolated from other families by tens of kilometers. They use objects reserved for the summer and buried when winter arrives, and vice versa. From one season to the other a person no longer is the same, because he or she no longer carries the same name and no longer defines his or her kinship the same way. Winter life, unlike summer life, is an intense, full and complete life. However, the ecological and climatic conditions, which regulate the life of the Eskimos, influence their perception of time only to the extent that they are the objects of the corresponding collective interpretation (Mauss and Beuchat 1906).

In continuation of the necessary social origin of the idea of time, Halbwachs states, a group's idea of its past is marked by striking events for the group, for example, the birth of children or marriages in a family, revolutions or wars, striking labor disputes in a country. Those memories, mobilized and shared with others at a given moment, are used only because they support the group in the definition it gives of itself at the present moment. They also support and reflect aspirations and collective tendencies in terms of actions and thoughts that are congruent with this definition, and they, once more, express the steps the group follows to perpetuate itself in its being. For example, the Way of the Cross followed by Jesus from Pilate to Calvary did not attract the attention of Christians until the fifteenth century when the disciples of Saint Francis made the reproduction of Jesus' suffering a spiritual exercise, explains Halbwachs (1941). In short, the Way of the Cross is a recent memory linked to new concerns! Those concerns are, in terms of knowledge, the way a group is building a definition of itself in present time. This also explains why memories can change and be forgotten when a group enters a new period of its life, because they no longer agree with the present collective conditions. On the contrary, other previously forgotten memories may reappear because they better accord with the way the group thinks and is trying to persist in the present (Halbwachs 1950).

However, to gain coherence, according to the immediate data of social consciousness, these memories must also be localized. As places change much less quickly than the group, they can, of course, contain many more memories! Halbwachs observes that the first Christians before long felt the need to locate some striking events in the life of Jesus around Jerusalem (Halbwachs 1941). For example, he emphasizes a belief that located David's and Isaiah's tombs in Bethlehem because they were supposed to be ancestors of Jesus. Jesus himself was supposed to be born in this place, whereas in reality nothing is known for sure on this point. However, the memories of the group are based in this spatial background, which at the same time confirms the certainty of the group's existence and persistence. In consecrated spaces, thanks to the spatial representation of memories, people have the feeling that a stream of uninterrupted religious thought has passed under the vaults. The place that persists itself symbolizes the permanence of faith in the midst of a profane world in perpetual motion.

The Laws of Evolution of the Collective Memory as a Collective Social Instinct

Lastly, evolution of the collective memory involves work on the particular memories; work, which is deemed necessary for the society to preserve itself. In this respect, Halbwachs, like Durkheim, is faithful to an organicist vision borrowed from biology (Marcel 2008): Society can be compared to a living organism whose relations are constrained by the conditions of its existence. The main support of relations in social life is their relation to the natural environment. The main problem a group must solve, according to Halbwachs, is its relationship with matter or, to be more precise, the way the group comes into contact with it, as it is difficult for collective consciousness to step out of itself and open itself up to what it is not. Insofar as human consciousness comes into contact with things, humans are forced to forget their fellow human beings. In order to act on matter, a consciousness must isolate itself and detach its attention from the life of the group (Halbwachs 1920: 89). In modern societies industrial workers are sacrificed, because they are devoted to work on matter and, consequently, have to detach themselves from concerns primarily devoted to human life, this is the condition for the whole group to feel its existence (Halbwachs 1938b). This primacy given to spatial collective representations is better understood retrospectively.

In this struggle for life, exercising its vital functions presupposes for a group a process of adaptation. The workings of a group on its collective memory can thus be seen as a paradigm case for such an adaptation process. Halbwachs's (1941) work on Christians figures as a case study[5] to introduce a general theory of collective memory, the results of which were be generalized. Halbwachs thought he could find four laws that showed how a religious group produced knowledge about its own persistence by reinforcing faith:

(1) A law of concentration: several facts can be located in the same place or in places very close to each other. In this case, everything happens as if the force of devotion needed several receptacles to pour into and not be exhausted. This diversification may reinforce belief, since we think of different memories while being in the same place. Without moving, the assembly of the faithful can embrace different memories in the same act of worship.

(2) A law of fragmentation: by an inverse process, the same fact that constitutes an interesting memory can be located in several distant places. For example, in Bethlehem two separate places correspond to the birth and the crib. Faith here finds several opportunities

to express itself in several different places and to review the various aspects of the single important lesson each one includes.

(3) Law of duality: two different locations of the same fact are accepted at the same time. For example, there are two paths of the passion of Christ. In this case, the memories belong to several groups: crusaders and natives, for example, each of which have their own tradition. Because each of them has its own place for the same memory, the integrity of the group and the strength of faith can be preserved.

(4) Finally, Halbwachs develops another law that we can phrase as follows: the more memories gain authority, the more they are detached from the reality of the past (Stoetzel 1978). They become legends, myths, gods, like the supernatural Christ. The ever-increasing group of Christians, who had not personally known Jesus, lost the memory of their prophet's strictly human life in order to cling to dogmas that underlined his divine nature. Conceived in this way, Jesus' life had only been a preparation for his death, which was now considered a supernatural event: a preparation for his resurrection. This is why collective memory can also relay myths, fantasized and distorted memories, on condition that they make sense for the group by symbolizing its unity and integrity in the present.

In short, the collective Christian memory adapts its memories of the details of the life of Christ and the associated places to each epoch. This adaptive work on memories illustrates the contemporary demands of Christianity, the contemporary needs and aspirations of Christians. And each time the group carries out any work on its memories, it does so as a means of preserving and consolidating the faith of the believers.

Conclusion

Durkheimian sociology, as a theory of knowledge, is linked to a social ontology that could be described as follows: collective life is understood as the group's approach to making itself last in time and space, just as every human being tries to survive in its environment. Many Durkheimians try to establish the conditions under which social ties can exist and can be maintained. In this sense, their sociology is a study of the social conditions of consensus and, more or less implicitly, associated with an organicist vision. Durkheim develops a theory of integration, of how and why individuals are bound by common goals. Robert Hertz endeavors to show that the collective representations of death are a means of linking the living and the dead, so that the disappearance of the deceased can be dealt with "smoothly" and without disturbing the community of the living. François Simiand conceives of the redundant economic cycles as an approach by the upper social classes to ensure that society anticipates its future state and in this way adapts to the transformations it undergoes.

Halbwachs also tries to understand how society, both by regulating the distribution of its population in space and by working on its memories, endeavors to maintain itself as such. What is peculiar are his works on spatial collective representations as categories considered to be the basis for the working of collective memory and thus for building knowledge in general. In this respect, Halbwachs is very much following and continuing Durkheim's project.

Jean-Christophe Marcel currently works at the Department of Sociology at the University of Burgundy. One of the leading experts on the work of Maurice Halbwachs, he has published extensively on the history of sociology and social theory. He studied the French reception of American sociology in *Reconstruire la sociologie avec les Américains?* (Dijon, 2017) and focused on the transformation of the Durkheimian sociology in *Le durkheimisme dans l'entre-deux-guerres* (Paris, 2001).

Notes

1. In particular, he systematically noted all his dreams, in order to show, and invalidate Bergson's theory, that dreams do not belong to a work of memory.
2. "En d'autres termes, de même qu'un corps vivant est soumis en partie aux conditions de la matière inerte, parce que, par tout un aspect de lui-même, il est une chose matérielle, une société, réalité psychique, ensemble de pensées et tendances collectives, il [sic] a cependant un corps organique, et participe aussi à la nature des choses physiques. C'est pourquoi elle s'enferme, à certains égards, elle se fixe dans des formes, dans des arrangements matériels qu'elle impose aux groupes dont elle est faite" (Halbwachs 1970: 168).
3. "Comprenons . . . que les formes matérielles de la société agissent sur elle, non point en vertu d'une contrainte physique, comme un corps agirait, sur un autre corps, mais par la conscience que nous en prenons, en tant que membres d'un groupe qui perçoivent son volume, sa structure physique, ses mouvements dans l'espace. Il y a là un genre de pensée ou de perception collective, qu'on pourrait appeler une donnée immédiate de la conscience sociale, qui tranche sur toutes les autres" (Halbwachs 1970: 182–83).

4. For a more comprehensive discussion of Halbwachs's critique of Durkheim's theory of suicide see Marcel (2000).
5. As far as the work on musicians Halbwachs (1950) could not achieve.

References

Durkheim, Émile. 1897. *Le Suicide*. Paris: Alcan.
———. 1898. "Représentations individuelles et représentations collectives." *Revue de métaphysique et de morale* 6: 273–302.
———. 1912. *Les formes élémentaires de la vie religieuse*. Paris: Alcan.
———. [1912] 1995. *The Elementary Forms of Religious Life*. New York: Free Press.
Durkheim, Émile, and Marcel Mauss. [1903] 1969. "De quelques formes primitives de classifications: Contribution à l'étude des représentations collectives." In *Œuvres II. Représentations collectives et diversité des civilisations* by Marcel Mauss, ed. Victor Karady, 13–89. Paris: Minuit.
Halbwachs, Maurice. 1918. "La doctrine d'Émile Durkheim." *Revue philosophique* 85: 353–411.
———. 1920. "Matière et société." *Revue philosophique* 45: 88–122.
———. 1925a. *Les origines du sentiment religieux d'après Durkheim*. Paris: Stock.
———. 1925b. *Les cadres sociaux de la mémoire*. Paris: Alcan.
———. 1930. *Les causes du suicide*. Paris: Alcan.
———. 1938a. *La psychologie collective*. Paris: Centre de Documentation Universitaire.
———. 1938b. *Esquisse d'une psychologie des classes sociales*. Paris: Rivière.
———. 1941. *La topographie légendaire des Evangiles en Terre Sainte*. Paris: PUF.
———. 1950. *La mémoire collective*. Paris: PUF.
———. [1938] 1970. *Morphologie sociale*. Paris: Colin.
Hirsch, Thomas. 2012. "Maurice Halbwachs et la sociologie religieuse." *Archives de sciences sociales des religions* 159: 225–45.
Hubert, Henri. 1905. "Étude sommaire de la représentations du temps dans la religion et la magie." *Annuaire de l'École pratique des hautes études*: 1–39.
Marcel, Jean-Christophe. 2000. "Maurice Halbwachs et le suicide: De la critique de Durkheim à la fondation d'une psychologie collective." In *Le Suicide un siècle après Durkheim*, ed. Massimo Borlandi and Mohamed Cherkaoui, 147–84. Paris: PUF.
———. 2001. *Le durkheimisme dans l'entre-deux-guerres*. Paris: PUF.
———. 2004. "Mauss et Halbwachs: Vers la fondation d'une psychologie collective." *Sociologie et sociétés* 26(2): 73–90.
———. 2008. "Organicisme et théorie des classes sociales chez Simiand et Halbwachs: Un héritage caché de Durkheim?" *Revue d'histoire des sciences humaines* 19: 143–60.
———. 2012. "Les durkheimiens face aux formes élémentaires (1912–1939)." *Année sociologique* 2(62): 465–81.

———. 2019. "La réception des formes par Mauss, 1912–1950." In *Les Formes élémentaires de la vie religieuse, cent ans après. Émile Durkheim et la religion*, ed. Matthieu Béra and Nicolas Sembel, 31–49. Paris: Garnier.

Mauss, Marcel. [1921] 1969. "L'expression obligatoire des sentiments (rituels oraux funéraires australiens)." In *Œuvres III. Cohésion sociale et divisions de la sociologie*, ed. Victor Karady, 269–78. Paris: Minuit.

Mauss, Marcel, and Henri Beuchat. 1906. "Essai sur les variations saisonnières des sociétés Eskimos: étude de morphologie sociale.'" *AS* 9: 39–132.

Stoetzel, Jean. 1978. *La psychologie sociale*. Paris: Flammarion.

Chapter 17

DURKHEIM'S QUEST

PHILOSOPHY BEYOND THE CLASSROOM AND THE LIBRARIES

Wendy James

Philosophy in the Fresh Air

I am not a philosopher, but I would like to start by picking up some striking thoughts clarified by Michel Foucault in his fairly recent introduction (now in English) to some of Immanuel Kant's earliest writing:[1]

> We should no longer be surprised by the promise made at the beginning of the *Anthropology* [1798], which was to study man as a "citizen of the world" . . . but not in the sense that he belongs to a given social group or such and such institution. He is *Weltbürger* purely and simply because he speaks. It is in the exchange of language that he manages on his own account both to attain and to realize the concrete universal. His living in the world is, originarily, residence in language. (Foucault 2008: 102)

The mainstream literature of philosophy has been produced by scholars who worked largely from the handwritten or published texts produced by their forebears. Their familiarity with ancient written languages from Europe or from Asia was often central to their debates; but how far did they seek deep meaning in the live world of spoken languages, especially perhaps through tackling issues of the translation of languages still unwritten? This is where the fieldworking anthropologist comes in; and where one has to recognize the connectedness of the human world, and indeed its history of complex, *live* interactions. These are shaped not only by language itself, but also by the varieties of patterned communication we exchange all the time through gesture, music, art, dance, individual and collective game-playing, not to mention productive co-operation—but also competition, even to the point of mutual harm. The world of Durkheimian sociology became ever closer to this perspective, in my view, as it distanced itself increasingly from the formal concepts and timeless imagery of academic philosophy. They sought ways of widening the scope of philosophy's questions. At first, they chose to investigate the relatively recent opening up of systematic studies of some of the world's "remotest" communities—that is, remote from any centers of "civilization," and apparently still steeped in ancient tradition.

Philosophers do not often consult maps or read detailed ethnography about non-literate people living in remote parts of the globe. But Émile Durkheim led the way with his focus on recently available ethnographic studies of Australian groups, and his colleagues followed, especially in their journal *L'Année sociologique* (AS). This focused on reviews of ethnographic work carried out far from the European or Asian heartlands of known history. Marcel Mauss's career had started with a focus on Indology, but a special interest in worldwide ethnography soon took over his teaching. This is clear from Nick Allen's (2000: 4–5, 149–50) listing of those lecture courses given by Mauss focusing on remote regions of the world, given from 1900 and into the late 1930s. Several of the best-known analytical essays of the Durkheimian group are striking for their colorful ethnographic examples and cross-comparisons. Most famously, perhaps, Mauss's ([1925] 1990) own "Essay on the Gift" provides memorable images such as the Maori *hau*, an extending and recursive "spirit of the gift" linking chains of givers and takers; the steadily circulating *kula* exchanges of the Trobriand Islanders of Melanesia, supporting economic and co-operative social relations between neighboring islands; alongside the dramatic Kwakiutl potlatch ceremonies of northwestern America, where competition between wealthy chiefs can become destructive. Such widely separated examples, from the farthest Australians to the Eskimos of the Arctic, were clearly chosen for special attention by Durkheim, Mauss, and their colleagues because they wished to explore the most general principles governing their lives, and to understand how these should be included as part of our common humanity. But the use of fresh, firsthand material from immediate oral sources, where translation was more than a matter of words alone, posed more questions than the philosopher could really answer from books in the library. The emergence of modern anthropological understanding owes a great deal to the way that today's fieldworker has come to engage as a fellow "human" being in reciprocal interactions on several levels with communities that are almost missing from standard written languages or historical testimony.

We might recall the example of Frank Hamilton Cushing, a young man from Pennsylvania who developed an early interest in Native American artifacts, and joined a museum expedition to the pueblos of New Mexico. He was able to stay on, spending some five years among the people of Zuñi from 1879, and subsequently publishing rich ethnographic studies. And over a century later, in the early 1990s, a Zuñi artist published drawings and cartoons, where we see the locals, all in full costume, giggling quite fondly as they remember Cushing and the strange things he did (see James 2003: Frontispiece, ii; 39–40). Through the interest that the Durkheimians took in his ethnographic accounts, for example, in Mauss's ([1938] 1985) use of the Zuñi material in his essay on "A Category of the Human Mind: the Notion of Person; the Notion of Self," we remember them too and can include them in our philosophical efforts to understand ourselves. The idea of "relationship" gives a pattern to our social lives with others; it is more than a simple concept of the difference between individual thought and the particular form of categories in the immediate social world. There are key interrelations within any social world, and often between social worlds, starting with those of gender and perhaps recurring over time between successive parental generations and their offspring. The concept of relation has a place as one of the standard range of philosophical categories, but despite its recognition by Charles Renouvier and its central relevance to the structure of Mauss ([1925] 1990) "Essay on the Gift," has not received the general attention it deserves from the Durkheimians or their followers, as Nick Allen (2000: 95–99) has argued. However, the concept of a relation, expressed often in reciprocal movement, in space, time, or communication, helps shape the various approaches of the social sciences today. A key case for them is surely the relation between male and female; it does appear in some areas of the work of the Durkheim group, but it is not often listed as a primary category on the philosophers' agenda. However, any serious focus on "sociality" must surely encompass those repeating patterns of human linkage through kinship, marriage and reproduction, which have been so central to sociology and social anthropology and are increasingly recognized by historians and evolutionary scientists—as explained by contributors to the volume on early human kinship edited by Nicholas Allen, Hilary Callan, Robin Dunbar, and Wendy James (2008). The varied set of geographically remote ethnographic studies selected in the key theoretical articles of the Durkheim group inevitably suggested too much of a "kaleidoscopic" pattern for humanity as a whole, of unrelated bits and pieces. But human history has rarely been randomly kaleidoscopic in this sense. Groups that have obviously changed through surviving evolutionary and historical pressures, at least, have also split up and migrated elsewhere, met others with whom they mixed and matched, and soon managed to transfer, and absorb, something of each other's language and cultural practices. We should remember that tremendous advances in the methods of history and archaeology have framed far more complex understandings of our own past than we had in Durkheim's day. There is a growing field of discussion around the new contributions by archaeologists evoking the potential imaginative stimulus of objects, and hence their impact on social activity. There is much of interest for Durkheimians in the early history of human communicative capacities, around which the "Lucy to Language" centenary project of the British Academy gathered scholars and new research from a wide range of disciplines. A broad overview is provided by the directors of the project in the volume edited by Robin Dunbar, Clive Gamble, and John Gowlett (2010), *Social Brain, Distributed Mind*. Clive Gamble has recently emphasized the relevance of the Durkheimian legacy to the ongoing work of archaeologists:

> The advantages of rediscovering Durkheim lie in the concept of the social brain . . . deliberately so named because it identifies social life as the operative dynamic in hominin evolution, a dynamic that not only has transformed the hardware of cognition but also explains the variety of collective representations arising from these modifications in deep hominin history. . . .
>
> To play its part in this endeavour, archaeology can now draw not only on Durkheim's agenda of the moral underpinnings of society but also the relational, rather than rational construction of cognition (Gamble 2010). The latter is summed up in the distributed mind model, where humans are constituted by their environment, and crucially, the materials and objects they interact with, as much as by their minds. (Gamble 2013: 133)

Thus, methods of making materials into instruments can generate new kinds of human interaction over time, and space; such as through the imaginative stimulus of making objects into containers—a gourd can carry fruit within it, maybe as a hut can be made to contain a family group, or a grave into which you can place the dead; or even a set of clothes for someone to wear (Gamble 2013: 134–36).

Durkheim's first major works on "The Division of Labor," "The Rules," and "Suicide" (1893; 1895; and 1897) were not really taken up by British scholars at the time. But a significant moment took place in 1898, when Marcel Mauss visited Oxford to present Edward Tylor at the Pitt Rivers Museum with a copy of the first volume of the journal AS. From that occasion onward, Mauss developed a lifelong relationship with British colleagues, visiting the country again in 1905, 1912, the 1920s, and during the 1930s when he lectured there (James 1998a: 3–8). Very soon after Durkheim's *Formes élémentaires* had appeared in 1912, it was quickly translated into English and helped shape the principle of ethnographic fieldwork as the proper basis of anthropology, as recognized by Bronisław Malinowski, Alfred Radcliffe-Brown, E. E. Evans-Pritchard, and their successors. Perhaps inevitably, as its fame grew, so did a number of simplifications and stereotypes of its argument about the solidarity of "social facts," the opposition between "the individual" and "society," or between sacred and profane. A more recent shift toward personal agency, individual experience, and memory in anthropology perhaps set Durkheim's *Formes* back in history, for some students. However, a fresh translation by Karen Fields with generally accessible, updated language and an illuminating introduction (Fields 1995), has rejuvenated interest in his ideas across the English-speaking countries.

Durkheim was always in search of the sources of what we take to be real in personal and religious experience. For him, the distinctly human means of knowing lay through what we might now call "sociality." This is an old term, used certainly in Enlightenment times and dating back to Latin roots. Now taken up widely in animal behavioral studies, the term is associated there with the kinds of practical co-operation that can lead to improved survival chances, as among honeybees or spiders. Of course, its parallel use across the science/humanities divide can obscure the main issues. In seeking to focus on the emergence of recognizably "human" features as distinct from those of which we are becoming increasingly aware of in "animal" social life, researchers today from both sides are looking for evidence of the specific qualities of interaction between individuals as such, whether in isolation or representing groups, as indicative of a personal, emotional, and anticipatory consciousness in a world shared with others. Terms such as "social intelligence" or "human sociality" for this kind of consciousness, start from "oneself" and presume a similar sense of self among others with whom one can engage in mutual communication. Interest in this approach relates not only to the creatively "interactive," other-oriented character of human sociality, but also to the role this context has played in the emergence of what is commonly understood these days as "culture" or "society" conceived of as an encompassing whole.

For Durkheim, we might suggest, the difference between the world of his readers and that of the Australians lay not in any essence, but simply in the way that the conventional elements of language, religious representation, and ceremonial action were configured in the regular practices of social life, thus providing the locally available material for personal and intellectual reflection. The configuration of the social world itself, for the Australians as for the all the world's peoples, was closely linked to ways in which "nature," space, and time were understood. Collective representations of the shapes of the natural world might even absorb and reflect back those of the human world, as with the common ways in which distinctions between animal identities might echo the diversity of human groups such as clans. Their interaction might be represented in mythical stories, rules of crisscrossing reciprocity between them through intermarriage, and ceremonial gatherings of the kind Durkheim was happy to call totemism. He did not dismiss such activities as mindless or so remote they were irrelevant to modern thought or life, however, but saw in them the beginnings of religion and science (Fields 1995: xxiv–xxvi).

The Durkheimian concept of society, despite the stereotypes, was by no means static. One of the most famous of the concepts he introduced was that of "effervescence": that is, the heightened emotional feeling, memory, and actions created by the very gathering of crowds, especially with loud speeches, music, and dancing, which could intensify religious or political emotion and lead to innovation and social change. From his vivid description of the excitements of the Australian corroboree he reflects more generally on connections between sacred gatherings and violence, even moving on to events of the French Revolution, and the Crusades (Durkheim [1912] 1995: 212–16).

The Growing Interest of the Durkheim Group in Africa

Following their early interest in some of the early ethnographic studies of "remote" peoples, the Durkheimians did move closer to a concern with the processes of world history than was usually found among mainstream philosophers. This is clear if we consider, for example, their growing interest in the African continent. As mentioned above, references in the key analytical essays to African cases are very rare. But if we consider Mauss specifically in this context, there is plenty to consider (James 1998b). And the first dozen volumes of the journal *L'Année sociologique* (1898–1913) offer plenty of reviews relating to Africa. I was honored to be invited to contribute an article myself on this theme to the centenary issue of AS, where plenty of detail is included (James 1998c). Africa's past, and indeed present, perhaps seemed too complex for the straightforward comparison of social types. Different socio-political or language-groups have been spilling over from one region to another for thousands of years, repeatedly creating history between themselves, quite apart from the complications of international contact and colonial control.

However, the reviews of African studies in the first series of AS, roughly a third each in French, German, and English, gradually became more numerous, especially in the last two issues before World War I (1910 and 1913). Marcel Mauss became one of the keenest reviewers, establishing an African presence in the very first issue of the journal. He wrote at some length on the West African travels of Mary Kingsley, commending her intimacy with the people she meets and the immediacy of her reports (Mauss 1898). Looking back over his continuing references to her work in West Africa, along with that of others, you can sense a movement toward that growing ambition to do field research himself in Morocco. In 1930, he eventually had the chance to spend a short time there, described in lively detail by Marcel Fournier (2006: 269–70). While making academic and diplomatic contacts, he clearly became fascinated by the country's complex social history and by a possession cult reflecting a long history among black Hausa speakers who for various historical reasons had moved north from their main homeland in Nigeria.

Mauss's writings in the *Manual of Ethnography* recently translated by Dominique Lussier ([1967] 2007) do not show him directly concerned with the abstract nature of "categories." But his presentations of methods of investigation are surely important for any developing philosophy of human life in action. Out of the nine very practically based chapters I will comment on just two that indicate his core sympathy for the ethnographic insights produced by personal encounter. Chapter 5 is on "Aesthetics," which explores first the way rhythm is embedded in our actions, perceptions, and communications; dance, music, and song; performances and artistic production. "Play" is treated at some length, including physical and verbal games; plastic arts—which he explains also involved rhythm; body decoration, cosmetics, and so on. "The forms of social life are in part common to ... the musical arts: rhetoric, mythology and theatre penetrate the whole life of a society" (Mauss [1967] 2007: 84). The chapter concludes with section on drama, which Mauss says "exists everywhere," referring initially to the extinct Tasmanians, the people of Tierra del Fuego, and among the Pygmies; and even mentioning archaeological

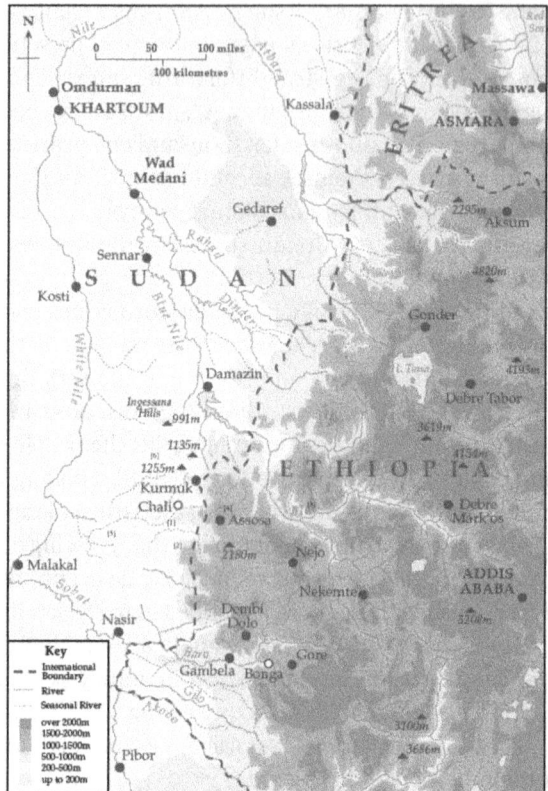

Figure 17.1. The Blue Nile Borderlands. Wendy James, *War and Survival in Sudan's Frontierlands: Voices from the Blue Nile* (Oxford: Oxford University Press, 2007).

evidence of the masquerade from the Middle Paleolithic. "The high point of dramatic art is to be found in religion; drama presents a large component of religion, and also of poetry. It corresponds to the search for another world" and "[i]n Africa one finds a highly developed epic poetry; the griots of Niger can recite ten or fifteen thousand verses" (Mauss 2007: 89–90).

Such points made by Mauss remind us that no language or musical style is static, and none exists in isolation from others. Translation goes on all the time, not only between languages or musical forms in the full sense, but often also between the way individual speakers or performers deploy a form at least partially familiar to each of them. There may be no "standard" way of pronouncing an unwritten tongue; in non-literate communities there may be quite a range of variation, where the upbringing and education of children is itself not linked to written texts but to oral or other interpersonal communication in the active world of finding or producing food, and shelter. Scholars such as Alan Barnard, whose work has helped bridge the gap between social/cultural anthropology and evolutionary thinking, considers that early forms of language may have been locally more numerous, and individuals more commonly multilingual, than has been supposed (Barnard 2016: 1–16, 83–88). It is surely through such constant interaction in culturally complex regions that historical shifts—even evolutionary shifts—commonly appear, in language, in music, in science, technology, art, and religion. While distinctions are being made all the time in one language, or musical style, perhaps they can often be heard from the perspective of another, and while "not understood" may be recognized as significant, or interesting, and "adopted"? Are such crisscrossing experiences, generating perhaps a touch of emotional "effervescence," part of the way that potentially lasting, even permanent, "categories" emerged in the past, as they certainly seem to do among ourselves today?

As I shall now illustrate with some examples from my own fieldwork, which goes back to the 1960s, there is no shortage of effervescence even in the remotest, most thinly populated but at the same time culturally complex parts of Africa.

Movements of Music and Dance over Space and Time in the Hills of Northeastern Africa

Archaeological and linguistic studies have recently been focusing on long-term continuities extending across the region I term the "Blue Nile Borderlands."

The dramatic escarpment shaping the western edge of the Ethiopian highlands and the extension of hills and valleys into the plains of Sudan has played a key part in the survival of many minority language groups. Reference is made in the chapter to James's research experience among, and between, a number of specific groups whose home areas are marked by numbers on the map: Uduk [1], Koma [2], Gumuz [3], Berta [4], Meban [5], and Jum Jum [6]. All are part of the broad Nilo-Saharan linguistic category. The Uduk and Koma tongues are key members of the Koman language family, known to have an ancient lineage, to which Gumuz is perhaps also related; Meban and Jum Jum belong to the well-known and widespread Nilotic family; and varieties of Berta constitute a relatively isolated group within Nilo-Saharan.

The Uduk language for example is claimed to have roots in the earliest forms of the Koman family some 7,000 years ago, as part of proto-Nilo-Saharan (Ehret 2001). A number of such minority languages survive in the hills, valleys, and plateaus of the region. The groups I came to know best were the Uduk (Sudan) and the Gumuz (Ethiopia). Some linguists regard both as belonging to the Koman family, though other experts doubt that Gumuz is properly seen as a member of this group—and regarded by them as a linguistic isolate (though has a relatively large population of native speakers).

Modern conditions over the last few decades of conflict, displacement, and flight to refugee camps have illustrated not only the potential capacities of the people for physical survival, but also the robust artistic and emotional appeal, even under such conditions, of the old forms of musical and other embodied cultural expression. My work in the region since the 1960s has offered me a glimpse into the creativity of such displaced peoples who are often in interesting contact with others, but also maintain links with past arts, especially music and storytelling. Background on the specific impact of civil war on local people in the Sudan and political change in Ethiopia can be found in James (2007), and many of the songs, dances, and some of the musical forms I shall mention briefly here can be viewed on a website designed to illustrate the same book.[2]

Across the borderlands between the high Ethiopian plateau and the plains of the Blue Nile Valley, many individuals speak languages other than their mother tongue. Some have picked up one or two others from neighbors, and many more are able to converse in national or regionally widespread tongues (Arabic, Oromo, Amharic, a few even in English), through engaging in trade, seasonal labor, or finding some educational opportunity. Regionally based healing cults have spread from time to time across the boundaries of language and local territories, together with a fairly mixed history of the spread and retreat of Islam and Christianity. The Uduk have taken over methods of divination from their Berta-speaking neighbors by burning ebony sticks over water; they have been drawn in to spiritual and prophet-led cults reaching them from the Nilotic-speaking Meban who have much in common with the Shilluk on the Nile River; and divination cults partly from another small Nilotic speaking group, Jum Jum (James 1979; 1988).

I did not have the chance to get to know the Gumuz as well as I had the Uduk in the 1960s. But what I can point to in some detail in the Gumuz case, echoed across several of the minorities across the whole mountain region, is the system of sister-exchange marriage

Figure 17.2. The fun of the *pumbulu*, 1975. © Wendy James 1975.

certainly still practiced in the 1970s (James 1986). Evidence shows that the Uduk certainly used to have this system, as did some of the Koma. Such levels of explicit social equality and practices of reciprocity, seemed to point to a deeper "conscience collective" than language differences themselves might indicate. Certainly in regard to gender issues, women in all the communities I was able to visit in the hilly borderlands linking Sudan and Ethiopia had a more open role in social and public life than they had among many of the larger national communities which now exert growing influence over them.

Across the hilly country, musical performances are widespread (and in the history of the local kingdoms on both the Ethiopian and Sudanese sides of the border, there is plenty of evidence that chiefs could call in bands of players from outlying villages to support special occasions). Many of the main local musical ensembles consist of a dozen or more men playing wind instruments and percussion with logs or sticks, while women—and quite a few men too—dance round in an anticlockwise circle. But there are also quite a number of musical styles cultivated particularly by women.

Girls create this "instrument" by slapping the holes they have carefully dug in suitably damp mud, and tuned with the palms of the hands, producing a light, bubbly music. I heard this often in the Uduk villages, where it is called *pumbulu*. Sometimes a couple of girls would each prepare a row of holes, and then play a duet. Other little girls would gather round and dance. After a few days, it rains again, the ground is turned to mud, and the instrument disappears. As I was taking an afternoon rest in the Gumuz village where I spent a few weeks in 1975, I was amazed to hear a sound I recognized as the *pumbulu*, quite nearby I went out and found a Gumuz girl playing on holes carefully excavated in the damp ground, just like the Uduk I remembered! But the holes were differently arranged—rather than six in a row, the Gumuz would prepare a square of four, and a fifth in the center.

An Ancient African Women's String Bow

Another instrument, called *dumbale* in Uduk, has long been played by women and girls. It consists of a bow, with a single string drawn across twice. It essentially for rhythm rather than melody, though pitch is altered by moving the thumb on the lower string and the chin on the upper. This instrument is found in several of the more "remote" parts of Africa, including the Congo forest. The sound of this light music also draws a little group of dancers.[3]

The major dance forms of the Uduk village are on a larger scale but consonant with these informal kinds of percussion music. The players themselves are adult men but everyone joins in the whirling, encircling movements, especially the diviners' initiation dance (originally taken over as part of a healing cult from the Jum Jum).

The Diviners' Dance

The cult of the *ngari* diviners had spread from Jum Jum hill community, speaking a marginal Nilotic language. It was particularly opposed by missionaries at the time. This picture was actually taken over a decade after they had been expelled, possibly accounting for the enthusiasm.[4] There were several other genres of celebratory ritual dancing current in the 1960s. Although big game hunting had more or less disappeared among the Uduk, I did happen to witness a similar dance starting up among the Gumuz in the 1970s, celebrating a leopard kill.

All these musical activities have rarely been static, and while recent decades have seen plenty of the spreading effects of the modern economy and the major religions into the less accessible parts of this border region, there has also been a lot of updating of the older forms, some borrowing and some re-invention of styles. During my time with

Figure 17.3. The Gumuz leopard celebration, 1975. © Wendy James 1975.

the Gumuz in the 1970s, I realized that they had a strong tradition of making and using drums, though I had not come across any drums as such among the Uduk during my visits in the 1960s.

Percussion Re-Invented in the Refugee Camp at Bonga

Oxfam, without realizing it, had provided unexpected help to the musicians in the Ethiopian refugee camp of Bonga, established mainly for Uduk speakers from the Sudan side in 1993, where I visited in 1994 and 2000. The plastic cans they provided for carrying water suggested many other uses! The "jerry-can" dance took the place of the beaten logs of the old *athele*, along with the homemade lyre, common across the Sudan.[5]

Then in my first visit of 1994, I had a real surprise. I suddenly heard of the revival of a "mythical" dance, the *Barangu*. I had been told firmly in the 1960s that the *Barangu* dance was obsolete, though the very name was familiar even to me. I already knew myths about this special dance, evoking the beginning of time. Everybody came; the giraffe high-stepping *tuku, tuku, tuku*, the elephant galumphing, the tortoise waddling, and so on; this happened, and that happened, people took sides, fire and language appeared with the help of the

Dog, human beings began to hunt the other animals, and permanent death displaced the older cycle of a return to life, made possible by the Moon Oil (James 1988: 31–41). I was amazed to learn that the *Barangu* dance itself was still remembered by one very small and remote village, whose people I had heard of but never met before. They came from a northwestern extremity of the main Uduk homeland in Sudan, but here in the refugee camp in Ethiopia were huddled up in the settlement with everyone else and there was general satisfaction at the chance to join in.[6]

Reviving the Barangu: A Dance from the Beginning of Time

A key lyric includes the lines "The gourd of old, how was it broken? The gourd was broken by the *wutule*." This catchy song can be "read" on various levels. It is a lament for death in general, evoking the old myth of the moon oil, once used to revive people after temporary death, until the gourd was dropped by the *wutule* lizard in a silly struggle, so that death, once died, became permanent (James 1979: 74–75). It recalls, in particular, deaths from fighting in the old days.

But to play such music and dance along with others in its rhythms was even more an evocation of the recent years of suffering. This was scarcely appreciated by the few international personnel who noticed the amount of dancing going on in the camp. One comment I heard from a UN protection officer who used to visit was "Dancing? Dancing? But they are refugees; they should be working, or doing something useful for themselves."

Concluding Comments

In 2012, we held a centenary celebration in Oxford to mark the original appearance of *Les formes élémentaires*, published as *Durkheim in Dialogue* (Hausner 2013). I would like briefly to recall Susan Stedman Jones's reminder, in her contribution to that volume, that Durkheim does not simply reject philosophy in favor of the empirical. "But he does specify support for a particular kind of philosophy, that is, one that accommodates representation, synthesis, subject-object relations and the idea of the conscience collective. And of course it must also be a philosophy that can accommodate history and change; it must logically accommodate changefulness" (Stedman Jones 2013: 159). I will conclude by returning to the same passage of Foucault's commentary on Kant with which I started: "The truth that anthropology brings to light is therefore not a truth anterior to language, and that the language will be entrusted to convey. It is a truth that is both more interior and more complex: it is in the very movement of the exchange, and that exchange realizes the universal truth of man." Foucault then explains in terms that could perhaps be read as evidence of Kant's work actually opening up early possibilities for a way forward through practical ethnography, later taken up particularly by the Durkheimian group, he continues: "From an anthropological perspective, then, truth takes its shape through the temporal dispersion of syntheses and in the movement of language and exchange . . . the universal emerges from the heart of experience in the movement of the *truly temporal* and the *actually exchanged*" (Foucault 2008: 102–3). It seems clear today, perhaps, reflecting on topics like "The Social Origins of Thought," that there is plenty for philosophers to find well away from the books and reading rooms, hidden out there in the real life and pulsating sounds of the market square or the dance-ground!

Wendy James is Emeritus Professor of Social Anthropology and Fellow of St. Cross College, Oxford. She is a member of the British Centre for Durkheimian Studies at the University of Oxford's Institute of Social and Cultural Anthropology. Her research focused on the ethnography of Sudan and Ethiopia. A former student of Edward E. Evans-Pritchard, she has always been conscious of a debt to the Durkheim school, as reflected in her book *The Ceremonial Animal: A New Portrait of Anthropology* (2003, Oxford University Press) as well as in the edited volume *Marcel Mauss: A Centenary Tribute* (1998, Berghahn, with Nick Allen).

Notes

1. This chapter draws on discussions on categories in the work of the Durkheim School held in Cologne in May 2017 and in June 2018, and the interdisciplinary exchanges we held there.
2. The website "Voices from the Blue Nile," www.voicesfromthebluenile.org uses photographs, recordings, and movie clips, with short explanatory paragraphs to illustrate something of my fieldwork among the Uduk speaking people of the Sudan (particularly James 2007). Scenes begin at home in the villages of the southern Blue Nile in the 1960s, and continue after the people were displaced to refugee camps in Ethiopia from the late 1980s, particularly in the large camp of Bonga, near Gambela, where I spent some months both in 1994 and in 2000.

The website includes eight screens, each containing six clips, each of which can be enlarged to full size. The screens are labeled as follows on the opening page of the website, with numbers added here for clarity in the citations and references used in this chapter: (1) Sounds of Work; (2) Memories of Home; (3) Survivors; (4) Children; (5) Songs; (6) 1960s (archival); (7) Dance and Music; (8) Future Horizons.

Citations in the text will be referenced in individual footnotes.

3. See "Voices from the Blue Nile," www.voicesfromthebluenile.org, Screen 6 (Archival, 1960s), and Screen 7 (Dance and Music), which both illustrate the *dumbale* bow being played. Screen 7 is a Hi-8 video with sound.
4. See Ibid., Screen 6 (Archival, 1960s).
5. See Ibid., Screen 7 (Dance and Music).
6. Ibid.

References

Allen, Nicholas J. 2000. *Categories and Classifications: Maussian Reflections on the Social.* Oxford: Berghahn.

Allen, Nicholas J., Hilary Callan, Robin Dunbar, and Wendy James, eds. 2008. *Early Human Kinship: From Sex to Social Reproduction.* Oxford: Wiley-Blackwell.

Barnard, Alan. 2016. *Language in Prehistory.* Cambridge: Cambridge University Press.

Dunbar, Robin, Clive Gamble, and John Gowlett, eds. 2010. *Social Brain, Distributed Mind.* Oxford: Oxford University Press.

Durkheim, Émile. 1893. *De la division du travail social.* Paris: Félix Alcan.

———. 1895. *Les règles de la méthode sociologique.* Paris: Félix Alcan.

———. 1897. *Le suicide: étude de sociologie.* Paris: Félix Alcan.

———. [1912] 1995. *The Elementary Forms of Religious Life*, trans. Karen E. Fields. New York: Free Press.

Ehret, Christophera. 2001. *A Historical-Comparative Reconstruction of Nilo-Saharan.* Cologne: Rüdiger Köppe Verlag.

Fields, Karen E. 1995. "Translator's Introduction: Religion as an Eminently Social Thing." In *The Elementary Forms of Religious Life* by Émile Durkheim, xvii–xxiii. Trans. Karen E. Fields. New York: Free Press.

Foucault, Michel. 2008. *Introduction to Kant's 'Anthropology'*, trans. Roberto Nigro and Kate Briggs. Los Angeles: Semiotext(e).

Fournier, Marcel. [1994] 2006. *Marcel Mauss: A Biography*, trans. Jane M. Todd. Princeton, NJ: Princeton University Press.

Gamble, Clive. 2010. "Technologies of Separation and the Evolution of Social Extension." In *Social Brain, Distributed Mind*, ed. Robin Dunbar, Clive Gamble, and John Gowlett, 17–42. Oxford: Oxford University Press.

———. 2013. "Durkheim and the Primitive Mind: An Archaeological Retrospective." In *Durkheim in Dialogue*, ed. Sondra L. Hausner, 124–42. Oxford: Berghahn.

Hausner, Sondra L., ed. 2013. *Durkheim in Dialogue: A Centenary Celebration of 'The Elementary Forms of Religious Life'*. Oxford: Berghahn.

James, Wendy. 1979. *'Kwanim Pa': The Making of the Uduk People; An Ethnographic Study of Survival in the Sudan-Ethiopian Borderlands*. Oxford: Clarendon Press.

———. 1986. "Lifelines: Exchange Marriage among the Gumuz." In *The Southern Marches of Imperial Ethiopia: Essays in Social Anthropology and History*, ed. Wendy James and Donald Donham, 119–47. Cambridge: Cambridge University Press. [2002 reissued in paperback with new preface; Oxford: James Currey).

———. 1988. *The Listening Ebony: Moral Knowledge, Religion and Power among the Uduk of Sudan*. Oxford: Clarendon Press [1999 reissued in paperback].

———. 1998a. "Introductory Essay: 'One of Us': Marcel Mauss and 'English' Anthropology." In *Marcel Mauss: A Centenary Tribute*, ed. Wendy James and Nicholas J. Allen, 3–28. Oxford: Berghahn.

———. 1998b. "Mauss in Africa: On Time, History and Politics." In *Marcel Mauss: A Centenary Tribute*, ed. Wendy James and Nicholas J. Allen, 226–48. Oxford: Berghahn.

———. 1998c. "The Treatment of African Ethnography in 'L'Année sociologique, (I–XII).'" *Année sociologique (AS)* 48 (1): 193–207.

———. 2003. *The Ceremonial Animal: A New Portrait of Anthropology*. Oxford: Oxford University Press [2004 reissued in paperback].

———. 2007. *War and Survival in Sudan's Frontierlands: Voices from the Blue Nile*. Oxford: Oxford University Press. [2009 reissued in paperback with new preface] accompanying website "Voices from the Blue Nile." Retrieved 30 April 2021 from www.voicesfromthebluenile.org.

Mauss, Marcel 1898. "Review of M. H. Kingsley." *AS* 1: 179–83.

———. [1938] 1985. "A Category of the Human Mind: The Notion of Person; the Notion of Self." In *The Category of the Person: Anthropology, Philosophy, History*, trans. Wilfred D. Halls, ed. Michael Carrithers, Steven Collins, and Steven Lukes, 1–25. Cambridge: Cambridge University Press.

———. [1925] 1990. *The Gift: The Form and Reason for Exchange in Archaic Societies*, trans. Wilfred D. Halls. London: Routledge. [First trans. 1954 by Ian Cunnison, introduced by Edward E. Evans-Pritchard. London: Cohen & West].

———. [1967] 2007. *Manual of Ethnography*, ed. and introduced by Nicholas J. Allen, trans. Dominique Lussier. Oxford: Berghahn.

Stedman Jones, Susan. 2013. "Durkheim, Anthropology and the Question of the Categories in 'Les formes élémentaires de la vie religieuse.'" In *Durkheim in Dialogue*, ed. Sondra L. Hausner, 143–64. Oxford: Berghahn.

INDEX

Abnormal Form, 92, 99
Aborigines, Australian, 63, 115, 123, 147
activity (category), 12, 59, 136, 196–97, 207–13, 217–19, 249, 261, 267
affliction (category), 136
Africa, 65, 300–303, 306
Althusser, Louis, 188
Americans, African, 104
Americans, Black, 90, 95, 104–7
Americans, Jewish, 95
Americans, Native, 297
Americans, transsexual, 95
Americans, White, 105
Amharic, 304
animism, 58, 60, 62–64, 82, 210
Année sociologique, 1, 5, 18, 21n1, 21n9, 47, 49, 51, 70, 149, 157, 159–60, 167, 221n2, 227, 242–43, 245–47, 251
anthropology, British, *see* British Anthropology
anthropology, social, 131, 153, 297
anti-magic, 142, 144, 149
anti-Semitism, 103
Arabic, 304
Aristotle, 6, 9, 19, 29–30, 33–34, 38, 59, 72–73, 81, 119–21, 124, 136, 140. *See also* categories, Aristotle
Australia, Australians, 63, 115, 138–39, 145–47, 159–60, 176, 181–82, 209, 296, 300. *See also* Aborigines, Australian
Azande, 115

Barangu, 307–8
Barthes, Roland, 274
becoming (category), 15, 77, 193, 195, 198–200, 263

beer, 149–52
Bergson, Henri, 14, 16–17, 53, 174–78, 187–89, 191–201, 202nn7–10, 216–18, 221, 221n4, 287
Berlin, 46, 228
Bernard, Claude, 3, 16, 114–17, 124
Berta, 303–4
Besnard, Philippe, 49
Bethlehem, 289–90
Beuchat, Henri, 6–8, 116, 288
Bianconi, Antoine, 3, 8, 11–12, 21n6
Blue Nile, 302–4, 309n2, 310n3
Boas, Franz, 14, 32–33, 37, 40, 42n6, 141, 147
Bordeaux, 14, 44–50, 53, 116
Borlandi, Massimo, 48, 51
Bouglé, Celestin, 9, 21n9
boundaries, 7, 17–18, 108n1, 144, 176, 223n12, 229–30, 237–38, 304
Bourdieu, Pierre, 2, 18, 54n9, 274, 276–78, 281
Bourgin, Hubert, 262
Brahma (Brahmā), 164–65
Brahmins, 162–64
British Anthropology, 15, 47, 66
British Social Anthropology, 2, 149

Cahen, Maurice, 151
Canguilhem, Georges, 188
cannibalism, 147
Capitol (Rome), 232
Cassirer, Ernst, 131
Castoriadis, Cornelius, 188, 199–200, 202n10
categories, Aristotle, 19, 29–30, 33–34, 38, 73, 81, 120, 124, 140

categories, Chinese, 248, 252, 254
categories de noir, 9
categories, general, 1–8, 10–19, 20n1, 21n4, 21n5, 21n10, 29–31, 33–34, 36–40, 41n2, 53, 70–77, 80, 83, 86–93, 95, 98, 100–106, 115, 117, 119–21, 124, 132–33, 136–44, 146, 150, 153, 156, 159, 170, 183, 190, 195–96, 198, 210, 214, 218, 220, 228, 235, 239n2, 244, 246, 248, 283, 286, 292, 297, 301, 303
categories, Hegelian, 131, 140
categories, Kantian, 29, 30–33, 37–38, 73, 79, 82, 120–21, 131, 140, 229
categories, neo-Kantian, 131
category project, 1–5, 8–9, 11–14, 16–17, 19, 21nn1–2, 21nn9–10, 70, 90, 93–94, 107, 114–15, 120, 124, 131–33, 138–39, 143, 145, 173, 187–92, 195–96, 198, 200–201, 207, 229
cause/causality (category), 3, 5–7, 11, 14, 17, 30, 33–38, 40, 42n4, 57, 59, 65, 79, 115, 121, 136, 138–40, 143, 150, 156, 207–15, 219–20, 222n8, 279
Cazeneuve, Jean, 274
Chavannes, Edouard, 242–43, 251
China, Chinese, 12, 18, 242–55, 255n2, 255n4, 256n8, 271n12
Christ, 291
Christianity, 10, 60, 81, 167, 289–91, 304
class (category), 13, 30–31, 38–39, 82, 84n5, 156, 188, 198, 233
Codrington, Robert, 59–61, 63, 65–66, 67nn5–6, 67nn9–10
Collège de Sociologie, 17, 229, 238
Comte, Auguste, 86–89, 93–94, 101
Congo, 306
co-operation, 77, 81, 296, 299
cosmology, 4–5, 12, 18, 123, 137, 149, 175, 257, 259, 261, 264, 267–68
Coulange, Fustel de, 230
crime, 15, 88, 90, 104–6
Cushing, Frank Hamilton, 297

Czarnowski, Stefan, 4, 14, 18, 227–30, 232–38, 239n5

dancing, 246–47, 300, 306, 308
Darlu, Alphonse, 10–11
Darwin, Charles, 32, 215
Daux, Auguste, 49
David (biblical), 289
Delacroix, Henri, 10
Deleuze, Gilles, 188, 193, 202n9
Dewey, John, 52
differentiation, 76–77, 80–81, 83, 193, 199, 212, 234, 260, 266
Digby, Sir Kenelm, 63
Dreyfus, Alfred, 175
Du Bois, W. E. B., 95, 106
Durkheim, Émile, 1–6, 9–19, 20n1, 29, 30, 37, 38–40, 41n2, 44–53, 53n1, 54n6, 65, 70–83, 83n2, 86, 87–103, 105–6, 108n1, 108n2, 113–22, 124, 131–33, 135–39, 141, 143–45, 147, 153, 156–61, 163, 170–78, 180–83, 187–92, 195–99, 201n2, 202n6, 202n9, 207, 209, 214–16, 218, 221n2, 222n7, 222n8, 223n10, 229–30, 233–35, 239n2, 243–44, 248–49, 275–76, 283–88, 290–92, 296–300, 308; and Aristotle, 120; and Bergson, 14, 16–17, 174–75, 188–89, 191–92, 195–96, 198, 202n4; and Bernard, 114–16; and Chinese cosmology, 12; death of, 4, 11, 149; and Freud, 53; and Granet, 12, 242–45, 247–48, 251; and Halbwachs, 283–84, 290–92; and Hume, 37, 41n2, 121; and Janet, 53; and justice, 86, 92–93, 99; and Kant, 73, 79, 98, 121, 229; and Mauss, 2, 3, 5, 12, 14–15, 21n2, 39, 40, 45–46, 48–53, 119–22, 140, 144, 147, 153, 163, 188–89, 201, 247, 251, 283, 286; and morality, 99–106; and Renouvier, 15; and start of category project, 70, 72, 90; and von Hartmann, 48; and Weber (L.), 11, 17, 208
Durkheim School, 1–4, 6–8, 9, 11, 13–15, 17, 21n1, 22n7,

114–15, 120, 131–33, 136, 141, 145, 149, 151, 207, 209, 214, 229–30, 239, 239n2
duties, moral, 98–99, 101

École normale supérieure, 45–46, 49, 52–53, 242, 278
effervescence, 16, 19, 30, 38, 41n2, 57, 115, 117–19, 121–24, 140, 170–77, 179, 181, 183, 196, 198, 211, 218, 222n7, 267, 284, 286, 300, 303
ego, 158–59
ENS, *see* École normale supérieure
epistemology, 1, 8, 29, 34, 37–40, 70–72, 74–75, 77–78, 80, 83, 90–91, 94, 116, 120, 192, 196, 220
epistemology, Humean, 38
epistemology, Kantian, 32–33
Eskimos, 33–34, 230, 235, 249, 288–289, 296
Espinas, Alfred, 174, 215, 221n1
Ethiopia, 19, 303–5, 307–8
Evans-Pritchard, E. E., 2, 36, 115, 299

Fauconnet, Paul, 11–12, 21n9
Figuier, Louis, 49
Fiji, 65
Fleck, Ludwik, 147
food, 8, 78, 82, 120, 144–53, 244, 303
force (category), 6, 133, 136, 138–39, 140, 142–44
Foucault, Michel, 2, 18, 188, 190, 274, 278–81, 295, 308–9
Fournier, Marcel, 1, 51, 54n8
Francis, St, 289
Frazer, James, 14–15, 32, 34–37, 47, 58, 65, 66n2, 67n12
freedom, 16, 42n6, 97, 138–43, 166, 193, 198, 214–15, 276

Garfinkel, Harold, 15, 88–90, 94–97, 100, 102, 105–07
Geertz, Clifford, 46, 255n3
Gellner, Ernest, 239n3
gender, 18, 88, 104, 118, 159, 264–68, 270n4, 297, 305
Gennep, Arnold van, 145, 230–31

genus (category), 75, 136–37, 190, 213, 247
Germany, Germans, 32, 34, 46, 49, 147, 149–50, 153
Ginzburg, Carlo, 46
God (Christian), 36, 133, 138, 165n5, 171, 227
god (general), 165n3, 202n6, 227, 231–32, 234, 239n4, 246
Goffman, Erving, 88, 95, 97, 106
Golden Bough, The, 58
Granet, Marcel, 11–12, 14, 18, 187, 229, 231, 237, 242–55, 255n8
Great Britain, 59, 60
Greece, Greeks, 144, 227
Grønbech, Vilhelm, 151
Groot, Jan Jakob Maria de, 12
Gumuz, 19, 303–4, 306–7
Gurvitch, Georges, 274–76

Halbwachs, Maurice, 11, 14, 17, 19, 21n9, 189, 192, 196–98, 283–92
Hamelin, Octave, 9, 48–49, 72
Hartmann, Eduard von, 47–48
Hegel, Georg W. F., 9, 131, 140, 149, 260. *See also* categories, Hegelian.
Hertz, Robert, 3, 8, 11, 14, 18, 230–31, 233–34, 257–60, 262–68, 270n2, 270n4, 270n10, 270n12, 291
Hindus, Hinduism, 148, 162, 164–67, 271n10
Hirst, Paul Q., 115
Homer, 157
homo duplex, 18, 213, 268–69
homo faber, 208–9, 222n4, 222n6
Howitt, Alfred, 181–82
Hubert, Henri, 1, 3–4, 6–9, 13, 15, 17, 35–37, 49, 57–59, 63, 66, 138–39, 143, 145, 147, 187, 189, 194–95, 208–10, 213–14, 216–19, 221n2, 222n8, 222n10, 227–31, 234, 236, 239n5, 278
Hume, David, 34–38, 40, 41n2, 119, 121. *See also* epistemology, Humean

Ibn Khaldoun, 239n3
India, 144, 148, 161, 163, 167

Intichiuma, 79
Iroquois, 63
Isaiah, 289

Janet, Pierre, 53
Japan, 243
Jesus, 289, 291. *See also* Christ
Johnson, Mark, 14, 38–40, 42n8
Jerusalem, 289
Jerusalem, Wilhelm, 9
Jum Jum, 303–4, 306
Jupiter Capitolinus, 232
justice, 86–97, 99, 101, 103, 108n1, 109n5, 133, 151

Kabylia, 276–77
Kant, Immanuel, 6, 9, 11, 14, 29–34, 37–38, 60–61, 72–74, 79, 82, 93, 98, 101, 119–21, 131, 136, 177, 229, 308. *See also* categories, Kantian; categories, neo-Kantian; epistemology, Kantian; philosophy, Kantian
King, John, 15, 62–65, 67n11
Kingsley, Mary, 301
kinship, 16, 118, 157–60, 176, 180, 182, 189–90, 243–44, 247, 250, 255n7, 288, 297
Koma, 303–5
König, René, 208
Krassowski, Jan Marian, 227
Krishna, 165
Kwakiutl, 147, 296

Laberthonnière, Lucien (abbot), 10
labor, collective, 15, 74, 76, 78
labor, co-operative, 77
labor, general, 15, 31, 70–72, 76–83, 84n6, 97, 99, 134–35, 137, 158, 160, 164, 171, 175, 178, 219, 244, 246, 254, 259–62, 264–65, 267, 270n4, 270n7, 270n9, 289, 304
labor, non-productive, 261–63, 265
labor, productive, 260–61, 263, 267
labor, ritual, 79
Lachelier, Jules, 10
Laclau, Ernesto, 200
Lakoff, George, 14, 38–40, 42n8
Lang, Andrew, 47, 63, 181
language, 8, 12–13, 31–33, 67n8, 81, 106, 121, 208–13, 219, 248, 253, 295–96, 298–307, 309

Latin, 47–48, 54n4, 150, 299
law, moral, 100, 268
law, natural, 6, 59, 119
law, Roman, 153
Leenhardt, Maurice, 21n7
Lefort, Claude, 200, 274, 276–77
Leipzig, 46
Leo the Hebrew, 45, 48
Léon, Xavier, 5, 72
Leroi-Gourhan, André, 2, 274
Le Roy, Edouard, 10
Lévi-Strauss, Claude, 2, 18, 36, 47, 54n3, 93, 97, 114, 124, 159, 188, 190, 198–201, 201n2, 274–78, 281
Lévy-Bruhl, Lucien, 131, 146–47, 188, 213, 285
Lewis, Ioan M., 239n3

Madagascar, 65
magic, 5, 34–36, 57–60, 63–66, 66n2, 67n12, 131, 138–39, 142–44, 149, 175, 194, 209–10, 213–14, 228, 238, 245, 264–65, 270n2, 278–80
Magna Mater, 231
Malinowski, Bronisław, 93, 141–43, 152, 299
mana, 6–8, 15, 35–37, 42n5, 57, 59–61, 63, 65–66, 67nn5–6, 67nn10–11, 67n13, 120, 138–39, 143–44, 150, 175–76, 207, 210, 219, 234, 236
Mannheim, Karl, 190
Maori, 147, 264, 296
Marett, Robert Ranulph, 15, 63–65, 67n12
Marillier, Léon, 63
Marxism, 71, 260–62, 270nn7–8, 276
matter, 13, 16, 19, 32, 53, 60, 63, 104, 114, 117, 119, 122, 123–24, 145, 148, 152, 193, 208, 210, 212–13, 277, 285, 288, 290, 296
Mauss, Marcel, 1–8, 11–15, 17, 19, 21n2, 21nn4–6, 21n10, 30, 36–37, 39–40, 42n7, 44–53, 53n1, 54nn4–5, 54nn7–8, 57–59, 63, 66, 90, 94, 116, 118–19, 120–23, 131–53, 156–57, 159–60, 163, 176, 187–89, 201, 202n6, 202n8, 208–9, 210,

213–16, 219–20, 221nn2–3, 222n8, 228–31, 235, 237, 247–49, 251, 259, 268, 271n12, 274–81, 283–84, 286, 288, 296, 299, 300–302; and Beuchat, 6–8, 288; and Durkheim, *see* Durkheim, Émile; and Hubert, 6–7, 15, 35–37, 57–59, 63, 66, 210, 219, 228–30, 278; and Weber (L.) 208–10, 213–14, 219, 221n3
Meban, 303–4
Meillet, Antoine, 12, 151
Melanesia, 59–61, 63, 65–66, 67n5, 138, 141, 152, 278, 296
Méliès, George, 131
mesmerism, 53
Métais, Pierre, 275
Mills, C. Wright, 106
Montesquieu, 47
morality, 99–102, 106–7, 174, 177, 179, 182–83, 268
morphology, social, 30–31, 38, 64, 160
Mouffe, Chantal, 200
Müller, Max, 14–15, 32–33, 60–61, 63–65, 67n7, 67n8, 67n9
music, 246–47, 296, 300–301, 303–6, 308, 310n2
mysticism, 53, 187
myths, mythology, 7, 16, 32, 58, 61–62, 67n8, 144, 146, 150, 162, 167n5, 172, 199, 215, 228, 245–47, 250, 267, 291, 300–301, 307, 308

Needham, Rodney, 2, 121–22, 265
Nigeria, 301
Nilotic, 303–4, 306
number (category), 136, 156

orenda, 36, 63
Oromo, 304
Ovid, 231–32, 239n4
Oxford, 32, 60, 299, 308

Paris, 5, 45, 228, 242–43
Parkin, Robert, 2, 259–60, 262
Parsons, Talcott, 15, 88–90, 94, 97, 103, 105–6
Peirce, Charles Sanders, 52
person (category), 5, 13, 136, 145, 156–57, 297

philosophy, Aristotelian, 72, 81
philosophy, general, 2, 6, 8, 10, 19, 21n5, 32, 34, 42n8, 47–49, 51, 58, 81, 84n5, 86, 88–90, 94–95, 106–7, 131–33, 160, 165–66, 187–89, 191–98, 208, 252, 295–96, 301, 308
philosophy, Kantian, 31–34, 93
philosophy, moral, 93, 95, 98
philosophy, Utilitarian, 93, 101
Piketty, Thomas, 106
Pitt Rivers Museum (Oxford), 299
place (category), 31, 136
pragmatism, 52, 71, 82, 195
psychic life, 78–79, 81, 83, 172

quantity (category), 7, 136

race, 88, 104, 106
racism, 103–4
Radcliffe-Brown, Alfred, 299
rationalism, 71, 73, 75, 177, 191, 202n7
reason (category), 8, 10, 32
reciprocity, 18, 92, 96, 102, 109, 133, 137, 140, 153, 276, 277, 300, 305
reference points, 76
reincarnation, 148–49
relation (category), 15, 74–77, 136, 161
relativism, 10, 14, 29, 30–32, 34, 36–37, 39–40, 213, 275
religion, 4–7, 9–11, 13, 15, 18, 36, 41n2, 47–48, 51, 57–66, 67n5, 67n8, 67n12, 87, 101, 114–15, 121, 134–35, 138, 140, 144, 146–49, 156, 160–61, 166, 171–77, 182–83, 194, 202n6, 208, 211–15, 217, 227–29, 231, 233–36, 238, 239n3, 243, 257–59, 264–65, 270n2, 270n3, 275, 284–86, 288–90, 299–300, 302–3
Renouvier, Charles, 9, 15, 72–75, 81, 297
repetition, 78–81, 83, 207, 219
Revolution, French, 173, 300
Ribot, Théodule, 49
ritual, 4, 16, 30, 38, 41n3, 48, 65, 67n6, 76–79, 87, 92, 93, 95, 118, 122, 124, 140, 146, 153, 161–62, 164, 173, 183, 211–12,

228, 230, 233, 235, 246, 250, 259, 266, 270n4, 275, 306
Robertson Smith, William, 47, 233
Romanticism, German, 60
Rome (ancient), 92, 94, 145, 229–32, 235–36, 271n10, 278

Sacks, Harvey, 88, 97, 100, 106–7
sacrifice, 16, 147, 161–62, 164, 232, 250, 260–61, 263, 268, 290
Sanskrit, 145, 157
Sapir, Edward, 33, 37
scholasticism, 72
Sens, Lycée, de 49, 50
SFP *see* Société Française de Philosophie
Shennong (spirit), 245
Shilluk, 304
Shiva, 164
Simmel, Georg, 153
Simon, Herbert, 106
Simondon, Gilbert, 2, 188
singing, 220, 246
slavery, 261
social fact(s), 5, 15–16, 18, 31, 36, 77, 79, 86–89, 91–96, 98, 100, 102, 105–7, 108n3, 113, 116, 133, 135, 138, 160–61, 199, 202n8, 249, 274–81, 299
social morphology, *see* morphology, social
Société Française de Philosophie, 2, 9, 10, 208
solidarity, 80, 96, 97, 100–101, 158, 160, 180, 183, 202n9, 247, 284, 299
Sorbonne, 5, 45–46
space (category), 4–8, 11, 17, 30, 38, 76–77, 82, 121–23, 136, 156, 160, 166, 189, 193, 195, 207, 215, 227–29, 233–38, 254, 266, 280, 285–87, 289, 291, 292n3, 297–98, 300
species (category), 136, 190
Spinoza, 48, 51, 202n9, 202n10
Stein, Rolf, 249
'Step of Yu', 250
Stiglitz, Joseph, 106
strength (category), 136
structuralism, 97, 188–89, 198, 200–201

substance (category), 6, 7, 11, 13, 133, 136, 140, 143–45, 147–50, 152–53, 156, 207, 220
Sudan, 19, 303–5, 307–8, 309n2
suicide, 47–48, 286–88, 293n4
synthesis, 10, 74, 76, 81, 83, 140–41, 143, 172, 179, 216, 279, 280, 308

Tacitus, 150, 152
Tasmania, 301
technology (category), 17, 182, 207–9, 213–15, 220–21, 221n1, 221n2, 222n4
Terminus (Roman god), 227, 231–32, 239n4
Tierra del Fuego, 301
time (category), 3–8, 17, 29–31, 38–39, 41n2, 75–76, 87, 123, 136, 156, 160, 165, 183, 189, 192–95, 197, 202, 207–9, 215–20, 222n4, 222n10, 223n12, 227–29, 254, 277, 280, 288–89, 291, 297–98, 300
Tiryakian, Edward, 50
totality (category), 16, 75, 77, 133–34, 136–39, 156–66, 202n9, 248, 275
totemism, 33, 139, 146–47, 176, 198–99, 300
transcendentalism, 72–73
truth, 82, 84n5, 195–96, 198, 281, 308, 309
Tylor, Edward B., 14–15, 32–35, 37, 47, 58, 60–64, 66, 66n2, 66n3, 67n5, 299

Uduk, 19, 303–8, 309n2
United States, 15, 62, 104, 105–7, 108n1
universalism, 14, 32, 36

value neutrality, 15, 102–3, 107
Vedic literature, 8, 16, 148, 161, 164–66
Vishnu, 164–65

wakan, 36
Warramunga, 181
Warsaw, 228
Way of the Cross, 289

Weber, Louis, 11, 16, 208–14, 219, 2221n3, 222n4
Weber, Max, 105, 109n7
Wittgenstein, Ludwig, 40, 89, 94, 106, 132
World War I, 2–4, 11, 89, 103, 145, 149, 229, 255n2, 260, 283, 301

World War II, 2, 152, 283

Yellow Emperor (the), 245
yin and yang, 12, 248, 252, 254
Yu the Great, 245, 250

Zuñi, 166, 297

www.ingramcontent.com/pod-product-compliance
Lightning Source LLC
Chambersburg PA
CBHW070803040426
42333CB00061B/1808